THE
RAMAYAN

Translated by RALPH T.H. GRIFFITH

VALMIKI

CLASSICS

First Published 2024
FiNGERPRINT! CLASSiCS
An imprint of Prakash Books India Pvt. Ltd

113/A, Darya Ganj,
New Delhi-110 002
Email: info@prakashbooks.com/sales@prakashbooks.com

 Fingerprint Publishing
 @FingerprintP
 @fingerprintpublishingbooks
www.fingerprintpublishing.com

ISBN: 978 93 6214 551 2

Contents

BOOK V

BOOK VI

BOOK

IV

BOOK

IV

Ráma's Lament

The princes stood by Pampá's side
   Which blooming lilies glorified.
   With troubled heart and sense o'erthrown
There Ráma made his piteous moan.
As the fair flood before him lay
The reason of the chief gave way;
And tender thoughts within him woke,
As to Sumitrá's son he spoke:

"How lovely Pampá's waters show,
Where streams of lucid crystal flow!
What glorious trees o'erhang the flood
Which blooms of opening lotus stud!
Look on the banks of Pampá where
Thick groves extend divinely fair;
And piles of trees, like hills in size,
Lift their proud summits to the skies.
But thought of Bharat's pain and toil,
And my dear spouse the giant's spoil,
Afflict my tortured heart and press
My spirit down with heaviness.
Still fair to me though sunk in woe
Bright Pampá and her forest show.
Where cool fresh waters charm the sight,

And flowers of every hue are bright.
The lotuses in close array
Their passing loveliness display,
And pard and tiger, deer and snake
Haunt every glade and dell and brake.
Those grassy spots display the hue
Of topazes and sapphires' blue,
And, gay with flowers of every dye,
With richly broidered housings vie.
What loads of bloom the high trees crown,
Or weigh the bending branches down!
And creepers tipped with bud and flower
Each spray and loaded limb o'erpower.
Now cool delicious breezes blow,
And kindle love's voluptuous glow,
When balmy sweetness fills the air,
And fruit and flowers and trees are fair.
Those waving woods, that shine with bloom,
Each varied tint in turn assume.
Like labouring clouds they pour their showers
In rain or ever-changing flowers.
Behold, those forest trees, that stand
High upon rock and table-land,
As the cool gales their branches bend,
Their floating blossoms downward send.
See, Lakshmaṇ, how the breezes play
With every floweret on the spray.
And sport in merry guise with all
The fallen blooms and those that fall.
See, brother, where the merry breeze
Shakes the gay boughs of flowery trees,
Disturbed amid their toil a throng
Of bees pursue him, loud in song.
The Koïls, mad with sweet delight,
The bending trees to dance invite;
And in its joy the wild wind sings
As from the mountain cave he springs.
On speed the gales in rapid course,
And bend the woods beneath their force,
Till every branch and spray they bind
In many a tangled knot entwined.

What balmy sweets those gales dispense
With cool and sacred influence!
Fatigue and trouble vanish: such
The magic of their gentle touch.
Hark, when the gale the boughs has bent
In woods of honey redolent,
Through all their quivering sprays the trees
Are vocal with the murmuring bees.
The hills with towering summits rise,
And with their beauty charm the eyes,
Gay with the giant trees which bright
With blossom spring from every height:
And as the soft wind gently sways
The clustering blooms that load the sprays,
The very trees break forth and sing
With startled wild bees' murmuring.
Thine eyes to yonder Cassias turn
Whose glorious clusters glow and burn.

Those trees in yellow robes behold,
Like giants decked with burnished gold.
Ah me, Sumitrá's son, the spring
Dear to sweet birds who love and sing,
Wakes in my lonely breast the flame
Of sorrow as I mourn my dame.
Love strikes me through with darts of fire,
And wakes in vain the sweet desire.
Hark, the loud Koïl swells his throat,
And mocks me with his joyful note.
I hear the happy wild-cock call
Beside the shady waterfall.
His cry of joy afflicts my breast
By love's absorbing might possessed.
My darling from our cottage heard
One morn in spring this shrill-toned bird,
And called me in her joy to hear
The happy cry that charmed her ear.
See, birds of every varied voice
Around us in the woods rejoice,
On creeper, shrub, and plant alight,
Or wing from tree to tree their flight.

Each bird his kindly mate has found,
And loud their notes of triumph sound,
Blending in sweetest music like
The distant warblings of the shrike.
See how the river banks are lined
With birds of every hue and kind.
Here in his joy the Koïl sings,
There the glad wild-cock flaps his wings.
The blooms of bright Aśokas where
The song of wild bees fills the air,
And the soft whisper of the boughs
Increase my longing for my spouse.
The vernal flush of flower and spray
Will burn my very soul away.
What use, what care have I for life
If I no more may see my wife
Soft speaker with the glorious hair,
And eyes with silken lashes fair?
Now is the time when all day long
The Koïls fill the woods with song.
And gardens bloom at spring's sweet touch
Which my beloved loved so much.
Ah me, Sumitrá's son, the fire
Of sorrow, sprung from soft desire,
Fanned by the charms the spring time shows,
Will burn my heart and end my woes,
Whose sad eyes look on each fair tree,
But my sweet love no more may see.
Ah me, Ah me, from hour to hour
Love in my soul will wax in power,
And spring, upon whose charms I gaze,
Whose breath the heat of toil allays,
With thoughts of her for whom I strain
My hopeless eyes, increase my pain.
As fire in summer rages through
The forests thick with dry bamboo,
So will my fawn eyed love consume
My soul o'erwhelmed with thoughts of gloom.
Behold, beneath each spreading tree
The peacocks dance in frantic glee,
And, stirred by all the gales that blow,

Their tails with jewelled windows glow,
Each bird, in happy love elate,
Rejoices with his darling mate.
But sights like these of joy and peace
My pangs of hopeless love increase.
See on the mountain slope above
The peahen languishing with love.
Behold her now in amorous dance
Close to her consort's side advance.
He with a laugh of joy and pride
Displays his glittering pinions wide;
And follows through the tangled dell
The partner whom he loves so well.
Ah happy bird! no giant's hate
Has robbed him of his tender mate;
And still beside his loved one he
Dances beneath the shade in glee.
Ah, in this month when flowers are fair
My widowed woe is hard to bear.
See, gentle love a home may find
In creatures of inferior kind.
See how the peahen turns to meet
Her consort now with love-drawn feet.

So, Lakshmaṇ, if my large-eyed dear,
The child of Janak still were here,
She, by love's thrilling influence led,
Upon my breast would lay her head.
These blooms I gathered from the bough
Without my love are useless now.
A thousand blossoms fair to see
With passing glory clothe each tree
That hangs its cluster-burthened head
Now that the dewy months are fled,
But, followed by the bees that ply
Their fragrant task, they fall and die.
A thousand birds in wild delight
Their rapture-breathing notes unite;
Bird calls to bird in joyous strain,
And turns my love to frenzied pain.
O, if beneath those alien skies,

There be a spring where Sítá lies,
I know my prisoned love must be
Touched with like grief, and mourn with me.
But ah, methinks that dreary clime
Knows not the touch of spring's sweet time.
How could my black eyed love sustain,
Without her lord, so dire a pain?
Or if the sweet spring come to her
In distant lands a prisoner,
How may his advent and her met
On every side with taunt and threat?
Ah, if the springtide's languor came
With soft enchantment o'er my dame,
My darling of the lotus eye,
My gently speaking love, would die;
For well my spirit knows that she
Can never live bereft of me
With love that never wavered yet
My Sítá's heart, on me is set,
Who, with a soul that ne'er can stray,
With equal love her love repay.
In vain, in vain the soft wind brings
Sweet blossoms on his balmy wings;
Delicious from his native snow,
To me like fire he seems to glow.
O, how I loved a breeze like this
When darling Sítá shared the bliss!
But now in vain for me it blows
To fan the fury of my woes.
That dark-winged bird that sought the skies
Foretelling grief with warning cries,
Sits on the tree where buds are gay,
And pours glad music from the spray.
That rover of the fields of air
Will aid my love with friendly care,
And me with gracious pity guide
To my large-eyed Videhan's side.
Hark, Lakshmaṇ, how the woods around
With love-inspiring chants resound,
Where birds in every bloom-crowned tree
Pour forth their amorous minstrelsy.

As though an eager gallant wooed
A gentle maid by love subdued,
Enamoured of her flowers the bee
Darts at the wind-rocked Tila tree.
Aśoka, brightest tree that grows,
That lends a pang to lovers' woes,
Hangs out his gorgeous bloom in scorn
And mocks me as I weep forlorn.
O Lakshmaṇ, turn thine eye and see
Each blossom-laden Mango tree,
Like a young lover gaily dressed
Whom fond desire forbids to rest.
Look, son of Queen Sumitrá through
The forest glades of varied hue,
Where blooms are bright and grass is green
The Kinnars with their loves are seen.
See, brother, see where sweet and bright
Those crimson lilies charm the sight,
And o'er the flood a radiance throw
Fair as the morning's roseate glow.
See, Pampá, most divinely sweet,
The swan's and mallard's loved retreat,
Shows her glad waters bright and clear,
Where lotuses their heads uprear
From the pure wave, and charm the view
With mingled tints of red and blue.
Each like the morning's early beams
Reflected in the crystal gleams;
And bees on their sweet toil intent
Weigh down each tender filament.
There with gay lawns the wood recedes;
There wildfowl sport amid the reeds,
There roedeer stand upon the brink,
And elephants descend to drink.
The rippling waves which winds make fleet
Against the bending lilies beat,
And opening bud and flower and stem
Gleam with the drops that hang on them.
Life has no pleasure left for me
While my dear queen I may not see,

Who loved so well those blooms that vie
With the full splendour of her eye.
O tyrant Love, who will not let
My bosom for one hour forget
The lost one whom I yearn to meet,
Whose words were ever kind and sweet.
Ah, haply might my heart endure
This hopeless love that knows not cure,
If spring with all his trees in flower
Assailed me not with ruthless power.
Each lovely scene, each sound and sight
Wherein, with her, I found delight,
Has lost the charm so sweet of yore,
And glads my widowed heart no more.
On lotus buds I seem to gaze,
Or blooms that deck Paláśa sprays;

But to my tortured memory rise
The glories of my darling's eyes.
Cool breezes through the forest stray
Gathering odours on their way,
Enriched with all the rifled scent
Of lotus flower and filament.
Their touch upon my temples falls
And Sítá's fragrant breath recalls.
Now look, dear brother, on the right
Of Pampá towers a mountain height
Where fairest Cassia trees unfold
The treasures of their burnished gold.
Proud mountain king! his woody side
With myriad ores is decked and dyed,
And as the wind-swept blossoms fall
Their fragrant dust is stained with all.
To yon high lands thy glances turn:
With pendent fire they flash and burn,
Where in their vernal glory blaze
Paláśa flowers on leafless sprays.
O Lakshmaṇ, look! on Pampá's side
What fair trees rise in blooming pride!
What climbing plants above them show

Or hang their flowery garlands low!
See how the amorous creeper rings
The wind-rocked trees to which she clings,
As though a dame by love impelled
With clasping arms her lover held.
Drunk with the varied scents that fill
The balmy air, from hill to hill,
From grove to grove, from tree to tree,
The joyous wind is wandering free.
These gay trees wave their branches bent
By blooms, of honey redolent.
There, slowly opening to the day,
Buds with dark lustre deck the spray.
The wild bee rests a moment where
Each tempting flower is sweet and fair,
Then, coloured by the pollen dyes,
Deep in some odorous blossom lies.
Soon from his couch away he springs:
To other trees his course he wings,
And tastes the honeyed blooms that grow
Where Pampá's lucid waters flow.
See, Lakshmaṇ, see, how thickly spread
With blossoms from the trees o'erhead,
That grass the weary traveller woos
With couches of a thousand hues,
And beds on every height arrayed
With red and yellow tints are laid,
No longer winter chills the earth:
A thousand flowerets spring to birth,
And trees in rivalry assume
Their vernal garb of bud and bloom.
How fair they look, how bright and gay
With tasselled flowers on every spray!
While each to each proud challenge flings
Borne in the song the wild bee sings.
That mallard by the river edge
Has bathed amid the reeds and sedge:
Now with his mate he fondly plays
And fires my bosom as I gaze.

Mandákiní is far renowned:
No lovelier flood on earth is found;
But all her fairest charms combined
In this sweet stream enchant the mind.
O, if my love were here to look
With me upon this lovely brook,
Never for Ayodhyá would I pine,
Or wish that Indra's lot were mine.
If by my darling's side I strayed
O'er the soft turf which decks the glade,
Each craving thought were sweetly stilled,
Each longing of my soul fulfilled.
But, now my love is far away,
Those trees which make the woods so gay,
In all their varied beauty dressed,
Wake thoughts of anguish in my breast.

That lotus-covered stream behold
Whose waters run so fresh and cold,

Sweet rill, the wildfowl's loved resort,
Where curlew, swan, and diver sport;
Where with his consort plays the drake,
And tall deer love their thirst to slake,
While from each woody bank is heard
The wild note of each happy bird.
The music of that joyous quire
Fills all my soul with soft desire;
And, as I hear, my sad thoughts fly
To Sítá of the lotus eye,
Whom, lovely with her moonbright cheek,
In vain mine eager glances seek.
Now turn, those chequered lawns survey
Where hart and hind together stray.
Ah, as they wander at their will
My troubled breast with grief they fill,
While torn by hopeless love I sigh
For Sítá of the fawn-like eye.
If in those glades where, touched by spring,
Gay birds their amorous ditties sing,
Mine own beloved I might see,

Then, brother, it were well with me:
If by my side she wandered still,
And this cool breeze that stirs the rill
Touched with its gentle breath the brows
Of mine own dear Videhan spouse.
For, Lakshmaṇ, O how blest are those
On whom the breath of Pampá blows,
Dispelling all their care and gloom
With sweets from where the lilies bloom!
How can my gentle love remain
Alive amid the woe and pain,
Where prisoned far away she lies,—
My darling of the lotus eyes?
How shall I dare her sire to greet
Whose lips have never known deceit?
How stand before the childless king
And meet his eager questioning?
When banished by my sire's decree,
In low estate, she followed me.
So pure, so true to every vow,
Where is my gentle darling now?
How can I bear my widowed lot,
And linger on where she is not,
Who followed when from home I fled
Distracted, disinherited?
My spirit sinks in hopeless pain
When my fond glances yearn in vain
For that dear face with whose bright eye
The worshipped lotus scarce can vie.
Ah when, my brother, shall I hear
That voice that rang so soft and clear,
When, sweetly smiling as she spoke,
From her dear lips gay laughter broke?
When worn with toil and love I strayed
With Sítá through the forest shade,
No trace of grief was seen in her,
My kind and thoughtful comforter.
How shall my faltering tongue relate
To Queen Kauśalyá Sítá's fate?
How answer when in wild despair
She questions, Where is Sítá, where?

Haste, brother, haste: to Bharat hie,
On whose fond love I still rely.
My life can be no longer borne,
Since Sítá from my side is torn."

Thus like a helpless mourner, bent
By sorrow, Ráma made lament;
And with wise counsel Lakshmaṇ tried
To soothe his care, and thus replied:
"O best of men, thy grief oppose,
Nor sink beneath thy weight of woes.
Not thus despond the great and pure
And brave like thee, but still endure.
Reflect what anguish wrings the heart
When loving souls are forced to part;
And, mindful of the coming pain,
Thy love within thy breast restrain.
For earth, though cooled by wandering streams,
Lies scorched beneath the midday beams.
Rávaṇ his steps to hell may bend,
Or lower yet in flight descend;
But be thou sure, O Raghu's son,
Avenging death he shall not shun.
Rise, Ráma, rise: the search begin,
And track the giant foul with sin.
Then shall the fiend, though far he fly,
Resign his prey or surely die.
Yea, though the trembling monster hide
With Sítá close to Diti's side,
E'en there, unless he yield the prize,
Slain by this wrathful hand he dies.
Thy heart with strength and courage stay,
And cast this weakling mood away.
Our fainting hopes in vain revive
Unless with firm resolve we strive.
The zeal that fires the toiler's breast
Mid earthly powers is first and best.
Zeal every check and bar defies,
And wins at length the loftiest prize,
In woe and danger, toil and care,
Zeal never yields to weak despair.

With zealous heart thy task begin,
And thou once more thy spouse shalt win.
Cast fruitless sorrow from thy soul,
Nor let this love thy heart control.
Forget not all thy sacred lore,
But be thy noble self once more."

He heard, his bosom rent by grief,
The counsel of his brother chief;
Crushed in his heart the maddening pain,
And rose resolved and strong again.
Then forth upon his journey went
The hero on his task intent,
Nor thought of Pampá's lovely brook,

Or trees which murmuring breezes shook,
Though on dark woods his glances fell,
On waterfall and cave and dell;
And still by many a care distressed
The son of Raghu onward pressed.
As some wild elephant elate
Moves through the woods in pride,
So Lakshman with majestic gait
Strode by his brother's side.
He, for his lofty spirit famed,
Admonished and consoled;
Showed Raghu's son what duty claimed,
And bade his heart be bold.
Then as the brothers strode apace
To Rishyamúka's height,
The sovereign of the Vánar race
Was troubled at the sight.
As on the lofty hill he strayed
He saw the chiefs draw near:
A while their glorious forms surveyed,
And mused in restless fear.
His slow majestic step he stayed
And gazed upon the pair.
And all his spirit sank dismayed
By fear too great to bear.
When in their glorious might the best

Of royal chiefs came nigh,
The Vánars in their wild unrest
Prepared to turn and fly.
They sought the hermit's sacred home
For peace and bliss ordained,
And there, where Vánars loved to roam,
A sure asylum gained.

CANTO

II

Sugríva's Alarm

Sugríva moved by wondering awe
The high-souled sons of Raghu saw,
In all their glorious arms arrayed;
And grief upon his spirit weighed.
To every quarter of the sky
He turned in fear his anxious eye,
And roving still from spot to spot
With troubled steps he rested not.
He durst not, as he viewed the pair,
Resolve to stand and meet them there;
And drooping cheer and quailing breast
The terror of the chief confessed.
While the great fear his bosom shook,
Brief counsel with his lords he took;
Each gain and danger closely scanned,
What hope in flight, what power to stand,
While doubt and fear his bosom rent,
On Raghu's sons his eyes he bent,
And with a spirit ill at ease
Addressed his lords in words like these:

"Those chiefs with wandering steps invade
The shelter of our pathless shade,

And hither come in fair disguise
Of hermit garb as Báli's spies."
Each lord beheld with troubled heart
Those masters of the bowman's art,
And left the mountain side to seek
Sure refuge on a loftier peak.
The Vánar chief in rapid flight
Found shelter on a towering height,
And all the band with one accord
Were closely gathered round their lord.
Their course the same, with desperate leap
Each made his way from steep to steep,
And speeding on in wild career
Filled every height with sudden fear.
Each heart was struck with mortal dread,
As on their course the Vánars sped,
While trees that crowned the steep were bent
And crushed beneath them as they went.
As in their eager flight they pressed
For safety to each mountain crest,
The wild confusion struck with fear
Tiger and cat and wandering deer.
The lords who watched Sugríva's will
Were gathered on the royal hill,
And all with reverent hands upraised
Upon their king and leader gazed.
Sugríva feared some evil planned,
Some train prepared by Báli's hand.
But, skilled in words that charm and teach,
Thus Hanumán began his speech:

"Dismiss, dismiss thine idle fear,
Nor dread the power of Báli here.
For this is Malaya's glorious hill
Where Báli's might can work no ill.
I look around but nowhere see
The hated foe who made thee flee,
Fell Báli, fierce in form and face:
Then fear not, lord of Vánar race.
Alas, in thee I clearly find
The weakness of the Vánar kind,

27

That loves from thought to thought to range,
Fix no belief and welcome change.
Mark well each hint and sign and scan,
Discreet and wise, thine every plan.
How may a king, with sense denied,
The subjects of his sceptre guide?"

Hanúmán, wise in hour of need,
Urged on the chief his prudent rede.
His listening ear Sugríva bent,
And spake in words more excellent:

"Where is the dauntless heart that free
From terror's chilling touch can see
Two stranger warriors, strong as those,
Equipped with swords and shafts and bows,
With mighty arms and large full eyes,
Like glorious children of the skies?
Báli my foe, I ween, has sent
These chiefs to aid his dark intent.
Hence doubt and fear disturb me still,
For thousands serve a monarch's will,
In borrowed garb they come, and those
Who walk disguised are counted foes.
With secret thoughts they watch their time,
And wound fond hearts that fear no crime.
My foe in state affairs is wise,
And prudent kings have searching eyes.
By other hands they strike the foe:
By meaner tools the truth they know.
Now to those stranger warriors turn,
And, less than king, their purpose learn.
Mark well the trick and look of each;
Observe his form and note his speech.
With care their mood and temper sound,
And, if their minds be friendly found,
With courteous looks and words begin
Their confidence and love to win.
Then as my friend and envoy speak,
And question what the strangers seek.
Ask why equipped with shaft and bow

Through this wild maze of wood they go.
If they, O chief, at first appear
Pure of all guile, in heart sincere,
Detect in speech and look the sin
And treachery that lurk within."

He spoke: the Wind-God's son obeyed.
With ready zeal he sought the shade,
And reached with hasty steps the wood
Where Raghu's son and Lakshmaṇ stood.

CANTO

III

Hanumán's Speech

The envoy in his faithful breast
Pondered Sugríva's high behest.
From Rishyamúka's peak he hied
And placed him by the princes' side.
The Wind-God's son with cautious art
Had laid his Vánar form apart,
And wore, to cheat the strangers eyes,
A wandering mendicant's disguise.
Before the heroes' feet he bent
And did obeisance reverent,
And spoke, the glorious pair to praise,
His words of truth in courteous phrase,
High honour duly paid, the best
Of all the Vánar kind addressed,
With free accord and gentle grace,
Those glories of their warrior race:
"O hermits, blest in vows, who shine
Like royal saints or Gods divine,
O best of young ascetics, say
How to this spot you found your way,

Scaring the troops of wandering deer
And silvan things that harbour here
Searching amid the trees that grow
Where Pampá's gentle waters flow.
And lending from your brows a gleam
Of glory to the lovely stream.
Who are you, say, so brave and fair,
Clad in the bark which hermits wear?
I see you heave the frequent sigh,
I see the deer before you fly.
While you, for strength and valour dread,
The earth, like lordly lions, tread,
Each bearing in his hand a bow,
Like Indra's own, to slay the foe.
With the grand paces of a bull,
So bright and young and beautiful.
The mighty arms you raise appear
Like trunks which elephants uprear,
And as you move this mountain-king
Is glorious with the light you bring.
How have you reached, like Gods in face,
Best lords of earth, this lonely place,

With tresses coiled in hermit guise,
And splendours of those lotus eyes?
As Gods who leave their heavenly sphere,
Alike your beauteous forms appear.
The Lords of Day and Night might thus
Stray from the skies to visit us.
Heroic youth, so broad of chest,
Fair with the beauty of the Blest,
With lion shoulders, tall and strong,
Like bulls who lead the lowing throng,
Your arms, unmatched for grace and length,
With massive clubs may vie in strength.
Why do no gauds those limbs adorn
Where priceless gems were meetly worn?
Each noble youth is fit, I deem,
To guard this earth, as lord supreme,
With all her woods and seas, to reign
From Meru's peak to Vindhya's chain.

Your smooth bows decked with dyes and gold
Are glorious in their masters' hold,
And with the arms of Indra vie
Which diamond splendours beautify.
Your quivers glow with golden sheen,
Well stored with arrows fleet and keen,
Each gleaming like a fiery snake
That joys the foeman's life to take.
As serpents cast their sloughs away
And all their new born sheen display,
So flash your mighty swords inlaid
With burning gold on hilt and blade.
Why are you silent, heroes? Why
My questions hear nor deign reply?
Sugríva, lord of virtuous mind,
The foremost of the Vánar kind,
An exile from his royal state,
Roams through the land disconsolate.
I, Hanumán, of Vánar race,
Sent by the king have sought this place,
For he, the pious, just, and true,
In friendly league would join with you.
Know, godlike youths, that I am one
Of his chief lords, the Wind-God's son.
With course unchecked I roam at will,
And now from Rishyamúka's hill,
To please his heart, his hope to speed,
I came disguised in beggar's weed."

Thus Hanúmán, well trained in lore
Of language, spoke, and said no more.
The son of Raghu joyed to hear
The envoy's speech, and bright of cheer
He turned to Lakshman by his side,
And thus in words of transport cried:

"The counselor we now behold
Of King Sugríva righteous-souled.
His face I long have yearned to see,
And now his envoy comes to me
With sweetest words in courteous phrase

31

Answer this mighty lord who slays
His foemen, by Sugríva sent,
This Vánar chief most eloquent.
For one whose words so sweetly flow
The whole Rig-veda needs must know,
And in his well-trained memory store
The Yajush and the Sáman's lore.
He must have bent his faithful ear
All grammar's varied rules to hear.
For his long speech how well he spoke!
In all its length no rule he broke.
In eye, on brow, in all his face
The keenest look no guile could trace.
No change of hue, no pose of limb
Gave sign that aught was false in him.
Concise, unfaltering, sweet and clear,
Without a word to pain the ear.
From chest to throat, nor high nor low,
His accents came in measured flow.
How well he spoke with perfect art
That wondrous speech that charmed the heart,
With finest skill and order graced
In words that knew nor pause nor haste!
That speech, with consonants that spring
From the three seats of uttering,
Would charm the spirit of a foe
Whose sword is raised for mortal blow.
How may a ruler's plan succeed
Who lacks such envoy good at need?
How fail, if one whose mind is stored
With gifts so rare assist his lord?
What plans can fail, with wisest speech
Of envoy's lips to further each?"

Thus Ráma spoke; and Lakshman taught
In all the art that utters thought,
To King Sugríva's learned spy
Thus made his eloquent reply:
"Full well we know the gifts that grace
Sugríva, lord of Vánar race,
And hither turn our wandering feet

That we that high-souled king may meet.
So now our pleasant task shall be
To do the words he speaks by thee."

His prudent speech the Vánar heard,
And all his heart with joy was stirred.
And hope that league with them would bring
Redress and triumph to his king.

CANTO

IV

Lakshman's Reply

Cheered by the words that Ráma spoke,
    Joy in the Vánar's breast awoke,
    And, as his friendly mood he knew,
His thoughts to King Sugríva flew:
"Again," he mused, "my high-souled lord
Shall rule, to kingly state restored;
Since one so mighty comes to save,
And freely gives the help we crave."

Then joyous Hanumán, the best
Of all the Vánar kind, addressed
These words to Ráma, trained of yore
In all the arts of speakers' lore:
"Why do your feet this forest tread
By silvan life inhabited,
This awful maze of tree and thorn
Which Pampá's flowering groves adorn?"
He spoke: obedient to the eye
Of Ráma, Lakshmaṇ made reply,
The name and fortune to unfold
Of Raghu's son the lofty-souled:
"True to the law, of fame unstained,

The glorious Daśaratha reigned,
And, steadfast in his duty, long
Kept the four castes from scathe and wrong.
Through his wide realm his will was done,
And, loved by all, he hated none.
Just to each creature great and small,
Like the Good Sire he cared for all.
The Ágnishṭom, as priests advised,
And various rites he solemnized,
Where ample largess ever paid
The Bráhmans for their holy aid.
Here Ráma stands, his heir by birth,
Whose name is glorious in the earth:
Sure refuge he of all oppressed,
Most faithful to his sire's behest.
He, Daśaratha's eldest born
Whom gifts above the rest adorn,
Lord of each high imperial sign,
The glory of his kingly line,
Reft of his right, expelled from home,
Came forth with me the woods to roam.
And Sítá too, his faithful dame,
Forth with her virtuous husband came,
Like the sweet light when day is done
Still cleaving to her lord the sun.
And me his sweet perfections drew
To follow as his servant true.
Named Lakshmaṇ, brother of my lord
Of grateful heart with knowledge stored
Most meet is he all bliss to share,
Who makes the good of all his care.
While, power and lordship cast away,
In the wild wood he chose to stay,
A giant came,—his name unknown,—
And stole the princess left alone.
Then Diti's son who, cursed of yore,
The semblance of a Rákshas wore,
To King Sugríva bade us turn
The robber's name and home to learn.
For he, the Vánar chief, would know
The dwelling of our secret foe.

Such words of hope spake Diti's son,
And sought the heaven his deeds had won.
Thou hast my tale. From first to last
Thine ears have heard whate'er has past.
Ráma the mighty lord and I
For refuge to Sugríva fly.
The prince whose arm bright glory gained,
O'er the whole earth as monarch reigned,
And richest gifts to others gave,
Is come Sugríva's help to crave;
Son of a king the surest friend
Of virtue, him who loved to lend
His succour to the suffering weak,
Is come Sugríva's aid to seek.
Yes, Raghu's son whose matchless hand
Protected all this sea-girt land,
The virtuous prince, my holy guide,
For refuge seeks Sugríva's side.
His favour sent on great and small
Should ever save and prosper all.
He now to win Sugríva's grace
Has sought his woodland dwelling-place.

Son of a king of glorious fame;—
Who knows not Daśaratha's name?—
From whom all princes of the earth
Received each honour due to worth;—
Heir of that best of earthly kings,
Ráma the prince whose glory rings
Through realms below and earth and skies,
For refuge to Sugríva flies.
Nor should the Vánar king refuse
The boon for which the suppliant sues,
But with his forest legions speed
To save him in his utmost need."

Sumitrá's son, his eyes bedewed
With piteous tears, thus sighed and sued.
Then, trained in all the arts that guide
The speaker, Hanumán replied:

"Yea, lords like you of wisest thought,
Whom happy fate has hither brought,
Who vanquish ire and rule each sense,
Must of our lord have audience.
Reft of his kingdom, sad, forlorn,
Once Báli's hate now Báli's scorn,
Defeated, severed from his spouse,
Wandering under forest boughs,
Child of the Sun, our lord and king
Sugríva will his succours bring,
And all our Vánar hosts combined
Will trace the dame you long to find."

With gentle tone and winning grace
Thus spake the chief of Vánar race,
And then to Raghu's son he cried:
"Come, haste we to Sugríva's side."

He spoke, and for his words so sweet
Good Lakshman paid all honour meet;
Then turned and cried to Raghu's son:
"Now deem thy task already done,
Because this chief of Vánar kind,
Son of the God who rules the wind,
Declares Sugríva's self would be
Assisted in his need by thee.
Bright gleams of joy his cheek o'erspread
As each glad word of hope he said;
And ne'er will one so valiant deign
To cheer our hearts with hope in vain."

He spoke, and Hanumán the wise
Cast off his mendicant disguise,
And took again his Vánar form,
Son of the God of wind and storm.
High on his ample back in haste
Raghu's heroic sons he placed,
And turned with rapid steps to find
The sovereign of the Vánar kind.

CANTO
V

The League

From Rishyamúka's rugged side
To Malaya's hill the Vánar hied,
And to his royal chieftain there
Announced the coming of the pair:
"See, here with Lakshmaṇ Ráma stands
Illustrious in a hundred lands.
Whose valiant heart will never quail
Although a thousand foes assail;
King Daśaratha's son, the grace
And glory of Ikshváku's race.
Obedient to his father's will
He cleaves to sacred duty still.
With rites of royal pomp and pride
His sire the Fire-God gratified;
Ten hundred thousand kine he freed,
And priests enriched with ample meed;
And the broad land protected, famed
For truthful lips and passions tamed.
Through woman's guile his son has made
His dwelling in the forest shade,
Where, as he lived with every sense
Subdued in hermit abstinence,
Fierce Rávaṇ stole his wife, and he
Is come a suppliant, lord, to thee.
Now let all honour due be paid
To these great chiefs who seek thine aid."
Thus spake the Vánar prince, and, stirred
With friendly thoughts, Sugríva heard.
The light of joy his face o'erspread,
And thus to Raghu's son he said:
"O Prince, in rules of duty trained,

Caring for all with love unfeigned,
Hanúmán's tongue has truly shown
The virtues that are thine alone.
My chiefest glory, gain, and bliss,
O stranger Prince, I reckon this,
That Raghu's son will condescend
To seek the Vánar for his friend.
If thou my true ally wouldst be
Accept the pledge I offer thee,
This hand in sign of friendship take,
And bind the bond we ne'er will break."

He spoke, and joy thrilled Ráma's breast;
Sugríva's hand he seized and pressed
And, transport beaming from his eye,
Held to his heart his new ally.
In wanderer's weed disguised no more,
His proper form Hanúmán wore.
Then, wood with wood engendering, came
Neath his deft hands the kindled flame.
Between the chiefs that fire he placed

With wreaths of flowers and worship graced.
And round its blazing glory went
The friends with slow steps reverent.

Thus each to other pledged and bound
In solemn league new transport found,
And bent upon his dear ally
The gaze he ne'er could satisfy.
"Friend of my soul art thou: we share
Each other's joy, each other's care;"
Thus in the bliss that thrilled his breast
Sugríva Raghu's son addressed.
From a high Sál a branch he tore
Which many a leaf and blossom bore,
And the fine twigs beneath them laid
A seat for him and Ráma made.
Then Hanumán with joyous mind,
Son of the God who rules the wind,
To Lakshman gave, his seat to be,

The gay branch of a Sandal tree.
Then King Sugríva with his eyes
Still trembling with the sweet surprise
Of the great joy he could not hide,
To Raghu's noblest scion cried:
"O Ráma, racked with woe and fear,
Spurned by my foes, I wander here.
Reft of my spouse, forlorn I dwell
Here in my forest citadel.
Or wild with terror and distress
Roam through the distant wilderness.
Vext by my brother Báli long
My soul has borne the scathe and wrong.
Do thou, whose virtues all revere,
Release me from my woe and fear.
From dire distress thy friend to free
Is a high task and worthy thee."

He spoke, and Raghu's son who knew
All sacred duties men should do.
The friend of justice, void of guile,
Thus answered with a gentle smile:
"Great Vánar, friends who seek my aid
Still find their trust with fruit repaid.
Báli, thy foe, who stole away
Thy wife this vengeful hand shall slay.
These shafts which sunlike flash and burn,
Winged with the feathers of the hern,
Each swift of flight and sure and dread,
With even knot and pointed head,
Fierce as the crashing fire-bolt sent
By him who rules the firmament,
Shall reach thy wicked foe and like
Infuriate serpents hiss and strike.
Thou, Vánar King, this day shalt see
The foe who long has injured thee
Lie, like a shattered mountain, low,
Slain by the tempest of my bow."

Thus Ráma spake: Sugríva heard,
And mighty joy his bosom stirred:

As thus his champion he addressed:
"Now by thy favour, first and best
Of heroes, shall thy friend obtain
His realm and darling wife again
Recovered from the foe.
Check thou mine elder brother's might;
That ne'er again his deadly spite
May rob me of mine ancient right,
Or vex my soul with woe."
The league was struck, a league to bring
To Sítá fiends, and Vánar king
Apportioned bliss and bale.
Through her left eye quick throbbings shot,
Glad signs the lady doubted not,
That told their hopeful tale.
The bright left eye of Báli felt
An inauspicious throb that dealt
A deadly blow that day.
The fiery left eyes of the crew
Of demons felt the throb, and knew
The herald of dismay.

CANTO

VI

★

The Tokens

With joy that sprang from hope restored
To Ráma spake the Vánar lord:
"I know, by wise Hanúmán taught,
Why thou the lonely wood hast sought.
Where with thy brother Lakshmaṇ thou
Hast sojourned, bound by hermit vow;
Have heard how Sítá, Janak's child,
Was stolen in the pathless wild,
How by a roving Rákshas she

Weeping was reft from him and thee;
How, bent on death, the giant slew
The vulture king, her guardian true,
And gave thy widowed breast to know
A solitary mourner's woe.
But soon, dear Prince, thy heart shall be
From every trace of sorrow free;

For I thy darling will restore,
Lost like the prize of holy lore.
Yea, though in heaven the lady dwell,
Or prisoned in the depths of hell,
My friendly care her way shall track
And bring thy ransomed darling back.
Let this my promise soothe thy care,
Nor doubt the words I truly swear.
Saints, fiends, and dwellers of the skies
Shall find thy wife a bitter prize,
Like the rash child who rues too late
The treacherous lure of poisoned cate.
No longer, Prince, thy loss deplore:
Thy darling wife will I restore.
'Twas she I saw: my heart infers
That shrinking form was doubtless hers,
Which gaint Rávaṇ, fierce and dread,
Bore swiftly through the clouds o'erhead
Still writhing in his strict embrace
Like helpless queen of serpent race,
And from her lips that sad voice came
Shrieking thine own and Lakshmaṇ's name.
High on a hill she saw me stand
With comrades twain on either hand.
Her outer robe to earth she threw,
And with it sent her anklets too.
We saw the glittering tokens fall;
We found them there and kept them all.
These will I bring: perchance thine eyes
The treasured spoils will recognize."

He ceased: then Raghu's son replied
To the glad tale, and eager cried:

"Bring them with all thy speed: delay
No more, dear friend, but haste away."

Thus Ráma spoke. Sugríva hied
Within the mountain's caverned side,
Impelled by love that stirred each thought
The precious tokens quickly brought,
And said to Raghu's son: Behold
This garment and these rings of gold.
In Ráma's hand with friendly haste
The jewels and the robe he placed.
Then, like the moon by mist assailed,
The tear-dimmed eyes of Ráma failed;
That burst of woe unmanned his frame,
Woe sprung from passion for his dame,
And with his manly strength o'erthrown,
He fell and cried, Ah me! mine own!
Again, again close to his breast
The ornaments and robe he pressed,
While the quick pants that shook his frame
As from a furious serpent came.
On his dear brother standing nigh
He turned at length his piteous eye;
And, while his tears increasing ran,
In bitter wail he thus began:
"Look, brother, and behold once more
The ornaments and robe she wore,
Dropped while the giant bore away
In cruel arras his struggling prey,
Dropped in some quiet spot, I ween,
Where the young grass was soft and green;
For still untouched by spot or stain
Their former beauty all retain."

He spoke with many a tear and sigh,
And thus his brother made reply:
"The bracelets thou hast fondly shown,
And earrings, are to me unknown,
But by long service taught I greet
The anklets of her honoured feet."

Then to Sugríva Ráma, best
Of Raghu's sons, these words addressed:

"Say to what quarter of the sky
The cruel fiend was seen to fly,
Bearing afar my captured wife,
My darling dearer than my life.
Speak, Vánar King, that I may know
Where dwells the cause of all my woe;
The fiend for whose transgression all
The giants by this hand shall fall.
He who the Maithil lady stole
And kindled fury in my soul,
Has sought his fate in senseless pride
And opened Death's dark portal wide.
Then tell me, Vánar lord, I pray,
The dwelling of my foe,
And he, beneath this hand, to-day
To Yáma's halls shall go."

CANTO
VII

Ráma Consoled

With longing love and woe oppressed
The Vánar chief he thus addressed:
And he, while sobs his utterance broke,
Raised up his reverent hands and spoke:

"O Raghu's son, I cannot tell
Where now that cruel fiend may dwell,
Declare his power and might, or trace
The author of his cursed race.
Still trust the promise that I make
And let thy breast no longer ache.

So will I toil, nor toil in vain,
That thou thy consort mayst regain.
So will I work with might and skill
That joy anew thy heart shall fill:
The valour of my soul display,
And Rávan and his legions slay.
Awake, awake! unmanned no more
Recall the strength was thine of yore.
Beseems not men like thee to wear
A weak heart yielding to despair.
Like troubles, too, mine eyes have seen,
Lamenting for a long-lost queen;
But, by despair unconquered yet,
My strength of mind I ne'er forget.
Far more shouldst thou of lofty soul
Thy passion and thy tears control,
When I, of Vánar's humbler strain,
Weep not for her in ceaseless pain.
Be firm, be patient, nor forget
The bounds the brave of heart have set
In loss, in woe, in strife, in fear,
When the dark hour of death is near.
Up! with thine own brave heart advise:
Not thus despond the firm and wise.
But he who gives his childish heart
To choose the coward's weakling part,
Sinks, like a foundered vessel, deep
In waves of woe that o'er him sweep.
See, suppliant hand to hand I lay,
And, moved by faithful love, I pray.
Give way no more to grief and gloom,
But all thy native strength resume.
No joy on earth, I ween, have they
Who yield their souls to sorrow's sway.
Their glory fades in slow decline:
'Tis not for thee to grieve and pine.
I do but hint with friendly speech
The wiser part I dare not teach.
This better path, dear friend, pursue,
And let not grief thy soul subdue."

Sugríva thus with gentle art
And sweet words soothed the mourner's heart,
Who brushed off with his mantle's hem
Tears from the eyes bedewed with them.
Sugríva's words were not in vain,
And Ráma was himself again,
Around the king his arms he threw
And thus began his speech anew:

"Whate'er a friend most wise and true,
Who counsels for the best, should do,
Whate'er his gentle part should be,
Has been performed, dear friend, by thee.
Taught by thy counsel, O my lord,
I feel my native strength restored.
A friend like thee is hard to gain,
Most rare in time of grief and pain.
Now strain thine utmost power to trace
The Maithil lady's dwelling place,
And aid me in my search to find
Fierce Rávaṇ of the impious mind.
Trust thou, in turn, thy loyal friend,
And say what aid this arm can lend
To speed thy hopes, as fostering rain
Quickens in earth the scattered grain.
Deem not those words, that seemed to spring
From pride, are false, O Vánar King.
None from these lips has ever heard,
None e'er shall hear, one lying word.
Again I promise and declare,
Yea, by my truth, dear friend, I swear."

Then glad was King Sugríva's breast,
And all his lords their joy confessed,
Stirred by sure hope of Ráma's aid,
And promise which the prince had made.

CANTO
VIII

Ráma's Promise

Doubt from Sugríva's heart had fled,
And thus to Raghu's son he said:
"No bliss the Gods of heaven deny.
Each views me with a favouring eye,
When thou, whom all good gifts attend,
Hast sought me and become my friend.
Leagued, friend, with thee in bold emprise
My arm might win the conquered skies;
And shall our banded strength be weak
To gain the realm which now I seek?
A happy fate was mine above
My kith and kin and all I love,
When, near the witness fire, I won
Thy friendship, Raghu's glorious son.
Thou too in ripening time shall see
Thy friend not all unworthy thee.
What gifts I have shall thus be shown:
Not mine the tongue to make them known.
Strong is the changeless bond that binds
The friendly faith of noble minds,
In woe, in danger, firm and sure
Their constancy and love endure.
Gold, silver, jewels rich and rare
They count as wealth for friends to share.

Yea, be they rich or poor and low,
Blest with all joys or sunk in woe,
Stained with each fault or pure of blame,
Their friends the nearest place may claim;
For whom they leave, at friendship's call,
Their gold, their bliss, their homes and all."

He spoke by generous impulse moved,
And Raghu's son his speech approved
Glancing at Lakshmaṇ by his side,
Like Indra in his beauty's pride.
The Vánar monarch saw the pair
Of mighty brothers standing there,
And turned his rapid eye to view
The forest trees that near him grew.
He saw, not far from where he stood,
A Sál tree towering o'er the wood.
Amid the thick leaves many a bee
Graced the scant blossoms of the tree,
From whose dark shade a bough, that bore
A load of leafy twigs, he tore,
Which on the grassy ground he laid
And seats for him and Ráma made.
Hanúmán saw them sit, he sought
A Sál tree's leafy bough and brought
The burthen, and with meek request
Entreated Lakshmaṇ, too, to rest.
There on the noble mountain's brow,
Strewn with the young leaves of the bough,
Sat Raghu's son in placid ease
Calm as the sea when sleeps the breeze.
Sugríva's heart with rapture swelled,
And thus, by eager love impelled,
He spoke in gracious tone, that, oft
Checked by his joy, was low and soft:
"I, by my brother's might oppressed,
By ceaseless woe and fear distressed,
Mourning my consort far away,
On Rishyamúka's mountain stray.
Expelled by Báli's cruel hate
I wander here disconsolate.
Do thou to whom all sufferers flee,
From his dread hand deliver me."

He spoke, and Ráma, just and brave,
Whose pious soul to virtue clave,
Smiled as in conscious might he eyed
The king of Vánars, and replied:

"Best fruit of friendship is the deed
That helps the friend in hour of need;
And this mine arm in death shall lay
Thy robber ere the close of day.
For see, these feathered darts of mine
Whose points so fiercely flash and shine,
And shafts with golden emblem, came
From dark woods known by Skanda's name,
Winged from the pinion of the hern
Like Indra's bolts they strike and burn.
With even knots and piercing head
Each like a furious snake is sped;
With these, to-day, before thine eye
Shall, like a shattered mountain, lie
Báli, thy dread and wicked foe,
O'erwhelmed in hideous overthrow."

He spoke: Sugríva's bosom swelled
With hope and joy unparalleled.
Then his glad voice the Vánar raised,
And thus the son of Raghu praised:
"Long have I pined in depth of grief;
Thou art the hope of all, O chief.
Now, Raghu's son, I hail thee friend,
And bid thee to my woes attend;
For, by my truth I swear it, now
Not life itself is dear as thou,
Since by the witness fire we met
And friendly hand in hand was set.
Friend communes now with friend, and hence
I tell with surest confidence,
How woes that on my spirit weigh
Consume me through the night and day."

For sobs and sighs he scarce could speak,
And his sad voice came low and weak,
As, while his eyes with tears o'erflowed,
The burden of his soul he showed.
Then by strong effort, bravely made,
The torrent of his tears he stayed,
Wiped his bright eyes, his grief subdued,

And thus, more calm, his speech renewed:
"By Báli's conquering might oppressed,
Of power and kingship dispossessed,
Loaded with taunts of scorn and hate
I left my realm and royal state.
He tore away my consort: she
Was dearer than my life to me,
And many a friend to me and mine
In hopeless chains was doomed to pine.
With wicked thoughts, unsated still,
Me whom he wrongs he yearns to kill;
And spies of Vánar race, who tried
To slay me, by this hand have died.
Moved by this constant doubt and fear
I saw thee, Prince, and came not near.
When woe and peril gather round
A foe in every form is found.
Save Hanumán, O Raghu's son,
And these, no friend is left me, none.
Through their kind aid, a faithful band
Who guard their lord from hostile hand,
Rest when their chieftain rests and bend
Their steps where'er he lists to wend,—
Through them alone, in toil and pain,
My wretched life I still sustain.

Enough, for thou hast heard in brief
The story of my pain and grief.
His mighty strength all regions know,
My brother, but my deadly foe.
Ah, if the proud oppressor fell,
His death would all my woe dispel.
Yea, on my cruel conqueror's fall
My joy depends, my life, my all.
This were the end and sure relief,
O Ráma, of my tale of grief.
Fair be his lot or dark with woe,
No comfort like a friend I know."

Then Ráma spoke: "O friend, relate
Whence sprang fraternal strife and hate,

49

That duly taught by thee, I may
Each foeman's strength and weakness weigh:
And skilled in every chance restore
The blissful state thou hadst before.
For, when I think of all the scorn
And bitter woe thou long hast borne,
My soul indignant swells with pain
Like waters flushed with furious rain.
Then, ere I string this bended bow,
Tell me the tale I long to know,
Ere from the cord my arrow fly,
And low in death thy foeman lie."

He spoke: Sugríva joyed to hear,
Nor less his lords were glad of cheer:
And thus to Ráma mighty-souled
The cause that moved their strife he told:

CANTO

IX

Sugríva's Story

"My brother, known by Báli's name,
Had won by might a conqueror's fame.
My father's eldest-born was he,
Well honoured by his sire and me.
My father died, and each sage lord
Named Báli king with one accord;
And he, by right of birth ordained,
The sovereign of the Vánars reigned.
He in his royal place controlled
The kingdom of our sires of old,
And I all faithful service lent
To aid my brother's government.
The fiend Máyáví,—him of yore

50

To Dundubhi his mother bore,—
For woman's love in strife engaged,
A deadly war with Báli waged.
When sleep had chained each weary frame
To vast Kishkindhá gates he came,
And, shouting through the shades of night,
Challenged his foeman to the fight.
My brother heard the furious shout,
And wild with rage rushed madly out,
Though fain would I and each sad wife
Detain him from the deadly strife.
He burned his demon foe to slay,
And rushed impetuous to the fray.
His weeping wives he thrust aside,
And forth, impelled by fury, hied;
While, by my love and duty led,
I followed where my brother sped.
Máyáví looked, and at the sight
Fled from his foes in wild affright.
The flying fiend we quickly viewed,
And with swift feet his steps pursued.
Then rose the moon, whose friendly ray
Cast light upon our headlong way.
By the soft beams was dimly shown
A mighty cave with grass o'ergrown.
Within its depths he sprang, and we
The demon's form no more might see.
My brother's breast was all aglow
With fury when he missed the foe,
And, turning, thus to me he said
With senses all disquieted:
"Here by the cavern's mouth remain;
Keep ear and eye upon the strain,
While I the dark recess explore
And dip my brand in foeman's gore."
I heard his angry speech, and tried
To turn him from his plan aside.
He made me swear by both his feet,
And sped within the dark retreat.
While in the cave he stayed, and I
Watched at the mouth, a year went by.

For his return I looked in vain,
And, moved by love, believed him slain.
I mourned, by doubt and fear distressed,
And greater horror seized my breast
When from the cavern rolled a flood,
A carnage stream of froth and blood;
And from the depths a sound of fear,
The roar of demons, smote mine ear;
But never rang my brother's shout
Triumphant in the battle rout.
I closed the cavern with a block,
Huge as a hill, of shattered rock.
Gave offerings due to Báli's shade,
And sought Kishkindhá, sore dismayed.
Long time with anxious care I tried
From Báli's lords his fate to hide,
But they, when once the tale was known,
Placed me as king on Báli's throne.
There for a while I justly reigned

And all with equal care ordained,
When joyous from the demon slain
My brother Báli came again.
He found me ruling in his stead,
And, fired with rage, his eyes grew red.
He slew the lords who made me king,
And spoke keen words to taunt and sting.
The kingly rank and power I held
My brother's rage with ease had quelled,
But still, restrained by old respect
For claims of birth, the thought I checked.
Thus having struck the demon down
Came Báli to his royal town.
With meek respect, with humble speech,
His haughty heart I strove to reach.
But all my arts were tried in vain,
No gentle word his lips would deign,
Though to the ground I bent and set
His feet upon my coronet:
Still Báli in his rage and pride
All signs of grace and love denied."

CANTO

X

Sugríva's Story

"I strove to soothe and lull to rest
The fury of his troubled breast:
"Well art thou come, dear lord," I cried.
"By whose strong arm thy foe has died.
Forlorn I languished here, but now
My saviour and defence art thou.
Once more receive this regal shade
Like the full moon in heaven displayed;
And let the chouries, thus restored,
Wave glorious o'er the rightful lord.
I kept my watch, thy word obeyed,
And by the cave a year I stayed.
But when I saw that stream of blood
Rush from the cavern in a flood,
My sad heart broken with dismay,
And every wandering sense astray,
I barred the entrance with a stone,—
A crag from some high mountain thrown—
Turned from the spot I watched in vain,
And to Kishkindhá came again.
My deep distress and downcast mien
By citizen and lord were seen.
They made me king against my will:
Forgive me if the deed was ill.
True as I ever was I see
My honoured king once more in thee;
I only ruled a while the state
When thou hadst left us desolate.
This town with people, lords, and lands,
Lay as a trust in guardian hands:
And now, my gracious lord, accept

The kingdom which thy servant kept.
Forgive me, victor of the foe,
Nor let thy wrath against me glow.
See joining suppliant hands I pray,
And at thy feet my head I lay.
Believe my words: against my will
The royal seat they made me fill.
Unkinged they saw the city, hence
They made me lord for her defence."

But Báli, though I humbly sued,
Reviled me in his furious mood:
"Out on thee, wretch!" in wrath he cried
With many a bitter taunt beside.
He summoned every lord, and all
His subjects gathered at his call.
Then forth his burning anger broke,
And thus amid his friends he spoke:
"I need not tell, for well ye know,
How fierce Máyáví, fiend and foe,
Came to Kishkindhá's gate by night,
And dared me in his wrath to fight.
I heard each word the demon said:
Forth from my royal hall I sped;
And, foe in brother's guise concealed,
Sugríva followed to the field.
The mighty demon through the shade
Beheld me come with one to aid:
Then shrinking from unequal fight,
He turned his back in swiftest flight.
From vengeful foes his life to save
He sought the refuge of a cave.
Then when I saw the fiend had fled
Within that cavern dark and dread,
Thus to my brother cruel-eyed,
Impatient in my wrath, I cried:
"I seek no more my royal town
Till I have struck the demon down.
Here by the cavern's mouth remain
Until my hand the foe have slain."
Upon his faith my heart relied,

And swift within the depths I hied.
A year went by: in every spot
I sought the fiend, but found him not.
At length my foe I saw and slew,
Whom long I feared when lost to view;
And all his kinsmen by his side
Beneath my vengeful fury died.
The monster, as he reeled and fell,
Poured forth his blood with roar and yell;
And, filling all the cavern, dyed
The portal with the crimson tide.
Upon my foeman slain at last
One look, one pitying look, I cast.
I sought again the light of day:
The cave was closed and left no way.
To the barred mouth I sadly came,
And called aloud Sugríva's name.
But all was still: no voice replied,

And hope within my bosom died.
With furious efforts, vain at first,
Through bars of rock my way I burst.
Then, free once more, the path that brought
My feet in safety home I sought.
'Twas thus Sugríva dared despise
The claim of brothers' friendly ties.
With crags of rock he barred me in,
And for himself the realm would win."

Thus Báli spoke in words severe;
And then, unmoved by ruth or fear,
Left me a single robe and sent
His brother forth in banishment.
He cast me out with scathe and scorn,
And from my side my wife was torn.
Now in great fear and ill at ease
I roam this land with woods and seas,
Or dwell on Rishyamúka's hill,
And sorrow for my consort still.
Thou hast the tale how first arose
This bitter hate of brother foes.

Such are the griefs neath which I pine,
And all without a fault of mine.
O swift to save in hour of fear,
My prayer who dread this Báli, hear
With gracious love assistance deign,
And mine oppressor's arm restrain."

Then Raghu's son, the good and brave,
With a gay laugh his answer gave:
"These shafts of mine which ne'er can fail,
Before whose sheen the sun grows pale,
Winged by my fury, fleet and fierce,
The wicked Báli's heart shall pierce.
Yea, mark the words I speak, so long
Shall live that wretch who joys in wrong,
Until these angered eyes have seen
The robber of thy darling queen.
I, taught by equal suffering, know
What waves of grief above thee flow.
This hand thy captive wife shall free,
And give thy kingdom back to thee."
Sugríva joyed as Ráma spoke,
And valour in his breast awoke.
His eye grew bright, his heart grew bold,
And thus his wondrous tale he told:

CANTO

XI

Dundubhi

"I doubt not, Prince, thy peerless might,
Armed with these shafts so keen and bright,
Like all-destroying fires of fate,
The worlds could burn and devastate.
But lend thou first thy mind and ear

Of Báli's power and might to hear.
How bold, how firm, in battle tried,
Is Báli's heart; and then decide.
From east to west, from south to north
On restless errand hurrying forth,
From farthest sea to sea he flies
Before the sun has lit the skies.
A mountain top he oft will seek,
Tear from its root a towering peak,
Hurl it aloft, as 'twere a ball,
And catch it ere to earth it fall.
And many a tree that long has stood
In health and vigour in the wood,
His single arm to earth will throw,
The marvels of his might to show.
Shaped like a bull, a monster bore
The name of Dundubhi of yore:
He matched in size a mountain height,
A thousand elephants in might.
By pride of wondrous gifts impelled,
And strength he deemed unparalleled,
To Ocean, lord of stream and brook,
Athirst for war, his way he took.
He reached the king of rolling waves
Whose gems are piled in sunless caves,
And threw his challenge to the sea;
"Come forth, O King, and fight with me."
He spoke, and from his ocean bed
The righteous monarch heaved his head,
And gave, sedate, his calm reply
To him whom fate impelled to die:
"Not mine, not mine the power," he cried,
"To cope with thee in battle tried;
But listen to my voice, and seek
The worthier foe of whom I speak.
The Lord of Hills, where hermits live
And love the home his forests give,
Whose child is Śankar's darling queen,
The King of Snows is he I mean.
Deep caves has he, and dark boughs shade
The torrent and the wild cascade.

From him expect the fierce delight
Which heroes feel in equal fight."

He deemed that fear checked ocean's king,
And, like an arrow from the string,
To the wild woods that clothe the side
Of Lord Himálaya's hills he hied.
Then Dundubhi, with hideous roar,
Huge fragments from the summit tore
Vast as Airávat, white with snow,
And hurled them to the plains below.
Then like a white cloud soft, serene,
The Lord of Mountains' form was seen.
It sat upon a lofty crest,
And thus the furious fiend addressed:
"Beseems thee not, O virtue's friend,
My mountain tops to rive and rend;

For I, the hermit's calm retreat,
For deeds of war am all unmeet."

The demon's eye with rage grew red,
And thus in furious tone he said:
"If thou from fear or sloth decline
To match thy strength in war with mine,
Where shall I find a champion, say,
To meet me burning for the fray?"
He spoke: Himálaya, skilled in lore
Of eloquence, replied once more,
And, angered in his righteous mind,
Addressed the chief of demon kind:
"The Vánar Báli, brave and wise,
Son of the God who rules the skies,
Sways, glorious in his high renown,
Kishkindhá his imperial town.
Well may that valiant lord who knows
Each art of war his might oppose
To thine, in equal battle set,
As Namuchi and Indra met.
Go, if thy soul desire the fray;
To Báli's city speed away,

And that unconquered hero meet
Whose fame is high for warlike feat."
He listened to the Lord of Snow,
And, his proud heart with rage aglow,
Sped swift away and lighted down
By vast Kishkindhá, Báli's town.
With pointed horns to strike and gore
The semblance of a bull he bore,
Huge as a cloud that downward bends
Ere the full flood of rain descends.
Impelled by pride and rage and hate,
He thundered at Kishkindhá's gate;
And with his bellowing, like the sound
Of pealing drums, he shook the ground,
He rent the earth and prostrate threw
The trees that near the portal grew.
King Báli from the bowers within
Indignant heard the roar and din.
Then, moonlike mid the stars, with all
His dames he hurried to the wall;
And to the fiend this speech, expressed
In clear and measured words, addressed:
"Know me for monarch. Báli styled,
Of Vánar tribes that roam the wild.
Say why dost thou this gate molest,
And bellowing thus disturb our rest?
I know thee, mighty fiend: beware
And guard thy life with wiser care."
He spoke: and thus the fiend returned,
While red with rage his eyeballs burned:
"What! speak when all thy dames are nigh
And hero-like thy foe defy?
Come, meet me in the fight this day,
And learn my strength by bold assay.
Or shall I spare thee, and relent
Until the coming night be spent?
Take then the respite of a night
And yield thee to each soft delight.
Then, monarch of the Vánar race
With loving arms thy friends embrace.
Gifts on thy faithful lords bestow,

Bid each and all farewell, and go.
Show in the streets once more thy face,
Install thy son to fill thy place.
Dally a while with each dear dame;
And then my strength thy pride shall tame
For, should I smite thee drunk with wine
Enamoured of those dames of thine,
Beneath diseases bowed and bent,
Or weak, unarmed, or negligent,
My deed would merit hate and scorn
As his who slays the child unborn."
Then Báli's soul with rage was fired,
Queen Tára and the dames retired;
And slowly, with a laugh of pride,
The king of Vánars thus replied:
"Me, fiend, thou deemest drunk with wine:
Unless thy fear the fight decline,
Come, meet me in the fray, and test
The spirit of my valiant breast."
He spoke in wrath and high disdain;
And, laying down his golden chain,
Gift of his sire Mahendra, dared
The demon, for the fray prepared;
Seized by the horns the monster, vast
As a huge hill, and held him fast,
Then fiercely dragged him round and round,
And, shouting, hurled him to the ground.
Blood streaming from his ears, he rose,
And wild with fury strove the foes.
Then Báli, match for Indra's might,
With every arm renewed the fight.
He fought with fists, and feet, and knees,
With fragments of the rock, and trees.
At last the monster's strength, assailed
By Śakra's conquering offspring, failed.
Him Báli raised with mighty strain
And dashed upon the ground again;
Where, bruised and shattered, in a tide
Of rushing blood, the demon died.
King Báli saw the lifeless corse,
And bending, with tremendous force

Raised the huge bulk from where it lay,
And hurled it full a league away.
As through the air the body flew,
Some blood-drops, caught by gales that blew,
Welled from his shattered jaw and fell
By Saint Matanga's hermit cell:
Matanga saw, illustrious sage,
Those drops defile his hermitage,

And, as he marvelled whence they came,
Fierce anger filled his soul with flame:
"Who is the villain, evil-souled,
With childish thoughts unwise and bold,
Who is the impious wretch," he cried,
"By whom my grove with blood is dyed?"

Thus spoke Matanga in his rage,
And hastened from the hermitage,
When lo, before his wondering eyes
Lay the dead bull of mountain size.
His hermit soul was nothing slow
The doer of the deed to know,
And thus the Vánar in a burst
Of wild tempestuous wrath he cursed:
"Ne'er let that Vánar wander here,
For, if he come, his death is near,
Whose impious hand with blood has dyed
The holy place where I abide,
Who threw this demon corse and made
A ruin of the pleasant shade.
If e'er he plant his wicked feet
Within one league of my retreat;
Yea, if the villain come so nigh
That very hour he needs must die.
And let the Vánar lords who dwell
In the dark woods that skirt my cell
Obey my words, and speeding hence
Find them some meeter residence.
Here if they dare to stay, on all
The terrors of my curse shall fall.
They spoil the tender saplings, dear

61

As children which I cherish here,
Mar root and branch and leaf and spray,
And steal the ripening fruit away.
One day I grant, no further hour,
To-morrow shall my curse have power,
And then each Vánar I may see
A stone through countless years shall be."
The Vánars heard the curse and hied
From sheltering wood and mountain side.
King Báli marked their haste and dread,
And to the flying leaders said:
"Speak, Vánar chiefs, and tell me why
From Saint Matanga's grove ye fly
To gather round me: is it well
With all who in those woodlands dwell?"
He spoke: the Vánar leaders told
King Báli with his chain of gold
What curse the saint had on them laid,
Which drove them from their ancient shade.
Then royal Báli sought the sage,
With reverent hands to soothe his rage.
The holy man his suppliant spurned,
And to his cell in anger turned.
That curse on Báli sorely pressed,
And long his conscious soul distressed.
Him still the curse and terror keep
Afar from Rishyamúka's steep.
He dares not to the grove draw nigh,
Nay scarce will hither turn his eye.
We know what terrors warm him hence,
And roam these woods in confidence.
Look, Prince, before thee white and dry
The demon's bones uncovered lie,
Who, like a hill in bulk and length,
Fell ruind for his pride of strength.
See those high Sál trees seven in row
That droop their mighty branches low,
These at one grasp would Báli seize,
And leafless shake the trembling trees.
These tales I tell, O Prince, to show
The matchless power that arms the foe.

How canst thou hope to slay him? how
Meet Báli in the battle now?"

Sugríva spoke and sadly sighed:
And Lakshman with a laugh replied:
"What show of power, what proof and test
May still the doubts that fill thy breast?"

He spoke. Sugríva thus replied:
"See yonder Sál trees side by side.
King Báli here would take his stand
Grasping his bow with vigorous hand,
And every arrow, keen and true,
Would strike its tree and pierce it through.
If Ráma now his bow will bend,
And through one trunk an arrow send;
Or if his arm can raise and throw
Two hundred measures of his bow,
Grasped by a foot and hurled through air,
The demon bull that moulders there,
My heart will own his might and fain
Believe my foe already slain."

Sugríva spoke inflamed with ire,
Scanned Ráma with a glance of fire,
Pondered a while in silent mood.
And thus again his speech renewed:
"All lands with Báli's glories ring,
A valiant, strong, and mighty king;
In conscious power unused to yield,
A hero first in every field.
His wondrous deeds his might declare,
Deeds Gods might scarcely do or dare;
And on this power reflecting still
I roam on Rishyamúka's hill.
Awed by my brother's might I rove,
In doubt and fear, from grove to grove,
While Hanumán, my chosen friend,
And faithful lords my steps attend;
And now, O true to friendship's tie,
I hail in thee my best ally.

My surest refuge from my foes,
And steadfast as the Lord of Snows.
Still, when I muse how strong and bold
Is cruel Báli, evil-souled,
But ne'er, O chief of Raghu's line,
Have seen what strength in war is thine,
Though in my heart I may not dare
Doubt thy great might, despise, compare,
Thoughts of his fearful deeds will rise
And fill my soul with sad surmise.
Speech, form, and trust which naught may move

Thy secret strength and glory prove,
As smouldering ashes dimly show
The dormant fires that live below."

He ceased: and Ráma answered, while
Played o'er his lips a gracious smile:
"Not yet convinced? This clear assay
Shall drive each lingering doubt away."
Thus Ráma spoke his heart to cheer,
To Dundubhi's vast frame drew near:
He touched it with his foot in play
And sent it twenty leagues away.
Sugríva marked what easy force
Hurled through the air that demon's corse
Whose mighty bones were white and dried,
And to the son of Raghu cried:
"My brother Báli, when his might
Was drunk and weary from the fight,
Hurled forth the monster body, fresh
With skin and sinews, blood and flesh.
Now flesh and blood are dried away,
The crumbling bones are light as hay,
Which thou, O Raghu's son, hast sent
Flying through air in merriment.
This test alone is weak to show
If thou be stronger or the foe.
By thee a heap of mouldering bone,
By him the recent corse was thrown.
Thy strength, O Prince, is yet untried:

64

Come, pierce one tree: let this decide.
Prepare thy ponderous bow and bring
Close to thine ear the straining string.
On yonder Sál tree fix thine eye,
And let the mighty arrow fly,
I doubt not, chief, that I shall see
Thy pointed shaft transfix the tree.
Then come, assay the easy task,
And do for love the thing I ask.
Best of all lights, the Day-God fills
With glory earth and sky:
Himálaya is the lord of hills
That heave their heads on high.
The royal lion is the best
Of beasts that tread the earth;
And thou, O hero, art confessed
First in heroic worth."

CANTO
XII

The Palm Trees

T hen Ráma, that his friend might know
His strength unrivalled, grasped his bow,
That mighty bow the foe's dismay,—
And on the string an arrow lay.
Next on the tree his eye he bent,
And forth the hurtling weapon went.
Loosed from the matchless hero's hold,
That arrow, decked with burning gold,
Cleft the seven palms in line, and through
The hill that rose behind them flew:
Six subterranean realms it passed,
And reached the lowest depth at last,
Whence speeding back through earth and air

It sought the quiver, and rested there.
Upon the cloven trees amazed,
The sovereign of the Vánars gazed.
With all his chains and gold outspread
Prostrate on earth he laid his head.
Then, rising, palm to palm he laid
In reverent act, obeisance made,
And joyously to Ráma, best
Of war-trained chiefs, these words addressed:

"What champion, Raghu's son, may hope
With thee in deadly fight to cope,
Whose arrow, leaping from the bow,
Cleaves tree and hill and earth below?
Scarce might the Gods, arrayed for strife
By Indra's self, escape, with life
Assailed by thy victorious hand:
And how may Báli hope to stand?
All grief and care are past away,
And joyous thoughts my bosom sway,
Who have in thee a friend, renowned,
As Varuṇ or as Indra, found.
Then on! subdue,—'tis friendship's claim,—
My foe who bears a brother's name.
Strike Báli down beneath thy feet:
With suppliant hands I thus entreat."
Sugríva ceased, and Ráma pressed
The grateful Vánar to his breast;
And thoughts of kindred feeling woke
In Lakshmaṇ's bosom, as he spoke:
"On to Kishkindhá, on with speed!
Thou, Vánar King, our way shalt lead,
Then challenge Báli forth to fight.
Thy foe who scorns a brother's right."
They sought Kishkindhá's gate and stood
Concealed by trees in densest wood,
Sugríva, to the fight addressed,
More closely drew his cinctured vest,
And raised a wild sky-piercing shout

To call the foeman Báli out.
Forth came impetuous Báli, stirred
To fury by the shout he heard.
So the great sun, ere night has ceased,
Springs up impatient to the east.
Then fierce and wild the conflict raged
As hand to hand the foes engaged,
As though in battle mid the stars
Fought Mercury and fiery Mars.
To highest pitch of frenzy wrought
With fists like thunderbolts they fought,
While near them Ráma took his stand,
And viewed the battle, bow in hand.
Alike they stood in form and might,
Like heavenly Aśvins paired in fight,
Nor might the son of Raghu know
Where fought the friend and where the foe;
So, while his bow was ready bent,
No life-destroying shaft he sent.
Crushed down by Báli's mightier stroke
Sugríva's force now sank and broke,
Who, hoping naught from Ráma's aid,
To Rishyamúka fled dismayed,
Weary, and faint, and wounded sore,
His body bruised and dyed with gore,
From Báli's blows, in rage and dread,
Afar to sheltering woods he fled.

Nor Báli farther dared pursue,
The curbing curse too well he knew.
"Fled from thy death!" the victor cried,
And home the mighty warrior hied.
Hanúmán, Lakshmaṇ, Raghu's son
Beheld the conquered Vánar run,
And followed to the sheltering shade
Where yet Sugríva stood dismayed.
Near and more near the chieftains came,
Then, for intolerable shame,
Not daring yet to lift his eyes,
Sugríva spoke with burning sighs:

"Thy matchless strength I first beheld,
And dared my foe, by thee impelled.
Why hast thou tried me with deceit
And urged me to a sure defeat?
Thou shouldst have said, "I will not slay
Thy foeman in the coming fray."
For had I then thy purpose known
I had not waged the fight alone."

The Vánar sovereign, lofty-souled,
In plaintive voice his sorrows told.
Then Ráma spake: "Sugríva, list,
All anger from thy heart dismissed,
And I will tell the cause that stayed
Mine arrow, and withheld the aid.
In dress, adornment, port, and height,
In splendour, battle-shout, and might,
No shade of difference could I see
Between thy foe, O King, and thee.
So like was each, I stood at gaze,
My senses lost in wildering maze,
Nor loosened from my straining bow
A deadly arrow at the foe,
Lest in my doubt the shaft should send
To sudden death our surest friend.
O, if this hand in heedless guilt
And rash resolve thy blood had spilt,
Through every land, O Vánar King,
My wild and foolish act would ring.
Sore weight of sin on him must lie
By whom a friend is made to die;
And Lakshmaṇ, I, and Sítá, best
Of dames, on thy protection rest.
On, warrior! for the fight prepare;
Nor fear again thy foe to dare.
Within one hour thine eye shall view
My arrow strike thy foeman through;
Shall see the stricken Báli lie
Low on the earth, and gasp and die.
But come, a badge about thee bind,
O monarch of the Vánar kind,

That in the battle shock mine eyes
The friend and foe may recognize.
Come, Lakshman, let that creeper deck
With brightest bloom Sugríva's neck,
And be a happy token, twined
Around the chief of lofty mind."

Upon the mountain slope there grew
A threading creeper fair to view,
And Lakshman plucked the bloom and round
Sugríva's neck a garland wound.
Graced with the flowery wreath he wore,
The Vánar chief the semblance bore
Of a dark cloud at close of day
Engarlanded with cranes at play,
In glorious light the Vánar glowed
As by his comrade's side he strode,
And, still on Ráma's word intent,
His steps to great Kishkindhá bent.

CANTO

XIII

The Return to Kishkindhá

Thus with Sugríva, from the side
Of Rishyamúka, Ráma hied,
And stood before Kishkindhá's gate
Where Báli kept his regal state.
The hero in his warrior hold
Raised his great bow adorned with gold,
And drew his pointed arrow bright
As sunbeams, finisher of fight.
Strong-necked Sugríva led the way
With Lakshman mighty in the fray.
Nala and Níla came behind

With Hanumán of lofty mind,
And valiant Tára, last in place,
A leader of the Vánar race.
They gazed on many a tree that showed
The glory of its pendent load,
And brook and limpid rill that made
Sweet murmurs as they seaward strayed.
They looked on caverns dark and deep,
On bower and glen and mountain steep,
And saw the opening lotus stud
With roseate cup the crystal flood,
While crane and swan and coot and drake
Made pleasant music on the lake,
And from the reedy bank was heard
The note of many a happy bird.
In open lawns, in tangled ways,
They saw the tall deer stand at gaze,
Or marked them free and fearless roam,
Fed with sweet grass, their woodland home.
At times two flashing tusks between
The wavings of the wood were seen,
And some mad elephant, alone,
Like a huge moving hill, was shown.
And scarcely less in size appeared
Great monkeys all with dust besmeared.
And various birds that roam the skies,
And silvan creatures, met their eyes,
As through the wood the chieftains sped,
And followed where Sugríva led.

Then Ráma, as their way they made,
Saw near at hand a lovely shade,
And, as he gazed upon the trees,
Spake to Sugríva words like these;
"Those stately trees in beauty rise,
Fair as a cloud in autumn skies.
I fain, my friend, would learn from thee
What pleasant grove is that I see."

Thus Ráma spake, the mighty souled;
And thus his tale Sugríva told:

70

"That, Ráma, is a wide retreat
That brings repose to weary feet.
Bright streams and fruit and roots are there,
And shady gardens passing fair.
There, neath the roof of hanging boughs,
The sacred Seven maintained their vows.
Their heads in dust were lowly laid,
In streams their nightly beds were made.
Each seventh night they broke their fast,
But air was still their sole repast,
And when seven hundred years were spent
To homes in heaven the hermits went.
Their glory keeps the garden yet,
With walls of stately trees beset.
Scarce would the Gods and demons dare,
By Indra led, to enter there.
No beast that roams the wood is found,
No bird of air, within the bound;
Or, thither if they idly stray,
They find no more their homeward way.
You hear at times mid dulcet tones
The chime of anklets, rings, and zones.
You hear the song and music sound,
And heavenly fragrance breathes around,
There duly burn the triple fires
Where mounts the smoke in curling spires,
And, in a dun wreath, hangs above
The tall trees, like a brooding dove.
Round branch and crest the vapours close
Till every tree enveloped shows
A hill of lazulite when clouds
Hang round it with their misty shrouds.
With Lakshmaṇ, lord of Raghu's line,
In reverent guise thine head incline,
And with fixt heart and suppliant hand
Give honour to the sainted band.
They who with faithful hearts revere
The holy Seven who harboured here,
Shall never, son of Raghu, know
In all their lives an hour of woe."

Then Ráma and his brother bent,
And did obeisance reverent
With suppliant hand and lowly head,
Then with Sugríva onward sped.
Beyond the sainted Seven's abode
Far on their way the chieftains strode,
And great Kishkindhá's portal gained,
The royal town where Báli reigned.
Then by the gate they took their stand
All ready armed a noble band,
And burning every one
To slay in battle, hand to hand,
Their foeman, Indra's son.

CANTO

XIV

The Challenge

They stood where trees of densest green
Wove round their forms a veiling screen.
O'er all the garden's pleasant shade
The eyes of King Sugríva strayed,

And, as on grass and tree he gazed,
The fires of wrath within him blazed.
Then like a mighty cloud on high,
When roars the tempest through the sky,
Girt by his friends he thundered out
His dread sky-rending battle-shout
Like some proud lion in his gait,
Or as the sun begins his state,
Sugríva let his quick glance rest
On Ráma whom he thus addressed:
"There is the seat of Báli's sway,
Where flags on wall and turret play,

Which mighty bands of Vánars hold,
Rich in all arms and store of gold.
Thy promise to thy mind recall
That Báli by thy hand shall fall.
As kindly fruits adorn the bough.
So give my hopes their harvest now."

In suppliant tone the Vánar prayed,
And Raghu's son his answer made:
"By Lakshman's hand this flowery twine
Was wound about thee for a sign.
The wreath of giant creeper throws
About thy form its brillant glows,
As though about the sun were set
The bright stars for a coronet.
One shaft of mine this day, dear friend,
Thy sorrow and thy fear shall end.
And, from the bowstring freed, shall be
Giver of freedom, King, to thee.
Then come, Sugríva, quickly show,
Where'er he lie, thy bitter foe;
And let my glance the wretch descry
Whose deeds, a brother's name belie.
Yea, soon in dust and blood o'erthrown
Shall Báli fall and gasp and groan.
Once let this eye the foeman see,
Then, if he live to turn and flee,
Despise my puny strength, and shame
With foul opprobrium Ráma's name.
Hast thou not seen his hand, O King,
Through seven tall trees one arrow wing?
Still in that strength securely trust,
And deem thy foeman in the dust.
In all my days, though surely tried
By grief and woe, I ne'er have lied;
And still by duty's law restrained
Will ne'er with falsehood's charge be stained.
Cast doubt away: the oath I sware
Its kindly fruit shall quickly bear,
As smiles the land with golden grain
By mercy of the Lord of rain.

Oh, warrior to the gate I defy
Thy foe with shout and battle-cry,
Till Báli with his chain of gold
Come speeding from his royal hold.
Proud hearts, with warlike fire aglow,
Brook not the challenge of a foe:
Each on his power and might relies,
And most before his ladies eyes.
King Báli loves the fray too well
To linger in his citadel,
And, when he hears thy battle-shout,
All wild for war will hasten out."
He spoke. Sugríva raised a cry
That shook and rent the echoing sky,
A shout so fierce and loud and dread
That stately bulls in terror fled,
Like dames who fly from threatened stain
In some ignoble monarch's reign.
The deer in wild confusion ran
Like horses turned in battle's van.
Down fell the birds, like Gods who fall
When merits fail, at that dread call.
So fiercely, boldened for the fray,
The offspring of the Lord of Day
Sent forth his furious shout as loud
As thunder from a labouring cloud,
Or, where the gale blows fresh and free,
The roaring of the troubled sea.

CANTO
XV

Tárá

That shout, which shook the land with fear,
   In thunder smote on Báli's ear,
   Where in the chamber barred and closed
The sovereign with his dame reposed.
Each amorous thought was rudely stilled,
And pride and rage his bosom filled.
His angry eyes flashed darkly red,
And all his native brightness fled,
As when, by swift eclipse assailed,
The glory of the sun has failed.
While in his fury uncontrolled
He ground his teeth, his eyeballs rolled,
He seemed a lake wherein no gem
Of blossom decks the lotus stem.
He heard, and with indignant pride
Forth from the bower the Vánar hied.
And the earth trembled at the beat
And fury of his hastening feet.
But Tárá to her consort flew,
Her loving arms around him threw,
And trembling and bewildered, gave
Wise counsel that might heal and save:
"O dear my lord, this rage control
That like a torrent floods thy soul,
And cast these idle thoughts away
Like faded wreath of yesterday,
O tarry till the morning light,
Then, if thou wilt, go forth and fight.

Think not I doubt thy valour, no;
Or deem thee weaker than thy foe,

75

Yet for a while would have thee stay
Nor see thee tempt the fight to-day.
Now list, my loving lord, and learn
The reason why I bid thee turn.
Thy foeman came in wrath and pride,
And thee to deadly fight defied.
Thou wentest out: he fought, and fled
Sore wounded and discomfited.
But yet, untaught by late defeat,
He comes his conquering foe to meet,
And calls thee forth with cry and shout:
Hence spring, my lord, this fear and doubt.
A heart so bold that will not yield,
But yearns to tempt the desperate field,
Such loud defiance, fiercely pressed,
On no uncertain hope can rest.
So lately by thine arm o'erthrown,
He comes not back, I ween, alone.
Some mightier comrade guards his side,
And spurs him to this burst of pride.
For nature made the Vánar wise:
On arms of might his hope relies;
And never will Sugríva seek
A friend whose power to save is weak.
Now listen while my lips unfold
The wondrous tale my Angad told.
Our child the distant forest sought,
And, learnt from spies, the tidings brought.
Two sons of Daśaratha, sprung
From old Ikshváku, brave and young,
Renowned in arms, in war untamed—
Ráma and Lakshmaṇ are they named—
Have with thy foe Sugríva made
A league of love and friendly aid.
Now Ráma, famed for exploit high,
Is bound thy brother's firm ally,
Like fires of doom that ruin all
He makes each foe before him fall.
He is the suppliant's sure defence,
The tree that shelters innocence.
The poor and wretched seek his feet:

In him the noblest glories meet.
With skill and knowledge vast and deep
His sire's commands he loved to keep;
With princely gifts and graces stored
As metals deck the Mountains' Lord.
Thou canst not, O my hero, stand
Before the might of Ráma's hand;
For none may match his powers or dare
With him in deeds of war compare.
Hear, I entreat, the words I say,
Nor lightly turn my rede away.
O let fraternal discord cease,
And link you in the bonds of peace.
Let consecrating rites ordain
Sugríva partner of thy reign.
Let war and thoughts of conflict end,
And be thou his and Ráma's friend,
Each soft approach of love begin,
And to thy soul thy brother win;
For whether here or there he be,
Thy brother still, dear lord, is he.
Though far and wide these eyes I strain
A friend like him I seek in vain.
Let gentle words his heart incline,
And gifts and honours make him thine,
Till, foes no more, in love allied,
You stand as brothers side by side.
Thou in high rank wast wont to hold
Sugríva, formed in massive mould;
Then come, thy brother's love regain,
For other aids are weak and vain.
If thou would please my soul, and still
Preserve me from all fear and ill,
I pray thee by thy love be wise
And do the thing which I advise.
Assuage thy fruitless wrath, and shun
The mightier arms of Raghu's son;
For Indra's peer in might is he,
A foe too strong, my lord, for thee."

The Fall of Báli

Thus Tárá with the starry eyes
  Her counsel gave with burning sighs.
  But Báli, by her prayers unmoved,
Spurned her advice, and thus reproved:
"How may this insult, scathe, and scorn
By me, dear love, be tamely born?
My brother, yea my foe, comes nigh
And dares me forth with shout and cry.
Learn, trembler! that the valiant, they
Who yield no step in battle fray,
Will die a thousand deaths but ne'er
An unavenged dishonour bear.
Nor, O my love, be thou dismayed
Though Ráma lend Sugríva aid,
For one so pure and duteous, one
Who loves the right, all sin will shun,
Release me from thy soft embrace,
And with thy dames thy steps retrace:
Enough already, O mine own,
Of love and sweet devotion shown.
Drive all thy fear and doubt away;
I seek Sugríva in the fray
His boisterous rage and pride to still,
And tame the foe I would not kill.
My fury, armed with brandished trees,
Shall strike Sugríva to his knees:

Nor shall the humbled foe withstand
The blows of my avenging hand,
When, nerved by rage and pride, I beat
The traitor down beneath my feet.

Thou, love, hast lent thine own sweet aid,
And all thy tender care displayed;
Now by my life, by these who yearn
To serve thee well, I pray thee turn.
But for a while, dear dame, I go
To come triumphant o'er the foe."

Thus Báli spake in gentlest tone:
Soft arms about his neck were thrown;
Then round her lord the lady went
With sad steps slow and reverent.
She stood in solemn guise to bless
With prayers for safety and success,
Then with her train her chamber sought
By grief and racking fear distraught.

With serpent's pantings fierce and fast
King Báli from the city passed.
His glance, as each quick breath he drew,
Around to find the foe he threw,
And saw where fierce Sugríva showed
His form with golden hues that glowed,
And, as a fire resplendent, stayed
To meet his foe in arms arrayed.
When Báli, long-armed chieftain, found
Sugríva stationed on the ground,
Impelled by warlike rage he braced
His warrior garb about his waist,
And with his mighty arm raised high
Rushed at Sugríva with a cry.
But when Sugríva, fierce and bold,
Saw Báli with his chain of gold,
His arm he heaved, his hand he closed,
And face to face his foe opposed.
To him whose eyes with fury shone,
In charge impetuous rushing on,
Skilled in each warlike art and plan,
Báli with hasty words began:
"My ponderous hand, to fight addressed
With fingers clenched and arm compressed
Shall on thy death doomed brow descend

And, crashing down, thy life shall end."
He spoke; and wild with rage and pride,
The fierce Sugríva thus replied:
"Thus let my arm begin the strife
And from thy body crush the life."

Then Báli, wounded and enraged,
With furious blows the battle waged.
Sugríva seemed, with blood-streams dyed,
A hill with fountains in his side.
But with his native force unspent
A Sál tree from the earth he rent,
And like the bolt of Indra smote
On Báli's head and chest and throat.
Bruised by the blows he could not shield,
Half vanquished Báli sank and reeled,
As sinks a vessel with her freight
Borne down by overwhelming weight.
Swift as Suparṇa's swiftest flight
In awful strength they rushed to fight:
So might the sun and moon on high
Encountering battle in the sky.
Fierce and more fierce, as fought the foes,
The furious rage of combat rose.
They warred with feet and arms and knees,
With nails and stones and boughs and trees,
And blows descending fast as rain
Dyed each dark form with crimson stain,
While like two thunder-clouds they met
With battle-cry and shout and threat.
Then Ráma saw Sugríva quail,
Marked his worn strength grow weak and fail.
Saw how he turned his wistful eye
To every quarter of the sky.
His friend's defeat he could not brook,
Bent on his shaft an eager look,
Then burned to slay the conquering foe,
And laid his arrow on the bow.
As to an orb the bow he drew
Forth from the string the arrow flew
Like Fate's tremendous discus hurled

By Yáma forth to end the world.
So loud the din that every bird
The bow-string's clans with terror heard,
And wildly fled the affrighted deer
As though the day of doom were near.
So, deadly as the serpent's fang,
Forth from the string the arrow sprang.
Like the red lightning's flash and flame
It flew unerring to its aim,
And, hissing murder through the air,
Pierced Báli's breast, and quivered there.
Struck by the shaft that flew so well
The mighty Vánar reeled and fell,
As earthward Indra's flag they pull
When Aśvíní's fair moon is full.

XVII

★

Báli's Speech

Like some proud tree before the blast
Brave Báli to the ground was cast,
Where prostrate in the dust he rolled
Clad in the sheen of glistening gold,

As when uptorn the standard lies
Of the great God who rules the skies.
When low upon the earth was laid
The lord whom Vánar tribes obeyed,
Dark as a moonless sky no more
His land her joyous aspect wore.
Though low in dust and mire was rolled
The form of Báli lofty-souled,
Still life and valour, might and grace
Clung to their well-loved dwelling-place.

That golden chain with rich gems set,
The choicest gift of Sákra, yet
Preserved his life nor let decay
Steal strength and beauty's light away.
Still from that chain divinely wrought
His dusky form a glory caught,
As a dark cloud, when day is done,
Made splendid by the dying sun.
As fell the hero, crushed in fight,
There beamed afar a triple light
From limbs, from chain, from shaft that drank
His life-blood as the warrior sank.
The never-failing shaft, impelled
By the great bow which Ráma held,
Brought bliss supreme, and lit the way
To Brahmá's worlds which ne'er decay.

Ráma and Lakshman nearer drew
The mighty fallen foe to view,
Mahendra's son, the brave and bold,
The monarch with his chain of gold,
With lustrous face and tawny eyes,
Broad chest, and arms of wondrous size,
Like Lord Mahendra fierce in fight,
Or Vishnu's never-conquered might,
Now fallen like Yayáti sent
From heaven, his store of merit spent,
Like the bright flame that pales and dies,
Like the great sun who fires the skies,
Doomed in the general doom to fall
When time shall end and ruin all.

The wounded Báli, when he saw
Ráma and Lakshman nearer draw,
Keen words to Raghu's son, impressed
With justice' holy stamp, addressed:

"What fame, from one thou hast not slain
In front of battle, canst thou gain,
Whose secret hand has laid me low
When madly fighting with my foe?

82

From every tongue thy glory rings,
A scion of a line of kings,
True to thy vows, of noblest race,
With every gentle gift and grace:
Whose tender heart for woe can feel,
And joy in every creature's weal:
Whose breast with high ambition swells,
Knows duty's claim and ne'er rebels.
They praise thy valour, patience, ruth,
Thy firmness, self-restraint, and truth:
Thy hand prepared for sin's control,
All virtues of a princely soul.
I thought of all these gifts of thine,
And glories of an ancient line,
I set my Tárá's tears at naught,
I met Sugríva and we fought.
O Ráma, till this fatal morn
I held that thou wouldst surely scorn
To strike me as I fought my foe
And thought not of a stranger's blow,
But now thine evil heart is shown,
A yawning well with grass o'ergrown.
Thou wearest virtue's badge, but guile
And meanest sin thy soul defile.
I took thee not for treacherous fire,
A sinner clad in saint's attire;
Nor deemed thou idly wouldst profess
The show and garb of righteousness.
In fenced town, in open land,
Ne'er hast thou suffered at this hand,
Nor canst of proud contempt complain:
Then wherefore is the guiltless slain?
My harmless life in woods I lead,
On forest fruits and roots I feed.
My foeman in the field I sought,
And ne'er with thee, O Ráma, fought.
Upon thy limbs, O King, I see
The raiment of a devotee;
And how can one like thee, who springs
From a proud line of ancient kings,
Beneath fair virtue's mask, disgrace

His lineage by a deed so base?
From Raghu is thy long descent,
For duteous deeds prëeminent:
Why, sinner clad in saintly dress,
Roamest thou through the wilderness?
Truth, valour, justice free from spot,
The hand that gives and grudges not,
The might that strikes the sinner down,
These bring a prince his best renown.
Here in the woods, O King, we live
On roots and fruit which branches give.

Thus nature framed our harmless race:
Thou art a man supreme in place.
Silver and gold and land provoke
The fierce attack, the robber's stroke,
Canst thou desire this wild retreat,
The berries and the fruit we eat?
'Tis not for mighty kings to tread
The flowery path, by pleasure led.
Theirs be the arm that crushes sin,
Theirs the soft grace to woo and win:
The steadfast will that guides the state,
Wise favour to the good and great;
And for all time are kings renowned
Who blend these arts and ne'er confound.
But thou art weak and swift to ire,
Unstable, slave of each desire.
Thou tramplest duty in the dust,
And in thy bow is all thy trust.
Thou carest naught for noble gain,
And treatest virtue with disdain,
While every sense its captive draws
To follow pleasure's changing laws.
I wronged thee not in word or deed,
But by thy deadly dart I bleed.
What wilt thou, mid the virtuous, say
To purge thy lasting stain away?
All these, O King, must sink to hell,
The regicide, the infidel,
He who in blood and slaughter joys,

A Bráhman or a cow destroys,
Untimely weds in law's despite
Scorning an elder brother's right,
Who dares his Teacher's bed ascend,
The miser, spy, and treacherous friend.
These impious wretches, one and all,
Must to the hell of sinners fall.
My skin the holy may not wear,
Useless to thee my bones and hair;
Nor may my slaughtered body be
The food of devotees like thee.
These five-toed things a man may slay
And feed upon the fallen prey;
The mailed rhinoceros may die,
And, with the hare his food supply.
Iguanas he may kill and eat,
With porcupine and tortoise meat.
But all the wise account it sin
To touch my bones and hair and skin.
My flesh they may not eat; and I
A useless prey, O Ráma, die.
In vain my Tárá reasoned well,
On dull deaf ears her counsel fell.
I scorned her words though sooth and sweet,
And hither rushed my fate to meet.
Ah for the land thou rulest! she
Finds no protection, lord, from thee,
Neglected like some noble dame
By a vile husband dead to shame.
Mean-hearted coward, false and vile,
Whose cruel soul delights in guile,
Could Daśaratha, noblest king,
Beget so mean and base a thing?
Alas! an elephant, in form
Of Ráma, in a maddening storm
Of passion casting to the ground
The girth of law that clipped him round,
Too wildly passionate to feel
The prick of duty's guiding steel,
Has charged me unawares, and dead
I fall beneath his murderous tread.

How, stained with this my base defeat,
How wilt thou dare, where good men meet,
To speak, when every tongue will blame
With keen reproach this deed of shame?
Such hero strength and valour, shown
Upon the innocent alone,
Thou hast not proved in manly strife
On him who robbed thee of thy wife.
Hadst thou but fought in open field
And met me boldly unconcealed,
This day had been thy fate to fall,
Slain by this hand, to Yáma's hall.
In vain I strove, and struck by thee
Fell by a hand I could not see.
Thus bites a snake, for sins of yore,
A sleeping man who wakes no more.
Sugríva's foeman thou hast killed,
And thus his heart's desire fulfilled;
But, Ráma, hadst thou sought me first,
And told the hope thy soul has nursed,
That very day had I restored
The Maithil lady to her lord;
And, binding Rávaṇ with a chain,
Had laid him at thy feet unslain.

Yea, were she sunk in deepest hell,
Or whelmed beneath the ocean's swell,
I would have followed on her track
And brought the rescued lady back,
As Hayagríva once set free
From hell the white Aśvatarí.
That when my spirit wings its flight
Sugríva reign, is just and right.
But most unjust, O King, that I,
Slain by thy treacherous hand, should lie.
Be still, my heart: this earthly state
Is darkly ruled by sovereign Fate.
The realm is lost and won: defy
Thy questioners with apt reply."

Ráma's Reply

He ceased: and Ráma's heart was stirred
At every keen reproach he heard.
There Báli lay, a dim dark sun,
His course of light and glory run:
Or like the bed of Ocean dried
Of his broad floods from side to side,
Or helpless, as the dying fire,
Hushed his last words of righteous ire.
Then Ráma, with his spirit moved,
The Vánar king in turn reproved:
"Why dost thou, Báli, thus revile,
And castest not a glance the while
On claims of duty, love, and gain,
And customs o'er the world that reign?
Why dost thou blame me, rash and blind,
Fickle as all thy Vánar kind,
Slighting each rule of ancient days
Which all the good and prudent praise?
This land, each hill and woody chase,
Belongs to old Ikshváku's race:
With bird and beast and man, the whole
Is ours to cherish and control.
Now Bharat, prompt at duty's call,
Wise, just, and true, is lord of all.
Each claim of law, love, gain he knows,
And wrath and favour duly shows.
A king from truth who never bends,
And grace with vigour wisely blends;
With valour worthy of his race,
He knows the claims of time and place.
Now we and other kings of might,

By his ensample taught aright,
The lands of every region tread
That justice may increase and spread.
While royal Bharat, wise and just,
Rules the broad earth, his glorious trust,
Who shall attempt, while he is lord,
A deed by Justice held abhorred?
We now, as Bharat has decreed,
Let justice guide our every deed,
And toil each sinner to repress
Who scorns the way of righteousness.
Thou from that path hast turned aside,
And virtue's holy law defied,
Left the fair path which kings should tread,
And followed pleasure's voice instead.
The man who cleaves to duty's law
Regards these three with filial awe—
The sire, the elder brother, third
Him from whose lips his lore he heard.
Thus too, for duty's sake, the wise
Regard with fond paternal eyes
The well-loved younger brother, one
Their lore has ripened, and a son.
Fine are the laws which guide the good,
Abstruse, and hardly understood;
Only the soul, enthroned within
The breast of each, knows right from sin.
But thou art wild and weak of soul,
And spurnest, like thy race, control;
The true and right thou canst not find,
The blind consulting with the blind.
Incline thine ear and I will teach
The cause that prompts my present speech.
This tempest of thy soul assuage,
Nor blame me in thine idle rage.
On this great sin thy thoughts bestow,
The sin for which I lay thee low.
Thou, Báli, in thy brother's life
Hast robbed him of his wedded wife,
And keepest, scorning ancient right,
His Rumá for thine own delight.

Thy son's own wife should scarcely be
More sacred in thine eyes than she.
All duty thou hast scorned, and hence
Comes punishment for dire offence.
For those who blindly do amiss
There is, I ween, no way but this:
To check the rash who dare to stray
From customs which the good obey,
I may not, sprung of Kshatriya line,

Forgive this heinous sin of thine:
The laws for those who sin like thee
The penalty of death decree.
Now Bharat rules with sovereign sway,
And we his royal word obey.
There was no hope of pardon, none,
For the vile deed that thou hast done,
That wisest monarch dooms to die
The wretch whose crimes the law defy;
And we, chastising those who err,
His righteous doom administer.
My soul accounts Sugríva dear
E'en as my brother Lakshman here.
He brings me blessing, and I swore
His wife and kingdom to restore:
A bond in solemn honour bound
When Vánar chieftains stood around.
And can a king like me forsake
His friend, and plighted promise break?
Reflect, O Vánar, on the cause,
The sanction of eternal laws,
And, justly smitten down, confess
Thou diest for thy wickedness.
By honour was I bound to lend
Assistance to a faithful friend;
And thou hast met a righteous fate
Thy former sins to expiate.
And thus wilt thou some merit win
And make atonement for thy sin.
For hear me, Vánar King, rehearse
What Manu spake in ancient verse,—

This holy law, which all accept
Who honour duty, have I kept:
"Pure grow the sinners kings chastise,
And, like the virtuous, gain the skies;
By pain or full atonement freed,
They reap the fruit of righteous deed,
While kings who punish not incur
The penalties of those who err."
Mándhátá once, a noble king,
Light of the line from which I spring,
Punished with death a devotee
When he had stooped to sin like thee;
And many a king in ancient time
Has punished frantic sinners' crime,
And, when their impious blood was spilt,
Has washed away the stain of guilt.
Cease, Báli, cease: no more complain:
Reproaches and laments are vain,
For thou art justly punished: we
Obey our king and are not free.
Once more, O Báli, lend thine ear
Another weightiest plea to hear.
For this, when heard and pondered well,
Will all complaint and rage dispel.
My soul will ne'er this deed repent,
Nor was my shaft in anger sent.
We take the silvan tribes beset
With snare and trap and gin and net,
And many a heedless deer we smite
From thickest shade, concealed from sight.
Wild for the slaughter of the game,
At stately stags our shafts we aim.
We strike them bounding scared away,
We strike them as they stand at bay,
When careless in the shade they lie,
Or scan the plain with watchful eye.
They turn away their heads; we aim,
And none the eager hunter blame.
Each royal saint, well trained in law
Of duty, loves his bow to draw

And strike the quarry, e'en as thou
Hast fallen by mine arrow now,
Fighting with him or unaware,—
A Vánar thou.—I little care.
But yet, O best of Vánars, know
That kings who rule the earth bestow
Fruit of pure life and virtuous deed,
And lofty duty's hard-won meed.
Harm not thy lord the king: abstain
From act and word that cause him pain;
For kings are children of the skies
Who walk this earth in men's disguise.
But thou, in duty's claims untaught,
Thy breast with blinding passion fraught,
Assailest me who still have clung
To duty, with thy bitter tongue."

He ceased: and Báli sore distressed
The sovereign claims of law confessed,
And freed, o'erwhelmed with woe and shame,
The lord of Raghu's race from blame.
Then, reverent palm to palm applied,
To Ráma thus the Vánar cried:
"True, best of men, is every word
That from thy lips these ears have heard,
It ill beseems a wretch like me
To bandy empty words with thee.
Forgive the angry taunts that broke
From my wild bosom as I spoke.
And lay not to my charge, O King,

My mad reproaches' idle sting.
Thou, in the truth by trial trained,
Best knowledge of the right hast gained:
And layest, just and pure within,
The meetest penalty on sin.
Through every bond of law I burst,
The boldest sinner and the worst.
O let thy right-instructing speech
Console my heart and wisely teach."

Like some sad elephant who stands
Fast sinking in the treacherous sands,
Thus Báli raised despairing eyes;
Then spake again with sobs and sighs:

"Not for myself, O King, I grieve,
For Tárá or the friends I leave,
As for sweet Angad, my dear son,
My noble, only little one.
For, nursed in luxury and bliss,
His father he will mourn and miss,
And like a stream whose fount is dry
Will waste away and sink and die,—
My own dear child, my only boy,
His mother Tárá's hope and joy.
Spare him, O son of Raghu, spare
The child entrusted to thy care.
My Angad and Sugríva treat
E'en as thy heart considers meet,
For thou, O chief of men, art strong
To guard the right and punish wrong.
O, if thou wilt thine ear incline
To hear these dying words of mine,
He and Sugríva will to thee
As Bharat and as Lakshmaṇ be.
Let not my Tárá, left forlorn,
Weep for Sugríva's wrathful scorn;
Nor let him, for her lord's offence,
Condemn her faithful innocence.
And well and wisely may he reign
If thy dear grace his power sustain:
If, following thee his friend and guide,
He turn not from thy hest aside:
Thus may he reign with glory, nay
Thus to the skies will win his way.
Though stayed by Tárá's fond recall,
By thy dear hand I longed to fall.
Against my brother rushed and fought,
And gained the death I long have sought."

Then Ráma thus the prince consoled
From whose clear eyes the mists were rolled:
"Grieve not for those thou leavest thus,
Nor tremble for thyself or us,
For we will deal with thine and thee
As duty and the laws decree.
He who exacts and he who pays,
Is justly slain or justly slays,
Shall in the life to come have bliss;
For each has done his task in this.
Thou, wandering from the right, art made
Pure by the forfeit thou hast paid.
Thy weight of sins is cast aside,
And duty's claim is satisfied.
Then grieve no more, O Prince, but clear
Thy bosom from all doubt and fear,
For fate, inexorably stern,
Thou hast no power to move or turn.
Thy princely Angad still will share
My tender love, Sugríva's care;
And to thy offspring shall be shown
Affection that shall match thine own."

CANTO
XIX

Tárá's Grief

N o answer gave the Vánar king
To Ráma's prudent counselling.
Battered and bruised by tree and stone,
By Ráma's arrow overthrown,
Fainting upon the ground he lay,
Gasping his troubled life away.

But Tárá in the Vánar's hall
Heard tidings of her husband's fall;
Heard that a shaft from Ráma's bow
Had laid the royal Báli low.
Her darling Angad by her side,
Distracted from her home she hied.
Then nigh the place of battle drew
The Vánars, Angad's retinue.
They saw the bow-armed Ráma: dread
Fell on them, and they turned and fled.
Like helpless deer, their leaders slain,
So wildly fled the startled train.
But Tárá saw, and nearer pressed,
And thus the flying band addressed:
"O Vánars, ye who ever stand
About our king, a trusty band,
Where is the lion master? why
Forsake ye thus your lord and fly?
Say, lies he dead upon the plain,
A brother by a brother slain,
Or pierced by shafts from Ráma's bow
That rain from far upon the foe?"

Thus Tárá questioned, and was still:
Then, wearers of each shape at will,
The Vánars thus with one accord
Answered the Lady of their lord:
"Turn, Tárá turn, and half undone
Save Angad thy beloved son.
There Ráma stands in death's disguise,
And conquered Báli faints and dies.
He by whose strong arm, thick and fast,
Uprooted trees and rocks were cast,
Lies smitten by a shaft that came
Resistless as the lightning flame.
When he, whose splendour once could vie
With Indra's, regent of the sky,
Fell by that deadly arrow, all
The Vánars fled who marked his fall.
Let all our chiefs their succours bring,
And Angad be anointed king;

94

For all who come of Vánar race
Will serve him set in Báli's place.
Or else our conquering foes to-day
Within our wall will force their way,
Polluting with their hostile feet
The chambers of thy loved retreat.
Great fear is on us, all and one.
Those who have wives and who have none,
They lust for power, are fierce and bold,
Or hate us for the strife of old."

She heard their speech as, sore afraid,
Arrested in their flight, they stayed,
And gave her answer as became
The spirit of so true a dame:
"Nay, what have I to do with pelf,
With son, with kingdom, or with self,
When he, my noble lord, who leads
The Vánars like a lion, bleeds?
His high-souled victor will I meet,
And throw me prostrate at his feet."

She hastened forth, her bosom rent
With anguish, weeping as she went,
And striking, mastered by her woes,
Her head and breast with frantic blows.
She hurried to the field and found
Her husband prostrate on the ground,
Who quelled the hostile Vánars' might,
Whose bank was never turned in flight:
Whose arm a massy rock could throw
As Indra hurls his bolts below:
Fierce as the rushing tempest, loud
As thunder from a labouring cloud:
Whene'er he roared his voice of fear
Struck terror on the boldest ear:
Now slain, as, hungry for the prey,
A tiger might a lion slay:
Or when, his serpent foe to seek,
Suparṇa with his furious beak
Tears up a sacred hillock, long

95

The reverence of a village throng,
Its altar with their offerings spread,
And the gay flag that waved o'erhead.
She looked and saw the victor stand
Resting upon his bow his hand:
And fierce Sugríva she descried,
And Lakshmaṇ by his brother's side.
She passed them by, nor stayed to view,
Swift to her husband's side she flew;
Then as she looked, her strength gave way,
And in the dust she fell and lay.
Then, as if startled ere the close
Of slumber, from the earth she rose.
Upon her dying husband, round
Whose soul the coils of Death were wound,
Her eyes in agony she bent
And called him with a shrill lament.
Sugríva, when he heard her cries,
And saw the queen with weeping eyes,
And youthful Angad standing there,
His load of grief could hardly bear.

CANTO
XX

Tárá's Lament

Again she bent her to the ground,
Her arms about her husband wound.
Sobbed on his breast, and sick and faint
With anguish poured her wild complaint:
"Brave in the charge of battle, boast
And glory of the Vánar host,
Why on the cold earth wilt thou lie
And give no answer when I cry?

96

Up, warrior, from thy lowly bed!
A meeter couch for thee is spread.
It ill beseems a glorious king
On the bare ground his limbs to fling.
Ah, surely must thy love be strong
For her whom thou hast governed long,
If thou, my hero, canst recline
On her cold breast forsaking mine.
Or, famed for justice through the land,
Thou on the road to heaven hast planned
Some city fairer far than this
To be thy new metropolis.
Are all our pleasures ended now,
With those delicious hours which thou
And I, dear lord, together spent
In woods that breathed the honey's scent?
Whelmed in my sorrow's boundless sea,
There is no joy, no hope, for me,
When my beloved lord, who led
The Vánars to the fight, is dead,
My widowed heart is stern and cold.
Or, at the sight mine eyes behold,
O'ermastered would it end this ache
And in a thousand fragments break.
Ah noble Vánar, doomed to pay
The penalty of all today—
Sugríva from his home expelled,
And Rumá from his arms withheld.
Our Vánar race and thee to save,
Wise counsel for thy weal I gave;
But thou, by wildest folly stirred,
Wouldst give no credence to my word,
And now wilt woo the nymphs above,
And shake their souls with pangs of love.
Ah, never could it be that thou
Beneath Sugríva's power shouldst bow,
Thy conqueror is none but Fate
Whose mandates all who breathe await.
And does no thrill of anguish run
Through the stern breast of Raghu's son,

Whose base hand dealt a coward's blow,
And smote thee fighting with thy foe?
Reft of my lord my days, alas!

In bitter bitter woe will pass:
And I, long blest with every good,
Must bear my dreary widowhood.
And when his uncle's brow is stern,
When his fierce eyes with fury burn,
Ah, what will be my Angad's fate,
So fair and young and delicate?
Come, darling, for the last sad sight,
Of thy dear sire who loved the right;
For soon thine eyes will long in vain
A look at that loved face to gain.
And, hero, as thy child draws near,
With tender words his spirit cheer;
Thy dying wishes gently speak,
And kiss him on the brows and cheek.
High fame, I ween, has Ráma won
By this great deed his hand has done,
His debt to brave Sugríva paid
And kept the promise that he made.
Be happy, King Sugríva, lord
Of Ramá to thine arms restored:
Enjoy uninterrupted reign,
For he, thy foe, at length is slain.
Dost thou not hear me speak, and why
Hast thou no word of soft reply?
Will thou not lift thine eyes and see
These dames who look to none but thee?"

From their sad eyes, as Tárá spoke,
The floods of bitter sorrow broke:
Then, pressing close to Angad's side,
Each lifted up her voice and cried:

"How couldst thou leave thine Angad thus,
And go, for ever go, from us—
Thy child so dear in brave attire,
Graced with the virtues of his sire?

If e'er in want of thought, O chief,
One deed of mine have caused thee grief,
Forgive my folly, I entreat,
And with my head I touch thy feet."

Again the hapless Tárá wept
As to her husband's side she crept,
And wild with sorrow and dismay
Sat on the ground where Báli lay.

CANTO

XXI

Hanumán's Speech

There, like a fallen star, the dame
   Fell by her lord's half lifeless frame;
   And Hanumán drew softly near,
And strove her grieving heart to cheer:
"By changeless law our bliss and woe
From ancient worth and folly flow.
What fruits soe'er we cull, the seeds
Were scattered by our former deeds.
Why mourn another's mournful fate,
And weep, thyself unfortunate?
Be calm, O thou whose heart is wise,
For none deserves another's sighs.
Look up, with idle sorrow strive:
Thy child, his heir, is yet alive.
Let needful rites be duly done,
Nor in thy woe forget thy son.
Regard the law which all obey:
They spring to life, they pass away.
Begin the task that bids thee rise,
And stay these tears, for thou art wise.
Our lord the king is doomed to die,

On whom ten million hearts rely.
Kind, liberal, patient, true, and just
Was he in whom they place their trust,
And now he seeks the land of those
Who for the right subdue their foes.
Each Vánar lord with all his train,
Each ranger of this wild domain,
And Angad here, thy darling, see
A governor and friend in thee.
These twain whose hearts with sorrow ache
The funeral rites shall undertake,
And Angad by his mother's care
Be king, his father's rightful heir.
Now let him pay, as laws require,
His sacred duty to his sire,
Nor one solemnity omit
Of all that mighty kings befit.
And when thy fond eye sees thine own
Dear Angad on his father's throne,
Then, lightened of its load of pain,
Thy spirit will have rest again."
She heard his speech, she heaved her head,
Looked upon Hanumán and said:

"Sweeter my slain lord's limbs to touch,
Than Angad or a hundred such.
No rule or right, a widowed dame,
O'er Angad or the realm I claim.
Sugríva is the uncle, he
In every act supreme must be.
I pray thee, chief, this plan resign,
Nor claim from me what ne'er is mine.
The father with his tender care
Guards the dear child the mother bare,
Where'er I be, no sweeter task,
No happier joy I hope or ask
Than thus to sit with loving eyes
And watch the bed where Báli lies.

100

Báli Dead

There breathing still with slow faint sighs
    Lay Báli on the ground: his eyes,

Damp with the tears of death, he raised,
On conquering Sugríva gazed,
And then in clearest speech expressed
The tender feelings of his breast:
"Not to my charge, Sugríva, lay
Thine injuries avenged to-day;
But rather blame resistless Fate
That urged me on infuriate.
Fate ne'er agreed our lives to bless
With simultaneous happiness:
To dwell like brothers side by side
In tender love was still denied.
The Vánars' realm is thine to-day:
Begin, O King, thy rightful sway;
For I must go at Yáma's call
To sojourn in his gloomy hall;
Must part and leave this very hour
My life, my realm, my kingly power,
And go instead of these to gain
Bright glory free from spot and stain.
Now at thy hands one boon I seek
With the last words my lips shall speak,
And, though it be no easy thing,
Perform the task I give thee, King.
This son of mine, no foolish boy,
Worthy of bliss and nursed in joy,—
See, prostrate on the ground he lies,
The hot tears welling from his eyes—

The child I love so well, more sweet
Than life itself, for woe unmeet,—
To him be kindly favour shown:
O guard and keep him as thine own.
Retain him ever by thy side,
His father, helper, friend, and guide.
From fear and woe his young life save,
And give him all his father gave.
Then Tárá's son in time shall be
Brave, resolute, and famed like thee,
And march before thee to the fight
Where stricken fiends shall own his might.
While yet a tender stripling, fame
Shall bruit abroad his warrior name,
And brightly shall his glory shine
For exploits worthy of his line.
Child of Susheṇ, my Tárá well
Obscurest lore can read and tell;
And, trained in wondrous art, divines
Each mystery of boding signs.
Her solemn warning ne'er despise,
Do boldly what her lips advise;
For things to come her eye can see,
And with her words events agree.
And for the son of Raghu's sake
The toil and danger undertake:
For breach of faith were grievous wrong,
Nor wouldst thou be unpunished long.
Now, brother, take this chain of gold,
Gift of celestial hands of old,
Or when I die its charm will flee,
And all its might be lost with me."

The loving speech Sugríva heard,
And all his heart with woe was stirred.
Remorse and gentle pity stole
Each thought of triumph from his soul:
Thus fades the light when Ráhu mars
The glory of the Lord of Stars.
All angry thoughts were stayed and stilled
And kindly love his bosom filled.

His brother's word the chief obeyed
And took the chain as Báli prayed.
On little Angad standing nigh
The dying hero fixed his eye,
And, ready from this world to part,
Spoke the fond utterance of his heart:

"Let time and place thy thoughts employ:
In woe be strong, be meek in joy.
Accept both pain and pleasure, still
Obedient to Sugríva's will.
Thou hast, my darling, from the first
With tender care been softly nursed;
But harder days, if thou wouldst win
Sugríva's love, must now begin.
To those who hate him ne'er incline,
Nor count his foe a friend of thine.
In all thy thoughts his welfare seek,
Obedient, lowly, faithful, meek.
Let no rash suit his bosom pain,
Nor yet from due requests abstain.
Each is a grievous fault, between
The two is found the happy mean."

Then Báli ceased: his eyeballs rolled
In stress of anguish uncontrolled
His massive teeth were bared to view,
And from the frame the spirit flew.
Their lord and leader dead, the crowd
Of noblest Vánars shrieked aloud:
"Since thou, O King, hast sought the skies
All desolate Kishkindhá lies.
Her woods, where Vánars loved to rove,
Are empty now, and hill and grove.
From every eye the light is fled,
Since thou, our mighty lord, art dead.
Thine was the unwearied arm that bore
The brunt of deadly fight of yore
With Golabh the Gandharva, when,
Lasting through five long years and ten,

The dreadful conflict knew no stay
In gloom of night, in glare of day;
And when the fifteenth year had past
Thy dire opponent fell at last.
If such a foeman fell beneath
Our hero's arm and awful teeth
Who freed us from our terror, how
Is conquering Báli fallen now?"

Then when they saw their leader slain
Great anguish seized the Vánar train,
Weeping their mighty chief, as when
In pastures near a lion's den
The cows by sudden fear are stirred,
Slain the bold bull who led the herd.
And hapless Tárá sank below
The whelming waters of her woe,
Looked upon Báli's face and fell
Beside him whom she loved go well,
Like a young creeper clinging round
A tall tree prostrate on the ground.

CANTO
XXIII

Tárá's Lament

S he kissed her lifeless husband's face,
She clasped him in a close embrace,
Laid her soft lips upon his head;
Then words like these the mourner said:

"No words of mine wouldst thou regard,
And now thy bed is cold and hard.
Upon the rude rough ground o'erthrown,
Beneath thee naught but sand and stone.

To thee the earth is dearer far
Than I and my caresses are,
If thou upon her breast wilt lie,
And to my words make no reply.
Ah my beloved, good and brave,
Bold to attack and strong to save,
Fate is Sugríva's thrall, and we
In him our lord and master see.
Lo, by thy bed, a mournful band,
Thy Vánar chiefs lamenting stand.
O hear thy nobles' groans and cries,
O mark thy Angad's weeping eyes,
O list to my entreaties, break
The chains of slumber and awake.
Ah me, my lord, this lowly bed
Where rest thy limbs and fallen head,
Is the cold couch where smitten lay
Thy foemen in the bloody fray.
O noble heart from blemish free,
Lover of war, beloved by me.
Why hast thou fled away and left
Thy Tárá of all hope bereft?
Unwise the father who allows
His child to be a warrior's spouse,
For, hero, see thy consort's fate,
A widow now most desolate,
For ever broken is my pride,
My hope of lasting bliss has died,
And sinking in the lowest deep
Of sorrow's sea I pine and weep.
Ah, surely not of earthly mould,
This stony heart is stern and cold,
Or, in a hundred pieces rent,
It had not lingered to lament.
Dead, dead! my husband, friend, and lord
In whom my loving hopes were stored,
First in the field, his foemen's dread,
My own victorious Báli, dead!
A woman when her lord has died,
Though children flourish by her side,
Though stores of gold her coffers fill,

105

Is called a lonely widow still.
Alas, thy bleeding gashes make
Around thy limbs a purple lake:
Thus slumbering was thy wont to lie
On cushions bright with crimson dye.
Dark streams of welling blood besmear
Thy limbs where dust and mire adhere,
Nor have I strength, weighed down by woe,
Mine arms about thy form to throw.
The issue of this day has brought
Sugríva all his wishes sought,
For Ráma shot one shaft and he
Is freed from fear and jeopardy.
Alas, alas, I may not rest
My head upon thy wounded breast,
Obstructed by the massive dart
Deep buried in thy bleeding heart."

Then Níla from his bosom drew
The fatal shaft that pierced him through,
Like some tremendous serpent deep
In caverns of a hill asleep.
As from the hero's wound it came,
Shot from the shaft a gleam of flame,
Like the last flashes of the sun
Descending when his course is run.
From the wide rent in crimson flood
Rushed the full stream of Báli's blood,
Like torrents down a mountain's side
With golden ore and copper dyed.
Then Tárá brushed with tender care
The dust of battle from his hair,
While her sad eyes poured down their rain
Upon her lord untimely slain.
Once more she looked upon the dead;
Then to her bright-eyed child she said:
"Turn hither, turn thy weeping eyes
Where low in death thy father lies.
By sinful deed and bitter hate
Our lord has met his mournful fate.
Bright as the sun at early morn

To Yáma's halls is Báli borne.
Then go, my child, salute the king,
From whom our bliss and honour spring."

Obedient to his mother's hest
His father's feet he gently pressed

With twining arms and lingering hands:
"Father," he cried, "here Angad stands."

Then Tárá: "Art thou stern and mute,
Regardless of thy child's salute?
Hast thou no blessing for thy son,
No word for little Angad, none?
O, hero, at thy lifeless feet
Here with my boy I take my seat,
As some sad mother of the herd,
By the fierce lion undeterred,
Lies moaning by the grassy dell
Wherein her lord and leader fell.
How, having wrought that awful rite,
The sacrifice of deadly fight,
Wherein the shaft by Ráma sped
Supplied the place of water shed,
How hast thou bathed thee at the end
Without thy wife her aid to lend?
Why do mine eyes no more behold
Thy bright beloved chain of gold,
Which, pleased with thee, the Immortals' King
About thy neck vouchsafed to fling?
Still lingering on thy lifeless face
I see the pride of royal race:
Thus when the sun has set, his glow
Still rests upon the Lord of Snow.
Alas my hero! undeterred
Thou wouldst not listen to my word.
With tears and prayers I sued in vain:
Thou wouldst not listen, and art slain.
Gone is my bliss, my glory: I
And Angad now with thee will die."

CANTO
XXIV

Sugríva's Lament

But when Sugríva saw her weep
O'erwhelmed in sorrow's rushing deep,
Swift through his bosom pierced the sting
Of anguish for the fallen king.
At the sad sight his eyes beheld
A flood of bitter tears outwelled,
And, with his bosom racked and rent,
To Ráma with his train he went.
He came with faltering steps and slow
Where Ráma held his mighty bow
And arrow like a venomed snake,
And to the son of Raghu spake:
"Well hast thou kept, O King, thy vow:
The promised fruit is gathered now.
But life is marred, my soul to-day
Turns sickening from all joy away.
For, while this queen laments and sighs
Amid a mourning people's cries,
And Angad weeps his father slain,
How can my heart delight to reign?
For outrage, fury, senseless pride,
My brother, doomed of yore, has died.
Yet, Raghu's son, in bitter woe
I mourn his fated overthrow.
Ah, better far in pain and ill
To dwell on Rishyamúka still
Than gain the heaven of Gods and all
Its pleasures by my brother's fall.
Did not he cry,—great-hearted foe,—
"Go, for I will not slay thee, Go"?
With his brave soul those words agree:

108

My speech, my deeds, are worthy me.
How can a brother counterweigh
His grievous loss with joys of sway,
And see with dull unpitying eye
So brave and good a brother die?
His lofty soul was nobly blind:
My death alas, he ne'er designed;
But I, urged blindly on by hate,
Sought with his life my rage to sate.
He smote me with a splintered tree:
I groaned aloud and turned to flee,
From stern reproaches he forbore,
And gently bade me sin no more.
Serene and dutiful and good
He kept the laws of brotherhood:
I, fierce and greedy, vengeful, base,
Showed all the vices of our race.
Ah me, dear friend, my brother's fate
Lays on my soul a crushing weight:
A sin no heart should e'er conceive,
But at the thought each soul should grieve:
Sin such as Indra's when his blow
Laid heavenly Viśvarúpa low.
Yet earth, the waters of the seas,
The race of women and the trees
Were fain upon themselves to take
The weight of sin for Indra's sake.
But who a Vánar's soul will free,
Or ease the load that crushes me?
Wretch that I am, I may not claim
The reverence due to royal name.
How shall I reign supreme, or dare
Affect the power I should not share?
Ah me, I sorrow for my sin,
The ruin of my race and kin,
Polluted by a hideous crime
World-hated till the end of time.
Alas, the floods of sorrow roll
With whelming force upon my soul:
So gathers the descending rain
In the deep hollow of the plain."

Ráma's Speech

T hen Raghu's son, whose feeling breast
    Shared the great woe that moved the rest,
    Strove with wise charm their grief to ease
And gently spoke in words like these:

"You ne'er can raise the dead to bliss
By agony of grief like this.
Cease your lament, nor leave undone
The funeral task you may not shun.
As nature orders o'er the dead.
Your tributary tears are shed,
But Fate, directing each event,
Is still the lord preëminent.
Yes, all obey the changeless laws
Of Fate the universal cause.
By Fate, the lives of all proceed,
That governs every word and deed,
None acts, none sees his hest obeyed,
But each and all by Fate are swayed.
The world its ordered course maintains,
And o'er that course Fate ever reigns.
Fate ne'er exceeds the rule of Fate:
Is ne'er too swift, is ne'er too late,
And making nature its ally
Forgets no life, nor passes by.
No kith and kin, no power and force
Can check or stay its settled course,
No friend or client, grace or charm,
That victor of the world disarm.
So all who see with prudent eyes
The hand of Fate must recognize,

For virtue rules, or love, or gain,
As Fate's unchanged decrees ordain.
Báli has died and won the meed
That waits in heaven on noble deed,
Throned in the seats the brave may reach
By liberal hand and gentle speech,
True to a warrior's duty, bold
In fight, the hero lofty-souled
Deigned not to guard his life: he died,
And now in heaven is glorified.
Then cease these tears and wild despair:
Turn to the task that claims your care,
For Báli's is the glorious fate
Which warriors count most fortunate."

When Ráma's speech had found a close,
Brave Lakshmaṇ, terror of his foes,
With wise and soothing words addressed
Sugríva still with woe oppressed:
"Arise Sugríva," thus he said,
"Perform the service of the dead.
Prepare with Tárá and her son
That Báli's rites be duly done.
A store of funeral wood provide
Which wind and sun and time have dried
And richest sandal fit to grace
The pyre of one of royal race.
With words of comfort soft and kind
Console poor Angad's troubled mind,
Nor let thy heart be thus cast down,
For thine is now the Vánars' town.
Let Angad's care a wreath supply,
And raiment rich with varied dye,
And oil and perfumes for the fire,
And all the solemn rites require.
Go, hasten to the town, O King,
And Tárá's little quickly bring.
A virtue is despatch: and speed
Is best of all in hour of need.
Go, let a chosen band prepare
The litter of the dead to bear.

For stout and tall and strong of limb
Must be the chiefs who carry him."

He spoke,—his friends' delight and pride,—
Then stood again by Ráma's side.
When Tára heard the words he said
Within the town he quickly sped,
And brought, on stalwart shoulders laid,
The litter for the rites arrayed,
Framed like a car for Gods, complete
With painted sides and royal seat,
With latticed windows deftly made,
And golden birds and trees inlaid:
Well joined and wrought in every part,
A marvel of ingenious art.
Where pleasure mounds in carven wood
And many a graven figure stood.
The best of jewels o'er it hung,
And wreaths of flowers around it clung,
And over all was raised on high
A canopy of saffron dye,
While like the sun of morning shone
The brilliant blooms that lay thereon.
That glorious litter Ráma eyed.
And spake to Lakshmaṇ by his side:
"Let Báli on the bier be placed
And with all funeral service graced."
Sugríva then with many a tear
Drew Báli's body to the bier
Whereon, with weeping Angad's aid,
The relics of the chief were laid
Neath many a vesture's varied fold,
And wreaths and ornaments and gold.
Then King Sugríva bade them speed
The obsequies by law decreed:
"Let Vánars lead the way and throw
Rich gems around them as they go,
And be the chosen bearers near
Behind them laden with the bier.
No costly rite may you deny,
Used when the proudest monarchs die:

As for a king of widest sway.
Perform his obsequies to-day."

Sugríva gave his high behest;
Then Princely Tára and the rest,
With little Angad weeping, led
The long procession of the dead.
Behind the funeral litter came,
With Tárá first, each widowed dame,
In tears and shrieks her loss deplored,
Add cried aloud, My lord! My lord!
While wood and hill and valley sent
In echoes back the shrill lament.
Then on a low and sandy isle
Was reared the hero's funeral pile
By crowds of toiling Vánars, where
The mountain stream ran fresh and fair,
The Vánar chiefs, a noble band,
Had laid the litter on the sand,
And stood a little space apart,
Each mourning in his inmost heart.
But Tárá, when her weeping eye
Saw Báli, on the litter lie,
Laid his dear head upon her lap,
And wailed aloud her dire mishap;
"O mighty Vánar, lord and king,
To whose fond breast I loved to cling,
Of goodly arms, wise, brave, and bold,
Rise, look upon me as of old.
Rise up, my sovereign, dost thou see
A crowd of subjects weep for thee?
Still o'er thy face, though breath has fled,
The joyous light of life is spread:
Thus around the sun, although he set,
A crimson glory lingers yet.
Death clad in Ráma's form to-day
Hast dragged thee from the world away.
One shaft from his tremendous bow
Dooms us to widowhood and woe.
Hast thou, O Vánar King, no eyes
Thy weeping wives to recognize,

Who for the length of way unmeet
Have followed thee with weary feet?
Yet every moon-faced beauty here
By thee, O King was counted dear.
Lord of the Vánar race, hast thou
No eyes to see Sugríva now?
About thee stands in mournful mood
A sore-afflicted multitude,
And Tára and thy lords of state
Around their monarch weep and wait.
Arise my lord, with gentle speech,
As was thy wont, dismissing each,
Then in the forest will we play
And love shall make our spirits gay."

The Vánar dames raised Tárá, drowned
In floods of sorrow, from the ground;
And Angad with Sugríva's aid,
O'erwhelmed with anguish and dismayed,
Weeping for his departed sire,
Placed Báli's body on the pyre:
Then lit the flame, and round the dead
Passed slowly with a mourner's tread.
Thus with full rites the funeral train
Performed the service for the slain,
Then sought the flowing stream and made
Libations to the parted shade.
There, setting Angad first in place,
The chieftains of the Vánar race,
With Tárá and Sugríva, shed
The water that delights the dead.

114

The Coronation

Each Vánar councillor and peer
In crowded numbers gathered near
Sugríva, mournful king, while yet
His vesture from the wave was wet,
Before the chief of Raghu's seed
Unwearied in each arduous deed,
They stood and raised the reverent hand
As saints before Lord Brahmá stand.
Then Hanumán of massive mould,
Like some tall hill of glistering gold,
Son of the God whose wild blasts shake
The forest, thus to Ráma spake:
"By thy kind favour, O my lord,
Sugríva, to his home restored
Triumphant, has regained to-day
His rank and power and royal sway.
He now will call each faithful friend,
Enter the city, and attend
With sage advice and prudent care
To every task that waits him there.
Then balm and unguent shall anoint
Our monarch, as the laws appoint,
And gems and precious wreaths shall be
His grateful offering, King, to thee.
Do thou, O Ráma, with thy friend
Thy steps within the city bend;
Our ruler on his throne install,
And with thy presence cheer us all."
Then, skilled in lore and arts that guide
The speaker, Raghu's son replied:
"For fourteen years I might not break

The mandate that my father spake;
Nor can I, till that time be fled,
The street of town or village tread.
Let King Sugríva seek the town
Most worthy of her high renown,
There let him be without delay
Anointed, and begin his sway."

This answered, to Sugríva then
Thus spake anew the king of men:
"Do thou who knowest right ordain
Prince Angad consort of thy reign;
For he is noble, true, and bold,
And trained a righteous course to hold
Gifts like his sire's that youth adorn
Born eldest to the eldest born.

This is the month of Śrávaṇ, first
Of those that see the rain-clouds burst.
Four months, thou knowest well, extends
The season when the rain descends.
No time for deeds of war is this:
Seek thou thy fair metropolis,
And I with Lakshmaṇ, O my friend,
The time upon this hill will spend.
An ample cavern opens there
Made lovely by the mountain air,
And lotuses and lilies fill
The pleasant lake and murmuring rill.
When Kártik's month shall clear the skies,
Then tempt the mighty enterprise.
Now, chieftain to thy home repair,
And be anointed sovereign there."

Sugríva heard: he bowed his head:
Within the lovely town he sped
Which Báli's royal will had swayed,
Where thousand Vánar chiefs arrayed
Gathered in order round their king,
And led him on with welcoming.
Low on the earth the lesser crowd

116

Fell in prostration as they bowed.
Sugríva looked with grateful eyes,
Spake to them all and bade them rise.
Then through the royal bowers he strode
Wherein the monarch's wives abode.
Soon from the inner chambers came
The Vánar of exalted fame;
And joyful friends drew near and shed
King-making balm upon his head,
Like Gods anointing in the skies
Their sovereign of the thousand eyes.
Then brought they, o'er their king to hold
The white umbrella decked with gold,
And chouries with their waving hair
In golden handles wondrous fair;
And fragrant herbs and seed and spice,
And sparkling gems exceeding price,
And every bloom from woods and leas,
And gum distilled from milky trees;
And precious ointment white as milk,
And spotless robes of cloth and silk,
Wreaths of sweet flowers whose glories gleam
In grassy grove, on lake or stream.
And fragrant sandal and each scent
That makes the soft breeze redolent;
Grain, honey, odorous seed, and store
Of oil and curd and golden ore;
A noble tiger's skin, a pair
Of sandals wrought with costliest care,
Eight pairs of damsels drawing nigh
Brought unguents stained with varied dye.
Then gems and cates and robes displayed
Before the twice-born priests were laid,
That they would deign in order due
To consecrate the king anew.
The sacred grass was duly spread
And sacrificial flame was fed,
Which Scripture-learned priests supplied
With oil which texts had sanctified.
Then, with all rites ordained of old,
High on the terrace bright with gold,

Whereon a glorious carpet lay,
And fresh-culled garlands sweet and gay,
Placed on his throne, Sugríva bent
His looks toward the Orient.
In horns from forehead of the bull,
In pitchers bright and beautiful,
In urns of gold the Vánara took
Pure water brought from stream and brook,
From every consecrated strand
And every sea that beats the land.
Then, as prescribed by sacred lore
And many a mighty sage of yore,
The leaders of the Vánars poured
The sacred water on their lord.
From every Vánar at the close
Of that imperial rite arose
Shouts of glad triumph, loud and long
Repeated by the high-souled throng.
Sugríva, when the rite was done,
Obeyed the hest of Raghu's son,
Prince Angad to his breast he strained,
And partner of his sway ordained.
Once more from all the host rang out
The loud huzza and joyful shout.
"Well done! well done!" each Vánar cried,
And good Sugríva glorified.

Then with glad voices loudly raised
Were Ráma and his brother praised;
And bright Kishkindhá shone that day
With happy throngs and banners gay.

Ráma on The Hill

But when the solemn rite was o'er,
And bold Sugríva reigned once more,
The sons of Raghu sought the hill,
Praśravaṇ of the rushing rill,
Where roamed the tiger and the deer,
And lions raised their voice of fear;
Thick set with trees of every kind,
With trailing shrubs and plants entwined;
Home of the ape and monkey, lair
Of mountain cat and pard and bear.
In cloudy gloom against the sky
The sanctifying hills rose high.
Pierced in their crest, a spacious cave
To Raghu's sons a shelter gave.
Then Ráma, pure from every crime,
In words well suited to the time
To Lakshmaṇ spake, whose faithful zeal
Watched humbly for his brother's weal:
"I love this spacious cavern where
There breathes a fresh and pleasant air.
Brave brother, let us here remain
Throughout the season of the rain.
For in mine eyes this mountain crest
Is above all, the loveliest.
Where copper-hued and black and white
Show the huge blocks that face the height;
Where gleams the shine of varied ore,
Where dark clouds hang and torrents roar;
Where waving woods are fair to see,
And creepers climb from tree to tree;
Where the gay peacock's voice is shrill,

And sweet birds carol on the hill;
Where odorous breath is wafted far
From Jessamine and Sinduvár;
And opening flowers of every hue
Give wondrous beauty to the view.
See, too, this pleasant water near
Our cavern home is fresh and clear;
And lilies gay with flower and bud
Are glorious on the lovely flood.
This cave that fares north and east
Will shelter us till rain has ceased;
And towering hills that rise behind
Will screen us from the furious wind.
Close by the cavern's portal lies
And level stone of ample size
And sable hue, a mighty block
Long severed from the parent rock.
Now let thine eye bent northward rest
A while upon that mountain crest,
High as a cloud that brings the rain,
And dark as iron rent in twain.
Look southward, brother, now and view
A cloudy pile of paler hue
Like Mount Kailása's topmost height
Where ores of every tint are bright.
See, Lakshman, see before our cave
That clear brook eastward roll its wave
As though 'twere Gangá's infant rill
Down streaming from the three-peaked hill.
See, by the water's gentle flow
Aśoka, sál, and sandal grow.
And every lovely tree most fair
With leaf and bud and flower is there.
See there, beneath the bending trees
That fringe her bank, the river flees,
Clothed with their beauty like a maid
In all her robes and gems arrayed,
While from the sedgy banks are heard
The soft notes of each amorous bird.
O see what lovely islets stud

Like gems the bosom of the flood,
And sárases and wild swans crowd
About her till she laughs aloud.
See, lotus blooms the brook o'erspread,
Some tender blue, some dazzling red,
And opening lilies white as snow
Their buds in rich profusion show.
There rings the joyous peacock's scream,
There stands the curlew by the stream,
And holy hermits love to throng
Where the sweet waters speed along.
Ranged on the grassy margin shine
Gay sandal trees in glittering line,
And all the wondrous verdure seems
The offspring of creative dreams.
O conquering Prince, there cannot be
A lovelier place than this we see.
Here sheltered on the beauteous height
Our days will pass in calm delight.
Nor is Kishkindhá's city, gay
With grove and garden, far away.
Thence will the breeze of evening bring
Sweet music as the minstrels sing;
And, when the Vánars dance, will come
The sound of tabour and of drum.
Again to spouse and realm restored,
Girt by his friends, the Vánar lord
Great glory has acquired; and how
Can he be less than happy now?"

This said, the son of Raghu made
His dwelling in that pleasant shade
Upon the mountain's shelving side
That sweetly all his wants supplied.
But still the hero's troubled mind
No comfort in his woe could find,
Yet mourning for his stolen wife
Dearer to Ráma than his life,
Chief when he saw the Lord of Night
Rise slowly o'er the eastern height,

He tossed upon his leafy bed
With eyes by sleep unvisited.
Outwelled the tears in ceaseless flow,
And every sense was numbed by woe.
Each pang that pierced the mourner through
Smote Lakshman's faithful bosom too,
Who, troubled for his brother's sake,
With wisest words the prince bespake:
"Arise, my brother, and be strong:
Thy hero heart has mourned too long.
Thou knowest well that tears and sighs
Will mar the mightiest enterprise.
Thine was the soul that loved to dare:
To serve the Gods was still thy care;
And ne'er may sorrow's sting subdue
A heart so resolute and true.
How canst thou hope to slay in fight
The giant cruel in his might?
Unwearied must the champion be
Who strives with such a foe as he.
Tear out this sorrow by the root;
Again be bold and resolute.
Arise, my brother, and subdue
The demon and his wicked crew.
Thou canst destroy the earth, her seas,
Her rooted hills and giant trees
Unseated by thy furious hand:
And shall one fiend thy power withstand?
Wait through this season of the rain
Till suns of autumn dry the plain,
Then shall thy giant foe, and all
His host and realm, before thee fall.
I wake thy valour that has slept
Amid the tears thine eyes have wept;
As drops of oil in worship raise
The dormant flame to sudden blaze."

The son of Raghu heard: he knew
His brother's rede was wise and true;
And, honouring his friendly guide,
In gentle words he thus replied:

"Whate'er a hero firm and bold,
Devoted, true, and lofty-souled
Should speak by deep affection led,
Such are the words which thou hast said.
I cast away each pensive thought
That brings the noblest plans to naught,
And each uninjured power will strain
Until the purposed end we gain.
Thy prudent words will I obey,
And till the close of rain-time stay,
When King Sugríva will invite
To action, and the streams be bright.
The hero saved in hour of need
Repays the debt with friendly deed:
But hated by the good are they
Who take the boon and ne'er repay."

CANTO
XXVIII

The Rains

"See, brother, see" thus Ráma cried
On Mályavat's dark-wooded side,
"A chain of clouds, like lofty hills,
The sky with gathering shadow fills.
Nine months those clouds have borne the load
Conceived from sunbeams as they glowed,
And, having drunk the seas, give birth,
And drop their offspring on the earth.
Easy it seems at such a time
That flight of cloudy stairs to climb,
And, from their summit, safely won,
Hang flowery wreaths about the sun.
See how the flash of evening's red
Fringes the fleecy clouds o'erhead

Till all the sky is streaked and lined
With bleeding wounds incarnadined,
Or the wide firmament above
Shows like a lover sick with love
And, pale with cloudlets, heaves a sigh
In the soft breeze that wanders by.
See, by the fervent heat embrowned,
How drenched with recent showers, the ground
Pours out in floods her gushing tears,
Like Sítá wild with torturing fears.
So softly blows this cloud-born breeze
Cool through the boughs of camphor trees
That one might hold it in the cup
Of hollowed hands and drink it up.
See, brother, where that rocky steep,
Where odorous shrubs in rain-drops weep,
Shows like Sugríva when they shed
Tne royal balm upon his head.
Like students at their task appear
These hills whose misty peaks are near:
Black deerskin garments wrought of cloud
Their forms with fitting mantles shroud,
Each torrent from the summit poured
Supplies the place of sacred cord.
And winds that in their caverns moan

Sound like the voice's undertone.
From east to west red lightnings flash,
And, quivering neath the golden lash,
The great sky like a generous steed
Groans inly at each call to speed.
Yon lightning, as it flashes through
The giant cloud of sable hue,
Recalls my votaress Sítá pressed
Mid struggles to the demon's breast.
See, on those mountain ridges stand
Sweet shrubs that bud and bloom expand.
The soft rain ends their pangs of grief,
And drops its pearls on flower and leaf.
But all their raptures stab me through
And wake my pining love anew.

Now through the air no wild bird flies,
Each lily shuts her weary eyes;
And blooms of opening jasmin show
The parting sun has ceased to glow.
No captain now for conquest burns,
But homeward with his host returns;
For roads and kings' ambitious dreams
Have vanished neath descending streams.
This is the watery month wherein
The Sámar's sacred chants begin.
Áshádha past, now Kośal's lord
The harvest of the spring has stored,
And dwells within his palace freed
From every care of pressing need.
Full is the moon, and fierce and strong
Impetuous Sarjú roars along
As though Ayodhyá's crowds ran out
To greet their king with echoing shout.
In this sweet time of ease and rest
No care disturbs Sugríva's breast,
The foe that marred his peace o'erthrown,
And queen and realm once more his own.
Alas, a harder fate is mine,
Reft both of realm and queen to pine,
And, like the bank which floods erode,
I sink beneath my sorrow's load.
Sore on my soul my miseries weigh,
And these long rains our action stay,
While Rávan seems a mightier foe
Than I dare hope to overthrow.
I saw the roads were barred by rain,
I knew the hopes of war were vain;
Nor could I bid Sugríva rise,
Though prompt to aid my enterprise.
E'en now I scarce can urge my friend
On whom his house and realm depend,
Who, after toil and peril past,
Is happy with his queen at last.
Sugríva after rest will know
The hour is come to strike the blow,
Nor will his grateful soul forget

My succour, or deny the debt
I know his generous heart, and hence
Await the time with confidence
When he his friendly zeal will show,
And brooks again untroubled flow."

CANTO
XXIX

Hanumán's Counsel

No flash of lightning lit the sky,
    No cloudlet marred the blue on high.
    The Saras missed the welcome rain,
The moon's full beams were bright again.
Sugríva, lapped in bliss, forgot
The claims of faith, or heeded not;
And by alluring joys misled
The path of falsehood learned to tread.
In careless ease he passed each hour,
And dallied in his lady's bower.
Each longing of his heart was stilled,
And every lofty hope fulfilled.
With royal Rumá by his side,
Or Tárá yet a dearer bride,

He spent each joyous day and night
In revelry and wild delight,
Like Indra whom the nymphs entice
To taste the joys of Paradise.
The power to courtiers' hands resigned,
To all their acts his eyes were blind.
All doubt, all fear he cast aside
And lived with pleasure for his guide.
But sage Hanúmán, firm and true,
Whose heart the lore of Scripture knew,

Well trained to meet occasion, trained
In all by duty's law ordained,
Strove with his prudent speech to find
Soft access to the monarch's mind.
He, skilled in every gentle art
Of eloquence that wins the heart,
Sugríva from his trance to wake,
His salutary counsel spake:

"The realm is won, thy name advanced,
The glory of thy house enhanced,
And now thy foremost care should be
To aid the friends who succoured thee.
He who is firm and faithful found
To friendly ties in honour bound,
Will see his name and fame increase
And his blest kingdom thrive in peace.
Wide sway is his who truly boasts
That friends and treasure, self and hosts,
All blent in one harmonious whole,
Are subject to his firm control.
Do thou, whose footsteps never stray
From the clear bounds of duty's way,
Assist, as honour bids thee, now
Thy friends, observant of thy vow.
For if all cares we lay not by,
And to our friend's assistance fly,
We, after, toil in idle haste,
And all the late endeavour waste.
Up! nor the promised help delay
Until the hour have slipped away.
Up! and with Raghu's son renew
The search for Sítá lost to view.
The hour is come: he hears the call,
But not on thee reproaches fall
From him who labours to repress
His eager spirit's restlessness.
Long joined to thee in friendly ties
He made thy fame and fortune rise,
In gentle gifts by none excelled.
In splendid might unparalleled.

Up, to his succour, King! repay
The favour of that prosperous day,
And to thy bravest captains send
Prompt mandates to assist thy friend.
The cry for help thou wilt not spurn
Although no grace demands return:
And wilt thou not thine aid afford
To him who realm and life restored?
Exert thy power, and thou hast won
The love of Daśaratha's son:
And wilt thou for his summons wait,
And, till he call thee, hesitate?
Think not the hero needs thy power
To save him in the desperate hour:
He with his arrows could subdue
The Gods and all the demon crew,
And only waits that he may see
Redeemed the promise made by thee.
For thee he risked his life and fought,
For thee that great deliverance wrought.
Then let us trace through earth and skies
His lady wheresoe'er she lies.
Through realms above, beneath, we flee,
And plant our footsteps on the sea.
Then why, O Lord of Vánars, still
Delay us waiting for thy will?
Give thy commands, O King, and say
What task has each and where the way.
Before thee myriad Vánars stand
To sweep through heaven, o'er seas and land."

Sugríva heard the timely rede
That roused him in the day of need,
And thus to Níla prompt and brave
His hest the imperial Vánar gave:
"Go, Níla, to the distant hosts
That keep in arms their several posts,
And all the armies that protect
The quarters, with their chiefs, collect.
To all the luminaries placed
In intermediate regions haste,

And bid each captain rise and lead
His squadrons to their king with speed.
Do thou meanwhile with strictest care
All that the time requires prepare.
The loitering Vánar who delays
To gather here ere thrice five days,
Shall surely die for his offence,
Condemned for sinful negligence."

Ráma's Lament

B ut Ráma in the autumn night
    Stood musing on the mountain height,
    While grief and love that scorned control
Shook with wild storms the hero's soul.
Clear was the sky, without a cloud
The glory of the moon to shroud.
And bright with purest silver shone
Each hill the soft beams looked upon.
He knew Sugríva's heart was bent
On pleasure, gay and negligent.
He thought on Janak's child forlorn
From his fond arms for ever torn.
He mourned occasion slipping by,
And faint with anguish heaved each sigh.

He sat where many a varied streak
Of rich ore marked the mountain peak.
He raised his eyes the sky to view,
And to his love his sad thoughts flew.
He heard the Sáras cry, and faint
With sorrow poured his love-born plaint:
"She, she who mocked the softest tone

Of wild birds' voices with her own,—
Where strays she now, my love who played
So happy in our hermit shade?
How can my absent love behold
The bright trees with their flowers of gold,
And all their gleaming glory see
With eyes that vainly look for me?
How is it with my darling when
From the deep tangles of the glen
Float carols of each bird elate
With rapture singing to his mate?
In vain my weary glances rove
From lake to hill, from stream to grove:
I find no rapture in the scene,
And languish for my fawn-eyed queen.
Ah, does strong love with wild unrest,
Born of the autumn, stir her breast?
And does the gentle lady pine
Till her bright eyes shall look in mine?"

Thus Raghu's son in piteous tone,
O'erwhelmed with sorrow, made his moan.
E'en as the bird that drinks the rains
To Indra thousand-eyed complains.
Then Lakshman who had wandered through
The copses where the berries grew,
Returning to the cavern found
His brother chief in sorrow drowned,
And pitying the woes that broke
The spirit of the hero spoke:

"Why cast thy strength of soul away,
And weakly yield to passion's sway?
Arise, my brother, do and dare
Ere action perish in despair.
Recall the firmness of thy heart,
And nerve thee for a hero's part.
Whose is the hand unscathed to sieze
The red flame quickened by the breeze?
Where is the foe will dare to wrong
Or keep the Maithil lady long?"

Then with pale lips that sorrow dried
The son of Raghu thus replied:
"Lord Indra thousand-eyed, has sent
The sweet rain from the firmament,
Sees the rich promise of the grain,
And turns him to his rest again.
The clouds with voices loud and deep,
Veiling each tree upon the steep,
Up on the thirsty earth have shed
Their precious burden and are fled.
Now in kings' hearts ambition glows:
They rush to battle with their foes;
But in Sugríva's sloth I see
No care for deeds of chivalry.
See, Lakshman, on each breezy height
A thousand autumn blooms are bright.
See how the wings of wild swans gleam
On every islet of the stream.
Four months of flood and rain are past:
A hundred years they seemed to last
To me whom toil and trouble tried,
My Sítá severed from my side.
She, gentlest woman, weak and young,
Still to her lord unwearied clung.
Still by the exile's side she stood
In the wild ways of Daṇḍak wood,
Like a fond bird disconsolate
If parted from her darling mate.
Sugríva, lapped in soft repose,
Untouched by pity for my woes,
Scorns the poor exile, dispossessed,
By Rávaṇ's mightier arm oppressed,
The wretch who comes to sue and pray
From his lost kingdom far away.
Hence falls on me the Vánar's scorn,
A suitor friendless and forlorn.
The time is come: with heedless eye
He sees the hour of action fly,—
Unmindful, now his hopes succeed,
Of promise made in stress of need.
Go seek him sunk in bliss and sloth,

131

Forgetful of his royal oath,
And as mine envoy thus upbraid
The monarch for his help delayed:
"Vile is the wretch who will not pay
The favour of an earlier day,
Hope in the supplicant's breast awakes,
And then his plighted promise breaks.
Noblest, mid all of women born,
Who keeps the words his lips have sworn,
Yea, if those words be good or ill,
Maintains his faith unbroken still.
The thankless who forget to aid
The friend who helped them when they prayed,
Dishonoured in their death shall lie,
And dogs shall pass their corpses by.
Sure thou wouldst see my strained arm hold
My bow of battle backed with gold,
Wouldst gaze upon its awful form
Like lightning flashing through the storm,
And hear the clanging bowstring loud
As thunder from a labouring cloud."

His valour and his strength I know:
But pleasure's sway now sinks them low,
With thee, my brother, for ally
That strength and valour I defy.

He promised, when the rains should end,
The succour of his arm to lend.
Those months are past: he dares forget,
And, lapped in pleasure, slumbers yet.
No thought disturbs his careless breast
For us impatient and distressed,
And, while we sadly wait and pine,
Girt by his lords he quaffs the wine.
Go, brother, go, his palace seek,
And boldly to Sugríva speak,
Thus give the listless king to know
What waits him if my anger glow:
Still open, to the gloomy God,
Lies the sad path that Báli trod.

132

"Still to thy plighted word be true,
Lest thou, O King, that path pursue.
I launched the shaft I pointed well.
And Báli, only Báli, fell.
But, if from truth thou dare to stray,
Both thee and thine this hand shall slay."
Thus be the Vánar king addressed,
Then add thyself what seems the best."

CANTO

XXXI

The Envoy

Thus Ráma spoke, and Lakshmaṇ then
Made answer to the prince of men:
"Yea, if the Vánar, undeterred
By fear of vengeance, break his word,
Loss of his royal power ere long
Shall pay the traitor for the wrong.
Nor deem I him so void of sense
To brave the bitter consequence.
But if enslaved to joy he lie,
And scorn thy grace with blinded eye,
Then let him join his brother slain:
Unmeet were such a wretch to reign.
Quick rises, kindling in my breast,
The wrath that will not be repressed,
And bids me in my fury slay
The breaker of his faith to-day.
Let Báli's son thy consort trace
With bravest chiefs of Vánar race."

Thus spoke the hero, and aglow
With rage of battle seized his bow.
But Ráma thus in gentler mood

133

With fitting words his speech renewed:
"No hero with a soul like thine
To paths of sin will e'er incline,
He who his angry heart can tame
Is worthiest of a hero's name.
Not thine, my brother, be the part
So alien from the tender heart,
Nor let thy feet by wrath misled
Forsake the path they loved to tread.
From harsh and angry words abstain:
With gentle speech a hearing gain,
And tax Sugríva with the crime
Of failing faith and wasted time."

Then Lakshmaṇ, bravest of the brave,
Obeyed the hest that Ráma gave,
To whom devoting every thought
The Vánar's royal town he sought.
As Mandar's mountain heaves on high
His curved peak soaring to the sky,
So Lakshmaṇ showed, his dread bow bent
Like Indra's in the firmament.
His brother's wrath, his brother's woe
Inflamed his soul to fiercest glow.
The tallest trees to earth were cast
As furious on his way he passed,
And where he stepped, so fiercely fleet,
The stones were shivered by his feet.
He reached Kishkindhá's city deep
Embosomed where the hills were steep,
Where street and open square were lined
With legions of the Vánar kind.
Then, as his lips with fury swelled,
The lord of Raghu's line beheld
A stream of Vánar chiefs outpoured
To do obeisance to their lord.
But when the mighty prince in view
Of the thick coming Vánars drew,
They turned them in amaze to seize
Crags of the rock and giant trees.
He saw, and fiercer waxed his ire,

As oil lends fury to the fire.
Scarce had the Vánar chieftains seen
That wrathful eye, that troubled mien
Fierce as the God's who rules the dead,
When, turned in wild affright, they fled.
Speeding in breathless terror all
Sought King Sugríva's council hall,
And there made known their tale of fear,
That Lakshman wild with rage, was near.
The king, untroubled by alarms,
Held Tárá in his amorous arms,
And in the distant bower with her
Heard not each clamorous messenger.
Then, summoned at the lords' behest
Forth from the city portals pressed,
Each like some elephant or cloud,
The Vánars in a trembling crowd:
Fierce warriors all with massive jaws
And terrors of their tiger claws,
Some matched ten elephants, and some
A hundred's strength could overcome.
Some chieftains, mightier than the rest,
Ten times a hundred's force possessed.
With eyes of fury Lakshman viewed
The Vánars' tree-armed multitude.
Thus garrisoned from side to side
The city walls assault defied.
Beyond the moat that girt the wall
Advanced the Vánar chiefs; and all
Upon the plain in firm brigade,
Impetuous warriors, stood arrayed.

Red at the sight flashed Lakshman's eyes,
His bosom heaved tumultuous sighs,
And forth the fire of fury broke
Like flame that flashes through the smoke.
Like some fierce snake the hero stood:
His bow recalled the expanded hood,
And in his shaft-head bright and keen
The flickering of its tongue was seen:
And in his own all-conquering might

The venom of its deadly bite.
Prince Angad marked his angry look,
And every hope his heart forsook.
Then, his large eyes with fury red,
To Angad Lakshmaṇ turned and said:

"Go tell the king that Lakshmaṇ waits
For audience at the city gates,
Whose heart, O tamer of thy foes,
Is heavy with his brother's woes.
Bid him to Ráma's word attend,
And ask if he will aid his friend.
Go, let the king my message learn:
Then hither with all speed return."

Prince Angad heard and wild with grief
Cried as he looked upon the chief:
"'Tis Lakshmaṇ's self: impelled by ire
He seeks the city of my sire."
At the fierce words and furious look
Of Raghu's son he quailed and shook.
Back through the city gates he sped,
And, laden with the tale of dread,
Sought King Sugríva, filled his ears
And Rumá's with his doubts and fears.
To Rumá and the king he bent,
And clasped their feet most reverent,
Clasped the dear feet of Tárá, too,
And told the startling tale anew.

But King Sugríva's ear was dulled,
By love and wine and languor lulled,
Nor did the words that Angad spake
The slumberer from his trance awake.
But soon as Raghu's son came nigh
The startled Vánars raised a cry,
And strove to win his grace, while dread
Each anxious heart disquieted.
They saw, and, as they gathered round,
Rose from the mighty throng a sound
Like torrents when they downward dash,

136

Or thunder with the lightning's flash.
The shouting of the Vánars broke
Sugríva's slumber, and he woke:
Still with the wine his eyes were red,
His neck with flowers was garlanded.
Roused at the voice of Angad came
Two Vánar lords of rank and fame;
One Yaksha, one Prabháva hight,—
Wise counsellors of gain and right.
They came and raised their voices high,
And told that Raghu's son was nigh:
"Two brothers steadfast in their truth,
Each glorious in the bloom of youth,
Worthy of rule, have left the skies,
And clothed their forms in men's disguise.
One at thy gates, in warlike hands
Holding his mighty weapon, stands.
His message is the charioteer
That brings the eager envoy near,
Urged onward by his bold intent,
And by the hest of Ráma sent."
The gathered Vánars saw and fled,
And raised aloud their cry of dread.
Son of Queen Tárá, Angad ran
To parley with the godlike man.
Still fiery-eyed with rage and hate
Stands Lakshman at the city gate,
And trembling Vánars scarce can fly
Scathed by the lightning of his eye.
"Go with thy son, thy kith and kin,
The favour of the prince to win,
And bow thy reverent head that so
His fiery wrath may cease to glow.
What righteous Ráma bids thee, do,
And to thy plighted word be true."

Hanumán's Counsel

Sugríva heard, and, trained and tried
In counsel, to his lords replied:
"No deed of mine, no hasty word
The anger of the prince has stirred.
But haply some who hate me still
And watch their time to work me ill,
Have slandered me to Raghu's son,
Accused of deeds I ne'er have done.
Now, O my lords—for you are wise—
Speak truly what your hearts advise,
And, pondering each event, inquire
The reason of the prince's ire.
No fear have I of Lakshmaṇ: none:
No dread of Raghu's mightier son.
But wrath, that fires a friendly breast
Without due cause, disturbs my rest.
With labour light is friendship gained,
But with severest toil maintained.
And doubt is strong, and faith is weak,

And friendship dies when traitors speak.
Hence is my troubled bosom cold
With fear of Ráma lofty-souled;
For heavy on my spirit weigh
His favours I can ne'er repay."

He ceased: and Hanumán of all
The Vánars in the council hall
In wisdom first, and rank, expressed
The thoughts that filled his prudent breast:
"No marvel thou rememberest yet

The service thou shouldst ne'er forget,
How the brave prince of Raghu's seed
Thy days from fear and peril freed;
And Báli for thy sake o'erthrew,
Whom Indra's self might scarce subdue.
I doubt not Ráma's anger burns
For the scant love thy heart returns.
For this he sends his brother, him
Whose glory never waxes dim.
Sunk in repose thy careless eye
Marks not the seasons as they fly,
Nor sees that autumn has begun
With dark blooms opening to the sun.
Clear is the sky: no cloudlet mars
The splendour of the shining stars.
The balmy air is soft and still,
And clear and bright are lake and rill.
Thou heedest not with blinded eyes
The hour for warlike enterprise.
Hence Lakshmaṇ hither comes to break
Thy slothful trance and bid thee wake.
Then, Monarch, with a patient ear
The high-souled Ráma's message hear,
Which, reft of wife and realm and friends,
Thus by another's mouth he sends.
Thou, Vánar King, hast done amiss:
And now I see no way but this:
Before his envoy humbly stand
And sue for peace with suppliant hand.
High duty bids a courtier seek
His master's weal, and freely speak.
So by no thought of fear controlled
My speech, O King, is free and bold,
For Ráma, if his anger glow,
Can, with the terrors of his bow
This earth with all the Gods subdue,
Gandharvas, and the demon crew.
Unwise to stir his wrathful mood
Whose favour must again be wooed.
And, most of all, unwise for one
Grateful like thee for service done.

Go with thy son and kinsmen: bend
Thy humble head and greet thy friend.
And, like a fond obedient spouse,
Be faithful to thy plighted vows."

CANTO

XXXIII

Lakshman's Entry

Through the fair city Lakshmaṇ came,
Invited in Sugríva's name.
Within the gates the guardian bands,
Of Vánars raised their suppliant hands,
And in their ordered ranks, amazed,
Upon the princely hero gazed,
They marked each burning breath he drew,
The fury of his soul they knew.
Their hearts were chilled with sudden fear:
They gazed, but dared not venture near,
Before his eyes the city, gay
With gems and flowery gardens, lay,
Where fane and palace rose on high,
And things of beauty charmed the eye.
Where trees of every blossom grew
Yielding their fruit in season due
To Vánars of celestial seed
Who wore each varied form at need,
Fair-faced and glorious with the shine
Of heavenly robes and wreaths divine.
There sandal, aloe, lotus bloomed,
And there delicious breath perfumed
The city's broad street, redolent
Of sugary mead and honey scent.
There many a lofty palace rose
Like Vindhya or the Lord of Snows,

And with sweet murmur sparkling rills
Leapt lightly down the sheltering hills.
On many a glorious palace, raised
For prince and noble, Lakshman gazed:
Like clouds of paly hue they shone
With fragrant wreaths that hung thereon:
There wealth of jewels was enshrined,
And fairer gems of womankind.
There gleamed, of noble height and size,
Like Indra's mansion in the skies,
Protected by a crystal fence
Of rock, the royal residence,
With roof and turret high and bright
Like Mount Kailása's loftiest height.
There blooming trees, Mahendra's gift,
High o'er the walls were seen to lift
Their golden fruited boughs, that made
With leaf and flower delicious shade.
He saw a band of Vánars wait,

Wielding their weapons, at the gate
Where golden portals flashed between
Celestial garlands red and green.
Within Sugríva's fair abode
Unchecked the mighty hero strode,
As when the sun of autumn shrouds
His glory in a pile of clouds.
Through seven wide courts he quickly passed,
And reached the royal tower at last,
Where seats were set with couch and bed
Of gold and silver richly spread.
While the young chieftain's feet drew near
The sound of music reached his ear,
As the soft breathings of the flute
Came blending with the voice and lute.
Then beauty showed her youth and grace
And varied charm of form and face:
Soft bright-eyed creatures, fair and young,—
Gay garlands round their necks were hung,
And greater charms to each were lent
By richest dress and ornament.

He saw the calm attendants wait
About their lord in careless state,
Heard women's girdles chime in sweet
Accordance with their tinkling feet.
He heard the anklet's silvery sound,
He saw the calm that reigned around,
And o'er him, as he listened, came
A rush of rage, a flood of shame.
He drew his bowstring: with the clang
From ease to west the welkin rang:
Then in his modest mood withdrew
A little from the ladies' view.
And sternly silent stood apart,
While wrath for Ráma filled his heart.
Sugríva knew the sounding string,
And at the call the Vánar king
Sprang swiftly from his golden seat,
And feared the coming prince to meet.
Then with cold lips that terror dried
To beauteous Tárá thus he cried:
"What cause of anger, O my spouse
Fair with the charm of lovely brows,
Sets Lakshmaṇ's gentle breast on fire,
And brings him in unwonted ire?
Say, canst thou see, O faultless dame,
A cause to fill his soul with flame?
For there must be a reason when
Such fury stirs the king of men.
Reveal the sin, if sin of mine
Anger the lord of Raghu's line.
Or go thyself, his rage subdue,
And with soft words his favour woo.
Soon as on thee his eyes are set
His heart this anger will forget,
For men like him of lofty mind
Are never stern with womankind.
First let thy gentle speech disarm
His fury, and his spirit charm,
And I, from fear of peril free,
The conqueror of his foes will see."

She heard: with faltering steps and slow,
With eyes that shone with trembling glow,
With gold-girt body gently bent
To meet the stranger prince she went.
When Lakshmaṇ saw the Vánar queen
With tranquil eyes and modest mien,
Before the dame he bent his head,
And anger, at her presence, fled.
Made bold by draughts of wine, and cheered
By Lakshmaṇ's look no more she feared,
And in the trust his favour lent
She thus addressed him eloquent:
"Whence springs thy burning fury? say:
Who dares thy will to disobey?
Who checks the maddened flames that seize
On forests full of withered trees?"

Then Lakshmaṇ spoke, her mind to ease,
His kind reply in words like these:

"Thy lord his days in pleasure spends,
Heedless of duty and of friends,
Nor dost thou mark, though fondly true,
The evil path his steps pursue.
He cares not for affairs of state,
Nor us forlorn and desolate,
But sits a mere spectator still,
A sensual slave to pleasure's will.
Four months were fixed, the time agreed
When he should help us in our need:
But, bound in toils of pleasure fast,
He sees not that the months are past.
Where beats the heart which draughts of wine
To virtue or to gain incline?
Hast thou not heard those draughts destroy
Virtue and gain and love and joy?
For those who, helped at need, refuse
Their aid in turn, their virtue lose:
And they who scorn a friend disdain
A treasure naught may buy again.
Thy lord has cast his friend away,

Nor feared from virtue's path to stray,
If this be true, declare, O dame
Who knowest duty's every claim,
What further work remains for us
Deceived and disappointed thus."
She listened, for his words were kind,
Where virtue showed with gain combined,
And thus in turn the prince addressed,
As hope was rising in his breast:
"No time, no cause of wrath I see
With those who live and honour thee:
And thou shouldst bear without offence
Thy servant's fitful negligence.
I know the seasons glide away,
While Ráma maddens at delay
I know what deed our thanks has earned,
I know that grace should be returned.
But still I know, whate'er befall,
That conquering love is lord of all;

Know where Sugríva's thoughts, possessed
By one absorbing passion, rest.
But he whom sensual joys debase
Heeds not the claim of time and place,
And sees not with his blinded sight
His duty or his gain aright.
O pardon him who loves me! spare
The Vánar caught in pleasure's snare,
And once again let Ráma grace
With favour him who rules our race.
E'en royal saints, whose chief delight
Was penance and austerest rite,
At love's commandment have unbent,
Beguiled by sweetest blandishment.
And know, Sugríva, roused at last,
The order to his lords has passed,
And, long by love and bliss delayed,
Wakes all on fire your hopes to aid.
A countless host his city fills,
New-gathered from a thousand hills:

Impetuous chiefs, who wear at need
Each varied form, his legions lead.
Come then, O hero, kept aloof
By modest awe, nor fear reproof:
A faithful friend untouched by blame
May look upon another's dame."

He passed within, by Tárá pressed,
And by his own impatient breast,
Refulgent there in sunlike sheen
Sugríva on his throne was seen.
Gay garlands round his neck were twined,
And Rumá by her lord recline.

CANTO

XXXIV

Lakshman's Speech

Sugríva started from his rest
With doubt and terror in his breast.
He heard the prince's furious tread
He saw his eyes glow fiercely red.
Swift sprang the monarch to his feet
Upstarting from his golden seat.
Rose Rumá and her fellows, too,
And closely round Sugríva drew,
As round the moon's full glory stand
Attendant stars in glittering band.
Sugríva glanced with reddened eyes,
Raised his joined hands in suppliant guise
Flew to the door, and rooted there
Stood like the tree that grants each prayer.
And Lakshman saw, and, fiercely moved,
With angry speech the king reproved:

"Famed is the prince who loves the truth,
Whose soul is touched with tender ruth,
Who, liberal, keeps each sense subdued,
And pays the debt of gratitude.
But all unmeet a king to be,
The meanest of the mean is he
Who basely breaks the promise made
To trusting friends who lent him aid.
He sins who for a steed has lied,
As if a hundred steeds had died:
Or if he lie, a cow to win,
Tenfold as heavy is the sin.
But if the lie a man betray,
Both he and his shall all decay.
O Vánar King, the thankless man
Is worthy of the general ban,
Who takes assistance of his friends,
And in his turn no service lends.
This verse of old by Brahmá sung
Is echoed now by every tongue.
Hear what He cried in angry mood
Bewailing man's ingratitude:
"For draughts of wine, for slaughtered cows,
For treacherous theft, for broken vows
A pardon is ordained: but none
For thankless scorn of service done."
Ungrateful, Vánar King, art thou,
And faithless to thy plighted vow.
For Ráma brought thee help, and yet
Thou shunnest to repay the debt:
Or, grateful, thou hadst surely pressed
To aid the hero in his quest.
Thou art, in vulgar pleasures drowned,
False to thy bond in honour bound.
Nor yet has Ráma's guileless heart
Discerned thee for the thing thou art—
A snake who holds the frogs that cries
And lures fresh victims as it dies.
Brave Ráma, born for glorious fate,
Has set thee in thy high estate,
And to the Vánars' throne restored,

Great-souled himself, their mean-souled lord.
Now if thy pride disown what he,
High thoughted prince, has done for thee,
Struck by his arrows shalt thou fall,
And Báli meet in Yáma's hall.
Still open, to the gloomy God,
Lies the sad path thy brother trod.
Then to thy plighted word be true,
Nor let thy steps that path pursue.
Methinks the shafts of Ráma, shot
Like thunderbolts, thou heedest not,
Who canst, absorbed in sensual bliss,
Thy promise from thy mind dismiss."

XXXV

Tárá's Speech

He ceased: and Tárá starry-eyed
Thus to the angry prince replied:
"Not to my lord shouldst thou address
A speech so fraught with bitterness:
Not thus reproached my lord should be,
And least of all, O Prince, by thee.
He is no thankless coward—no—
With spirit dead to valour's glow.
From paths of truth he never strays,
Nor wanders in forbidden ways.
Ne'er will Sugríva's heart forget,
By Ráma saved, the lasting debt.
Still in his grateful breast will live
The succour none but he could give.
Restored to fame by Ráma's grace,
To empire o'er the Vánar race,
From ceaseless dread and toil set free,

Restored to Rumá and to me:
By grief and care and exile tried,
New to the bliss so long denied,
Like Viśvámitra once, alas,
He marks not how the seasons pass.
That saint ten thousand years remained,
By sweet Ghritáchí's love enchained,
And deemed those years, that flew away
So lightly, but a single day.
O, if those years unheeded flew
By him who times and seasons knew,
Unequalled for his lofty mind,
What marvel meaner eyes are blind?
Then be not angry, Raghu's son,
And let thy brother feel for one
Who many a weary year has spent
Stranger to love and blandishment.
Let not this wrath thy soul inflame,
Like some mean wretch unknown to fame:
For high and noble hearts like thine
Love mercy and to ruth incline,
Calm and deliberate, and slow
With anger's raging fire to glow.
At length, O righteous prince, relent,
Nor let my words in vain be spent,
This sudden blaze of fury slake,
I pray thee for Sugríva's sake.
He would renounce at Ráma's call
Rumá and Angad, me and all
Who call him lord: his gold and grain,
The favour of his friend to gain.
His arm shall slay the fiend more base
In soul than all his impious race,
And happy Ráma reunite
To Sítá, rival in delight
Of the triumphant Moon when he
Rejoins his darling Rohiṇí.
Ten million million demons guard
The gates of Lanká firmly barred.
All hope until that host be slain,
To smite the robber king is vain.

Nor with Sugríva's aid alone
May king and host be overthrown.
Thus ere he died—for well he knew—
Spake Báli, and his words are true.
I know not what his proofs might be,
But speak the words he spake to me.
Hence far and wide our lords are sent
To raise the mightiest armament,
For their return Sugríva waits
Ere he can sally from his gates.
Still is the oath Sugríva swore
Kept firmly even as before:
And the great host this day will be
Assembled by the king's decree,
Ten thousand thousand troops, who wear
The form of monkey and of bear,
Prepared for thee the war to wage:
Then let thy wrath no longer rage.
The matrons of the Vánar race
See marks of fury in thy face;
They see thine eyes like blood are red,
And will not yet be comforted."

CANTO
XXXVI

Sugríva's Speech

She ceased: and Lakshman gave assent,
Won by her gentle argument.
So Tárá's pleading, just and mild,
His softening heart had reconciled.
His altered mood Sugríva saw,
And cast aside the fear and awe
Like raiment heavy with the rain
Which on his troubled soul had lain.

Then quickly to the ground he threw
His flowery garland, bright of hue,
Which round his royal neck he wore,
And, sobered, was himself once more.
Then turning to the princely man
In soothing words the king began:
"My glory, wealth, and royal sway
To other hands had passed away:
But Ráma to my rescue came,
And gave me back my power and fame.
O Lakshman, say, whose grateful heart

Could nurse the hope to pay in part,
By service of a life, the deed
Of Ráma sprung of heavenly seed?
His foeman Rávan shall be slain,
And Sítá shall be his again.
The hero's side I will not leave,
But he the conquest shall achieve.
What need of help has he who drew
His bow, and one great arrow flew
Through seven tall trees, a mountain rent,
And cleft the earth with force unspent?
What aid needs he who shook his bow,
And at the sound the earth below
With hill and wood and rooted rock
Quaked feverous with the thunder shock?
Yet all my legions will I bring,
And follow close the warrior king
Marching on his impetuous way
Fierce Rávan and his hosts to slay.
If I be guilty of offence,
Careless through love or negligence,
Let him his loyal slave forgive;
For error cleaves to all who live."

Thus king Sugríva, good and brave,
In humble words his answer gave,
Softened was Lakshman's angry mood
Who thus his friendly speech renewed:
"My brother, Vánar King, will see

A champion and a friend in thee.
So strong art thou, so brave and bold,
So pure in thought, so humble-souled,
That thou deservest well to reign
And all a monarch's bliss to gain.
Lend thou my brother aid, and all
His foes beneath his arm will fall.
Full well the words thou speakest suit
A chieftain wise and resolute.
With grateful heart that loves the right,
And foot that never yields in fight.
O come, and my sad brother cheer
Who mourns the wife he holds so dear.
O pardon, friend, my harsh address,
And Ráma's frantic bitterness."

CANTO

XXXVII

The Gathering

He ceased: and King Sugríva cried
To sage Hanúmán by his side:
"Summon the Vánar legions, those
Who dwell about the Lord of Snows:
Those who in Vindhyan groves delight,
Kailása's, or Mahendra's height,
Dwell on the Five bright Peaks, or where
Mandar's white summit cleaves the air:
Wherever they are wandring free
In highlands by the western sea,
On that east hill whence springs the sun,
Or where he sinks when day is done.
Call the great chiefs whose legions fill
The forests of the Lotus Hill,
Where every one in strength and size

With the stupendous Anjan vies.
Call those, with tints of burnished gold
Whom Maháśaila's caverns hold:
Those who on Dhúmra roam, or hide
In the wild woods on Meru's side.
Call those who, brilliant as the sun,
On high Maháruṇ leap and run,
Quaffing sweet juices that distil
From odorous trees upon the hill,
Call those whom tranquil haunts delight,
Where dwell the sage and anchorite
In groves that through their wide extent
Exhale a thousand blossoms' scent.
Send out, send out: from coast to coast
Assemble all the Vánar host:
With force, with words, with gifts of price
Compel, admonish and entice.
Already envoys have been sent
To warn them of their lord's intent.
Let others urged by thee repeat
My mandate that their steps be fleet.
Those lords who yielding to the sway
Of love's delight would fain delay,
Urge hither with the utmost speed,
Or with thee to my presence lead:
And those who linger to the last
Until ten days be come and passed,
And dare their sovereign to defy,
For their offence shall surely die.
Thousands, yea millions, shall there be,
Obedient to their king's decree,
The lions of the Vánar race,
Assembled from each distant place,
Forth shall they haste like hills in size,
Or mighty clouds that veil the skies,
And swiftly speeding on their way
Bring all our legions in array."

He ceased: the son of Váyu heard,
Submissive to his sovereign's word;
And sent his rapid envoys forth

To east and west and south and north.
They bent their airy course afar
Along the paths of bird and star,
And sped through ether farther yet
Where Vishṇu's splendid sphere is set.
By sea, on hill, by wood and lake
They called to arms for Ráma's sake,
As each with terror in his breast
Obeyed his awful king's behest.
Three million Vánars, fierce and strong
As Anjan's self, a wondrous throng
Sped from the spot where Ráma still
Gazed restless from the woody hill.
Ten million others, brave and bold,
With coats that shone like burning gold,
Came flying from the mountain crest
Where sinks the weary sun to rest.
Impetuous from the northern skies,
Where Mount Kailása's summits rise,
Ten hundred millions hasted, hued
Like manes of lions, ne'er subdued:
The dwellers on Himálaya's side,
Whose food his roots and fruit supplied,
With rangers of the Vindhyan chain
And neighbours of the Milky Main.
Some from the palm groves where they fed,
Some from the woods of betel sped:
In countless numbers, fierce and brave,
They came from mountain, lake, and cave.

As on their way the Vánars went
To rouse each distant armament,
They chanced that wondrous tree to view
That on Himálaya's summit grew.
Of old upon that sacred height
Was wrought Maheśvar's glorious rite,
Which every God in heaven beheld,
And his glad heart with triumph swelled.
There from pure seed at random sown
Bright plants with luscious fruit had grown,
And, sweet as Amrit to the taste,

The summit of the mountain graced.
Who once should eat the virtuous fruit
That sprang from so divine a root,
One whole revolving moon should be
From every pang of hunger free.
The Vánars culled the fruit they found
Ripe on the sacrificial ground
With rare celestial odours sweet,
To lay them at Sugríva's feet.
Those noble envoys scoured the land
To summon every Vánar band
Then swiftly homeward at the head
Of countless armaments they sped.
They gathered by Kishkindhá's wall.
They thronged Sugríva's palace hall,
And, richly laden, bare within
That fruit of heavenly origin.
Their gifts before their king they spread,
And thus in tones of triumph said:

"Through every land our way we took
To visit hill and wood and brook,
And all thy hosts from east to west
Flock hither at their lord's behest."
Sugríva with delighted look
The present of his envoys took,
Then bade them go, with gracious speech
Rewarding and dismissing each.

Sugríva's Departure

Thus all the princely Vánars, true
To their appointed tasks, withdrew.
Sugríva deemed already done
The work he planned for Raghu's son.
Then Lakshmaṇ gently spoke and cheered
Sugríva for his valour feared:
"Now, chieftain, if thy will be so,
Forth from Kishkindhá let us go."
Sugríva's heart swelled high with pride
As to the prince he thus replied:
"Come, speed we forth without delay:
'Tis mine thy mandate to obey."
Sugríva bade the dames adieu,
And Tárá and the rest withdrew.
Then at their chieftain's summons came
The Vánars first in rank and fame,
A trusty brave and reverent band,
Meet e'en before a queen to stand.
They at his call made haste to bring
The litter of the glorious king.
"Mount, O my friend." Sugríva cried,
And straight Sumitrá's son complied.
Then took by Lakshmaṇ's side his place
The sovereign of the woodland race,
Upraised by Vánars, fleet and strong,
Who bore the glittering load along.
On high above his royal head
A paly canopy was spread,
And chouries white in many a hand
The forehead of the monarch fanned,

And shell and drum and song and shout
Pealed round him as the king passed out.

About the monarch went a throng
Of Vánar warriors brave and strong,
As onward to the mountain shade
Where Ráma dwelt his way he made.
Soon as the lovely spot he viewed
Where Ráma lived in solitude,
The Vánar monarch, far-renowed,
With Lakshman, lightly stepped to ground,
And to the son of Raghu went
Joining his raised hands reverent.
As their great leader raised his hands,
So suppliant stood the Vánar bands.
Well pleased the son of Raghu saw
Those legions, hushed in reverent awe,
Stand silent like the tranquil floods
That raise their hands of lotus buds.
But Ráma, when the king, to greet
His friend, had bowed him at his feet,
Raised him who ruled the Vánar race,
And held him in a close embrace:
Then, when his arms he had unknit,
Besought him by his side to sit,
And thus with gentle words the best
Of men the Vánar king addressed:
"The prince who well his days divides,
And knows aright the times and tides
To follow duty, joy, or gain,
He, only he, deserves to reign.
But he who wealth and virtue leaves,
And every hour to pleasure cleaves,
Falls from his bliss like him who wakes
From slumber on a branch that breaks.
True king is he who smites his foes,
And favour to his servants shows,
And of that fruit makes timely use
Which virtue, wealth, and joy produce.
The hour is come that bids thee rise
To aid me in my enterprise.

Then call thy nobles to debate,
And with their help deliberate."

"Lost was my power," the king replied,
"All strength had fled, all hope had died.
The Vánars owned another lord,
But by thy grace was all restored.
All this, O conqueror of the foe,
To thee and Lakshman's aid I owe.
And his should be the villain's shame
Who durst deny the sacred claim.
These Vánar chiefs of noblest birth
Have at my bidding roamed the earth,
And brought from distant regions all
Our legions at their monarch's call:
Fierce bears with monkey troops combined,
And apes of every varied kind,
Terrific in their forms, who dwell
In grove and wood and bosky dell:
The bright Gandharvas' brood, the seed
Of Gods, they change their shapes at need.
Each with his legions in array,
Hither, O Prince, they make their way.
They come: and tens of millions swell
To numbers that no tongue may tell.
For thee their armies will unite
With chiefs, Mahendra's peers in might.
From Meru and from Vindhya's chain
They come like clouds that bring the rain.
These round thee to the war will go,
To smite to earth thy demon foe;
Will slay the Rákshas and restore
Thy consort when the fight is o'er."

157

The Vánar Host

Then Ráma, best of all who guide
Their steps by duty, thus replied:
"What marvel if Lord Indra send
The kindly rain, O faithful friend?
If, thousand-rayed, the God of Day
Drive every darksome cloud away?
Or, rising high, the Lord of Night
Flood the broad heaven with silver light?
What marvel, King, that one like thee
The glory of his friends should be?
No marvel, O my lord, that thou
Hast shown thy noble nature now.
Thy heart, Sugríva, well I know:
Naught from thy lips but truth may flow,
With thee for friend and champion all
My foes beneath my arm will fall.
The Rákshas, when my queen he stole,
Brought sure destruction on his soul,
Like Anuhláda who beguiled
Queen Śachí called Puloma's child.
Yes, near, Sugríva, is the day
When I my demon foe shall slay,
As conquering Indra in his ire
Slew Queen Paulomí's haughty sire."

He ceased: thick clouds of dust rose high
To every quarter of the sky:
The very sun grew faint and pale
Behind the darkly-gathering veil.
The mighty clouds that hung o'erhead
From east to west thick darkness spread,

And earth to her foundations shook
With hill and forest, lake and brook.
Then hidden was the ground beneath
Fierce warriors armed with fearful teeth,
Hosts numberless, each lord in size
A match for him who rules the skies:
From many a sea and distant hill,
From rock and river, lake and rill.
Some like the morning sun were bright,
Some, like the moon, were silver white:
These green as lotus fibres, those
White-coated from their native snows.
Then Śatabali came in view
Girt by a countless retinue.
Like some gold mountain high in air
Tárá's illustrious sire was there.
There Rumá`s father, far-renowned,
With tens of thousands ranged around.
There, tinted like the tender green
Of lotus filaments, was seen,
Compassed by countless legions, one
Whose face was as the morning sun,
Hanúmán's father good and great,
Kesarí, wisest in debate.
There the proud king Gaváksha, feared
For his strong warrior arm, appeared.
There Dhúmra, mighty lord, the dread
Of foes, his ursine legions led.
There Panas, first for warlike fame,
With twenty million warriors came.
There glorious Níla, dark of hue,
Arrayed his countless troops in view.
There moved lord Gavaya brave and bold,
Resplendent like a hill of gold,
And near him Darímukha stood
With millions from the hill and wood
And Dwivid famed for strength and speed,
And Mamda, both of Aśvin seed.
There Gaja, strong and glorious, led
The countless troops around him spread,
And Jámbaván the king whose sway

159

The bears delighted to obey,
With swarming myriads onward pressed
True to his lord Sugríva's hest;
And princely Ruman, dear to fame,
Led millions whom no hosts could tame,
All these and many a chief beside
Came onward fierce in warlike pride.
They covered all the plain, and still
Pressed forward over wood and hill.
In rows for many a league around
They rested on the grassy ground;
Or to Sugríva made their way,
Like clouds about the Lord of Day,
And to the king their proud heads bent
In power and might preeminent.
Sugríva then to Ráma sped,
And raised his reverent hands, and said
That every chief from coast to coast
Was present with his warrior host.

CANTO

XL

The Army of the East

With practised eye the king reviewed
The Vánars' countless multitude,
And, joying that his hest was done,
Thus spake to Raghu's mighty son:
"See, all the Vánar hosts who fear
My sovereign might are gathered here.
Chiefs strong as Indra's self, who speed
Wher'er they list, these armies lead.
Fierce and terrific to the view
As Daityas or the Dánav crew,

Famed in all lands for souls afire
With lofty thoughts, they never tire,
O'er hill and vale they wander free,
And islets of the distant sea.
And these gathered myriads, all
Will serve thee, Ráma, at thy call.
Whate'er thy heart advises, say:
Thy mandates will the host obey."

Then answered Ráma, as he pressed
The Vánar monarch to his breast:
"O search for my lost Sítá, strive
To find her if she still survive:
And in thy wondrous wisdom trace
Fierce Rávaṇ to his dwelling-place.
And when by toil and search we know
Where Sítá lies and where the foe,
With thee, dear friend, will I devise
Fit means to end the enterprise.
Not mine, not Lakshmaṇ's is the power
To guide us in the doubtful hour.
Thou, sovereign of the Vánars, thou
Must be our hope and leader now."

He ceased: at King Sugríva's call
Near came a Vánar strong and tall.
Huge as a towering mountain, loud
As some tremendous thunder cloud,
A prince who warlike legions led:
To him his sovereign turned and said:
"Go, take ten thousand of our race
Well trained in lore of time and place,
And search the eastern region; through
Groves, woods, and hills thy way pursue.
There seek for Sítá, trace the spot
Where Rávaṇ hides, and weary not.
Search for the captive in the caves
Of mountains, and by woods and waves.
To Sarjú, Kaúsikí, repair,
Bhagírath's daughter fresh and fair.
Search mighty Yamun's peak, explore

161

Swift Yamuná's delightful shore,
Sarasvati and Sindhu's tide,
And rapid Śona's pebbly side.
Then roam afar by Mahí's bed
Where Kálamahí's groves are spread.
Go where the silken tissue shines,
Go to the land of silver mines.
Visit each isle and mountain steep
And city circled by the deep,
And distant villages that high
About the peaks of Mandar lie.
Speed over Yavadwipa's land,
And see Mount Śiśir proudly stand
Uplifting to the skies his head
By Gods and Dánavs visited.
Search each ravine and mountain pass,
Each tangled thicket deep in grass.
Search every cave with utmost care
If haply Ráma's queen be there.
Then pass beyond the sounding sea
Where heavenly beings wander free,
And Śona's waters swift and strong
With ruddy billows foam along.
Search where his shelving banks descend,
Search where the hanging woods extend.
Try if the pathless thickets screen
The robber and the captive queen.
Search where the torrent floods that rend
The mountain to the plains descend:
Search dark abysses where they rave,
Search mountain slope and wood and cave
Then on with rapid feet and gain
The inlands of the fearful main
Where, tortured by the tempest's lash,
Against rude rocks the billows dash:
An ocean like a sable cloud,
Whose margent monstrous serpents crowd:

An ocean rising with a roar
To beat upon an iron shore.
On, onward still! your feet shall tread

Shores of the sea whose waves are red,
Where spreading wide your eyes shall see
The guilt-tormenting cotton tree
And the wild spot where Garuḍ dwells
Which gems adorn and ocean shells,
High as Kailása, nobly decked,
Wrought by the heavenly architect.
Huge giants named Mandehas there
In each foul shape they love to wear,
Numbing the soul with terror's chill,
Hang from the summit of the hill.
When darts the sun his earliest beam
They plunge them in the ocean stream,
New vigour from his rays obtain,
And hang upon the rocks again.
Speed onward still: your steps shall be
At length beside the Milky Sea
Whose every ripple as it curls
Gleams glorious with its wealth of pearls.
Amid that sea like pale clouds spread
The white Mount Rishabh rears his head.
About the mountain's glorious waist
Woods redolent of bloom are braced.
A lake where lotuses unfold
Their silver buds with threads of gold,
Sudarśan ever bright and fair
Where white swans sport, lies gleaming there,
The wandering Kinnar's dear resort,
Where heavenly nymphs and Yakshas sport.
On! leave the Milky Sea behind:
Another flood your search shall find,
A waste of waters, wild and drear,
That chills each living heart with fear.
There see the horse's awful head,
Wrath-born, that flames in Ocean's bed.
There rises up a fearful cry
From the sea things that move thereby,
When, helpless, powerless for flight,
They gaze upon the horrid sight.
Past to the northern shore, and then
Beyond the flood three leagues and ten

Your wondering glances will behold
Mount Játarúpa bright with gold.
There like the young moon pale of hue
The monstrous serpent will ye view,
The earth's supporter, whose bright eyes
Resemble lotus leaves in size.
He rests upon the mountain's brow,
And all the Gods before him bow.
Ananta with a thousand heads
His length in robes of azure spreads.
A triple-headed palm of gold—
Meet standard for the lofty-souled—
Springs towering from the mountain's crest
Beneath whose shade he loves to rest,
So that in eastern realms each God
May use it as a measuring-rod.
Beyond, with burning gold aglow,
The eastern steep his peaks will show,
Which in unrivalled glory rise
A hundred leagues to pierce the skies,
And all the neighbouring air is bright
With golden trees that clothe the height.
A lofty peak uprises there
Ten leagues in height and one league square
Saumanas, wrought of glistering gold,
Ne'er to be loosened from its hold.
There his first step Lord Vishnu placed
When through the universe he paced,
And with his second lightly pressed
The loftiest peak of Meru's crest.
When north of Jambudwíp the sun

A portion of his course has run,
And hangs above this mountain height,
Then creatures see the genial light.
Vaikhánases, saints far renowned,
And Bálakhilyas love the ground
Where in their glory half divine,
Touched by the morning glow, they shine
The light that flashes from that steep
Illumines all Sudarśandwíp,

And on each creature, as it glows,
The sight and strength of life bestows.
Search well that mountain's woody side
If Rávaṇ there his captive hide.
The rising sun, the golden hill
The air with growing splendours fill,
Till flashes from the east the red
Of morning with the light they shed.
This, where the sun begins his state,
Is earth and heaven's most eastern gate.
Through all the mountain forest seek
By waterfall and cave and peak.
Search every nook and bosky dell,
If Rávaṇ there with Sítá dwell.
There, Vánars, there your steps must stay:
No farther eastward can ye stray.
Beyond no sun, no moon gives light,
But all is sunk in endless night.
Thus far, O Vánar lords, may you
O'er sea and land your search pursue.
But wild and dark and known to none
Is the drear space beyond the sun.
That mountain whence the sun ascends
Your long and weary journey ends.
Now go, and in a month return,
And let success my praises earn.
He who beyond tho month shall stay
Will with his life the forfeit pay."

The Army of the South

He gathered next a chosen band
For service in the southern land.
He summoned Níla son of Fire,
And, offspring of the eternal Sire,
Jámbaván bold and strong and tall,
And Hanumán, the best of all,
And many a valiant lord beside,
With Angad for their chief and guide.
"Go forth," he cried, "with all this host
Exploring to the southern coast:
The thousand peaks that Vindhya shows
Where every tree and creeper grows:
Where Narmadá's sweet waters run,
And serpents bask them in the sun:
Where Krishṇaveṇí's currents flee,
And sparkles fair Godávarí.
Through Mekhal pass and Utkal's land:
Go where Daśárṇa's cities stand.
Avantí seek, of high renown,
And Abravanti's glorious town.
Search every hill and brook and cave
Where Daṇḍak's woods their branches wave
Ayomukh's woody hill explore
Whose sides are bright with richest ore,
Lifting his glorious head on high
From bloomy groves that round him lie.

Search well his forests where the breeze
Blows fragrant from the sandal trees.
Then will you see Káverí's stream
Whose pleasant waters glance and gleam,

And to the lovely banks entice
The sportive maids of Paradise.
High on the top of Malaya's hill,
In holy musing, calm and still,
Sits, radiant as the Lord of Light,
Agastya, noblest anchorite.
Soon as that lofty-thoughted lord
His high permission shall accord,
Pass Támraparṇí's flood whose isles
Are loved by basking crocodiles.
The sandal woods that fringe her side
Those islets and her waters hide;
While, like an amorous matron, she
Speeds to her own dear lord the sea.
Thence hasting on your way behold
The Páṇḍyas' gates of pearl and gold.
Then, with your task maturely planned,
On ocean's shore your feet will stand.
Where, by Agastya's high decree,
Mahendra, planted in the sea,
With tinted peaks against the tide
Rises in solitary pride,
And glorious in his golden glow
Spurns back the waves that beat below.
Fair mountain, bright with creepers' bloom
And every tint that trees assume,
Where Yaksha, God, and heavenly maid
Meet wandering in the lovely shade,
At changing moon and solemn tide
By Indra's presence glorified.
One hundred leagues in fair extent
An island fronts the continent:
No man may tread its glittering shore,
With utmost heed that isle explore,
For the fair country owns the sway
Of Rávaṇ whom we burn to slay.
A mighty monster stands to keep
The passage of the southern deep.
Lifting her awful arms on high
She grasps e'en shadows as they fly.
Speed through that isle, and onward still

Where in mid sea the Flowery Hill
Raises on high his bloomy head
By saints and angels visited.
There, with a hundred gleaming peaks
Bright as the sun, the sky he seeks,
One glorious peak the Lord of Day
Gilds ever with his loving ray;
Thereon ne'er yet the glances fell
Of thankless wretch or infidel.
Bow to that hill in reverence due,
And then once more your search pursue.
Beyond that glorious mountain hie,
And Súryaván, proud hill is nigh.
Your rapid course yet farther bend
Where Vaidyut's airy peaks ascend.
There trees of noblest sort, profuse
Of wealth, their kindly gifts produce.
Their precious fruits, O Vánars, taste,
The honey sip, and onward haste.
Next will ye see Mount Kunjar rise,
Who cheers with beauty hearts and eyes.
There is Agastya's mansion, decked
By heaven's all moulding architect.
Near Bhogavatí stands, the place
Where dwell the hosts of serpent race:
A broad-wayed city, walled and barred,
Which watchful legions keep and guard,
The fiercest of the serpent youth,
Each awful for his venomed tooth:
And throned in his imperial hall
Is Vásuki who rules them all.
Explore the serpent city well,
Search town and tower and citadel,
And scan each field and wood that lies
Around it, with your watchful eyes.
Beyond that spot your way pursue:
A noble mountain shall ye view,
Named Rishabh, like a mighty bull,
With gems made bright and beautiful.

All trees of sandal flourish there
Of heavenly fragrance, rich and rare.
But, though they tempt your longing eyes,
Avoid to touch them, and be wise.
For Rohitas, a guardian band
Of fierce Gandharvas, round them stand,
Who five bright sovereign lords obey,
In glory like the God of Day.
Here by good deeds a home is won
With shapes like fire, the moon, the sun.
Here they who merit heaven by worth
Dwell on the confines of the earth.
There stay: beyond it, dark and drear,
Lies the departed spirits' sphere,
And, girt with darkness, far from bliss,
Is Yáma's sad metropolis.
So far, my lords, o'er land and sea
Your destined course is plain and free.
Beyond your steps you may not set,
Where living thing ne'er journeyed yet.
With utmost care these realms survey,
And all you meet upon the way.
And, when the lady's course is traced,
Back to your king, O Vánars, haste.
And he who tells me he has seen,
After long search, the Maithil queen,
Shall gain a noble guerdon: he
In power and bliss shall equal me.
Dear as my very life, above
His fellows in his master's love;
I call him, yea though stained with crime,
My kinsman from that happy time."

The Army of the West

Then to Sushen Sugríva bent,
And thus addressed him reverent:
"Two hundred thousand of our best
With thee, my lord, shall seek the west.
Explore Suráshtra's] distant plain,
Explore Váhlíka's wild domain,
And all the pleasant brooks that flee
Through mountains to the western sea.
Search clustering groves on mountain heights,
And woods the home of anchorites.
Search where the breezy hills are high,
Search where the desert regions lie.
Search all the western land beset
With woody mountains like a net.
The country`s farthest limit reach,
And stand upon the ocean beach.
There wander through the groves of palm
Where the soft air is full of balm.
Through grassy dell and dark ravine
Seek Rávan and the Maithil queen.
Go visit Somagiri's steep
Where Sindhu mingles with the deep.
There lions, borne on swift wings, roam
The levels of their mountain home,
And elephants and monsters bear,
Caught from the ocean, to their lair.
You Vánars, changing forms at will,
With rapid search must scour the hill,
And his sky-kissing peak of gold
Where loveliest trees their blooms unfold.
There golden-peaked, ablaze with light,

Uprises Páriyátra's height
Where wild Gandharvas, fierce and fell,
In bands of countless myriads dwell.
Pluck ye no fruit within the wood;
Beware the impious neighbourhood,
Where, very mighty, strong, and hard
To overcome, the fruit they guard.
Yet search for Janak's daughter still,
For Vánars there need fear no ill.
Near, bright as turkis, Vajra named,
There stands a hill of diamond framed.
Soaring a hundred leagues in pride,
With trees and creepers glorified.
Search there each cave and dark abyss
By waterfall and precipice.
Far in that sea the wild waves beat
On Chakraván's firm-rooted feet.
Where the great discus, thousand rayed,
By Vísvakarmá's art was made.
When Panchajan the fiend was slain.
And Hayagríva, fierce in vain,

Thence taking shell and discus went
Lord Vishṇu, God preëminent.
On! sixty thousand hills of gold
With wondering eyes shall ye behold,
Where in his glory every one
Is brilliant as the morning sun.
Full in the midst King Meru, best
Of mountains, lifts his lofty crest,
On whom of yore, as all have heard,
The sun well-pleased this boon conferred:
"On thee, O King, on thee and thine
Light, day and night, shall ever shine.
Gandharvas, Gods who love thee well
And on thy sacred summits dwell,
Undimmed in lustre, bright and fair,
The golden sheen shall ever share."
The Vísvas, Vasus, they who ride
The tempest, every God beside,
Draw nigh to Meru's lofty crest

When evening darkens in the west,
And to the parting Lord of Day
The homage of their worship pay,
Ere yet a while, unseen of all,
Behind Mount Asta's peaks he fall.
Wrought by the heavenly artist's care
A glorious palace glitters there,
And round about it sweet birds sing
Where the gay trees are blossoming:
The home of Varuṇ high-souled lord,
Wrist-girded with his deadly cord.
With ten tall stems, a palm between
Meru and Asta's hill is seen:
Pure silver from the base it springs,
And far and wide its lustre flings.
Seek Rávaṇ and the dame by brook,
In pathless glen, in leafy nook
On Meru's crest a hermit lives
Bright with the light that penance gives:
Sávarṇi is he named, renowned
As Brahmá's peer, with glory crowned.
There bowing down in reverence speak
And ask him of the dame you seek.
Thus far the splendid Lord of Day
Pursues through heaven his ceaseless way,
Shedding on every spot his light;
Then sinks behind Mount Asta's height,
Thus far advance: the sunless sea
Beyond is all unknown to me.
Susheṇ of mighty arm, long tried
In peril, shall your legions guide.
Receive his words with high respect,
And ne'er his lightest wish neglect.
He is my consort's sire, and hence
Deserves the utmost reverence."

The Army of the North

Forth went the legions of the west:
And wise Sugríva addressed
Śatabal, summoned from the crowd.
To whom the sovereign cried aloud:
"Go forth, O Vánar chief, go forth,
Explore the regions of the north.
Thy host a hundred thousand be,
And Yáma's sons attend on thee.
With dauntless courage, strength, and skill
Search every river, wood, and hill.
Through every land in order go
Right onward to the Hills of Snow.
Search mid the peaks that shine afar,
In woods of Lodh and Deodár.
Search if with Janak's daughter, screened
By sheltering rocks, there lie the fiend.

The holy grounds of Soma tread
By Gods and minstrels visited.
Reach Kála's mount, and flats that lie
Among the peaks that tower on high.
Then leave that hill that gleams with ore,
And fair Sudarśan's heights explore.
Then on to Devasakhá hie,
Loved by the children of the sky.
A dreary land you then will see
Without a hill or brook or tree,
A hundred leagues, bare, wild, and dread
In lifeless desolation, spread.
Pursue your onward way, and haste
Through the dire horrors of the waste

Until triumphant with delight
You reach Kailása's glittering height.
There stands a palace decked with gold,
For King Kuvera wrought of old,
A home the heavenly artist planned
And fashioned with his cunning hand.
There lotuses adorn the flood
With full-blown flower and opening bud
Where swans and mallards float, and gay
Apsarases come down to play.
There King Vaiśravaṇ's self, the lord
By all the universe adored,
Who golden gifts to mortals sends,
Lives with the Guhyakas his friends.
Search every cavern in the steep,
And green glens where the moonbeams sleep,
If haply in that distant ground
The robber and the dame be found.
Then on to Krauncha's hill, and through
His fearful pass your way pursue:
Though dark and terrible the vale
Your wonted courage must not fail.
There through abyss and cavern seek,
On lofty ridge, and mountain peak,
On, on! pursue your journey still
By valley, lake, and towering hill.
Reach the North Kurus' land, where rest
The holy spirits of the blest:
Where golden buds of lilies gleam
Resplendent on the silver stream,
And leaves of azure turkis throw
Soft splendour on the waves below.
Bright as the sun at early morn
Fair pools that happy clime adorn,
Where shine the loveliest flowers on stems
Of crystal and all valued gems.
Blue lotuses through all the land
The glories of their blooms expand,
And the resplendent earth is strown
With peerless pearl and precious stone.

There stately trees can scarce uphold
The burthen of their fruits of gold,
And ever flaunt their gay attire
Of flower and leaf like flames of fire.
All there sweet lives untroubled spend
In bliss and joy that know not end,
While pearl-decked maidens laugh, or sing
To music of the silvery string.
Still on your forward journey keep,
And rest you by the northern deep,
Where springing from the billows high
Mount Somagiri seeks the sky,
And lightens with perpetual glow
The sunless realm that lies below.
There, present through all life's extent,
Dwells Brahmá Lord preëminent,
And round the great God, manifest
In Rudra forms high sages rest.
Then turn, O Vánars: search no more,
Nor tempt the sunless, boundless shore."

CANTO
XLIV

The Ring

B ut special counselling he gave
To Hanumán the wise and brave:

To him on whom his soul relied,
With friendly words the monarch cried:
"O best of Vánars, naught can stay
By land or sea thy rapid way,
Who through the air thy flight canst bend,
And to the Immortals' home ascend.

175

All realms, I ween, are known to thee
With every mountain, lake, and sea.
In strength and speed which naught can tire
Thou, worthy rival of thy sire
The mighty monarch of the wind,
Where'er thou wilt a way canst find.
Exert thy power, O swift and strong,
Bring back the lady lost so long,
For time and place, O thou most wise,
Lie open to thy searching eyes."

When Ráma heard that special hest
To Hanumán above the rest,
He from the monarch's favour drew
Hope of success and trust anew
That he on whom his lord relied,
In toil and peril trained and tried,
Would to a happy issue bring
The task commanded by the king.
He gave the ring that bore his name,
A token for the captive dame,
That the sad lady in her woe
The missive of her lord might know.
"This ring," he said, "my wife will see,
Nor fear an envoy sent by me.
Thy valour and thy skill combined,
Thy resolute and vigorous mind,
And King Sugríva's high behest,
With joyful hopes inspire my breast."

CANTO
XLV

The Departure

Away, away the Vánars sped
Like locusts o'er the land outspread.
To northern realms where rising high
The King of Mountains cleaves the sky,
Fierce Śatabal with vast array
Of Vánar warriors led the way.
Far southward, as his lord decreed,
Wise Hanumán, the Wind-God's seed,
With Angad his swift way pursued,
And Tára's warlike multitude,
Strong Vinata with all his band
Betook him to the eastern land,
And brave Sushen in eager quest
Sped swiftly to the gloomy west.
Each Vánar chieftain sought with speed
The quarter by his king decreed,
While from his legions rose on high
The shout and boast and battle cry:
"We will restore the dame and beat
The robber down beneath our feet.
My arm alone shall win the day
From Rávan met in single fray,
Shall rob the robber of his life,
And rescue Ráma's captive wife
All trembling in her fear and woe.
Here, comrades, rest: no farther go:
For I will vanquish hell, and she
Shall by this arm again be free.
The rooted mountains will I rend,
The mightiest trees will break and bend,
Earth to her deep foundations cleave,

And make the calm sea throb and heave.
A hundred leagues from steep to steep
In desperate bound my feet shall leap.
My steps shall tread unchecked and free,
Through woods, o'er land and hill and sea,
Range as they list from flood to fell,
And wander through the depths of hell."

XLVI

Sugríva's Tale

"How, King," cried Ráma, "didst thou gain
Thy lore of sea and hill and plain?"
"I told thee how," Sugríva said,
"From Báli's arm Máyáví fled
To Malaya's hill, and strove to save
His life by hiding in the cave.
I told how Báli sought, to kill
His foe, the hollow of the hill;
Nor need I, King, again unfold
The wondrous tale already told.
Then, wandering forth, my way I took
By many a town and wood and brook.
I roamed the earth from place to place,
Till, like a mirror's polished face,
The whole broad disk, that lies between
Its farthest bounds, mine eyes had seen.
I wandered first to eastern skies
Where fairest trees rejoiced mine eyes,
And many a cave and wooded hill
Where lilies robed the lake and rill.
There metal dyes that hill adorn
Whence springs the sun to light the morn.

There, too, I viewed the Milky sea,
Where nymphs of heaven delight to be.
Then to the south I made my way
From regions of the rising day,
And roamed o'er Vindhya, where the breeze
Is odorous of sandal trees.
Still in my fear I found no rest:
I sought the regions of the west,
And gazed on Asta, where the sun

Sinks when his daily course is run.
Then from that noblest hill I fled
And to the northern country sped,
Saw Himaván, and Meru's steep,
And stood beside the northern deep.
But when, by Báli's might oppressed,
E'en in those wilds I could not rest,
Came Hanumán the wise and brave,
And thus his prudent counsel gave:
"'I told thee how Matanga cursed
Thy tyrant, that his head should burst
In pieces, should he dare invade
The precincts of that tranquil shade.
There may we dwell in peace and be
From thy oppressor's malice free."
We went to Rishyamúka's hill,
And spent our days secure from ill
Where, with that curse upon his head,
The cruel Báli durst not tread."

XLVII

The Return

Thus forth in quest of Sítá went
The legions King Sugríva sent.
To many a distant town they hied
By many a lake and river's side.
As their great sovereign's order taught,
Through valleys, plains, and groves they sought.
They toiled unresting through the day:
At night upon the ground they lay
Where the tall trees, whose branches swayed
Beneath their fruit, gave pleasant shade.
Then, when a weary month was spent,
Back to Praśravaṇ's hill they went,
And stood with faces of despair
Before their king Sugríva there.
Thus, having wandered through the east,
Great Vinata his labours ceased,
And weary of the fruitless pain
Returned to meet the king again,
Brave Śatabali to the north
Had led his Vánar legions forth.
Now to Sugríva he sped
With all his host dispirited.
Sushen the western realms had sought,
And homeward now his legions brought.
All to Sugríva came, where still
He sat with Ráma on the hill.
Before their sovereign humbly bent
And thus addressed him reverent:
"On every hill our steps have been,
By wood and cave and deep ravine;
And all the wandering brooks we know

180

Throughout the land that seaward flow,
Our feet by thy command have traced
The tangled thicket and the waste,
And dens and dingles hard to pass
for creeping plants and matted grass.
Well have we searched with toil and pain,
And monstrous creatures have we slain
But Hanumán of noblest mind
The Maithil lady yet will find;
For to his quarter of the sky
The robber fiend was seen to fly."

CANTO

XLVIII

The Asur's Death

But Hanumán still onward pressed
With Tára, Angad, and the rest,
Through Vindhya's pathless glens he sped
And left no spot unvisited.
He gazed from every mountain height,
He sought each cavern dark as night,
And wandered through the bloomy shade
By pool and river and cascade,
But, though they sought in every place,
Of Sítá yet they found no trace.
On fruit and woodland berries fed
Through many a lonely wild they sped,
And reached at last, untouched by fear,
A desert terrible and drear:
A fruitless waste, a land of gloom
Where trees were bare of leaf and bloom,
Where every scanty stream was dried,
And niggard earth her roots denied.
No elephants through all the ground,

No buffaloes or deer are found.
There roams no tiger, pard, or bear,
No creature of the wood is there.
No bird displays his glittering wings,
No tree, no shrub, no creeper springs.
There rise no lilies from the flood,
Resplendent with their flower and bud,
Where the delighted bees may throng
About the fragrance with their song.
There lived a hermit Kaṇḍu named,
For truth and wealth of penance famed.
Whom fervent zeal and holy rite
Had dowered with all-surpassing might.
His little son, a ten year child—
So chanced it—perished in the wild.
His death with fury stirred the sage,
Who cursed the forest in his rage,
Doomed from that hour to shelter none,
A waste for bird and beast to shun.

They searched by every forest edge,
They searched each cave and mountain ledge,
And thickets whence the water fell
Wandering through the tangled dell.
Striving to do Sugríva's will
They roamed along each leafy rill.
But vain were all endeavours, vain
The careful search, the toil and pain.
Through one dark grove they scarce could wind,
So thick were creepers intertwined.
There as they struggled through the wood
Before their eyes an Asur stood.
High as a towering hill, his pride
The very Gods in heaven defied.
When on the fiend their glances fell
Each braced him for the combat well.
The demon raised his arm on high,
And rushed upon them with a cry.
Him Angad smote,—for, sure, he thought
This was the fiend they long had sought.

From his huge mouth by Angad felled,
The blood in rushing torrents welled,
As, like a mountain from his base
Uptorn, he dropped upon his face.
Thus fell the mighty fiend: and they
Through the thick wood pursued their way;
Then, weary with the toil, reclined
Where leafy boughs to shade them twined.

CANTO
XLIX

Angad's Speech

Then Angad spake: "We Vánars well
Have searched each valley, cave, and dell,
And hill, and brook, and dark recess,
And tangled wood, and wilderness.
But all in vain: no eye has seen
The robber or the Maithil queen.
A dreary time has passed away,
And stern is he we all obey.
Come, cast your grief and sloth aside:
Again be every effort tried;
So haply may our toil attain
The sweet success that follows pain.
Laborious effort, toil, and skill,
The firm resolve, the constant will
Secure at last the ends we seek:
Hence, O my friends, I boldly speak.
Once more then, noble hearts, once more
Let us to-day this wood explore,
And, languor and despair subdued,
Purchase success with toil renewed.
Sugríva is a king austere,

And Ráma's wrath we needs must fear.
Come, Vánars, ye think it wise,
And do the thing that I advise."

Then Gandhamádan thus replied
With lips that toil and thirst had dried;
"Obey his words, for wise and true
Is all that he has counselled you.
Come, let your hosts their toil renew
And search each grove and desert through,
Each towering hill and forest glade.
By lake and brook and white cascade,
Till every spot, as our great lord
Commanded, be again explored."

Uprose the Vánars one and all,
Obedient to the chieftain's call,
And over the southern region sped
Where Vindhya's tangled forests spread.
They clomb that hill that towers on high
Like a huge cloud in autumn's sky,
Where many a cavern yawns, and streaks
Of radiant silver deck the peaks.
In eager search they wandered through
The forests where the Lodh trees grew,
Where the dark leaves were thick and green,
But found not Ráma's darling queen.
Then faint with toil, their hearts depressed,
Descending from the mountain's crest,
Their weary limbs a while to ease
They lay beneath the spreading trees.

The Enchanted Cave

Angad and Tára by his side,
Again rose Hanumán and tried
Each mountain cavern, dark and deep,
And stony pass and wooded steep,
The lion's and the tiger's home,
By rushing torrents white with foam.
Then with new ardour, south and west,
O'er Vindhya's height the search they pressed.
The day prescribed was near and they
Still wandered on their weary way.
They reached the southern land beset
With woody mountains like a net.
At length a mighty cave they spied
That opened in a mountain's side.
Where many a verdant creeper grew
And o'er the mouth its tendrils threw.
Thence issued crane, and swan, and drake,
And trooping birds that love the lake.
The Vánars rushed within to cool
Their fevered lips in spring or pool.
Vast was the cavern dark and dread,
Where not a ray of light was shed;
Yet not the more their eyesight failed,

Their courage sank or valour quailed.
On through the gloom the Vánars pressed
With hunger, thirst, and toil distressed,
Poor helpless wanderers, sad, forlorn,
With wasted faces wan and worn.
At length, when life seemed lost for aye,
They saw a splendour as of day,

A wondrous forest, fair and bright,
Where golden trees shot flamy light.
And lotus-covered pools were there
With pleasant waters fresh and fair,
And streams their rippling currents rolled
By seats of silver and of gold.
Fair houses reared their stately height
Of burnished gold and lazulite,
And glorious was the lustre thrown
Through lattices of precious stone.
And there were flowers and fruit on stems
Of coral decked with rarest gems,
And emerald leaves on silver trees,
And honeycomb and golden bees.
Then as the Vánars nearer drew,
A holy woman met their view,
Around her form was duly tied
A garment of the blackdeer's hide.
Pure votaress she shone with light
Of fervent zeal and holy rite.
Then Hanumán before the rest
With reverent words the dame addressed:
"Who art thou? say: and who is lord
Of this vast cave with treasures stored?"

CANTO
LI

Svayamprabhá

"Assailed by thirst and hunger, dame,
Within a gloomy vault we came.
We saw the cavern opening wide,
And straight within its depths we hied.
But utterly amazed are we

At all the marvels that we see.
Whose are the golden trees that gleam
With splendour like the morning's beam?
These cates of noblest sort? these roots?
This wondrous store of rarest fruits?
Whose are these calm and cool retreats,
These silver homes and golden seats,
And lattices of precious stones?
Who is the happy lord that owns
The golden trees, of rarest scent,
Neath loads of fruit and blossom bent?
Who, strong in holy zeal, had power
To deck the streams with richest dower,
And bade the lilies bright with gold
The glory of their blooms unfold,
Where fish in living gold below
The sheen of changing colours show?
Thine is the holy power, I ween,
That beautified the wondrous scene;
But if another's, lady, deign
To tell us, and the whole explain."

To him the lady of the cave
In words like these her answer gave:
"Skilled Maya framed in days of old
This magic wood of growing gold.
The chief artificer in place
Was he of all the Dánav race.
He, for his wise enchantments famed,
This glorious dwelling planned and framed
He for a thousand years endured
The sternest penance, and secured
From Brahmá of all boons the best,
The knowledge Uśanas possessed.
Lord, by that boon, of all his will,
He fashioned all with perfect skill;
And, with his blissful state content,
In this vast grove a season spent.
By Indra's jealous bolt he fell
For loving Hemá's charms too well.

And Brahmá on that nymph bestowed
The treasures of this fair abode,
Wherein her tranquil days to spend
In happiness that ne'er may end.
Sprung of a lineage old and high,
Merusávarṇi's daughter, I
Guard ever for that heavenly dame
This home, Svayamprabhá my name,—
For I have loved the lady long,
So skilled in arts of dance and song.
But say what cause your steps has led
The mazes of this grove to tread.

How, strangers did ye chance to spy
The wood concealed from wanderer's eye?
Tell clearly why ye come: but first
Eat of this fruit and quench your thirst."

The Exit

"Ráma," he cried, "a prince whose sway
All peoples of the earth obey,
To Daṇḍak's tangled forest came
With his brave brother and his dame.
From that dark shade of forest boughs
The giant Rávaṇ stole his spouse.
Our king Sugríva's orders send
These Vánars forth to aid his friend,
That so the lady be restored
Uninjured to her sorrowing lord.
With Angad and the rest, this band
Has wandered through the southern land,
With careful search in every place

The lady and the fiend to trace.
We roamed the southern region o'er,
And stood upon the ocean's shore.
By hunger pressed our strength gave way;
Beneath the spreading trees we lay,
And cried, worn out with toil and woe,
"No farther, comrades, can we go."
Then as our sad eyes looked around
We spied an opening in the ground,
Where all was gloomy dark behind
The creeping plants that o'er it twined.
Forth trooping from the dark-recess
Came swans and mallards numberless,
With drops upon their shining wings
As newly bathed where water springs.
"On, comrades, to the cave," I cried
And all within the portal hied.
Each clasping fast another's hand
Far onward pressed the Vánar band;
And still, as thirst and hunger drove,
We traced the mazes of the grove.
Here thou with hospitable care
Hast fed us with the noblest fare,
Preserving us, about to die,
With this thy plentiful supply.
But how, O pious lady, say,
May we thy gracious boon repay?"

He ceased: the ascetic dame replied:
"Well, Vánars, am I satisfied.
A life of holy works I lead,
And from your hands no service need."
Then spake again the Vánar chief:
"We came to thee and found relief.
Now listen to a new distress,
And aid us, holy votaress.
Our wanderings in this vasty cave
Exhaust the time Sugríva gave.
Once more then, lady, grant release,
And let thy suppliants go in peace
Again upon their errand sped,

For King Sugríva's ire we dread.
And the great task our sovereign set,
Alas, is unaccomplished yet."

Thus Hanumán their leader prayed,
And thus the dame her answer made:
"Scarce may the living find their way
Returning hence to light of day;
But I will free you through the might
Of penance, fast, and holy rite.
Close for a while your eyes, or ne'er
May you return to upper air."
She ceased: the Vánars all obeyed;
Their fingers on their eyes they laid,
And, ere a moment's time had fled,
Were through the mazy cavern led.
Again the gracious lady spoke,
And joy in every bosom woke:
"Lo, here again is Vindhya's hill,
Whose valleys trees and creepers fill;
And, by the margin of the sea,
Praśravaṇ where you fain would be."
With blessings then she bade adieu,
And swift within the cave withdrew.

CANTO
LIII

Angad's Counsel

They looked upon the boundless main
The awful seat of Varuṇ's reign.
And heard his waters roar and rave
Terrific with each crested wave.
Then, in the depths of sorrow drowned,
They sat upon the bosky ground,

And sadly, as they pondered, grieved
For days gone by and naught achieved.
Pain pierced them through with sharper sting
When, gazing on the trees of spring,
They saw each waving bough that showed
The treasures of its glorious load,
And helpless, fainting with the weight
Of woe they sank disconsolate.
Then, lion-shouldered, stout and strong,
The noblest of the Vánar throng,
Angad the prince imperial rose,
And, deeply stricken by the woes
That his impetuous spirit broke,
Thus gently to the chieftains spoke:
"Mark ye not, Vánars, that the day
Our monarch fixed has passed away?
The month is lost in toil and pain,
And now, my friends, what hopes remain?
On you, in lore of counsel tried,
Our king Sugríva most relied.
Your hearts, with strong affection fraught,

His weal in every labour sought,
And the true valour of your band
Was blazoned wide in every land.
Forth on the toilsome search you sped,
By me—for so he willed it—led,
To us, of every hope bereft,
Death is the only refuge left.
For none a happy life may see
Who fails to do our king's decree.
Come, let us all from food abstain,
And perish thus, since hope is vain.
Stern is our king and swift to ire,
Imperious, proud, and fierce like fire,
And ne'er will pardon us the crime
Of fruitless search and wasted time.
Far better thus to end our lives,
And leave our wealth, our homes and wives,
Leave our dear little ones and all,
Than by his vengeful hand to fall.

Think not Sugríva's wrath will spare
Me Báli's son, imperial heir:
For Raghu's royal son, not he,
To this high place anointed me.
Sugríva, long my bitter foe,
With eager hand will strike the blow,
And, mindful of the old offence,
Will slay me now for negligence,
Nor will my pitying friends have power
To save me in the deadly hour.
No—here, O chieftains, will I lie
By ocean's marge, and fast and die."

They heard the royal prince declare
The purpose of his fixt despair;
And all, by common terror moved,
His speech in these sad words approved:
"Sugríva's heart is hard and stern,
And Ráma's thoughts for Sítá yearn.
Our forfeit lives will surely pay
For idle search and long delay,
And our fierce king will bid us die
The favour of his friend to buy."

Then Tára softly spake to cheer
The Vánars' hearts oppressed by fear:
"Despair no more, your doubts dispel:
Come in this ample cavern dwell.
There may we live in blissful ease
Mid springs and fruit and bloomy trees,
Secure from every foe's assault,
For magic framed the wondrous vault.
Protected there we need not fear
Though Ráma and our king come near;
Nor dread e'en him who batters down
The portals of the foeman's town."

Hanumán's Speech

But Hanumán, while Tára, best
Of splendid chiefs his thought expressed,
Perceived that Báli's princely son
A kingdom for himself had won.
His keen eye marked in him combined
The warrior's arm, the ruler's mind,
And every noble gift should grace
The happy sovereign of his race:
Marked how he grew with ripening age
More glorious and bold and sage,—
Like the young moon that night by night
Shines on with ever waxing light,—
Brave as his royal father, wise
As he who counsels in the skies:
Marked how, forwearied with the quest,
He heeded not his liege's hest,
But Tára's every word obeyed
Like Indra still by Śukra swayed.
Then with his prudent speech he tried
To better thoughts the prince to guide,
And by division's skilful art
The Vánars and the youth to part:
"Illustrious Angad, thou in fight
Hast far surpassed thy father's might,
Most worthy, like thy sire of old,
The empire of our race to hold.
The Vánars' fickle people range
From wish to wish and welcome change.
Their wives and babes they will not leave
And to their new-made sovereign cleave.
No art, no gifts will draw away

The Vánars from Sugríva's sway,
Through hope of wealth, through fear of pain
Still faithful will they all remain.
Thou fondly hopest in this cave
The vengeance of the foe to brave.
But Lakshmaṇ's arm a shower will send
Of deadly shafts those walls to rend.
Like Indra's bolts his shafts have power
To cleave the mountain like a flower.
O Angad, mark my counsel well:
If in this cave thou choose to dwell,

These Vánar hosts with one accord
Will quit thee for their lawful lord,
And turn again with thirsty eyes
To wife and babe and all they prize.
Thou in the lonely cavern left
Of followers and friends bereft,
Wilt be in all thy woe, alas,
Weak as a blade of trembling grass:
And Lakshmaṇ's arrows, keen and fierce
From his strong bow, thy heart will pierce.
But if in lowly reverence meek
Sugríva's court with us thou seek,
He, as thy birth demands, will share
The kingdom with the royal heir.
Thy loving kinsman, true and wise,
Looks on thee still with favouring eyes.
Firm in his promise, pure is he,
And ne'er will vex or injure thee.
He loves thy mother, lives for her
A faithful friend and worshipper.
That mother's love thou mayst not spurn:
Her only child, return, return."

Angad's Reply

"What truth or justice canst thou find,"
    Cried Angad, "in Sugríva's mind?
    Where is his high and generous soul,
His purity and self-control?
How is he worthy of our trust,
Righteous, and true, and wise, and just,
Who, shrinking not from sin and shame,
Durst take his living brother's dame?
Who, when, in stress of mortal strife
His noble brother fought for life,
Against the valiant warrior barred
The portal which he stood to guard?
Can he be grateful—he who took
The hand of Ráma, and forsook
That friend who saved him in his woes,
To whom his life and fame he owes?
Ah no! his heart is cold and mean,
What bids him search for Ráma's queen?
Not honour's law, not friendship's debt,
But angry Lakshman's timely threat.
No prudent heart will ever place
Its trust in one so false and base,
Who heeds not friendship, kith or kin,
Who scorns the law and cleaves to sin.
But true or false, whate'er he be,
One consequence I clearly see;
Me, in my youth anointed heir
Against his wish, he will not spare,
But strike with eager hand the blow
That rids him of a household foe.
Shall I of power and friends despoiled,

In all my purpose crossed and foiled,—
Shall I Kishkindhá seek, and wait,
Like some poor helpless thing, my fate?
The cruel wretch through lust of sway
Will seize upon his hapless prey,
And to a prison's secret gloom
The remnant of my years will doom.
'Tis better far to fast and die
Than hopeless bound in chains to lie,
Your steps, O Vánars, homeward bend
And leave me here my life to end.
Better to die of hunger here
Than meet at home the fate I fear.
Go, bow you at Sugríva's feet,
And in my name the monarch greet.
Before the sons of Raghu bend,
And give the greeting that I send.
Greet kindly Rumá too, for she
A son's affection claims from me,
And gently calm with friendly care
My mother Tárá's wild despair;
Or when she hears her darling's fate
The queen will die disconsolate."

Thus Angad bade the chiefs adieu:
Then on the ground his limbs he threw
Where sacred Darbha grass was spread,
And wept as every hope had fled.
The moving words of Angad drew
Down aged cheeks the piteous dew.
And, as the chieftains' eyes grew dim,
They swore to stay and die with him.
On holy grass whose every blade
Was duly, pointing southward, laid,
The Vánars sat them down and bent
Their faces to the orient,
While "Here, O comrades, let us die
With Angad," was the general cry.

Sampáti

Then came the vultures' mighty king
Where sat the Vánars sorrowing,—
Sampáti, best of birds that fly
On sounding pinions through the sky,
Jaṭáyus' brother, famed of old,
Most glorious and strong and bold.
Upon the slope of Vindhya's hill
He saw the Vánars calm and still.

These words he uttered while the sight
Filled his fierce spirit with delight:
"Behold how Fate with changeless laws
Within his toils the sinner draws,
And brings me, after long delay,
A rich and noble feast to-day,
These Vánars who are doomed to die
My hungry maw to satisfy."

He spoke no more: and Angad heard
The menace of the mighty bird;
And thus, while anguish filled his breast,
The noble Hanumán addressed:
"Vivasvat's son has sought this place
For vengeance on the Vánar race.
See, Yáma, wroth for Sítá's sake,
Is come our guilty lives to take.
Our king's decree is left undone,
And naught achieved for Raghu's son.
In duty have we failed, and hence
Comes punishment for dire offence.
Have we not heard the marvels wrought

By King Jaṭáyus, how he fought
With Rávaṇ's might, and, nobly brave,
Perished, the Maithil queen to save?
There is no living creature, none,
But loves to die for Raghu's son,
And in long toils and dangers we
Have placed our lives in jeopardy.
Blest is Jaṭáyus, he who gave
His life the Maithil queen to save,
And proved his love for Ráma well
When by the giant's hand he fell.
Now raised to bliss and high renown
He fears not fierce Sugríva's frown.
Alas, alas! what miseries spring
From that rash promise of the king!
His own sad death, and Ráma sent
With Lakshmaṇ forth to banishment:
The Maithil lady borne away:
Jaṭáyus slain in mortal fray:
The fall of Báli when the dart
Of Ráma quivered in his heart:
And, after toil and pain and care,
Our misery and deep despair."

He ceased: the feathered monarch heard,
His heart with ruth and wonder stirred:
"Whose is that voice," the vulture cried,
"That tells me how Jaṭáyus died,
And shakes my inmost soul with woe
For a loved brother's overthrow?
After long days at length I hear
The glorious name of one so dear.
Once more, O Vánar chieftains, tell
How King Jaṭáyus fought and fell.
But first your aid, I pray you, lend,
And from this peak will I descend.
The sun has burnt my wings, and I
No longer have the power to fly."

Angad's Speech

Though grief and woe his utterance broke
They trusted not the words he spoke;
But, looking still for secret guile,
Reflected in their hearts a while:
"If on our mangled limbs he feed,
We gain the death ourselves decreed."
Then rose the Vánar chiefs, and lent
Their arms to aid the bird's descent;
And Angad spake: "There lived of yore
A noble Vánar king who bore
The name of Riksharajas, great
And brave and strong and fortunate.
His sons were like their father: fame
Knows Báli and Sugríva's name.
Praised in all lands, a glorious king
Was Báli, and from him I spring.
Brave Ráma, Daśaratha's heir,
A glorious prince beyond compare,
His sire and duty's law obeyed,
And sought the depths of Daṇḍak' shade
Sítá his well-beloved dame,
And Lakshmaṇ, with the wanderer came.
A giant watched his hour, and stole
The sweet delight of Ráma's soul.
Jaṭáyus, Daśaratha's friend,
Swift succour to the dame would lend.
Fierce Rávaṇ from his car he felled,
And for a time the prize withheld.
But bleeding, weak with years, and tired,
Beneath the demon's blows expired,
Due rites at Ráma's hands obtained,

And bliss that ne'er shall minish, gained.
Then Ráma with Sugríva made
A covenant for mutual aid,
And Báli, to the field defied,
By conquering Ráma's arrow died.
Sugríva then, by Ráma's grace,
Was monarch of the Vánar race.
By his command a mighty host
Seeks Ráma's queen from coast to coast.
Sent forth by him, in every spot
We looked for her, but find her not.
Vain is the toil, as though by night
We sought to find the Day-God's light.
In lands unknown at length we found
A spacious cavern under ground,
Whose vaults that stretch beneath the hill
Were formed by Maya's magic skill.
Through the dark maze our steps were bent,
And wandering there a month we spent,

And lost, in fruitless error, thus
The days our king allotted us.
Thus we though faithful have transgressed,
And failed to keep our lord's behest.
No chance of safety can we see,
No lingering hope of life have we.
Sugríva's wrath and Ráma's hate
Press on our souls with grievous weight:
And we, because 'tis vain to fly,
Resolve at length to fast and die."

LVIII

Tidings of Sítá

The piteous tears his eye bedewed
  As thus his speech the bird renewed;
  "Alas my brother, slain in fight
By Rávan's unresisted might!
I, old and wingless, weak and worn,
O'er his sad fate can only mourn.
Fled is my youth: in life's decline
My former strength no more is mine.
Once on the day when Vritra died,
We brothers, in ambitious pride,
Sought, mounting with adventurous flight,
The Day-God garlanded with light.
On, ever on we urged our way
Where fields of ether round us lay,
Till, by the fervent heat assailed,
My brother's pinions flagged and failed.
I marked his sinking strength, and spread
My stronger wings to screen his head,
Till, all my feathers burnt away,
On Vindhya's hill I fell and lay.
There in my lone and helpless state
I heard not of my brother's fate."

Thus King Sampáti spoke and sighed:
And royal Angad thus replied:
"If, brother of Jatáyus, thou
Hast heard the tale I told but now,
Obedient to mine earnest prayer
The dwelling of that fiend declare.
O, say where cursed Rávan dwells,
Whom folly to his death impels."

He ceased. Again Sampáti spoke,
And hope in every breast awoke:
"Though lost my wings, and strength decayed,
Yet shall my words lend Ráma aid.
I know the worlds where Vishṇu trod,
I know the realm of Ocean's God;
How Asurs fought with heavenly foes,
And Amrit from the churning rose.
A mighty task before me lies,
To prosper Ráma's enterprise,
A task too hard for one whom length
Of days has rifled of his strength.
I saw the cruel Rávaṇ bear
A gentle lady through the air.
Bright was her form, and fresh and young,
And sparkling gems about her hung.
"O Ráma, Ráma!" cried the dame,
And shrieked in terror Lakshmaṇ's name,
As, struggling in the giant's hold,
She dropped her gauds of gems and gold.
Like sun-light on a mountain shone
The silken garments she had on,
And glistened o'er his swarthy form
As lightning flashes through the storm.
That giant Rávaṇ, famed of old,
Is brother of the Lord of Gold.
The southern ocean roars and swells
Round Lanká, where the robber dwells
In his fair city nobly planned
And built by Viśvakarmá's hand.
Within his bower securely barred,
With monsters round her for a guard,
Still in her silken vesture clad
Lies Sítá, and her heart is sad.
A hundred leagues your course must be
Beyond this margin of the sea.
Still to the south your way pursue,
And there the giant Rávaṇ view.
Then up, O Vánars, and away!
For by my heavenly lore I say,
There will you see the lady's face,

202

And hither soon your steps retrace.
In the first field of air are borne
The doves and birds that feed on corn.
The second field supports the crows
And birds whose food on branches grows.
Along the third in balanced flight
Sail the keen osprey and the kite.
Swift through the fourth the falcon springs
The fifth the slower vulture wings.
Up to the sixth the gay swans rise,

Where royal Vainateya flies.
We too, O chiefs, of vulture race,
Our line from Vinatá may trace,
Condemned, because we wrought a deed
Of shame, on flesh and blood to feed.
But all Suparṇa's wondrous powers
And length of keenest sight are ours,
That we a hundred leagues away
Through fields of air descry our prey.
Now from this spot my gazing eye
Can Rávaṇ and the dame descry.
Devise some plan to overleap
This barrier of the briny deep.
Find the Videhan lady there,
And joyous to your home repair.
Me too, O Vánars, to the side
Of Varuṇ's home the ocean, guide,
Where due libations shall be paid
To my great-hearted brother's shade."

Sampáti's Story

They heard his counsel to the close,
Then swiftly to their feet they rose;
And Jámbaván with joyous breast
The vulture king again addressed:

"Where, where is Sítá? who has seen,
Who borne away the Maithil queen?
Who would the lightning flight withstand
by Lakshman's hand?"
Again Sampáti spoke to cheer
The Vánars as they bent to hear:
"Now listen, and my words shall show
What of the Maithil dame I know,
And in what distant prison lies
The lady of the long dark eyes.
Scorched by the fiery God of Day,
High on this mighty hill I lay.
A long and weary time had passed,
And strength and life were failing fast.
Yet, ere the breath had left my frame,
My son, my dear Supárśva, came.
Each morn and eve he brought me food,
And filial care my life renewed.
But serpents still are swift to ire,
Gandharvas slaves to soft desire,
And we, imperial vultures, need
A full supply our maws to feed.
Once he turned at close of day,
Stood by my side, but brought no prey.
He looked upon my ravenous eye,
Heard my complaint and made reply:

"Borne on swift wings ere day was light
I stood upon Mahendra's height,
And, far below, the sea I viewed
And birds in countless multitude.
Before mine eyes a giant flew
Whose monstrous form was dark of hue
And struggling in his grasp was borne
A lady radiant as the morn.
Swift to the south his course he bent,
And cleft the yielding element.
The holy spirits of the air
Came round me as I marvelled there,
And cried as their bright legions met:
"O say, is Sítá living yet?"
Thus cried the saints and told the name
Of him who held the struggling dame.
Then while mine eye with eager look
Pursued the path the robber took,
I marked the lady's streaming hair,
And heard her cry of wild despair.
I saw her silken vesture rent
And stripped of every ornament,
Thus, O my father, fled the time:
Forgive, I pray, the heedless crime."
In vain the mournful tale I heard
My pitying heart to fury stirred,
What could a helpless bird of air,
Reft of his boasted pinions, dare?
Yet can I aid with all that will
And words can do, and friendly skill."

CANTO
LX

Sampáti's Story

Then from the flood Sampáti paid
  Due offerings to his brother's shade.
  He bathed him when the rites were done,
And spake again to Báli's son:
"Now listen, Prince, while I relate
How first I learned the lady's fate.
Burnt by the sun's resistless might
I fell and lay on Vindhya's height.
Seven nights in deadly swoon I passed,
But struggling life returned at last.
Around I bent my wondering view,
But every spot was strange and new.
I scanned the sea with eager ken,
And rock and brook and lake and glen,
I saw gay trees their branches wave,
And creepers mantling o'er the cave.
I heard the wild birds' joyous song,
And waters as they foamed along,
And knew the lovely hill must be
Mount Vindhya by the southern sea.

Revered by heavenly beings, stood
Near where I lay, a sacred wood,
Where great Niśakar dwelt of yore
And pains of awful penance bore.
Eight thousand seasons winged their flight
Over the toiling anchorite—
Upon that hill my days were spent,—
And then to heaven the hermit went.
At last, with long and hard assay,
Down from that height I made my way,

And wandered through the mountain pass
Rough with the spikes of Darbha grass.
I with my misery worn, and faint
Was eager to behold the saint:
For often with Jaṭáyus I
Had sought his home in days gone by.
As nearer to the grove I drew
The breeze with cooling fragrance blew,
And not a tree that was not fair,
With richest flower and fruit was there.
With anxious heart a while I stayed
Beneath the trees' delightful shade,
And soon the holy hermit, bright
With fervent penance, came in sight.
Behind him bears and lions, tame
As those who know their feeder, came,
And tigers, deer, and snakes pursued
His steps, a wondrous multitude,
And turned obeisant when the sage
Had reached his shady hermitage.
Then came Niśakar to my side
And looked with wondering eyes, and cried:
"I knew thee not, so dire a change
Has made thy form and feature strange.
Where are thy glossy feathers? where
The rapid wings that cleft the air?
Two vulture brothers once I knew:
Each form at will could they endue.
They of the vulture race were kings,
And flew with Mátariśva's wings.
In human shape they loved to greet
Their hermit friend, and clasp his feet.
The younger was Jaṭáyus, thou
The elder whom I gaze on now.
Say, has disease or foeman's hate
Reduced thee from thy high estate?"

Sampáti's Story

"Ah me! o'erwhelmed with shame and weak
With wounds," I cried, "I scarce can speak.
My hapless brother once and I
Our strength of flight resolved to try.
And by our foolish pride impelled
Our way through realms of ether held.
We vowed before the saints who tread
The wilds about Kailása's head,
That we with following wings would chase
The swift sun to his resting place.
Up on our soaring pinions through
The fields of cloudless air we flew.
Beneath us far, and far away,
Like chariot wheels bright cities lay,
Whence in wild snatches rose the song
Of women mid the gay-clad throng,
With sounds of sweetest music blent
And many a tinkling ornament.
Then as our rapid wings we strained
The pathway of the sun we gained.
Beneath us all the earth was seen
Clad in her garb of tender green,
And every river in her bed
Meandered like a silver thread.
We looked on Meru far below
And Vindhya and the Lord of Snow,
Like elephants that bend to cool
Their fever in a lilied pool.
But fervent heat and toil o'ercame
The vigour of each yielding frame,
Our weary hearts began to quail,

And wildered sense to reel and fail.
We knew not, fainting and distressed,
The north or south or east or west.
With a great strain mine eyes I turned
Where the fierce sun before me burned,
And seemed to my astonished eyes
The equal of the earth in size.
At length, o'erpowered, Jaṭáyus fell
Without a word to say farewell,
And when to earth I saw him hie
I followed headlong from the sky.
With sheltering wings I intervened
And from the sun his body screened,
But lost, for heedless folly doomed,
My pinions which the heat consumed.
In Janasthán, I hear them say,
My hapless brother fell and lay.
I, pinionless and faint and weak,
Dropped upon Vindhya's woody peak.
Now with my swift wings burnt away,
Reft of my brother and my sway,
From this tall mountain's summit I
Will cast me headlong down and die."

CANTO
LXII

Sampáti's Story

"As to the saint I thus complained
My bitter tears fell unrestrained.
He pondered for a while, then broke
The silence, and thus calmly spoke:
"Forth from thy sides again shall spring,
O royal bird, each withered wing,
And all thine ancient power and might

Return to thee with strength of sight.
A noble deed has been foretold
In prophecy pronounced of old:
Nor dark to me are future things,
Seen by the light which penance brings.
A glorious king shall rise and reign,
The pride of old Ikshváku's strain.
A good and valiant prince, his heir,
Shall the dear name of Ráma bear.
With his brave brother Lakshmaṇ he
An exile in the woods shall be,
Where Rávaṇ, whom no God may slay,
Shall steal his darling wife away.
In vain the captive will be wooed
With proffered love and dainty food,
She will not hear, she will not taste:
But, lest her beauty wane and waste,
Lord Indra's self will come to her
With heavenly food, and minister.
Then envoys of the Vánar race
By Ráma sent will seek this place.
To them, O roamer of the air,
The lady's fate shalt thou declare.
Thou must not move—so maimed thou art
Thou canst not from this spot depart.
Await the day and moment due,
And thy burnt wings will sprout anew.
I might this day the boon bestow
And bid again thy pinions grow,
But wait until thy saving deed
The nations from their fear have freed.
Then for this glorious aid of thine
The princes of Ikshváku's line,
And Gods above and saints below
Eternal gratitude shall owe.
Fain would mine aged eyes behold
That pair of whom my lips have told,
Yet wearied here I must not stay,
But leave my frame and pass away."

Sampáti's Story

"With this and many a speech beside
My failing heart he fortified,
With glorious hope my breast inspired,
And to his holy home retired.
I scaled the mountain height, to view
The region round, and looked for you.
In ceaseless watchings night and day
A hundred seasons passed away,
And by the sage's words consoled
I wait the hour and chance foretold.
But since Niśakar sought the skies,
And cast away all earthly ties,
Full many a care and doubt has pressed
With grievous weight upon my breast.
But for the saint who turned aside
My purpose I had surely died.
Those hopeful words the hermit spake,
That bid me live for Ráma's sake,
Dispel my anguish as the light
Of lamp and torch disperse the night."

He ceased: and in the Vánars' view
Forth from his side young pinions grew,
And boundless rapture filled his breast
As thus the chieftains he addressed:
"Joy, joy! the pinions, which the Lord
Of Day consumed, are now restored
Through the dear grace & boundless might
Of that illustrious anchorite.
The fire of youth within me burns,
And all my wonted strength returns.

Onward, ye Vánars, toil strive,
And you shall find the dame alive.
Look on these new-found wings, and hence
Be strong in surest confidence."
Swift from the crag he sprang to try
His pinions in his native sky.
His words the chieftains' doubts had stilled,
And every heart with courage filled.

CANTO
LXIV

The Sea

Shouts of triumphant joy outrang
As to their feet the Vánars sprang:
And, on the mighty task intent,
Swift to the sea their steps they bent.
They stood and gazed upon the deep,
Whose billows with a roar and leap
On the sea banks ware wildly hurled,—
The mirror of the mighty world.
There on the strand the Vánars stayed
And with sad eyes the deep surveyed,
Here, as in play, his billows rose,
And there he slumbered in repose.
Here leapt the boisterous waters, high
As mountains, menacing the sky,
And wild infernal forms between
The ridges of the waves were seen.

They saw the billows rave and swell,
And their sad spirits sank and fell;
For ocean in their deep despair
Seemed boundless as the fields of air.
Then noble Angad spake to cheer

The Vánars and dispel their fear:
"Faint not: despair should never find
Admittance to a noble mind.
Despair, a serpent's mortal bite,
Benumbs the hero's power and might."

Then passed the weary night, and all
Assembled at their prince's call,
And every lord of high estate
Was gathered round him for debate.
Bright was the chieftains' glorious band
Round Angad on the ocean strand,
As when the mighty Storm-Gods meet
Round Indra on his golden seat.
Then princely Angad looked on each,
And thus began his prudent speech:
"What chief of all our host will leap
A hundred leagues across the deep?
Who, O illustrious Vánars, who
Will make Sugríva's promise true,
And from our weight of fear set free
The leaders of our band and me?
To whom, O warriors, shall we owe
A sweet release from pain and woe,
And proud success, and happy lives
With our dear children and our wives,
Again permitted by his grace
To look with joy on Ráma's face,
And noble Lakshman, and our lord
The king, to our sweet homes restored?"
Thus to the gathered lords he spoke;
But no reply the silence broke.
Then with a sterner voice he cried:
"O chiefs, the nation's boast and pride,
Whom valour strength and power adorn,
Of most illustrious lineage born,
Where'er you will you force a way,
And none your rapid course can stay.
Now come, your several powers declare.
And who this desperate leap will dare?"

CANTO
LXV

The Council

But none of all the host was found
To clear the sea with desperate bound,
Though each, as Angad bade, declared
His proper power and what he dared.
Then spake good Jámbaván the sage,
Chief of them all for reverend age;
"I, Vánar chieftains, long ago
Limbs light to leap could likewise show,
But now on frame and spirit weighs
The burthen of my length of days.
Still task like this I may not slight,
When Ráma and our king unite.
So listen while I tell, O friends,
What lingering strength mine age attends.
If my poor leap may aught avail,
Of ninety leagues, I will not fail.
Far other strength in youth's fresh prime
I boasted, in the olden time,
When, at Prahláda's solemn rite,
I circled in my rapid flight
Lord Vishṇu, everlasting God,
When through the universe he trod.
But now my limbs are weak and old,
My youth is fled, its fire is cold,
And these exhausted nerves to strain
In such a task were idle pain."

Then Angad due obeisance paid,
And to the chief his answer made:
"Then I, ye noble Vánars, I
Myself the mighty leap will try:

214

Although perchance the power I lack
To leap from Lanká's island back."

Thus the impetuous chieftain cried,
And Jámbaván the sage replied:
"Whate'er thy power and might may be,
This task, O Prince, is not for thee.
Kings go not forth themselves, but send
The servants who their best attend.
Thou art the darling and the boast,
The honoured lord of all the host.
In thee the root, O Angad, lies
Of our appointed enterprise;
And thee, on whom our hopes depend,
Our care must cherish and defend."

Then Báli's noble son replied:
"Needs must I go, whate'er betide,
For, if no chief this exploit dare,
What waits us all save blank despair,—
Upon the ground again to lie
In hopeless misery, fast, and die?
For not a hope of life I see
If we neglect our king's decree."
Then spoke the aged chief again:
"Nay our attempt shall not be vain,
For to the task will I incite
A chieftain of sufficient might."

CANTO
LXVI

Hanumán

The chieftain turned his glances where
The legions sat in mute despair;
And then to Hanumán, the best
Of Vánar lords, these words addressed:
"Why still, and silent, and apart,
O hero of the dauntless heart?
Thou keepest treasured in thy mind
The laws that rule the Vánar kind,
Strong as our king Sugríva, brave
As Ráma's self to slay or save.
Through every land thy praise is heard,
Famous as that illustrious bird,
Aríshṭanemi's son, the king
Of every fowl that plies the wing.
Oft have I seen the monarch sweep
With sounding pinions o'er the deep,
And in his mighty talons bear
Huge serpents struggling through the air.
Thy arms, O hero, match in might
The ample wings he spreads for flight;
And thou with him mayest well compare
In power to do, in heart to dare.
Why, rich in wisdom, power, and skill,
O hero, art thou lingering still?
An Apsaras the fairest found
Of nymphs for heavenly charms renowned,
Sweet Punjikasthalá, became
A noble Vánar's wedded dame.
Her heavenly title heard no more,
Anjaná was the name she bore,
When, cursed by Gods, from heaven she fell

In Vánar form on earth to dwell,
New-born in mortal shape the child
Of Kunjar monarch of the wild.
In youthful beauty wondrous fair,
A crown of flowers about her hair,
In silken robes of richest dye
She roamed the hills that kiss the sky.
Once in her tinted garments dressed
She stood upon the mountain crest,
The God of Wind beside her came,
And breathed upon the lovely dame.
And as he fanned her robe aside
The wondrous beauty that he eyed
In rounded lines of breast and limb
And neck and shoulder ravished him;
And captured by her peerless charms
He strained her in his amorous arms.
Then to the eager God she cried
In trembling accents, terrified:
"Whose impious love has wronged a spouse
So constant in her nuptial vows?"
He heard, and thus his answer made:
"O, be not troubled, nor afraid,
But trust, and thou shalt know ere long
My love has done thee, sweet, no wrong,
So strong and brave and wise shall be
The glorious child I give to thee.
Might shall be his that naught can tire,
And limbs to spring as springs his sire."
Thus spoke the God; the conquered dame
Rejoiced in heart nor feared the shame.
Down in a cave beneath the earth
The happy mother gave thee birth.
Once o'er the summit of the wood
Before thine eyes the new sun stood.
Thou sprangest up in haste to seize
What seemed the fruitage of the trees.
Up leapt the child, a wondrous bound,
Three hundred leagues above the ground,
And, though the angered Day-God shot
His fierce beams on him, feared him not.

Then from the hand of Indra came
A red bolt winged with wrath and flame.
The child fell smitten on a rock,
His cheek was shattered by the shock,
Named Hanumán thenceforth by all
In memory of the fearful fall.
The wandering Wind-God saw thee lie
With bleeding cheek and drooping eye,
And stirred to anger by thy woe
Forbade each scented breeze to blow.
The breath of all the worlds was stilled,
And the sad Gods with terror filled
Prayed to the Wind, to calm the ire
And soothe the sorrow of the sire.
His fiery wrath no longer glowed,
And Brahmá's self the boon bestowed
That in the brunt of battle none
Should slay with steel the Wind-God's son.
Lord Indra, sovereign of the skies,
Bent on thee all his thousand eyes,
And swore that ne'er the bolt which he
Hurls from the heaven should injure thee.
'Tis thine, O mighty chief, to share
The Wind-God's power, his son and heir.
Sprung from that glorious father thou,
And thou alone, canst aid us now.
This earth of yore, through all her climes,
I circled one-and-twenty times,
And gathered, as the Gods decreed,
Great store of herbs from hill and mead,
Which, scattered o'er the troubled wave,
The Amrit to the toilers gave.

But now my days are wellnigh told,
My strength is gone, my limbs are old,
And thou, the bravest and the best,
Art the sure hope of all the rest.
Now, mighty chief, the task assay:
Thy matchless power and strength display.
Rise up, O prince, our second king,

218

And o'er the flood of ocean spring.
So shall the glorious exploit vie
With his who stepped through earth and sky."
He spoke: the younger chieftain heard,
His soul to vigorous effort stirred,
And stood before their joyous eyes
Dilated in gigantic size.

CANTO
LXVII

Hanumán's Speech

S oon as his stature they beheld,
    Their fear and sorrow were dispelled;
    And joyous praises loud and long
Rang out from all the Vánar throng.
On the great chief their eyes they bent
In rapture and astonishment,
As, when his conquering foot he raised,
The Gods upon Náráyaṇ gazed.
He stood amid the joyous crowd,
Bent to the chiefs, and cried aloud:
"The Wind-God, Fire's eternal friend,
Whose blasts the mountain summits rend,
With boundless force that none may stay,
Takes where he lists his viewless way.
Sprung from that glorious father, I
In power and speed with him may vie,
A thousand times with airy leap
Can circle loftiest Meru's steep:
With my fierce arms can stir the sea
Till from their bed the waters flee
And rush at my command to drown
This land with grove and tower and town.

I through the fields of air can spring
Far swifter than the feathered King,
And leap before him as he flies,
On sounding pinions through the skies.
I can pursue the Lord of Light
Uprising from the eastern height,
And reach him ere his course be sped
With burning beams engarlanded.
I will dry up the mighty main,
Shatter the rocks and rend the plain.
O'er earth and ocean will I bound,
And every flower that grows on ground,
And bloom of climbing plants shall show
Strewn on the ground, the way I go,
Bright as the lustrous path that lies
Athwart the region of the skies.
The Maithil lady will I find,—
Thus speaks mine own prophetic mind,—
And cast in hideous ruin down
The shattered walls of Lanká's town."

Still on the chief in rapt surprise
The Vánar legions bent their eyes,
And thus again sage Jámbaván
Addressed the glorious Hanumán:
"Son of the Wind, thy promise cheers
The Vánars' hearts, and calms their fears,
Who, rescued from their dire distress,
With prospering vows thy way will bless.
The holy saints their favour lend,
And all our chiefs the deed commend
Urging thee forward on thy way:
Arise then, and the task assay.
Thou art our only refuge; we,
Our lives and all, depend on thee."

Then sprang the Wind-God's son the best
Of Vánars, on Mahendra's crest,
And the great mountain rocked and swayed
By that unusual weight dismayed,
As reels an elephant beneath

The lion's spring and rending teeth.
The shady wood that crowned him shook,
The trembling birds the boughs forsook,
And ape and pard and lion fled
From brake and lair disquieted.

BOOK

V

BOOK

V

Hanumán's Leap

Thus Rávaṇ's foe resolved to trace
The captive to her hiding-place
Through airy pathways overhead
Which heavenly minstrels visited.
With straining nerve and eager brows,
Like some strong husband of the cows,
In ready might he stood prepared
For the bold task his soul has dared.
O'er gem-like grass that flashed and glowed
The Vánar like a lion strode.
Roused by the thunder of his tread,
The beasts to shady coverts fled.
Tall trees he crushed or hurled aside,
And every bird was terrified.
Around him loveliest lilies grew,
Pale pink, and red, and white, and blue,
And tints of many a metal lent
The light of varied ornament.
Gandharvas, changing forms at will,
And Yakshas roamed the lovely hill,
And countless Serpent-Gods were seen
Where flowers and grass were fresh and green.
As some resplendent serpent takes
His pastime in the best of lakes,

So on the mountain's woody height
The Vánar wandered with delight.
Then, standing on the flowery sod,
He paid his vows to saint and God.
Svayambhu and the Sun he prayed,
And the swift Wind to lend him aid,
And Indra, sovereign of the skies,
To bless his hardy enterprise.
Then once again the chief addressed
The Vánars from the mountain crest:
"Swift as a shaft from Ráma's bow
To Rávaṇ's city will I go,
And if she be not there will fly
And seek the lady in the sky;
Or, if in heaven she be not found,
Will hither bring the giant bound."

He ceased; and mustering his might
Sprang downward from the mountain height,
While, shattered by each mighty limb,
The trees unrooted followed him.
The shadow on the ocean cast
By his vast form, as on he passed,
Flew like a ship before the gale
When the strong breeze has filled the sail,
And where his course the Vánar held
The sea beneath him raged and swelled.
Then Gods and all the heavenly train
Poured flowerets down in gentle rain;
Their voices glad Gandharvas raised,
And saints in heaven the Vánar praised.
Fain would the Sea his succour lend
And Raghu's noble son befriend.
He, moved by zeal for Ráma's sake,
The hill Maináka thus bespake:
"O strong Maináka, heaven's decree
In days of old appointed thee
To be the Asurs bar, and keep
The rebels in the lowest deep.
Thou guardest those whom heaven has cursed
Lest from their prison-house they burst,

And standest by the gates of hell
Their limitary sentinel.
To thee is given the power to spread
Or spring above thy watery bed.
Now, best of noble mountains, rise
And do the thing that I advise.
E'en now above thy buried crest
Flies mighty Hanumán, the best
Of Vánars, moved for Ráma's sake
A wonderous deed to undertake.
Lift up thy head that he may stay
And rest him on his weary way."

He heard, and from his watery shroud,
As bursts the sun from autumn cloud,
Rose swifty, crowned with plant and tree,
And stood above the foamy sea.
There with his lofty peaks upraised
Bright as a hundred suns he blazed,
And crest and crag of burnished gold
Flashed on the flood that round him rolled.

The Vánar thought the mountain rose
A hostile bar to interpose,
And, like a wind-swept cloud, o'erthrew
The glittering mountain as he flew.
Then from the falling hill rang out
A warning voice and joyful shout.
Again he raised him high in air
To meet the flying Vánar there,
And standing on his topmost peak
In human form began to speak:
"Best of the Vánars' noblest line,
A mighty task, O chief, is thine.
Here for a while, I pray thee, light
And rest upon the breezy height.
A prince of Raghu's line was he
Who gave his glory to the Sea,
Who now to Ráma's envoy shows
High honour for the debt he owes.
He bade me lift my buried head

227

Uprising from my watery bed,
And woo the Vánar chief to rest
A moment on my glittering crest.
Refresh thy weary limbs, and eat
My mountain fruits for they are sweet.
I too, O chieftain, know thee well;
Three worlds thy famous virtues tell;
And none, I ween, with thee may vie
Who spring impetuous through the sky.
To every guest, though mean and low,
The wise respect and honour show;
And how shall I neglect thee, how
Slight the great guest so near me now?
Son of the Wind, 'tis thine to share
The might of him who shakes the air;
And,—for he loves his offspring,—he
Is honoured when I honour thee.
Of yore, when Krita's age was new,
The little hills and mountains flew
Where'er they listed, borne on wings
More rapid than the feathered king's.
But mighty terror came on all
The Gods and saints who feared their fall.
And Indra in his anger rent
Their pinions with the bolts he sent.
When in his ruthless fury he
Levelled his flashing bolt at me,
The great-souled Wind inclined to save,
And laid me neath the ocean's wave.
Thus by the favour of the sire
I kept my cherished wings entire;
And for this deed of kindness done
I honour thee his noble son.
O come, thy weary limbs relieve,
And honour due from me receive."
"I may not rest," the Vánar cried;
"I must not stay or turn aside.
Yet pleased am I, thou noblest hill,
And as the deed accept thy will."

Thus as he spoke he lightly pressed
With his broad hand the mountain's crest,
Then bounded upward to the height
Of heaven, rejoicing in his might,
And through the fields of boundless blue,
The pathway of his father, flew.
Gods, saints, and heavenly bards beheld
That flight that none had paralleled,
Then to the Nágas' mother came
And thus addressed the sun-bright dame:
"See, Hanumán with venturous leap
Would spring across the mighty deep,—
A Vánar prince, the Wind-God's seed:
Come, Surasá, his course impede.
In Rákshas form thy shape disguise,
Terrific, like a hill in size:
Let thy red eyes with fury glow,
And high as heaven thy body grow.
With fearful tusks the chief defy,
That we his power and strength may try.
He will with guile thy hold elude,
Or own thy might, by thee subdued."

Pleased with the grateful honours paid,
The godlike dame their words obeyed,
Clad in a shape of terror she
Sprang from the middle of the sea,
And, with fierce accents that appalled
All creatures, to the Vánar called:
"Come, prince of Vánars, doomed to be
My food this day by heaven's decree.
Such boon from ages long ago
To Brahmá's favouring will I owe."

She ceased, and Hanumán replied,
By shape and threat unterrified:
"Brave Ráma with his Maithil spouse
Lodged in the shade of Daṇḍak's boughs,
Thence Rávan king of giants stole
Sítá the joy of Ráma's soul.

By Ráma's high behest to her
I go a willing messenger;
And never shouldst them hinder one
Who toils for Daśaratha's son.
First captive Sítá will I see,
And him who sent and waits for me,
Then come and to thy will submit,
Yea, by my truth I promise it."
"Nay, hope not thus thy life to save;
Not such the boon that Brahmá gave.
Enter my mouth," was her reply,
"Then forward on thy journey hie!"

"Stretch, wider stretch thy jaws," exclaimed
The Vánar chief, to ire inflamed;
And, as the Rákshas near him drew,
Ten leagues in height his stature grew.
Then straight, her threatening jaws between,
A gulf of twenty leagues was seen.
To fifty leagues he waxed, and still
Her mouth grew wider at her will.
Then smaller than a thumb became,
Shrunk by his power, the Vánar's frame.
He leaped within, and turning round
Sprang through the portal at a bound.
Then hung in air a moment, while
He thus addressed her with a smile:
"O Daksha's child, farewell at last!
For I within thy mouth have passed.
Thou hast the gift of Brahmá's grace:
I go, the Maithil queen to trace."
Then, to her former shape restored,
She thus addressed the Vánar lord:
"Then forward to the task, and may
Success and joy attend thy way!
Go, and the rescued lady bring
In triumph to her lord and king."

Then hosts of spirits as they gazed
The daring of the Vánar praised.
Through the broad fields of ether, fast

Garuḍ's royal self, he passed,
The region of the cloud and rain,
Loved by the gay Gandharva train,
Where mid the birds that came and went
Shone Indra's glorious bow unbent,
And like a host of wandering stars
Flashed the high Gods' celestial cars.
Fierce Sinhiká who joyed in ill
And changed her form to work her will,
Descried him on his airy way
And marked the Vánar for her prey.
"This day at length," the demon cried,
"My hunger shall be satisfied,"
And at his passing shadow caught
Delighted with the cheering thought.
The Vánar felt the power that stayed
And held him as she grasped his shade,
Like some tall ship upon the main
That struggles with the wind in vain.
Below, above, his eye he bent
And scanned the sea and firmament.
High from the briny deep upreared
The monster's hideous form appeared,
"Sugríva's tale," he cried, "is true:
This is the demon dire to view
Of whom the Vánar monarch told,
Whose grasp a passing shade can hold."
Then, as a cloud in rain-time grows
His form, dilating, swelled and rose.
Wide as the space from heaven to hell
Her jaws she opened with a yell,
And rushed upon her fancied prey
With cloud-like roar to seize and slay.
The Vánar swift as thought compressed
His borrowed bulk of limb and chest,
And stood with one quick bound inside
The monstrous mouth she opened wide.
Hid like the moon when Ráhu draws
The orb within his ravening jaws.
Within that ample cavern pent
The demon's form he tore and rent,

And, from the mangled carcass freed,
Came forth again with thought-like speed.

Thus with his skill the fiend he slew,
Then to his wonted stature grew.
The spirits saw the demon die
And hailed the Vánar from the sky:
"Well hast thou fought a wondrous fight
Nor spared the fiend's terrific might,
On, on! perform the blameless deed,
And in thine every wish succeed.
Ne'er can they fail in whom combine
Such valour, thought, and skill as thine."

Pleased with their praises as they sang,
Again through fields of air he sprang,
And now, his travail wellnigh done,
The distant shore was almost won.
Before him on the margent stood
In long dark line a waving wood,
And the fair island, bright and green
With flowers and trees, was clearly seen,
And every babbling brook that gave
Her lord the sea a tribute wave.
He lighted down on Lamba's peak
Which tinted metals stain and streak,
And looked where Lanká's splendid town
Shone on the mountain like a crown.

Lanká

The glorious sight a while he viewed,
Then to the town his way pursued.
Around the Vánar as he went
Breathed from the wood delicious scent,
And the soft grass beneath his feet
With gem-like flowers was bright and sweet.
Still as the Vánar nearer drew
More clearly rose the town to view.
The palm her fan-like leaves displayed,
Priyálas lent their pleasant shade,
And mid the lower greenery far
Conspicuous rose the Kovidár.
A thousand trees mid flowers that glowed
Hung down their fruit's delicious load,
And in their crests that rocked and swayed
Sweet birds delightful music made.
And there were pleasant pools whereon
The glories of the lotus shone;
And gleams of sparkling fountains, stirred
By many a joyous water-bird.
Around, in lovely gardens grew
Blooms sweet of scent and bright of hue,
And Lanká, seat of Rávan's sway,
Before the wondering Vánar lay:
With stately domes and turrets tall,
Encircled by a golden wall,
And moats whose waters were aglow
With lily blossoms bright below:
For Sítá's sake defended well
With bolt and bar and sentinel,
And Rákshases who roamed in bands

With ready bows in eager hands.
He saw the stately mansions rise
Like pale-hued clouds in autumn skies;
Where noble streets were broad and bright,
And banners waved on every height.
Her gates were glorious to behold
Rich with the shine of burnished gold:
A lovely city planned and decked
By heaven's creative architect,
Fairest of earthly cities meet
To be the Gods' celestial seat.
The Vánar by the northern gate
Thus in his heart began debate
"Our mightiest host would strive in vain
To take this city on the main:
A city that may well defy
The chosen warriors of the sky;
A city never to be won
E'en by the arm of Raghu's son.
Here is no hope by guile to win
The hostile hearts of those within.
'Twere vain to war, or bribe, or sow
Dissension mid the Vánar foe.
But now my search must I pursue
Until the Maithil queen I view:
And, when I find the captive dame,
Make victory mine only aim.
But, if I wear my present shape,
How shall I enter and escape
The Rákshas troops, their guards and spies,
And sleepless watch of cruel eyes?
The fiends of giant race who hold
This mighty town are strong and bold;
And I must labour to elude
The fiercely watchful multitude.
I in a shape to mock their sight
Must steal within the town by night,
Blind with my art the demons' eyes,
And thus achieve my enterprise.
How may I see, myself unseen
Of the fierce king, the captive queen,

And meet her in some lonely place,
With none beside her, face to face?"

When the bright sun had left the skies
The Vánar dwarfed his mighty size,

And, in the straitest bounds restrained,
The bigness of a cat retained.
Then, when the moon's soft light was spread,
Within the city's walls he sped.

CANTO
III

The Guardian Goddess

There from the circling rampart's height
He gazed upon the wondrous sight;
Broad gates with burnished gold displayed,
And courts with turkises inlaid;
With gleaming silver, gems, and rows
Of crystal stairs and porticoes.
In semblance of a Rákshas dame
The city's guardian Goddess came,—
For she with glances sure and keen
The entrance of a foe had seen,—
And thus with fury in her eye
Addressed him with an angry cry:
"Who art thou? what has led thee, say,
Within these walls to find thy way?
Thou mayst not enter here in spite
Of Rávaṇ and his warriors' might."
"And who art thou?" the Vánar cried,
By form and frown unterrified,
"Why hast thou met me by the gate,
And chid me thus infuriate?"

He ceased: and Lanká made reply:
"The guardian of the town am I,
Who watch for ever to fulfil
My lord the Rákshas monarch's will.
But thou shalt fall this hour, and deep
Shall be thy never-ending sleep."

Again he spake: "In spite of thee
This golden city will I see.
Her gates and towers, and all the pride
Of street and square from side to side,
And freely wander where I please
Amid her groves of flowering trees;
On all her beauties sate mine eye.
Then, as I came, will homeward hie."

Swift with an angry roar she smote
With her huge hand the Vánar's throat.
The smitten Vánar, rage-impelled,
With fist upraised the monster felled:
But quick repented, stirred with shame
And pity for a vanquished dame,
When with her senses troubled, weak
With terror, thus she strove to speak:
"O spare me thou whose arm is strong:
O spare me, and forgive the wrong.
The brave that law will ne'er transgress
That spares a woman's helplessness.
Hear, best of Vánars, brave and bold,
What Brahmá's self of yore foretold;
"Beware," he said, "the fatal hour
When thou shalt own a Vánar's power.
Then is the giants' day of fear,
For terror and defeat are near."
Now, Vánar chief, o'ercome by thee,
I own the truth of heaven's decree.
For Sítá's sake will ruin fall
On Rávaṇ, and his town, and all."

Within the City

The guardian goddess thus subdued,
The Vánar chief his way pursued,
And reached the broad imperial street
Where fresh-blown flowers were bright and sweet.
The city seemed a fairer sky
Where cloud-like houses rose on high,
Whence the soft sound of tabors came
Through many a latticed window frame,
And ever and anon rang out
The merry laugh and joyous shout.
From house to house the Vánar went
And marked each varied ornament,
Where leaves and blossoms deftly strung
About the crystal columns hung.
Then soft and full and sweet and clear
The song of women charmed his ear,
And, blending with their dulcet tones,
Their anklets' chime and tinkling zones.
He heard the Rákshas minstrel sing
The praises of their matchless king;
And softly through the evening air
Came murmurings of text and prayer.
Here moved a priest with tonsured head,
And there an eager envoy sped,
Mid crowds with hair in matted twine
Clothed in the skins of deer and kine,—
Whose only arms, which none might blame,
Were blades of grass and holy flame
There savage warriors roamed in bands
With clubs and maces in their hands,
Some dwarfish forms, some huge of size,

With single ears and single eyes.
Some shone in glittering mail arrayed
With bow and mace and flashing blade;
Fiends of all shapes and every hue,
Some fierce and foul, some fair to view.

He saw the grisly legions wait
In strictest watch at Rávan's gate,
Whose palace on the mountain crest
Rose proudly towering o'er the rest,
Fenced with high ramparts from the foe,
And lotus-covered moats below.
But Hanumán, unhindered, found
Quick passage through the guarded bound,
Mid elephants of noblest breed,
And gilded car and neighing steed.

[I omit Canto V. which corresponds to chapter XI. in Gorresio's edition. That scholar justly observes: "The eleventh chapter, Description of Evening, is certainly the work of the Rhapsodists and an interpolation of later date. The chapter might be omitted without any injury to the action of the poem, and besides the metre, style, conceits and images differ from the general tenour of the poem; and that continual repetition of the same sounds at the end of each hemistich which is not exactly rime, but assonance, reveals the artificial labour of a more recent age." The following sample will probably be enough.

Fair shone the moon, as if to lend
His cheering light to guide a friend,
And, circled by the starry host,
Looked down upon the wild sea-coast.
The Vánar cheiftain raised his eyes,
And saw him sailing through the skies
Like a bright swan who joys to take
His pastime on a silver lake;
Fair moon that calms the mourner's pain.
Heaves up the waters of the main,
And o'er the life beneath him throws
A tender light of soft repose,
The charm that clings to Mandar's hill,

Gleams in the sea when winds are still,
And decks the lilly's opening flower,
Showed in that moon her sweetest power.

I am unable to show the difference of style in a translation.]

CANTO
VI

The Court

The palace gates were guarded well
  By many a Rákshas sentinel,
  And far within, concealed from view,
Were dames and female retinue
For charm of form and face renowned;
Whose tinkling armlets made a sound,
Clashed by the wearers in their glee,
Like music of a distant sea.
The hall beyond the palace gate,
Rich with each badge of royal state,
Where lines of noble courtiers stood,
Showed like a lion-guarded wood.
There the wild music rose and fell
Of drum and tabor and of shell,
Through chambers at each holy tide
By solemn worship sanctified.
Through grove and garden, undismayed,
From house to house the Vánar strayed,
And still his wondering glances bent
On terrace, dome, and battlement:
Then with a light and rapid tread
Prahasta's home he visited,
And Kumbhakarṇa's courtyard where
A cloudy pile rose high in air;

And, wandering o'er the hill, explored
The garden of each Rákshas lord.
Each court and grove he wandered through,
Then nigh to Rávaṇ's palace drew.
She-demons watched it foul of face,
Each armed with sword and spear and mace,
And warrior fiends of every hue,
A strange and fearful retinue.
There elephants in many a row,
The terror of the stricken foe.
Huge Airávat, deftly trained
In battle-fields, stood ready chained.
Fair litters on the ground were set
Adorned with gems and golden net.
Gay bloomy creepers clothed the walls;
Green bowers were there and picture halls,
And chambers made for soft delight.
Broad banners waved on every height.
And from the roof like Mandar's hill
The peacock's cry came loud and shrill.

CANTO

VII

Rávan's Palace

He passed within the walls and gazed
On gems and gold that round him blazed,
And many a latticed window bright
With turkis and with lazulite.

Through porch and ante-rooms he passed
Each richer, fairer than the last;
And spacious halls where lances lay,
And bows and shells, in fair array:
A glorious house that matched in show

All Paradise displayed below.
Upon the polished floor were spread
Fresh buds and blossoms white and red,
And women shone, a lovely crowd,
As lightning flashes through a cloud:
A palace splendid as the sky
Which moon and planets glorify:
Like earth whose towering hills unfold
Their zones and streaks of glittering gold;
Where waving on the mountain brows
The tall trees bend their laden boughs,
And every bough and tender spray
With a bright load of bloom is gay,
And every flower the breeze has bent
Fills all the region with its scent.
Near the tall palace pale of hue
Shone lovely lakes where lilies blew,
And lotuses with flower and bud
Gleamed on the bosom of the flood.
There shone with gems that flashed afar
The marvel of the Flower-named car,
Mid wondrous dwellings still confessed
Supreme and nobler than the rest.
Thereon with wondrous art designed
Were turkis birds of varied kind.
And many a sculptured serpent rolled
His twisted coil in burnished gold.
And steeds were there of noblest form
With flying feet as fleet as storm:
And elephants with deftest skill
Stood sculptured by a silver rill,
Each bearing on his trunk a wreath
Of lilies from the flood beneath.
There Lakshmí, beauty's heavenly queen,
Wrought by the artist's skill, was seen
Beside a flower-clad pool to stand
Holding a lotus in her hand.

The Enchanted Car

There gleamed the car with wealth untold
Of precious gems and burnished gold;
Nor could the Wind-God's son withdraw
His rapt gaze from the sight he saw,
By Viśvakarmá's self proclaimed
The noblest work his hand had framed.
Uplifted in the air it glowed
Bright as the sun's diurnal road.
The eye might scan the wondrous frame
And vainly seek one spot to blame,
So fine was every part and fair
With gems inlaid with lavish care.
No precious stones so rich adorn
The cars wherein the Gods are borne,
Prize of the all-resistless might
That sprang from pain and penance rite,
Obedient to the master's will
It moved o'er wood and towering hill,
A glorious marvel well designed
By Viśvakarmá's artist mind,
Adorned with every fair device
That decks the cars of Paradise.
Swift moving as the master chose
It flew through air or sank or rose,
And in its fleetness left behind
The fury of the rushing wind:
Meet mansion for the good and great,
The holy, wise, and fortunate.
Throughout the chariot's vast extent
Were chambers wide and excellent,
All pure and lovely to the eyes

As moonlight shed from cloudless skies.
Fierce goblins, rovers of the night
Who cleft the clouds with swiftest flight
In countless hosts that chariot drew,
With earrings clashing as they flew.

CANTO

IX

The Ladies' Bower

W here stately mansions rose around,
A palace fairer still he found,
Whose royal height and splendour showed
Where Rávaṇ's self, the king, abode.
A chosen band with bow and sword
Guarded the palace of their lord,
Where Ráksha's dames of noble race
And many a princess fair of face
Whom Rávaṇ's arm had torn away
From vanquished kings in slumber lay.

There jewelled arches high o'erhead
An ever-changing lustre shed
From ruby, pearl, and every gem
On golden pillars under them.
Delicious came the tempered air
That breathed a heavenly summer there,
Stealing through bloomy trees that bore
Each pleasant fruit in endless store.
No check was there from jealous guard,
No door was fast, no portal barred;
Only a sweet air breathed to meet
The stranger, as a host should greet
A wanderer of his kith and kin
And woo his weary steps within.

He stood within a spacious hall
With fretted roof and painted wall,
The giant Rávaṇ's boast and pride,
Loved even as a lovely bride.
'Twere long to tell each marvel there,
The crystal floor, the jewelled stair,
The gold, the silver, and the shine
Of chrysolite and almandine.
There breathed the fairest blooms of spring;
There flashed the proud swan's silver wing,
The splendour of whose feathers broke
Through fragrant wreaths of aloe smoke.
"'Tis Indra's heaven," the Vánar cried,
Gazing in joy from side to side;
"The home of all the Gods is this,
The mansion of eternal bliss."
There were the softest carpets spread,
Delightful to the sight and tread,
Where many a lovely woman lay
O'ercome by sleep, fatigued with play.
The wine no longer cheered the feast,
The sound of revelry had ceased.
The tinkling feet no longer stirred,
No chiming of a zone was heard.
So when each bird has sought her nest,
And swans are mute and wild bees rest,
Sleep the fair lilies on the lake
Till the sun's kiss shall bid them wake.
Like the calm field of winter's sky
Which stars unnumbered glorify,
So shone and glowed the sumptuous room
With living stars that chased the gloom.
"These are the stars," the chieftain cried,
"In autumn nights that earth-ward glide,
In brighter forms to reappear
And shine in matchless lustre here."
With wondering eyes a while he viewed
Each graceful form and attitude.
One lady's head was backward thrown,
Bare was her arm and loose her zone.
The garland that her brow had graced

Hung closely round another's waist.
Here gleamed two little feet all bare
Of anklets that had sparkled there,
Here lay a queenly dame at rest
In all her glorious garments dressed.
There slept another whose small hand
Had loosened every tie and band,
In careless grace another lay
With gems and jewels cast away,
Like a young creeper when the tread
Of the wild elephant has spread
Confusion and destruction round,
And cast it flowerless to the ground.
Here lay a slumberer still as death,
Save only that her balmy breath
Raised ever and anon the lace
That floated o'er her sleeping face.
There, sunk in sleep, an amorous maid
Her sweet head on a mirror laid,
Like a fair lily bending till
Her petals rest upon the rill.
Another black-eyed damsel pressed
Her lute upon her heaving breast,
As though her loving arms were twined
Round him for whom her bosom pined.
Another pretty sleeper round
A silver vase her arms had wound,
That seemed, so fresh and fair and young
A wreath of flowers that o'er it hung.
In sweet disorder lay a throng
Weary of dance and play and song,
Where heedless girls had sunk to rest
One pillowed on another's breast,
Her tender cheek half seen beneath
Bed roses of the falling wreath,
The while her long soft hair concealed
The beauties that her friend revealed.
With limbs at random interlaced
Round arm and leg and throat and waist,
That wreath of women lay asleep
Like blossoms in a careless heap.

Rávan Asleep

Apart a dais of crystal rose
With couches spread for soft repose,
Adorned with gold and gems of price
Meet for the halls of Paradise.
A canopy was o'er them spread
Pale as the light the moon beams shed,
And female figures, deftly planned,
The faces of the sleepers fanned,
There on a splendid couch, asleep
On softest skins of deer and sheep.
Dark as a cloud that dims the day
The monarch of the giants lay,
Perfumed with sandal's precious scent
And gay with golden ornament.

His fiery eyes in slumber closed,
In glittering robes the king reposed
Like Mandar's mighty hill asleep
With flowery trees that clothe his steep.
Near and more near the Vánar
The monarch of the fiends to view,
And saw the giant stretched supine
Fatigued with play and drunk with wine.
While, shaking all the monstrous frame,
His breath like hissing serpents' came.
With gold and glittering bracelets gay
His mighty arms extended lay
Huge as the towering shafts that bear
The flag of Indra high in air.
Scars by Airávat's tusk impressed
Showed red upon his shaggy breast.

And on his shoulders were displayed
The dints the thunder-bolt had made.
The spouses of the giant king
Around their lord were slumbering,
And, gay with sparkling earrings, shone
Fair as the moon to look upon.
There by her husband's side was seen
Mandodarí the favourite queen,
The beauty of whose youthful face
Beamed a soft glory through the place.
The Vánar marked the dame more fair
Than all the royal ladies there,
And thought, "These rarest beauties speak
The matchless dame I come to seek.
Peerless in grace and splendour, she
The Maithil queen must surely be."

CANTO

XI

The Banquet Hall

But soon the baseless thought was spurned
And longing hope again returned:
"No: Ráma's wife is none of these,
No careless dame that lives at ease.
Her widowed heart has ceased to care
For dress and sleep and dainty fare.
She near a lover ne'er would lie
Though Indra wooed her from the sky.
Her own, her only lord, whom none
Can match in heaven, is Raghu's son."

Then to the banquet hall intent
On strictest search his steps he bent.
He passed within the door, and found

Fair women sleeping on the ground,
Where wearied with the song, perchance,
The merry game, the wanton dance,
Each girl with wine and sleep oppressed
Had sunk her drooping head to rest.
That spacious hall from side to side
With noblest fare was well supplied;
There quarters of the boar, and here
Roast of the buffalo and deer,
There on gold plate, untouched as yet
The peacock and the hen were set.
There deftly mixed with salt and curd
Was meat of many a beast and bird,
Of kid and porcupine and hare,
And dainties of the sea and air.
There wrought of gold, ablaze with shine
Of precious stones, were cups of wine.
Through court and bower and banquet hall
The Vánar passed and viewed them all;
From end to end, in every spot,
For Sítá searched, but found her not.

CANTO

XII

The Search Renewed

Again the Vánar chief began
Each chamber, bower, and hall to scan.
In vain: he found not her he sought,
And pondered thus in bitter thought:
"Ah me the Maithil queen is slain:
She, ever true and free from stain,
The fiend's entreaty has denied,
And by his cruel hand has died.
Or has she sunk, by terror killed,

When first she saw the palace filled
With female monsters evil miened
Who wait upon the robber fiend?
No battle fought, no might displayed,
In vain this anxious search is made;
Nor shall my steps, made slow by shame,
Because I failed to find the dame,
Back to our lord the king be bent,
For he is swift to punishment.
In every bower my feet have been,
The dames of Rávaṇ have I seen;
But Ráma's spouse I seek in vain,
And all my toil is fruitless pain.
How shall I meet the Vánar band
I left upon the ocean strand?
How, when they bid me speak, proclaim
These tidings of defeat and shame?
How shall I look on Angad's eye?
What words will Jámbaván reply?
Yet dauntless hearts will never fail
To win success though foes assail,
And I this sorrow will subdue
And search the palace through and through,
Exploring with my cautious tread
Each spot as yet unvisited."

Again he turned him to explore
Each chamber, hall, and corridor,
And arbour bright with scented bloom,
And lodge and cell and picture-room.

With eager eye and noiseless feet
He passed through many a cool retreat
Where women lay in slumber drowned;
But Sítá still was nowhere found.

CANTO
XIII

Despair And Hope

Then rapid as the lightning's flame
From Rávaṇ's halls the Vánar came.
Each lingering hope was cold and dead,
And thus within his heart he said:
"Alas, my fruitless search is done:
Long have I toiled for Raghu's son;
And yet with all my care have seen
No traces of the ravished queen.
It may be, while the giant through
The lone air with his captive flew,
The Maithil lady, tender-souled,
Slipped struggling from the robber's hold,
And the wild sea is rolling now
O'er Sítá of the beauteous brow.
Or did she perish of alarm
When circled by the monster's arm?
Or crushed, unable to withstand
The pressure of that monstrous hand?
Or when she spurned his suit with scorn,
Her tender limbs were rent and torn.
And she, her virtue unsubdued,
Was slaughtered for the giant's food.
Shall I to Raghu's son relate
His well-beloved consort's fate,
My crime the same if I reveal
The mournful story or conceal?
If with no happier tale to tell
I seek our mountain citadel,
How shall I face our lord the king,
And meet his angry questioning?

How shall I greet my friends, and brook
The muttered taunt, the scornful look?
How to the son of Raghu go
And kill him with my tale of woe?
For sure the mournful tale I bear
Will strike him dead with wild despair.
And Lakshmaṇ ever fond and true,
Will, undivided, perish too.
Bharat will learn his brother's fate,
And die of grief disconsolate,
And sad Śatrughna with a cry
Of anguish on his corpse will die.
Our king Sugríva, ever found
True to each bond in honour bound,
Will mourn the pledge he vainly gave,
And die with him he could not save.
Then Rumá his devoted wife
For her dead lord will leave her life,
And Tárá, widowed and forlorn,
Will die in anguish, sorrow-worn.
On Angad too the blow will fall
Killing the hope and joy of all.
The ruin of their prince and king
The Vánars' souls with woe will wring.
And each, overwhelmed with dark despair,
Will beat his head and rend his hair.
Each, graced and honoured long, will miss
His careless life of easy bliss,
In happy troops will play no more
On breezy rock and shady shore,
But with his darling wife and child
Will seek the mountain top, and wild
With hopeless desolation, throw
Himself, his wife, and babe, below.
Ah no: unless the dame I find
I ne'er will meet my Vánar kind.
Here rather in some distant dell
A lonely hermit will I dwell,
Where roots and berries will supply
My humble wants until I die;

Or on the shore will raise a pyre
And perish in the kindled fire.
Or I will strictly fast until
With slow decay my life I kill,
And ravening dogs and birds of air
The limbs of Hanumán shall tear.
Here will I die, but never bring
Destruction on my race and king.
But still unsearched one grove I see
With many a bright Aśoka tree.
There will I enter in, and through
The tangled shade my search renew.
Be glory to the host on high,
The Sun and Moon who light the sky,
The Vasus and the Maruts' train,
Ádityas and the Aśvins twain.
So may I win success, and bring
The lady back with triumphing."

CANTO
XIV

The Asoka Grove

He cleared the barrier at a bound;
He stood within the pleasant ground,
And with delighted eyes surveyed
The climbing plants and varied shade,
He saw unnumbered trees unfold
The treasures of their pendent gold,
As, searching for the Maithil queen,
He strayed through alleys soft and green;
And when a spray he bent or broke
Some little bird that slept awoke.
Whene'er the breeze of morning blew,

Where'er a startled peacock flew,
The gaily coloured branches shed
Their flowery rain upon his head
That clung around the Vánar till
He seemed a blossom-covered hill,
The earth, on whose fair bosom lay
The flowers that fell from every spray,
Was glorious as a lovely maid
In all her brightest robes arrayed,
He saw the breath of morning shake
The lilies on the rippling lake
Whose waves a pleasant lapping made
On crystal steps with gems inlaid.
Then roaming through the enchanted ground,
A pleasant hill the Vánar found,
And grottoes in the living stone
With grass and flowery trees o'ergrown.
Through rocks and boughs a brawling rill
Leapt from the bosom of the hill,
Like a proud beauty when she flies
From her love's arms with angry eyes.

He clomb a tree that near him grew
And leafy shade around him threw.
"Hence," thought the Vánar, "shall I see
The Maithil dame, if here she be,
These lovely trees, this cool retreat
Will surely tempt her wandering feet.
Here the sad queen will roam apart.
And dream of Ráma in her heart."

Sítá

Fair as Kailása white with snow
He saw a palace flash and glow,
A crystal pavement gem-inlaid,
And coral steps and colonnade,
And glittering towers that kissed the skies,
Whose dazzling splendour charmed his eyes.
There pallid, with neglected dress,
Watched close by fiend and giantess,
Her sweet face thin with constant flow
Of tears, with fasting and with woe;
Pale as the young moon's crescent when
The first faint light returns to men:
Dim as the flame when clouds of smoke
The latent glory hide and choke;
Like Rohiṇí the queen of stars
Oppressed by the red planet Mars;
From her dear friends and husband torn,
Amid the cruel fiends, forlorn,
Who fierce-eyed watch around her kept,
A tender woman sat and wept.
Her sobs, her sighs, her mournful mien,
Her glorious eyes, proclaimed the queen.
"This, this is she," the Vánar cried,
"Fair as the moon and lotus-eyed,
I saw the giant Rávan bear
A captive through the fields of air.
Such was the beauty of the dame;
Her form, her lips, her eyes the same.
This peerless queen whom I behold
Is Ráma's wife with limbs of gold.

Best of the sons of men is he,
And worthy of her lord is she."

Hanumán's Lament

Then, all his thoughts on Sítá bent,
The Vánar chieftain made lament:
"The queen to Ráma's soul endeared,
By Lakshmaṇ's pious heart revered,
Lies here,—for none may strive with Fate,
A captive, sad and desolate.
The brothers' might full well she knows,
And bravely bears the storm of woes,
As swelling Gangá in the rains
The rush of every flood sustains.
Her lord, for her, fierce Báli slew,
Virádha's monstrous might o'erthrew,
For her the fourteen thousand slain
In Janasthán bedewed the plain.
And if for her Ikshváku's son
Destroyed the world 'twere nobly done.
This, this is she, so far renowned,
Who sprang from out the furrowed ground,
Child of the high-souled king whose sway
The men of Míthilá obey:
The glorious lady wooed and won
By Daśaratha's noblest son;
And now these sad eyes look on her
Mid hostile fiends a prisoner.
From home and every bliss she fled
By wifely love and duty led,
And heedless of a wanderer's woes,

A life in lonely forests chose.
This, this is she so fair of mould.
Whose limbs are bright as burnished gold.

Whose voice was ever soft and mild,
Who sweetly spoke and sweetly smiled.
O, what is Ráma's misery! how
He longs to see his darling now!
Pining for one of her fond looks
As one athirst for water brooks.
Absorbed in woe the lady sees
No Rákshas guard, no blooming trees.
Her eyes are with her thoughts, and they
Are fixed on Ráma far away."

CANTO
XVII

Sítá's Guard

His pitying eyes with tears bedewed,
The weeping queen again he viewed,
And saw around the prisoner stand
Her demon guard, a fearful band.
Some earless, some with ears that hung
Low as their feet and loosely swung:
Some fierce with single ears and eyes,
Some dwarfish, some of monstrous size:
Some with their dark necks long and thin
With hair upon the knotty skin:
Some with wild locks, some bald and bare,
Some covered o'er with bristly hair:
Some tall and straight, some bowed and bent
With every foul disfigurement:
All black and fierce with eyes of fire,
Ruthless and stern and swift to ire:

Some with the jackal's jaw and nose,
Some faced like boars and buffaloes:
Some with the heads of goats and kine,
Of elephants, and dogs, and swine:
With lions' lips and horses' brows,
They walked with feet of mules and cows:
Swords, maces, clubs, and spears they bore
In hideous hands that reeked with gore,
And, never sated, turned afresh
To bowls of wine and piles of flesh.
Such were the awful guards who stood
Round Sítá in that lovely wood,
While in her lonely sorrow she
Wept sadly neath a spreading tree.
He watched the spouse of Ráma there
Regardless of her tangled hair,
Her jewels stripped from neck and limb,
Decked only with her love of him.

CANTO
XVIII

Rávan

While from his shelter in the boughs
     The Vánar looked on Ráma's spouse
     He heard the gathered giants raise
The solemn hymn of prayer and praise.—
Priests skilled in rite and ritual, who
The Vedas and their branches knew.
Then, as loud strains of music broke
His sleep, the giant monarch woke.
Swift to his heart the thought returned
Of the fair queen for whom he burned;
Nor could the amorous fiend control
The passion that absorbed his soul.

In all his brightest garb arrayed
He hastened to that lovely shade,
Where glowed each choicest flower and fruit,
And the sweet birds were never mute,
And tall deer bent their heads to drink
On the fair streamlet's grassy brink.
Near that Aśoka grove he drew,—
A hundred dames his retinue.
Like Indra with the thousand eyes
Girt with the beauties of the skies.
Some walked beside their lord to hold
The chouries, fans, and lamps of gold.
And others purest water bore
In golden urns, and paced before.
Some carried, piled on golden plates,
Delicious food of dainty cates;
Some wine in massive bowls whereon
The fairest gems resplendent shone.
Some by the monarch's side displayed,
Wrought like a swan, a silken shade:
Another beauty walked behind,
The sceptre to her care assigned.
Around the monarch gleamed the crowd
As lightnings flash about a cloud,
And each made music as she went
With zone and tinkling ornament.
Attended thus in royal state
The monarch reached the garden gate,
While gold and silver torches, fed
With scented oil a soft light shed.

He, while the flame of fierce desire
Burnt in his eyes like kindled fire,
Seemed Love incarnate in his pride,
His bow and arrows laid aside.
His robe, from spot and blemish free
Like Amrit foamy from the sea,
Hung down in many a loosened fold
Inwrought with flowers and bright with gold.
The Vánar from his station viewed,
Amazed, the wondrous multitude,

Where, in the centre of that ring
Of noblest women, stood the king,
As stands the full moon fair to view,
Girt by his starry retinue.

CANTO
XIX

Sítá's Fear

Then o'er the lady's soul and frame
A sudden fear and trembling came,
When, glowing in his youthful pride,
She saw the monarch by her side.
Silent she sat, her eyes depressed,
Her soft arms folded o'er her breast,
And,—all she could,—her beauties screened
From the bold gazes of the fiend.
There where the wild she-demons kept
Their watch around, she sighed and wept.
Then, like a severed bough, she lay
Prone on the bare earth in dismay.
The while her thoughts on love's fleet wings
Flew to her lord the best of kings.
She fell upon the ground, and there
Lay struggling with her wild despair,
Sad as a lady born again
To misery and woe and pain,
Now doomed to grief and low estate,
Once noble fair and delicate:
Like faded light of holy lore,
Like Hope when all her dreams are o'er;
Like ruined power and rank debased,
Like majesty of kings disgraced:
Like worship foiled by erring slips,
The moon that labours in eclipse;

259

A pool with all her lilies dead,
An army when its king has fled:
So sad and helpless wan and worn,
She lay among the fiends forlorn.

CANTO

XX

Rávan's Wooing

With amorous look and soft address
The fiend began his suit to press:
"Why wouldst thou, lady lotus-eyed,
From my fond glance those beauties hide?
Mine eager suit no more repel:
But love me, for I love thee well.
Dismiss, sweet dame, dismiss thy fear;
No giant and no man is near.
Ours is the right by force to seize
What dames soe'er our fancy please.
But I with rude hands will not touch
A lady whom I love so much.
Fear not, dear queen: no fear is nigh:
Come, on thy lover's love rely,
Some little sign of favor show,
Nor lie enamoured of thy woe.
Those limbs upon that cold earth laid,
Those tresses twined in single braid,
The fast and woe that wear thy frame,
Beseem not thee, O beauteous dame.
For thee the fairest wreaths were meant,
The sandal and the aloe's scent,
Rich ornaments and pearls of price,
And vesture meet for Paradise.
With dainty cates shouldst thou be fed,
And rest upon a sumptuous bed.

And festive joys to thee belong,
The music, and the dance and song.
Rise, pearl of women, rise and deck
With gems and chains thine arms and neck.
Shall not the dame I love be seen
In vesture worthy of a queen?
Methinks when thy sweet form was made
His hand the wise Creator stayed;
For never more did he design
A beauty meet to rival thine.
Come, let us love while yet we may,
For youth will fly and charms decay,
Come cast thy grief and fear aside,
And be my love, my chosen bride.
The gems and jewels that my hand
Has reft from every plundered land,—
To thee I give them all this day,
And at thy feet my kingdom lay.

The broad rich earth will I o'errun,
And leave no town unconquered, none;
Then of the whole an offering make
To Janak, dear, for thy sweet sake.
In all the world no power I see
Of God or man can strive with me.
Of old the Gods and Asurs set
In terrible array I met:
Their scattered hosts to earth I beat,
And trod their flags beneath my feet.
Come, taste of bliss and drink thy fill,
And rule the slave who serves thy will.
Think not of wretched Ráma: he
Is less than nothing now to thee.
Stript of his glory, poor, dethroned,
A wanderer by his friends disowned,
On the cold earth he lays his head,
Or is with toil and misery dead.
And if perchance he lingers yet,
His eyes on thee shall ne'er be set.
Could he, that mighty monarch, who
Was named Hiraṇyakaśipu,

Could he who wore the garb of gold
Win Glory back from Indra's hold?
O lady of the lovely smile,
Whose eyes the sternest heart beguile,
In all thy radiant beauty dressed
My heart and soul thou ravishest.
What though thy robe is soiled and worn,
And no bright gems thy limbs adorn,
Thou unadorned art dearer far
Than all my loveliest consorts are.
My royal home is bright and fair;
A thousand beauties meet me there,
But come, my glorious love, and be
The queen of all those dames and me."

CANTO
XXI

Sítá's Scorn

She thought upon her lord and sighed,
And thus in gentle tones replied:
"Beseems thee not, O King, to woo
A matron, to her husband true.
Thus vainly one might hope by sin
And evil deeds success to win.
Shall I, so highly born, disgrace
My husband's house, my royal race?
Shall I, a true and loyal dame,
Defile my soul with deed of shame?"

Then on the king her back she turned,
And answered thus the prayer she spurned:
"Turn, Rávaṇ, turn thee from thy sin;
Seek virtue's paths and walk therein.
To others dames be honour shown;

Protect them as thou wouldst thine own.
Taught by thyself, from wrong abstain
Which, wrought on thee, thy heart would pain.
Beware: this lawless love of thine
Will ruin thee and all thy line;
And for thy sin, thy sin alone,
Will Lanká perish overthrown.
Dream not that wealth and power can sway
My heart from duty's path to stray.
Linked like the Day-God and his shine,
I am my lord's and he is mine.
Repent thee of thine impious deed;
To Ráma's side his consort lead.
Be wise; the hero's friendship gain,
Nor perish in his fury slain.
Go, ask the God of Death to spare,
Or red bolt flashing through the air,
But look in vain for spell or charm
To stay my Ráma's vengeful arm.
Thou, when the hero bends his bow,
Shalt hear the clang that heralds woe,
Loud as the clash when clouds are rent
And Indra's bolt to earth is sent.
Then shall his furious shafts be sped,
Each like a snake with fiery head,
And in their flight shall hiss and flame
Marked with the mighty archer's name.
Then in the fiery deluge all
Thy giants round their king shall fall."

Rávan's Threat

Then anger swelled in Rávaṇ's breast,
Who fiercely thus the dame addressed:
"'Tis ever thus: in vain we sue
To woman, and her favour woo.
A lover's humble words impel
Her wayward spirit to rebel.
The love of thee that fills my soul
Still keeps my anger in control,
As charioteers with bit and rein
The swerving of the steed restrain.
The love that rules me bids me spare
Thy forfeit life, O thou most fair.
For this, O Sítá, have I borne
The keen reproach, the bitter scorn,
And the fond love thou boastest yet
For that poor wandering anchoret;
Else had the words which thou hast said
Brought death upon thy guilty head.
Two months, fair dame, I grant thee still
To bend thee to thy lover's will.
If when that respite time is fled
Thou still refuse to share my bed,
My cooks shall mince thy limbs with steel
And serve thee for my morning meal."

The minstrel daughters of the skies
Looked on her woe with pitying eyes,
And sun-bright children of the Gods
Consoled the queen with smiles and nods.
She saw, and with her heart at ease,

Addressed the fiend in words like these;
"Hast thou no friend to love thee, none
In all this isle to bid thee shun
The ruin which thy crime will bring
On thee and thine, O impious King?
Who in all worlds save thee could woo
Me, Ráma's consort pure and true,
As though he tempted with his love
Queen Śachí on her throne above?
How canst thou hope, vile wretch, to fly
The vengeance that e'en now is nigh,
When thou hast dared, untouched by shame,
To press thy suit on Ráma's dame?
Where woods are thick and grass is high
A lion and a hare may lie;
My Ráma is the lion, thou
Art the poor hare beneath the bough.
Thou railest at the lord of men,
But wilt not stand within his ken.
What! is that eye unstricken yet
Whose impious glance on me was set?
Still moves that tongue that would not spare
The wife of Daśaratha's heir?"

Then, hissing like a furious snake,
The fiend again to Sítá spake:
"Deaf to all prayers and threats art thou,
Devoted to thy senseless vow.
No longer respite will I give,
And thou this day shalt cease to live;
For I, as sunlight kills the morn,
Will slay thee for thy scathe and scorn."

The Rákshas guard was summoned: all
The monstrous crew obeyed the call,
And hastened to the king to take
The orders which he fiercely spake:
"See that ye guard her well, and tame,
Like some wild thing, the stubborn dame,
Until her haughty soul be bent

By mingled threat and blandishment."
The monsters heard: away he strode,
And passed within his queens' abode.

CANTO

XXIII

The Demons' Threats

Then round the helpless Sítá drew
With fiery eyes the hideous crew,
And thus assailed her, all and each,
With insult, taunt, and threatening speech:
"What! can it be thou prizest not
This happy chance, this glorious lot,
To be the chosen wife of one
So strong and great, Pulastya's son?
Pulastya—thus have sages told—
Is mid the Lords of Life enrolled.
Lord Brahmá's mind-born son was he,
Fourth of that glorious company.
Viśravas from Pulastya sprang,—
Through all the worlds his glory rang.
And of Viśravas, large-eyed dame!
Our king the mighty Rávaṇ came.
His happy consort thou mayst be:
Scorn not the words we say to thee."

One awful demon, fiery-eyed,
Stood by the Maithil queen and cried:
'Come and be his, if thou art wise,
Who smote the sovereign of the skies,
And made the thirty Gods and three,
O'ercome in furious battle, flee.

Thy lover turns away with scorn
From wives whom grace and youth adorn.
Thou art his chosen consort, thou
Shall be his pride and darling now."

Another, Vikatá by name,
In words like these addressed the dame:
"The king whose blows, in fury dealt,
The Nágas and Gandharvas felt,
In battle's fiercest brunt subdued,
Has stood by thee and humbly wooed.
And wilt thou in thy folly miss
The glory of a love like this?
Scared by his eye the sun grows chill,
The wanderer wind is hushed and still.
The rains at his command descend,
And trees with new-blown blossoms bend.
His word the hosts of demons fear,
And wilt thou, dame, refuse to hear?
Be counselled; with his will comply,
Or, lady, thou shalt surely die."

CANTO
XXIV

Sítá's Reply

Still with reproaches rough and rude
Those fiends the gentle queen pursued:
"What! can so fair a life displease,
To dwell with him in joyous ease?
Dwell in his bowers a happy queen
In silk and gold and jewels' sheen?
Still must thy woman fancy cling
To Ráma and reject our king?

Die in thy folly, or forget
That wretched wandering anchoret.
Come, Sítá, in luxurious bowers
Spend with our lord thy happy hours;
The mighty lord who makes his own
The treasures of the worlds o'erthrown."

Then, as a tear bedewed her eye,
The hapless lady made reply:
"I loathe, with heart and soul detest
The shameful life your words suggest.
Eat, if you will, this mortal frame:
My soul rejects the sin and shame.
A homeless wanderer though he be,
In him my lord, my life I see,
And, till my earthly days be done,
Will cling to great Ikshváku's son."

Then with fierce eyes on Sítá set
They cried again with taunt and threat:
Each licking with her fiery tongue
The lip that to her bosom hung,
And menacing the lady's life
With axe, or spear or murderous knife:
"Hear, Sítá, and our words obey,
Or perish by our hands to-day.
Thy love for Raghu's son forsake,
And Rávaṇ for thy husband take,
Or we will rend thy limbs apart
And banquet on thy quivering heart.
Now from her body strike the head,
And tell the king the dame is dead.
Then by our lord's commandment she
A banquet for our band shall be.
Come, let the wine be quickly brought
That frees each heart from saddening thought.
Then to the western gate repair,
And we will dance and revel there."

Sítá's Lament

On the bare earth the lady sank,
   And trembling from their presence shrank
   Like a strayed fawn, when night is dark,
And hungry wolves around her bark.

Then to a shady tree she crept,
And thought upon her lord and wept.
By fear and bitter woe oppressed
She bathed the beauties of her breast
With her hot tears' incessant flow,
And found no respite from her woe.
As shakes a plantain in the breeze
She shook, and fell on trembling knees;
While at each demon's furious look
Her cheek its native hue forsook.
She lay and wept and made her moan
In sorrow's saddest undertone,
And, wild with grief, with fear appalled,
On Ráma and his brother called:
"O dear Kauśalyá, hear me cry!
Sweet Queen Sumitrá, list my sigh!
True is the saw the wise declare:
Death comes not to relieve despair.
'Tis vain for dame or man to pray;
Death will not hear before his day;
Since I, from Ráma's sight debarred,
And tortured by my cruel guard,
Still live in hopeless woe to grieve
And loathe the life I may not leave,
Here, like a poor deserted thing,
My limbs upon the ground I fling,

And, like a bark beneath the blast,
Shall sink oppressed with woes at last.
Ah, blest are they, supremely blest,
Whose eyes upon my lord may rest;
Who mark his lion port, and hear
His gentle speech that charms the ear.
Alas, what antenatal crime,
What trespass of forgotten time
Weighs on my soul, and bids me bow
Beneath this load of misery now?"

CANTO
XXVI

Sítá's Lament

"I Ráma's wife, on that sad day,
By Rávaṇ's arm was borne away,
Seized, while I sat and feared no ill,
By him who wears each form at will.
A helpless captive, left forlorn
To demons' threats and taunts and scorn,
Here for my lord I weep and sigh,
And worn with woe would gladly die.
For what is life to me afar
From Ráma of the mighty car?
The robber in his fruitless sin
Would hope his captive's love to win.
My meaner foot shall never touch
The demon whom I loathe so much.
The senseless fool! he knows me not,
Nor the proud soul his love would blot.
Yea, limb from limb will I be rent,
But never to his prayer consent;
Be burnt and perish in the fire,
But never meet his base desire.

My lord was grateful, true and wise,
And looked on woe with pitying eyes;
But now, recoiling from the strife
He pities not his captive wife.
Alone in Janasthán he slew
The thousands of the Rákshas crew.
His arm was strong, his heart was brave,
Why comes he not to free and save?
Why blame my lord in vain surmise?
He knows not where his lady lies.
O, if he knew, o'er land and sea
His feet were swift to set me free;
This Lanká, girdled by the deep,
Would fall consumed, a shapeless heap,
And from each ruined home would rise
A Rákshas widow's groans and cries."

CANTO

XXVII

Trijatá's Dream

Their threats unfeared, their counsel spurned,
The demons' breasts with fury burned.
Some sought the giant king to bear
The tale of Sítá's fixt despair.
With threats and taunts renewed the rest
Around the weeping lady pressed.
But Trijaṭá, of softer mould,
A Rákshas matron wise and old,
With pity for the captive moved,
In words like these the fiends reproved:
"Me, me," she cried, "eat me, but spare
The spouse of Daśaratha's heir.
Last night I dreamt a dream; and still
The fear and awe my bosom chill;

For in that dream I saw foreshown
Our race by Ráma's hand o'erthrown.
I saw a chariot high in air,
Of ivory exceeding fair.
A hundred steeds that chariot drew
As swiftly through the clouds it flew,
And, clothed in white, with wreaths that shone,
The sons of Raghu rode thereon.
I looked and saw this lady here,
Clad in the purest white, appear
High on the snow white hill whose feet
The angry waves of ocean beat.
And she and Ráma met at last
Like light and sun when night is past.
Again I saw them side by side.
On Rávan's car they seemed to ride,
And with the princely Lakshman flee
To northern realms beyond the sea.

Then Rávan, shaved and shorn, besmeared
With oil from head to foot, appeared.
He quaffed, he raved: his robes were red:
Fierce was his eye, and bare his head.
I saw him from his chariot thrust;
I saw him rolling in the dust.
A woman came and dragged away
The stricken giant where he lay,
And on a car which asses drew
The monarch of our race she threw.
He rose erect, he danced and laughed,
With thirsty lips the oil he quaffed,
Then with wild eyes and streaming mouth
Sped on the chariot to the south.
Then, dropping oil from every limb,
His sons the princes followed him,
And Kumbhakarna, shaved and shorn,
Was southward on a camel borne.
Then royal Lanká reeled and fell
With gate and tower and citadel.
This ancient city, far-renowned:
All life within her walls was drowned;

272

And the wild waves of ocean rolled
O'er Lanká and her streets of gold.
Warned by these signs I bid you fly;
Or by the hand of Ráma die,
Whose vengeance will not spare the life
Of one who vexed his faithful wife.
Your bitter taunts and threats forgo:
Comfort the lady in her woe,
And humbly pray her to forgive;
For so you may be spared and live."

[Instead of advancing the story it goes back to Canto XVII, containing a lamentation of Sítá after Rávaṇ has left her, and describes the the auspicious signs sent to cheer her, the throbbing of her left eye, arm, and side. The Canto is found in the Bengal recension. Gorresio translates it. and observes: "I think that Chapter XXVIII.—The Auspicious Signs— is an addition, a later interpolation by the Rhapsodists. It has no bond of connexion either with what precedes or follows it, and may be struck out not only without injury to, but positively to the advantage of the poem. The metre in which this chapter is written differs from that which is generally adopted in the course of the poem."]

CANTO
XXX

Hanumán's Deliberation

The Vánar watched concealed: each word
Of Sítá and the fiends he heard,
And in a maze of anxious thought
His quick-conceiving bosom wrought.
"At length my watchful eyes have seen,
Pursued so long, the Maithil queen,
Sought by our Vánar hosts in vain
From east to west, from main to main.
A cautious spy have I explored

The palace of the Rákhshas lord,
And thoroughly learned, concealed from sight,
The giant monarch's power and might.
And now my task must be to cheer
The royal dame who sorrows here.
For if I go, and soothe her not,
A captive in this distant spot,
She, when she finds no comfort nigh,
Will sink beneath her woes and die.
How shall my tale, if unconsoled
I leave her, be to Ráma told?
How shall I answer Raghu's son,
"No message from my darling, none?"
The husband's wrath, to fury fanned,
Will scorch me lifeless where I stand,
Or if I urge my lord the king
To Lanká's isle his hosts to bring,
In vain will be his zeal, in vain
The toil, the danger, and the pain.
Yea, this occasion must I seize
That from her guard the lady frees,
To win her ear with soft address
And whisper hope in dire distress.
Shall I, a puny Vánar, choose
The Sanskrit men delight to use?
If, as a man of Bráhman kind,
I speak the tongue by rules refined,
The lady, yielding to her fears,
Will think 'tis Rávaṇ's voice she hears.
I must assume my only plan—
The language of a common man.
Yet, if the lady sees me nigh,

In terror she will start and cry;
And all the demon band, alarmed,
Will come with various weapons armed,
With their wild shouts the grove will fill,
And strive to take me, or to kill.
And, at my death or capture, dies
The hope of Ráma`s enterprise.
For none can leap, save only me,

A hundred leagues across the sea.
It is a sin in me, I own,
To talk with Janak's child alone.
Yet greater is the sin if I
Be silent, and the lady die.
First I will utter Ráma's name,
And laud the hero's gifts and fame.
Perchance the name she holds so dear
Will soothe the faithful lady's fear."

CANTO

XXXI

Hanumán's Speech

Then in sweet accents low and mild
The Vánar spoke to Janak's child:
"A noble king, by sin unstained,
The mighty Daśaratha reigned.
Lord of the warrior's car and steed,
The pride of old Ikshváku's seed.
A faithful friend, a blameless king,
Protector of each living thing.
A glorious monarch, strong to save,
Blest with the bliss he freely gave.
His son, the best of all who know
The science of the bended bow,
Was moon-bright Ráma, brave and strong,
Who loved the right and loathed the wrong,
Who ne'er from kingly duty swerved,
Loved by the lands his might preserved.
His feet the path of law pursued;
His arm rebellious foes subdued.
His sire's command the prince obeyed
And, banished, sought the forest shade,
Where with his wife and brother he

Wandered a saintly devotee.
There as he roamed the wilds he slew
The bravest of the Rákshas crew.
The giant king the prince beguiled,
And stole his consort, Janak's child.
Then Ráma roamed the country round,
And a firm friend, Sugríva, found,
Lord of the Vánar race, expelled
From his own realm which Báli held,
He conquered Báli and restored
The kingdom to the rightful lord.
Then by Sugríva's high decree
The Vánar legions searched for thee,
Sampáti's counsel bade me leap
A hundred leagues across the deep.
And now my happy eyes have seen
At last the long-sought Maithil queen.
Such was the form, the eye, the grace
Of her whom Ráma bade me trace."

He ceased: her flowing locks she drew
To shield her from a stranger's view;
Then, trembling in her wild surprise,
Raised to the tree her anxious eyes.

CANTO
XXXII

Sítá's Doubt

Her eyes the Maithil lady raised
And on the monkey speaker gazed.
She looked, and trembling at the sight
Wept bitter tears in wild affright.
She shrank a while with fear distraught,
Then, nerved again, the lady thought:

"Is this a dream mine eyes have seen,
This creature, by our laws unclean?
O, may the Gods keep Ráma, still,
And Lakshmaṇ, and my sire, from ill!
It is no dream: I have not slept,
But, trouble-worn, have watched and wept
Afar from that dear lord of mine
For whom in ceaseless woe I pine,
No art may soothe my wild distress
Or lull me to forgetfulness.
I see but him: my lips can frame
No syllable but Ráma's name.
Each sight I see, each sound I hear,
Brings Ráma to mine eye or ear,
The wish was in my heart, and hence
The sweet illusion mocked my sense.
'Twas but a phantom of the mind,
And yet the voice was soft and kind.
Be glory to the Eternal Sire,
Be glory to the Lord of Fire,
The mighty Teacher in the skies,
And Indra with his thousand eyes,
And may they grant the truth to be
E'en as the words that startled me."

CANTO

XXXIII

The Colloquy

Down from the tree Hanumán came
And humbly stood before the dame.
Then joining reverent palm to palm
Addressed her thus with words of balm:
"Why should the tears of sorrow rise,
Sweet lady, to those lovely eyes,

As when the wind-swept river floods
Two half expanded lotus buds?
Who art thou, O most fair of face?
Of Asur, or celestial race?
Did Nága mother give thee birth?
For sure thou art no child of earth.
Do Rudras claim that heavenly form?
Or the swift Gods who ride the storm?
Or art thou Rohiṇí the blest,
That star more lovely than the rest,—
Reft from the Moon thou lovest well
And doomed a while on earth to dwell?
Or canst thou, fairest wonder, be
The starry queen Arundhatí,
Fled in thy wrath or jealous pride
From her dear lord Vaśishṭha's side?
Who is the husband, father, son
Or brother, O thou loveliest one,
Gone from this world in heaven to dwell,
For whom those eyes with weeping swell?
Yet, by the tears those sweet eyes shed,
Yet, by the earth that bears thy tread,
By calling on a monarch's name,
No Goddess but a royal dame.
Art thou the queen, fair lady, say,
Whom Rávaṇ stole and bore away?
Yea, by that agony of woe,
That form unrivalled here below,
That votive garb, thou art, I ween,
King Janak's child and Ráma's queen."

Hope at the name of Ráma woke,
And thus the gentle lady spoke:
"I am that Sítá wooed and won
By Daśaratha's royal son,
The noblest of Ikshváku's line;
And every earthly joy was mine.
But Ráma left his royal home
In Daṇḍak's tangled wilds to roam.
Where with Sumitrá's son and me,

He lived a saintly devotee.
The giant Rávaṇ came with guile
And bore me thence to Lanká's isle.
Some respite yet the fiend allows,
Two months of life, to Ráma's spouse.
Two moons of hopeless woe remain,
And then the captive will be slain."

CANTO
XXXIV

Hanumán's Speech

Thus spoke the dame in mournful mood,
  And Hanumán his speech renewed:
  "O lady, by thy lord's decree
I come a messenger to thee.
Thy lord is safe with steadfast friends,
And greeting to his queen he sends,
And Lakshmaṇ, ever faithful bows
His reverent head to Ráma's spouse."

Through all her frame the rapture ran,
As thus again the dame began:
"Now verily the truth I know
Of the wise saw of long ago:
"Once only in a hundred years
True joy to living man appears."

He marked her rapture-beaming hue,
And nearer to the lady drew,
But at each onward step he took
Suspicious fear her spirit shook.
"Alas, Alas," she cried in fear.
"False is the tale I joyed to hear.

'Tis Rávaṇ, 'tis the fiend, who tries
To mock me with a new disguise.
If thou, to wring my woman's heart,
Hast changed thy shape by magic art,
And wouldst a helpless dame beguile,
The wicked deed is doubly vile.
But no: that fiend thou canst not be:
Such joy I had from seeing thee.
But if my fancy does not err,
And thou art Ráma's messenger,
The glories of my lord repeat:
For to these ears such words are sweet."

The Vánar knew the lady's thought,
And gave the answer fondly sought:

"Bright as the sun that lights the sky
Dear as the Moon to every eye.
He scatters blessings o'er the land
Like bounties from Vaiśravaṇ's hand.
Like Vishṇu strong and unsubdued,
Unmatched in might and fortitude.
Wise, truthful as the Lord of Speech,
With gentle words he welcomes each.
Of noblest mould and form is he,
Like love's incarnate deity.
He quells the fury of the foe,
And strikes when justice prompts the blow.
Safe in the shadow of his arm
The world is kept from scathe and harm.
Now soon shall Rávaṇ rue his theft,
And fall, of realm and life bereft.
For Ráma's wrathful hand shall wing
His shafts against the giant king.
The day, O Maithil Queen, is near
When he and Lakshmaṇ will be here,
And by their side Sugríva lead
His countless hosts of Vánar breed.
Sugríva's servant, I, by name
Hanumán, by his order came.

With desperate leap I crossed the sea
To Lanká's isle in search of thee,
No traitor, gentle dame, am I:
Upon my word and faith rely."

CANTO

XXXV

Hanumán's Speech

With joyous heart she heard him tell
    Of the great lord she loved so well,
    And in sweet accents, soft and low,
Spoke, half forgetful of her woe:
"How didst thou stand by Ráma's side?
How came my lord and thou allied?
How met the people of the wood
With men on terms of brotherhood?
Declare each grace and regal sign
That decks the lords of Raghu's line.
Each circumstance and look relate:
Tell Ráma's form and speech, and gait."

"Thy fear and doubt," he cried, "dispelled,
Hear, lady, what mine eyes beheld.
Hear the imperial signs that grace
The glory of Ikshváku's race.
With moon-bright face and lotus eyes,
Most beautiful and good and wise,
With sun-like glory round his head,
Long-suffering as the earth we tread,
He from all foes his realm defends.
Yea, o'er the world his care extends.
He follows right in all his ways,
And ne'er from royal duty strays.

He knows the lore that strengthens kings;
His heart to truth and honour clings.
Each grace and gift of form and mind
Adorns that prince of human kind;
And virtues like his own endue
His brother ever firm and true.
O'er all the land they roamed distraught,
And thee with vain endeavour sought,
Until at length their wandering feet
Trod wearily our wild retreat.
Our banished king Sugríva spied
The princes from the mountain side.
By his command I sought the pair
And led them to our monarch there.
Thus Ráma and Sugríva met,
And joined the bonds that knit them yet,
When each besought the other's aid,
And friendship and alliance made.
An arrow launched from Ráma's bow
Laid Báli dead, Sugríva's foe.
Then by commandment of our lord
The Vánar hosts each land explored.
We reached the coast: I crossed the sea
And found my way at length to thee."

CANTO

XXXVI

Ráma's Ring

"Receive," he cried, "this precious ring,
Sure token from thy lord the king:
The golden ring he wont to wear:
See, Ráma's name engraven there."
Then, as she took the ring he showed,
The tears that spring of rapture flowed.

She seemed to touch the hand that sent
The dearly valued ornament,
And with her heart again at ease,
Replied in gentle words like these:
"O thou, whose soul no fears deter,
Wise, brave, and faithful messenger!
And hast thou dared, o'er wave and foam,
To seek me in the giants' home?
In thee, true messenger, I find
The noblest of thy woodland kind.
Who couldst, unmoved by terror, brook
On Rávaṇ, king of fiends, to look.

Now may we commune here as friends,
For he whom royal Ráma sends
Must needs be one in danger tried,
A valiant, wise, and faithful guide.
Say, is it well with Ráma still?
Lives Lakshmaṇ yet untouched by ill?
Then why should Ráma's hand be slow
To free his consort from her woe?
Why spare to burn, in search of me,
The land encircled by the sea?
Can Bharat send no army out
With banners, cars and battle shout?
Cannot thy king Sugríva lend
His legions to assist his friend?"

His hands upon his head he laid
And thus again his answer made:
"Not yet has Ráma learnt where lies
His lady of the lotus eyes,
Or he like Indra from the sky
To Śachí's aid, to thee would fly.
Soon will he hear the tale, and then,
Roused to revenge, the lord of men
Will to the giants' island lead
Fierce myriads of the woodland breed,
Bridging his conquering way, and make
The town a ruin for thy sake.
Believe my words, sweet dame; I swear

By roots and fruit, my woodland fare,
By Meru's peak and Vindhya's chain,
And Mandar of the Milky Main,
Soon shalt thou see thy lord, though now
He waits upon Praśravaṇ's brow,
Come glorious as the breaking morn,
Like Indra on Airávat borne.
For thee he looks with longing eyes;
The wood his scanty food supplies.
For thee his brow is pale and worn,
For thee are meat and wine forsworn.
Thine image in his heart he keeps,
For thee by night he wakes and weeps.
Or if perchance his eyes he close
And win brief respite from his woes,
E'en then the name of Sítá slips
In anguish from his murmuring lips.
If lovely flowers or fruit he sees,
Which women love, upon the trees,
To thee, to thee his fancy flies.
And 'Sítá! O my love!' he cries."

CANTO
XXXVII

Sítá's Speech

"Thou bringest me," she cried again,
  "A mingled draught of bliss and pain:
  Bliss, that he wears me in his heart,
Pain, that he wakes and weeps apart,
O, see how Fate is king of all,
Now lifts us high, now bids us fall,
And leads a captive bound with cord
The meanest slave, the proudest lord,
Thus even now Fate's stern decree

Has struck with grief my lord and me.
Say, how shall Ráma reach the shore
Of sorrow's waves that rise and roar,
A shipwrecked sailor, well nigh drowned
In the wild sea that foams around?
When will he smite the demon down,
Lay low in dust the giants' town,
And, glorious from his foes' defeat,
His wife, his long-lost Sítá, meet?
Go, bid him speed to smite his foes
Before the year shall reach its close.
Ten months are fled but two remain,
Then Rávan's captive must be slain.
Oft has Vibhishan, just and wise,
Besought him to restore his prize.
But deaf is Rávan's senseless ear:
His brother's rede he will not hear.
Vibhishan's daughter loves me well:
From her I learnt the tale I tell.
Avindhya prudent, just, and old,
The giant's fall has oft foretold;
But Fate impels him to despise
His word on whom he most relies.
In Ráma's love I rest secure,
For my fond heart is true and pure,
And him, my noblest lord, I deem
In valour, power, and might supreme."

As from her eyes the waters ran,
The Vánar chief again began:
"Yea, Ráma, when he hears my tale,
Will with our hosts these walls assail.
Or I myself, O Queen, this day
Will bear thee from the fiend away,
Will lift thee up, and take thee hence
To him thy refuge and defence;
Will take thee in my arms, and flee
To Ráma far beyond the sea;
Will place thee on Praśravan hill
Where Raghu's son is waiting still."

"How canst thou bear me hence?" she cried,
"The way is long, the sea is wide.
To bear my very weight would be
A task too hard for one like thee."

Swift rose before her startled eyes
The Vánar in his native size,
Like Mandar's hill or Meru's height,
Encircled with a blaze of light.
"O come," he cried, "thy fears dispel,
Nor doubt that I will bear thee well.
Come, in my strength and care confide,
And sit in joy by Ráma's side."

Again she spake: "I know thee now,
Brave, resolute, and strong art thou;
In glory like the Lord of Fire
With storm-swift feet which naught may tire
But yet with thee I may not fly:
For, borne so swiftly through the sky,
Mine eyes would soon grow faint and dim,
My dizzy brain would reel and swim,
My yielding arms relax their hold,
And I in terror uncontrolled
Should fall into the raging sea
Where hungry sharks would feed on me.
Nor can I touch, of free accord,
The limbs of any save my lord.
If, by the giant forced away,
In his enfolding arms I lay,
Not mine, O Vánar, was the blame;
What could I do, a helpless dame?
Go, to my lord my message bear,
And bid him end my long despair."

Again the Vánar chief replied,
With her wise answer satisfied:
"Well hast thou said: thou canst not brave
The rushing wind, the roaring wave.
Thy woman's heart would sink with fear
Before the ocean shore were near.
And for thy dread lest limb of thine
Should for a while be touched by mine,
The modest fear is worthy one
Whose cherished lord is Raghu's son.
Yet when I sought to bear thee hence
I spoke the words of innocence,
Impelled to set the captive free
By friendship for thy lord and thee.
But if with me thou wilt not try
The passage of the windy sky,
Give me a gem that I may show,
Some token which thy lord may know."

Again the Maithil lady spoke,
While tears and sobs her utterance broke:
"The surest of all signs is this,
To tell the tale of vanished bliss.
Thus in my name to Ráma speak:
"Remember Chitrakúṭa's peak
And the green margin of the rill
That flows beside that pleasant hill,
Where thou and I together strayed
Delighting in the tangled shade.
There on the grass I sat with thee
And laid my head upon thy knee.

There came a greedy crow and pecked
The meat I waited to protect
And, heedless of the clods I threw,
About my head in circles flew,
Until by darling hunger pressed
He boldly pecked me on the breast.
I ran to thee in rage and grief
And prayed for vengeance on the thief.
Then Ráma from his slumber rose
And smiled with pity at my woes.
Upon my bleeding breast he saw
The scratches made by beak and claw.
He laid an arrow on his bow,
And launched it at the shameless crow.
That shaft, with magic power endued,
The bird, where'er he flew, pursued,
Till back to Raghu's son he fled
And bent at Ráma's feet his head.
Couldst thou for me with anger stirred
Launch that dire shaft upon a bird,
And yet canst pardon him who stole
The darling of thy heart and soul?
Rise up, O bravest of the brave,
And come in all thy might to save.
Come with the thunders of thy bow,
And smite to earth the Rákshas foe."

She ceased; and from her glorious hair
She took a gem that sparkled there
A token which her husband's eyes
With eager love would recognize.
His head the Vánar envoy bent
In low obeisance reverent.
And on his finger bound the gem
She loosened from her diadem.

[I omit two Cantos of dialogue. Sítá tells Hanumán again to convey her message to Ráma and bid him hasten to rescue her. Hanumán replies as before that there is no one on earth equal to Ráma, who will soon come and destroy Rávan. There is not a new idea in the two Cantos: all is reiteration.]

XLI

The Ruin of the Grove

Dismissed with every honour due
The Vánar from the spot withdrew.
Then joyous thought the Wind-God's son:
"The mighty task is wellnigh done.
The three expedients I must leave;
The fourth alone can I achieve.
These dwellers in the giants' isle
No arts of mine can reconcile.
I cannot bribe: I cannot sow
Dissension mid the Rákshas foe.
Arts, gifts, address, these fiends despise;
But force shall yet their king chastise.
Perchance he may relent when all
The bravest of his chieftains fall.
This lovely grove will I destroy,
The cruel Rávan's pride and joy.
The garden where he takes his ease
Mid climbing plants and flowery trees
That lift their proud tops to the skies,
Dear to the tyrant as his eyes.
Then will he rouse in wrath, and lead
His legions with the car and steed
And elephants in long array,
And seek me thirsty for the fray.
The Rákshas legions will I meet,
And all his bravest host defeat;
Then, glorious from the bloody plain,
Turn to my lord the king again."

Then every lovely tree that bore
Fair blossoms, from the soil he tore,

Till each green bough that lent its shade
To singing birds on earth was laid.
The wilderness he left a waste,
The fountains shattered and defaced:
O'erthrew and levelled with the ground
Each shady seat and pleasure-mound.
Each arbour clad with climbing bloom,
Each grotto, cell, and picture room,
Each lawn by beast and bird enjoyed,
Each walk and terrace was destroyed.
And all the place that was so fair
Was left a ruin wild and bare,
As if the fury of the blast
Or raging fire had o'er it passed.

CANTO

XLII

The Giants Roused

The cries of startled birds, the sound
Of tall trees crashing to the ground,
Struck with amaze each giant's ear,
And filled the isle with sudden fear.
Then, wakened by the crash and cries,
The fierce shefiends unclosed their eyes,
And saw the Vánar where he stood
Amid the devastated wood.
The more to scare them with the view
To size immense the Vánar grew;
And straight the Rákshas warders cried
Janak's daughter terrified
"Whose envoy, whence, and who is he,
Why has he come to talk with thee?
Speak, lady of the lovely eyes,
And let not fear thy joy disguise."

Then thus replied the Maithil dame
Of noble soul and perfect frame.
"Can I discern, with scanty skill,
These fiends who change their forms at will?
'Tis yours to say: your kin you meet;
A serpent knows a serpent's feet.

I weet not who he is: the sight
Has filled my spirit with affright."
Some pressed round Sítá in a ring;
Some bore the story to their king:
"A mighty creature of our race,
In monkey form, has reached the place.
He came within the grove," they cried,
"He stood and talked by Sítá's side,
He comes from Indra's court to her,
Or is Kuvera's messenger;
Or Ráma sent the spy to seek
His consort, and her wrongs to wreak.
His crushing arm, his trampling feet
Have marred and spoiled that dear retreat,
And all the pleasant place which thou
So lovest is a ruin now.
The tree where Sítá sat alone
Is spared where all are overthrown.
Perchance he saved the dame from harm:
Perchance the toil had numbed his arm."

Then flashed the giant's eye with fire
Like that which lights the funeral pyre.
He bade his bravest Kinkars speed

And to his feet the spoiler lead.
Forth from the palace, at his hest,
Twice forty thousand warriors pressed.
Burning for battle, strong and fierce,
With clubs to crush and swords to pierce,
They saw Hanúmán near a porch,
And, thick as moths around a torch,
Rushed on the foe with wild attacks
Of mace and club and battle-axe.

As round him pressed the Rákshas crowd,
The wondrous monkey roared aloud,
That birds fell headlong from the sky:
Then spake he with a mighty cry:
"Long life to Daśaratha's heir,
And Lakshmaṇ, ever-glorious pair!
Long life to him who rules our race,
Preserved by noblest Ráma's grace!
I am the slave of Kośal's king,
Whose wondrous deeds the minstrels sing.
Hanúmán I, the Wind-God's seed:
Beneath this arm the foemen bleed.
I fear not, unapproached in might,
A thousand Rávaṇ's ranged for fight,
Although in furious hands they rear
The hill and tree for sword and spear,
I will, before the giants' eyes,
Their city and their king chastise;
And, having communed with the dame,
Depart in triumph as I came."

At that terrific roar and yell
The heart of every giant fell.
But still their king's command they feared
And pressed around with arms upreared.
Beside the porch a club was laid:
The Vánar caught it up, and swayed
The weapon round his head, and slew
The foremost of the Rákshas crew.
Thus Indra vanquished, thousand-eyed,
The Daityas who the Gods defied.
Then on the porch Hanúmán sprang,
And loud his shout of triumph rang.
The giants looked upon the dead,
And turning to their monarch fled.
And Rávaṇ with his spirit wrought
To frenzy by the tale they brought,
Urged to the fight Prahasta's son,
Of all his chiefs the mightiest one.

The Ruin of The Temple

The Wind-God's son a temple scaled
    Which, by his fury unassailed,
    High as the hill of Meru, stood
Amid the ruins of the wood;
And in his fury thundered out
Again his haughty battle-shout:
"I am the slave of Kośal's King
Whose wondrous deeds the minstrels sing."
Forth hurried, by that shout alarmed,
The warders of the temple armed
With every weapon haste supplied,
And closed him in on every side,
With bands that strove to pierce and strike
With shaft and axe and club and pike.
Then from its base the Vánar tore
A pillar with the weight it bore.
Against the wall the mass he dashed,
And forth the flames in answer flashed,
That wildly ran o'er roofs and wall
In hungry rage consuming all.
He whirled the pillar round his head
And struck a hundred giants dead.
Then high upheld on air he rose
And called in thunder to his foes:
"A thousand Vánar chiefs like me
Roam at their will o'er land and sea,
Terrific might we all possess:
Our stormy speed is limitless.
And all, unconquered in the fray,
Our king Sugríva's word obey.
Backed by his bravest myriads, he

293

Our warrior lord will cross the sea.
Then Lanká's lofty towers, and all
Your hosts and Rávan's self shall fall.
None shall be left unslaughtered; none
Who braves the wrath of Raghu's son."

CANTO

XLIV

Jambumáli's Death

Then Jambumáli, pride and boast
    For valour of the Rákshas host,
    Prahasta's son supremely brave,
Obeyed the hest that Rávan gave:
Fierce warrior with terrific teeth,
With saguine robes and brilliant wreath.
A bow like Indra's own, and store

Of glittering shafts the chieftain bore.
And ever as the string he tried
The weapon with a roar replied,
Loud as the crashing thunder sent
By him who rules the firmament.
Soon as the foeman came in view
Borne on a car which asses drew,
The Vánar chieftain mighty-voiced
Shouted in triumph and rejoiced.
Prahasta's son his bow-string drew,
And swift the winged arrows flew,
One in the face the Vánar smote,
Another quivered in his throat.
Ten from the deadly weapon sent
His brawny arms and shoulders rent.
Then as he felt each galling shot
The Vánar's rage waxed fiercely hot.

He looked, and saw a mass of stone
That lay before his feet o'erthrown.
The mighty block he raised and threw,
And crashing through the air it flew.
But Jambumáli shunned the blow,
And rained fresh arrows from his bow.
The Vánar's limbs were red with gore:
A Sál tree from the earth he tore,
And, ere he hurled it undismayed,
Above his head the missile swayed.
But shafts from Jambumáli's bow
Cut through it ere his hand could throw.
And thigh and arm and chest and side
With streams of rushing blood were dyed.
Still unsubdued though wounded oft
The shattered trunk he raised aloft,
And down with well-directed aim
On Jambumáli's chest it came.
There crushed upon the trampled grass
He lay an undistinguished mass,
The foeman's eye no more could see
His head or chest or arm or knee.
And bow and car and steeds and store
Of glittering shafts were seen no more.

When Jambumáli's death he heard,
King Rávaṇ's heart with rage was stirred
And forth his general's sons he sent,
For power and might preeminent.

The Seven Defeated

Forth went the seven in brave attire,
In glory brilliant as the fire,
Impetuous chiefs with massive bows,
The quellers of a host of foes:
Trained from their youth in martial lore,
And masters of the arms they bore:
Each emulous and fiercely bold,
And banners wrought with glittering gold
Waved o'er their chariots, drawn at speed
By coursers of the noblest breed.
On through the ruins of the grove
At Hanumán they fiercely drove,
And from the ponderous bows they strained
A shower of deadly arrows rained.
Then scarce was seen the Vánar's form
Enveloped in the arrowy storm.
So stands half veiled the Mountains' King
When rainy clouds about him cling.
By nimble turn, by rapid bound
He shunned the shafts that rained around,
Eluding, as in air he rose,
The rushing chariots of his foes.
The mighty Vánar undismayed
Amid his archer foemen played,
As plays the frolic wind on high
Mid bow-armed clouds that fill the sky.
He raised a mighty roar and yell
That fear on all the army fell,
And then, his warrior soul aglow
With fury, rushed upon the foe,

Some with his open hand he beat
To death and trampled with his feet;
Some with fierce nails he rent and slew,
And others with his fists o'erthrew;
Some with his legs, as on he rushed,
Some with his bulky chest he crushed;
While some struck senseless by his roar
Dropped on the ground and breathed no more,
The remnant, seized with sudden dread,
Turned from the grove and wildly fled.
The trampled earth was thickly strown
With steed and car and flag o'erthrown,
And the red blood in rivers flowed
From slaughtered fiends o'er path and road.

CANTO

XLVI

The Captains

Mad with the rage of injured pride
King Rávaṇ summoned to his side
The valiant five who led his host,
Supreme in war and honoured most.
"Go forth," he cried, "with car and steed,
And to my feet this monkey lead,
But watch each chance of time and place
To seize this thing of silvan race.
For from his wondrous exploits he
No monkey of the woods can be,

But some new kind of creature meant
To work us woe, by Indra sent.
Gandharvas, Nágas, and the best
Of Yakshas have our might confessed.

Have we not challenged and subdued
The whole celestial multitude?
Yet will you not, if you are wise,
A chief of monkey race despise.
For I myself have Báli known,
And King Sugríva's power I own.
But none of all their woodland throng
Was half so terrible and strong."

Obedient to the words he spake
They hastened forth the foe to take.
Swift were the cars whereon they rode,
And bright their weapons flashed and glowed.
They saw: they charged in wild career
With sword and mace and axe and spear.
From Durdhar's bow five arrows sped
And quivered in the Vánar's head.
He rose and roared: the fearful sound
Made all the region echo round.
Then from above his weight he threw
On Durdhar's car that near him drew.
The weight that came with lightning speed
Crushed pole and axle, car and steed.
It shattered Durdhar's head and neck,
And left him lifeless mid the wreck.
Yúpáksha saw the warrior die,
And Virúpáksha heard his cry,
And, mad for vengeance for the slain,
They charged their Vánar foe again.
He rose in air: they onward pressed
And fiercely smote him on the breast.
In vain they struck his iron frame:
With eagle swoop to earth he came,
Tore from the ground a tree that grew
Beside him, and the demons slew.
Then Bhásakama raised his spear,
And Praghas with a laugh drew near,
And, maddened at the sight, the two
Against the undaunted Vánar flew.
As from his wounds the torrents flowed,
Like a red sun the Vánar showed.

He turned, a mountain peak to seize
With all its beasts and snakes and trees.
He hurled it on the pair: and they
Crushed, overwhelmed, beneath it lay.

CANTO

XLVII

The Death of Aksha

But Rávaṇ, as his fury burned,
His eyes on youthful Aksha turned,
Who rose impetuous at his glance
And shouted for his bow and lance.
He rode upon a glorious car
That shot the light of gems afar.
His pennon waved mid glittering gold
And bright the wheels with jewels rolled,
By long and fierce devotion won
That car was splendid as the sun.
With rows of various weapons stored;
And thought-swift horses whirled their lord
Racing along the earth, or rose
High through the clouds whene'er he chose.
Then fierce and fearful war between
The Vánar and the fiend was seen.
The Gods and Asurs stood amazed,
And on the wondrous combat gazed.
A cry from earth rose long and shrill,
The wind was hushed, the sun grew chill.
The thunder bellowed from the sky,
And troubled ocean roared reply.
Thrice Aksha strained his dreadful bow,
Thrice smote his arrow on the foe,
And with full streams of crimson bled
Three gashes in the Vánar's head.

Then rose Hanúmán in the air
To shun the shafts no life could bear.
But Aksha in his car pursued,
And from on high the fight renewed
With storm of arrows, thick as hail
When angry clouds some hill assail.
Impatient of that arrowy shower
The Vánar chief put forth his power,
Again above his chariot rose
And smote him with repeated blows.
Terrific came each deadly stroke:
Breast neck and arm and back he broke;
And Aksha fell to earth, and lay
With all his life-blood drained away.

Hanumán Captured

To Indrajít the bold and brave
      The giant king his mandate gave:
      "O trained in warlike science, best
In arms of all our mightiest,
Whose valour in the conflict shown
To Asurs and to Gods is known,
The Kinkars whom I sent are slain,
And Jambumálí and his train;
The lords who led our giant bands
Have fallen by the monkey's hands;
With shattered cars the ground is spread,
And Aksha lies amid the dead.
Thou art my best and bravest: go,
Unmatched in power, and slay the foe."

He heard the hest: he bent his head;
Athirst for battle forth he sped.
Four tigers fierce, of tawny hue,
With fearful teeth, his chariot drew.

Hanúmán heard his strong bow clang,
And swiftly from the earth he sprang,
While weak and ineffective fell
The archer's shafts though pointed well.
The Rákshas saw that naught might kill
The wondrous foe who mocked his skill,
And launched a magic shaft to throw
A binding spell about his foe.
Forth flew the shaft: the mystic charm
Stayed his swift feet and numbed his arm,
Through all his frame he felt the spell,
And motionless to earth he fell.
Nor would the reverent Vánar loose
The bonds that bound him as a noose.
He knew that Brahmá's self had charmed
The weapon that his might disarmed.

They saw him helpless on the ground,
And all the giants pressed around,
And bonds of hemp and bark were cast
About his limbs to hold him fast.
They drew the ropes round feet and wrists;
They beat him with their hands and fists,
And dragged him as they strained the cord
With shouts of triumph to their lord.

Rávan

On the fierce king Hanúmán turned
His angry eyes that glowed and burned.
He saw him decked with wealth untold
Of diamond and pearl and gold,
And priceless was each wondrous gem
That sparkled in his diadem.
About his neck rich chains were twined,
The best that fancy e'er designed,
And a fair robe with pearls bestrung
Down from his mighty shoulders hung.
Ten heads he reared, as Mandar's hill
Lifts woody peaks which tigers fill,
Bright were his eyes, and bright, beneath,
The flashes of his awful teeth.
His brawny arms of wondrous size
Were decked with rings and scented dyes.
His hands like snakes with five long heads
Descending from their mountain beds.
He sat upon a crystal throne
Inlaid with wealth of precious stone,
Whereon, of noblest work, was set
A gold-embroidered coverlet.
Behind the monarch stood the best
Of beauteous women gaily dressed,
And each her giant master fanned,
Or waved a chourie in her hand.
Four noble courtiers wise and good
In counsel, near the monarch stood,
As the four oceans ever stand
About the sea-encompassed land.
Still, though his heart with rage was fired,

The Vánar marvelled and admired:
"O what a rare and wondrous sight!
What beauty, majesty, and might!
All regal pomp combines to grace
This ruler of the Rákshas race.
He, if he scorned not right and law,
Might guide the world with tempered awe:
Yea, Indra and the Gods on high
Might on his saving power rely."

CANTO

L

Prahasta's Questions

Then fierce the giant's fury blazed
    As on Hanúmán's form he gazed,
    And shaken by each wild surmise
He spake aloud with flashing eyes:
"Can this be Nandi standing here,
The mighty one whom all revere?
Who once on high Kailása's hill
Pronounced the curse that haunts me still?
Or is the woodland creature one
Of Asur race, or Bali's son?
The wretch with searching question try:
Learn who he is, and whence; and why
He marred the glory of the grove,
And with my captains fiercely strove."

Prahasta heard his lord's behest,
And thus the Vánar chief addressed:
"O monkey stranger be consoled:
Fear not, and let thy heart be bold.
If thou by Indra's mandate sent
Thy steps to Lanká's isle hast bent,

With fearless words the cause explain,
And freedom thou shalt soon regain.
Or if thou comest as a spy
Despatched by Vishṇu in the sky,
Or sent by Yáma, or the Lord
Of Riches, hast our town explored;
Proved by the prowess thou hast shown
No monkey save in form alone;
Speak boldly all the truth, and be
Released from bonds, unharmed and free.
But falsehood spoken to our king
Swift punishment of death will bring."

He ceased: the Vánar made reply;
"Not Indra's messenger am I,
Nor came I hither to fulfil
Kuvera's hest or Vishṇu's will.
I stand before the giants here
A Vánar e'en as I appear.
I longed to see the king: 'twas hard
To win my way through gate and guard.
And so to gain my wish I laid
In ruin that delightful shade.
No fiend, no God of heavenly kind
With bond or chain these limbs may bind.
The Eternal Sire himself of old
Vouchsafed the boon that makes me bold,
From Brahmá's magic shaft released
I knew the captor's power had ceased,
The fancied bonds I freely brooked,
And thus upon the king have looked.
My way to Lanká have I won,
A messenger from Raghu's son."

Hanumán's Reply

"My king Sugríva greets thee fair,
And bids me thus his rede declare.
Son of the God of Wind, by name
Hanumán, to this isle I came.
To set the Maithil lady free
I crossed the barrier of the sea.
I roamed in search of her and found
Her weeping in that lovely ground.
Thou in the lore of duty trained,
Who hast by stern devotion gained
This wondrous wealth and power and fame
Shouldst fear to wrong another's dame.
Hear thou my counsel, and be wise:
No fiend, no dweller in the skies
Can bear the shafts by Lakshman shot,
Or Ráma when his wrath is hot.
O Giant King, repent the crime
And soothe him while there yet is time.
Now be the Maithil queen restored
Uninjured to her sorrowing lord.
Soon wilt thou rue thy dire mistake:
She is no woman but a snake,
Whose very deadly bite will be
The ruin of thy house and thee.
Thy pride has led thy thoughts astray,
That fancy not a hand may slay
The monarch of the giants, screened
From mortal blow of God and fiend.
Sugríva still thy death may be:
No Yaksha, fiend, or God is he,
And Ráma from a woman springs,

The mortal seed of mortal kings.
O think how Báli fell subdued;
Think on thy slaughtered multitude.
Respect those brave and strong allies;
Consult thy safety, and be wise.
I, even I, no helper need
To overthrow, with car and steed,
Thy city Lanká half divine:
The power but not the will is mine.
For Raghu's son, before his friend
The Vánar monarch, swore to end
With his own conquering arm the life
Of him who stole his darling wife.
Turn, and be wise, O Rávaṇ turn;
Or thou wilt see thy Lanká burn,
And with thy wives, friends, kith and kin
Be ruined for thy senseless sin."

CANTO
LII

Vibhishan's Speech

Then Rávaṇ spake with flashing eye:
"Hence with the Vánar: let him die."
Vibhishan heard the stern behest,
And pondered in his troubled breast;
Then, trained in arts that soothe and please
Addressed the king in words like these:

"Revoke, my lord, thy fierce decree,
And hear the words I speak to thee.
Kings wise and noble ne'er condemn
To death the envoys sent to them.
Such deed the world's contempt would draw
On him who breaks the ancient law.

Observe the mean where justice lies,
And spare his life but still chastise."

Then forth the tyrant's fury broke,
And thus in angry words he spoke:
"O hero, when the wicked bleed
No sin or shame attends the deed.
The Vánar's blood must needs be spilt,
The penalty of heinous guilt."

Again Vibhishaṇ made reply:
"Nay, hear me, for he must not die.
Hear the great law the wise declare:
"Thy foeman's envoy thou shalt spare."
'Tis true he comes an open foe:
'Tis true his hands have wrought us woe,
But law allows thee, if thou wilt,
A punishment to suit the guilt.
The mark of shame, the scourge, the brand,
The shaven head, the wounded hand.
Yea, were the Vánar envoy slain,
Where, King of giants, were the gain?
On them alone, on them who sent
The message, be the punishment.
For spake he well or spake he ill,
He spake obedient to their will,
And, if he perish, who can bear
Thy challenge to the royal pair?
Who, cross the ocean and incite
Thy death-doomed enemies to fight?"

Observe the mean, who flies the line
And speaks his ire-inspired disdain,

They forth the giant's tail to smoke,
And thus in angry words he spoke,
"O heinous offender, who dared
No sense of shame or dread displayed,
They,
The penalty of heinous guilt.

CANTO
LIII

The Punishment

K ing Rávaṇ, by his pleading moved,
The counsel of the chief approved:
"Thy words are wise and true: to kill
An envoy would beseem us ill.
Yet must we for his crime invent
Some fitting mode of punishment.
The tail, I fancy, is the part
Most cherished by a monkey's heart.
Make ready: set his tail aflame,
And let him leave us as he came,
And thus disfigured and disgraced
Back to his king and people haste."

The giants heard their monarch's speech;
And, filled with burning fury, each
Brought strips of cotton cloth, and round
The monkey's tail the bandage wound.
As round his tail the bands they drew
His mighty form dilating grew
Vast as the flame that bursts on high
Where trees are old and grass is dry.
Each band and strip they soaked in oil,
And set on fire the twisted coil.
Delighted as they viewed the blaze,
The cruel demons stood at gaze:
And mid loud drums and shells rang out
The triumph of their joyful shout.
They pressed about him thick and fast
As through the crowded streets he passed,
Observing with attentive care
Each rich and wondrous structure there,

Still heedless of the eager cry
That rent the air, The spy! the spy!

Some to the captive lady ran,
And thus in joyous words began:
"That copper-visaged monkey, he
Who in the garden talked with thee,
Through Lanká's town is led a show,
And round his tail the red flames glow."
The mournful news the lady heard
That with fresh grief her bosom stirred.
Swift to the kindled fire she went
And prayed before it reverent:
"If I my husband have obeyed,
And kept the ascetic vows I made,
Free, ever free, from stain and blot,
O spare the Vánar; harm him not."

Then leapt on high the flickering flame
And shone in answer to the dame.
The pitying fire its rage forbore:
The Vánar felt the heat no more.
Then, to minutest size reduced,
The bonds that bound his limbs he loosed,
And, freed from every band and chain,
Rose to his native size again.
He seized a club of ponderous weight
That lay before him by the gate,
Rushed at the fiends that hemmed him round,
And laid them lifeless on the ground.
Through Lanká's town again he strode,
And viewed each street and square and road,—
Still wreathed about with harmless blaze,
A sun engarlanded with rays.

The Burning of Lanká

"What further deed remains to do
To vex the Rákshas king anew?
The beauty of his grove is marred,
Killed are the bravest of his guard.
The captains of his host are slain;
But forts and palaces remain,
Swift is the work and light the toil
Each fortress of the foe to spoil."

Reflecting thus, his tail ablaze
As through the cloud red lightning plays,
He scaled the palaces and spread
The conflagration where he sped.
From house to house he hurried on,
And the wild flames behind him shone.
Each mansion of the foe he scaled,
And furious fire its roof assailed
Till all the common ruin shared:
Vibhishaṇ's house alone was spared.
From blazing pile to pile he sprang,
And loud his shout of triumph rang,
As roars the doomsday cloud when all
The worlds in dissolution fall.
The friendly wind conspired to fan
The hungry flames that leapt and ran,
And spreading in their fury caught
The gilded walls with pearls inwrought,
Till each proud palace reeled and fell
As falls a heavenly citadel.

Loud was the roar the demons raised
Mid walls that split and beams that blazed,
As each with vain endeavour strove
To stay the flames in house or grove.
The women, with dishevelled hair,
Flocked to the roofs in wild despair,
Shrieked out for succour, wept aloud,
And fell, like lightning from a cloud.
He saw the flames ascend and curl
Round turkis, diamond, and pearl,
While silver floods and molten gold
From ruined wall and latice rolled.
As fire grows fiercer as he feeds
On wood and grass and crackling reeds,
So Hanúmán the ruin eyed
With fury still unsatisfied.

CANTO
LV

Fear for Sítá

B ut other thoughts resumed their sway
When Lanká's town in ruin lay;
And, as his bosom felt their weight
He stood a while to meditate.
"What have I done?", he thought with shame,
"Destroyed the town with hostile flame.
O happy they whose firm control
Checks the wild passion of the soul;
Who on the fires of anger throw
The cooling drops that check their glow.
But woe is me, whom wrath could lead
To do this senseless shameless deed.
The town to fire and death I gave,

Nor thought of her I came to save,—
Doomed by my own rash folly, doomed
To perish in the flames consumed.
If I, when anger drove me wild,
Have caused the death of Janak's child,
The kindled flame shall end my woe,
Or the deep fires that burn below,
Or my forsaken corse shall be
Food for the monsters of the sea.
How can I meet Sugríva? how
Before the royal brothers bow,—
I whose rash deed has madly foiled,
The noble work in which we toiled?
Or has her own bright virtue shed
Its guardian influence round her head?
She lives untouched,—the peerless dame;
Flame has no fury for the flame.
The very fire would ne'er consent
To harm a queen so excellent,—
The high-souled Ráma's faithful wife,
Protected by her holy life.
She lives, she lives. Why should I fear
For one whom Raghu's sons hold dear?
Has not the pitying fire that spared
The Vánar for the lady cared?"

Such were his thoughts: he pondered long,
And fear grew faint and hope grew strong.
Then round him heavenly voices rang,
And, sweetly tuned, his praises sang:
"O glorious is the exploit done
By Hanumán the Wind-God's son.
The flames o'er Lanká's city rise:
The giants' home in ruin lies.
O'er roof and wall the fires have spread,
Nor harmed a hair of Sítá's head."

Mount Arishta

He looked upon the burning waste,
Then sought the queen in joyous haste,
With words of hope consoled her heart,
And made him ready to depart.

He scaled Arishṭa's glorious steep
Whose summits beetled o'er the deep.
The woods in varied beauty dressed
Hung like a garland round his crest,
And clouds of ever changing hue
A robe about his shoulders threw.
On him the rays of morning fell
To wake the hill they loved so well,
And bid unclose those splendid eyes
That glittered in his mineral dyes.
He woke to hear the music made
By thunders of the white cascade,
While every laughing rill that sprang
From crag to crag its carol sang.
For arms, he lifted to the stars
His towering stems of Deodárs,
And morning heard his pealing call
In tumbling brook and waterfall.
He trembled when his woods were pale
And bowed beneath the autumn gale,
And when his vocal reeds were stirred
His melancholy moan was heard.

Far down against the mountain's feet
The Vánar heard the wild waves beat;
Then turned his glances to the north.

313

Sprang from the peak and bounded forth,
The mountain felt the fearful shock
And trembled through his mass of rock.
The tallest trees were crushed and rent
And headlong to the valley sent,
And as the rocking shook each cave
Loud was the roar the lions gave.
Forth from the shaken cavern came
Fierce serpents with their tongues aflame;
And every Yaksha, wild with dread,
And Kinnar and Gandharva, fled.

CANTO
LVII

Hanumán's Return

Still, like a winged mountain, he
Sprang forward through the airy sea,
And rushing through the ether drew
The clouds to follow as he flew,
Through the great host around him spread,
Grey, golden, dark, and white, and red.
Now in a sable cloud immersed,
Now from its gloomy pall he burst,
Like the bright Lord of Stars concealed
A moment, and again revealed.
Sunábha passed, he neared the coast
Where waited still the Vánar host.
They heard a rushing in the skies,
And lifted up their wondering eyes.
His wild triumphant shout they knew
That louder still and louder grew,
And Jámbaván with eager voice
Called on the Vánars to rejoice:
"Look he returns, the Wind-God's son,

And full success his toils have won;
Triumphant is the shout that comes
Like music of a thousand drums."

Up sprang the Vánars from the ground
And listened to the wondrous sound
Of hurtling arm and thigh as through
The region of the air he flew,
Loud as the wind, when tempests rave,
Roars in the prison of the cave.
From crag to crag, from height to height;
They bounded in their mad delight,
And when he touched the mountain's crest,
With reverent welcome round him pressed.
They brought him of their woodland fruits,
They brought him of the choicest roots,
And laughed and shouted in their glee
The noblest of their chiefs to see.
Nor Hanumán delayed to greet
Sage Jámbaván with reverence meet;
To Angad and the chiefs he bent
For age and rank preëminent,
And briefly spoke: "These eyes have seen,
These lips addressed, the Maithil queen."
They sat beneath the waving trees,
And Angad spoke in words like these:
"O noblest of the Vánar kind
For valour power and might combined,
To thee triumphant o'er the foe
Our hopes, our lives and all we owe.
O faithful heart in perils tried,

Which toil nor fear could turn aside,
Thy deed the lady will restore,
And Ráma's heart will ache no more."

The Feast of Honey

They rose in air: the region grew
Dark with their shadow as they flew.
Swift to a lovely grove they came
That rivalled heavenly Nandan's fame;
Where countless bees their honey stored,—
The pleasance of the Vánars' lord,
To every creature fenced and barred,
Which Dadhimukh was set to guard,
A noble Vánar, brave and bold,
Sugríva's uncle lofty-souled.
To Angad came with one accord
The Vánars, and besought their lord
That they those honeyed stores might eat
That made the grove so passing sweet.

He gave consent: they sought the trees
Thronged with innumerable bees.
They rifled all the treasured store,
And ate the fruit the branches bore,
And still as they prolonged the feast
Their merriment and joy increased.
Drunk with the sweets, they danced and bowed,
They wildly sang, they laughed aloud,
Some climbed and sprang from tree to tree,
Some sat and chattered in their glee.
Some scaled the trees which creepers crowned,
And rained the branches to the ground.
There with loud laugh a Vánar sprang
Close to his friend who madly sang,
In doleful mood another crept
To mix his tears with one who wept.

Then Dadhimukh with fury viewed
The intoxicated multitude.
He looked upon the rifled shade,
And all the ruin they had made;
Then called with angry voice, and strove
To save the remnant of the grove.
But warning cries and words were spurned,
And angry taunt and threat returned.
Then fierce and wild contention rose:
With furious words he mingled blows.
They by no shame or fear withheld,
By drunken mood and ire impelled,
Used claws, and teeth, and hands, and beat
The keeper under trampling feet.

[Three Cantos consisting of little but repetitions are omitted. Dadhimukh escapes from the infuriated monkeys and hastens to Sugríva to report their misconduct. Sugríva infers that Hanumán and his band have been successful in their search, and that the exuberance of spirits and the mischief complained of, are but the natural expression of their joy. Dadhimukh obtains little sympathy from Sugríva, and is told to return and send the monkeys on with all possible speed.]

CANTO
LXV

The Tidings

O
n to Praśravaṇ's hill they sped
Where blooming trees their branches spread.
To Raghu's sons their heads they bent
And did obeisance reverent.
Then to their king, by Angad led,
Each Vánar chieftain bowed his head;
And Hanumán the brave and bold
His tidings to the monarch told;

But first in Ráma's hand he placed
The gem that Sítá's brow had graced:
"I crossed the sea: I searched a while
For Sítá in the giants' isle.
I found her vext with taunt and threat
By demon guards about her set.
Her tresses twined in single braid,
On the bare earth her limbs were laid.
Sad were her eyes: her cheeks were pale
As shuddering flowers in winter's gale.
I stood beside the weeping dame,
And gently whispered Ráma's name:
With cheering words her grief consoled,
And then the whole adventure told.
She weeps afar beyond the sea,
And her true heart is still with thee.
She gave a sign that thou wouldst know,
She bids thee think upon the crow,
And bright mark pressed upon her brow
When none was nigh but she and thou.
She bids thee take this precious stone,
The sea-born gem thou long hast known.
"And I," she said, "will dull the sting
Of woe by gazing on the ring.
One little month shall I sustain
This life oppressed with woe and pain:
And when the month is ended, I
The giants' prey must surely die.'"

CANTO
LXVI

Ráma's Speech

There ceased the Vánar: Ráma pressed
The treasured jewel to his breast,
And from his eyes the waters broke
As to the Vánar king he spoke:
"As o'er her babe the mother weeps,
This flood of tears the jewel steeps.
This gem that shone on Sítá's head
Was Janak's gift when we were wed,
And the pure brow that wore it lent
New splendour to the ornament.
This gem, bright offspring of the wave,
The King of Heaven to Janak gave,
Whose noble sacrificial rite
Had filled the God with new delight.
Now, as I gaze upon the prize,
Methinks I see my father's eyes.
Methinks I see before me stand
The ruler of Videha's land.
Methinks mine arms are folded now
Round her who wore it on her brow.
Speak, Hanumán, O say, dear friend,
What message did my darling send?
O speak, and let thy words impart
Their gentle dew to cool my heart.
Ah, 'tis the crown of woe to see
This gem and ask "Where, where is she?"
If for one month her heart be strong,
Her days of life will yet be long.
But I, with naught to lend relief,
This very day must die of grief.
Come, Hanumán, and quickly guide

The mourner to his darling's side.
O lead me—thou hast learnt the way—
I cannot and I will not stay.
How can my gentle love endure,
So timid, delicate, and pure,
The dreadful demons fierce and vile
Who watch her in the guarded isle?
No more the light of beauty shines
From Sítá as she weeps and pines.
But pain and sorrow, cloud on cloud
Her moonlight glory dim and shroud.
O speak, dear Hanumán, and tell
Each word that from her sweet lips fell,
Her words, her words alone can give
The healing balm to make me live."

BOOK

VI

BOOK

IV

Ráma's Speech

The son of Raghu heard, consoled,
The wondrous tale Hanumán told;
And, as his joyous hope grew high,
In friendly words he made reply:

"Behold a mighty task achieved,
Which never heart but his conceived.
Who else across the sea can spring,
Save Váyu and the Feathered King?
Who, pass the portals strong and high
Which Nágas, Gods, and fiends defy,
Where Rávan's hosts their station keep,—
And come uninjured o'er the deep?
By such a deed the Wind-God's son
Good service to the king has done,
And saved from ruin and disgrace
Lakshmaṇ and me and Raghu's race.
Well has he planned and bravely fought,
And with due care my lady sought.
But of the sea I sadly think,
And the sweet hopes that cheered me sink.
How can we cross the leagues of foam
That keep us from the giant's home?
What can the Vánar legions more
Than muster on the ocean shore?"

323

Sugríva's Speech

He ceased: and King Sugríva tried
To calm his grief, and thus replied:
"'Be to thy nobler nature true,
Nor let despair thy soul subdue.
This cloud of causeless woe dispel,
For all as yet has prospered well,
And we have traced thy queen, and know
The dwelling of our Rákshas foe.
Arise, consult: thy task must be
To cast a bridge athwart the sea,
The city of our foe to reach
That crowns the mountain by the beach;

And when our feet that isle shall tread,
Rejoice and deem thy foeman dead.
The sea unbridged, his walls defy
Both fiends and children of the sky,
Though at the fierce battalions' head
Lord Indra's self the onset led.
Yea, victory is thine before
The long bridge touch the farther shore,
So fleet and fierce and strong are these
Who limb them as their fancies please.
Away with grief and sad surmise
That mar the noblest enterprise,
And with their weak suspicion blight
The sage's plan, the hero's might.
Come, this degenerate weakness spurn,
And bid thy dauntless heart return,
For each fair hope by grief is crossed
When those we love are dead or lost.

Arise, O best of those who know,
Arm for the giant's overthrow.
None in the triple world I see
Who in the fight may equal thee;
None who before thy face may stand
And brave the bow that arms thy hand,
Trust to these mighty Vánars: they
With full success thy trust will pay,
When thou shalt reach the robber's hold,
And loving arms round Sítá fold."

CANTO

III

Lanká

He ceased: and Raghu's son gave heed,
Attentive to his prudent rede:
Then turned again, with hope inspired,
To Hanumán, and thus inquired:

"Light were the task for thee, I ween,
To bridge the sea that gleams between
The mainland and the island shore.
Or dry the deep and guide as o'er.
Fain would I learn from thee whose feet
Have trod the stones of every street,
Of fenced Lanká's towers and forts,
And walls and moats and guarded ports,
And castles where the giants dwell,
And battlemented citadel.
O Váyu's son, describe it all,
With palace, fort, and gate, and wall."

He ceased: and, skilled in arts that guide
The eloquent, the chief replied:

"Vast is the city, gay and strong,
Where elephants unnumbered throng,
And countless hosts of Rákshas breed
Stand ready by the car and steed.
Four massive gates, securely barred,
All entrance to the city guard,
With murderous engines fixt to throw
Bolt, arrow, rock to check the foe,
And many a mace with iron head
That strikes at once a hundred dead.
Her golden ramparts wide and high
With massy strength the foe defy,
Where inner walls their rich inlay
Of coral, turkis, pearl display.
Her circling moats are broad and deep,
Where ravening monsters dart and leap.
By four great piers each moat is spanned
Where lines of deadly engines stand.
In sleepless watch at every gate
Unnumbered hosts of giants wait,
And, masters of each weapon, rear
The threatening pike and sword and spear.
My fury hurled those ramparts down,
Filled up the moats that gird the town,
The piers and portals overturned,
And stately Lanká spoiled and burned.
Howe'er we Vánars force our way
O'er the wide seat of Varuṇ's sway,
Be sure that city of the foe
Is doomed to sudden overthrow,
Nay, why so vast an army lead?
Brave Angad, Dwivid good at need,
Fierce Mainda, Panas famed in fight,
And Níla's skill and Nala's might,
And Jámbaván the strong and wise,
Will dare the easy enterprise.
Assailed by these shall Lanká fall
With gate and rampart, tower and wall.
Command the gathering, chief: and they
In happy hour will haste away."

326

The March

He ceased; and spurred by warlike pride
The impetuous son of Raghu cried:
"Soon shall mine arm with wrathful joy
That city of the foe destroy.
Now, chieftain, now collect the host,
And onward to the southern coast!
The sun in his meridian tower
Gives glory to the Vánar power.
The demon lord who stole my queen
By timely flight his life may screen.
She, when she knows her lord is near,
Will cling to hope and banish fear,
Saved like a dying wretch who sips
The drink of Gods with fevered lips.
Arise, thy troops to battle lead:
All happy omens counsel speed.
The Lord of Stars in favouring skies
Bodes glory to our enterprise.
This arm shall slay the fiend; and she,
My consort, shall again be free.

Mine upward-throbbing eye foreshows
The longed-for triumph o'er my foes.
Far in the van be Níla's post,
To scan the pathway for the host,
And let thy bravest and thy best,
A hundred thousand, wait his hest.
Go forth, O warrior Níla, lead
The legions on through wood and mead
Where pleasant waters cool the ground,
And honey, flowers, and fruit abound.

Go, and with timely care prevent
The Rákshas foeman's dark intent.
With watchful troops each valley guard
Ere brooks and fruits and roots be marred
And search each glen and leafy shade
For hostile troops in ambuscade.
But let the weaklings stay behind:
For heroes is our task designed.
Let thousands of the Vánar breed
The vanguard of the armies lead:
Fierce and terrific must it be
As billows of the stormy sea.
There be the hill-huge Gaja's place,
And Gavaya's, strongest of his race,
And, like the bull that leads the herd,
Gaváksha's, by no fears deterred
Let Rishabh, matchless in the might
Of warlike arms, protect our right,
And Gandhamádan next in rank
Defend and guide the other flank.
I, like the God who rules the sky
Borne on Airávat mounted high
On stout Hanúmán's back will ride,
The central host to cheer and guide.
Fierce as the God who rules below,
On Angad's back let Lakshman show
Like him who wealth to mortals shares,
The lord whom Sárvabhauma bears.
The bold Sushen's impetuous might,
And Vegadarsí's piercing sight,
And Jámbaván whom bears revere,
Illustrious three, shall guard the rear."
He ceased, the royal Vánar heard,
And swift, obedient to his word,
Sprang forth in numbers none might tell
From mountain, cave, and bosky dell,
From rocky ledge and breezy height,
Fierce Vánars burning for the fight.
And Ráma's course was southward bent
Amid the mighty armament.
On, joyous, pressed in close array

The hosts who owned Sugríva's sway,
With nimble feet, with rapid bound
Exploring, ere they passed, the ground,
While from ten myriad throats rang out
The challenge and the battle shout.
On roots and honeycomb they fed,
And clusters from the boughs o'erhead,
Or from the ground the tall trees tore
Rich with the flowery load they bore.
Some carried comrades, wild with mirth,
Then cast their riders to the earth,
Who swiftly to their feet arose
And overthrew their laughing foes.
While still rang out the general cry,
"King Rávan and his fiends shall die,"
Still on, exulting in the pride
Of conscious strength, the Vánars hied,
And gazed where noble Sahya, best
Of mountains, raised each towering crest.
They looked on lake and streamlet, where
The lotus bloom was bright and fair,
Nor marched—for Ráma's hest they feared
Where town or haunt of men appeared.
Still onward, fearful as the waves
Of Ocean when he roars and raves,
Led by their eager chieftains, went
The Vánars' countless armament.
Each captain, like a noble steed
Urged by the lash to double speed.
Pressed onward, filled with zeal and pride,
By Ráma's and his brother's side,
Who high above the Vánar throng
On mighty backs were borne along,
Like the great Lords of Day and Night
Seized by eclipsing planets might.
Then Lakshman radiant as the morn,
On Angad's shoulders high upborne.
With sweet consoling words that woke
New ardour, to his brother spoke:
"Soon shalt thou turn, thy queen regained
And impious Rávan's life-blood drained,

In happiness and high renown
To dear Ayodhyá's happy town.
I see around exceeding fair
All omens of the earth and air.
Auspicious breezes sweet and low
To greet the Vánar army blow,
And softly to my listening ear
Come the glad cries of bird and deer.
Bright is the sky around us, bright
Without a cloud the Lord of Light,
And Śukra with propitious love
Looks on thee from his throne above.
The pole-star and the Sainted Seven
Shine brightly in the northern heaven,
And great Triśanku, glorious king,

Ikshváku's son from whom we spring,
Beams in unclouded glory near
His holy priest whom all revere.
Undimmed the two Viśákhás shine,
The strength and glory of our line,
And Nairrit's influence that aids
Our Rákshas foemen faints and fades.
The running brooks are fresh and fair,
The boughs their ripening clusters bear,
And scented breezes gently sway
The leaflet of the tender spray.
See, with a glory half divine
The Vánars' ordered legions shine,
Bright as the Gods' exultant train
Who saw the demon Tárak slain.
O let thine eyes these signs behold,
And bid thy heart be glad and bold."
The Vánar squadrons densely spread
O'er all the country onward sped,
While rising from the rapid beat
Of bears' and monkeys' hastening feet.
Dust hid the earth with thickest veil,
And made the struggling sunbeams pale.
Now where Mahendra's peaks arise
Came Ráma of the lotus eyes

And the long arm's resistless might,
And clomb the mountain's wood-crowned height.
Thence Daśaratha's son beheld
Where billowy Ocean rose and swelled,
Past Malaya's peaks and Sahya's chain

The Vánar legions reached the main,
And stood in many a marshalled band
On loud-resounding Ocean's strand.
To the fair wood that fringed the tide
Came Daśaratha's son, and cried:
"At length, my lord Sugríva, we
Have reached King Varuṇ's realm the sea,
And one great thought, still-vexing, how
To cross the flood, awaits us now.
The broad deep ocean, that denies
A passage, stretched before us lies.
Then let us halt and plan the while
How best to storm the giant's isle."

He ceased: Sugríva on the coast
By trees o'ershadowed stayed the host,
That seemed in glittering lines to be
The bright waves of a second sea.
Then from the shore the captains gazed
On billows which the breezes raised
To fury, as they dashed in foam
O'er Varuṇ's realm, the Asurs' home:
The sea that laughed with foam, and danced
With waves whereon the sunbeams glanced:
Where, when the light began to fade,
Huge crocodiles and monsters played;
And, when the moon went up the sky,
The troubled billows rose on high
From the wild watery world whereon
A thousand moons reflected shone:
Where awful serpents swam and showed
Their fiery crests which flashed and glowed,
Illumining the depths of hell,
The prison where the demons dwell.
The eye, bewildered, sought in vain

The bounding line of sky and main:
Alike in shade, alike in glow
Were sky above and sea below.
There wave-like clouds by clouds were chased,
Here cloud-like billows roared and raced:
Then shone the stars, and many a gem
That lit the waters answered them.
They saw the great-souled Ocean stirred
To frenzy by the winds, and heard,
Loud as ten thousand drums, the roar
Of wild waves dashing on the shore.
They saw him mounting to defy
With deafening voice the troubled sky.
And the deep bed beneath him swell
In fury as the billows fell.

CANTO
V

Ráma's Lament

There on the coast in long array
The Vánars' marshalled legions lay,
Where Níla's care had ordered well
The watch of guard and sentinel,
And Mainda moved from post to post
With Dwivid to protect the host.

Then Ráma stood by Lakshman's side,
And mastered by his sorrow cried:
"My brother dear, the heart's distress,
As days wear on, grows less and less.
But my deep-seated grief, alas,
Grows fiercer as the seasons pass.
Though for my queen my spirit longs,
And broods indignant o'er my wrongs,

Still wilder is my grief to know
That her young life is passed in woe.
Breathe, gentle gale, O breathe where she
Lies prisoned, and then breathe on me,

And, though my love I may not meet,
Thy kiss shall be divinely sweet.
Ah, by the giant's shape appalled,
On her dear lord for help she called,
Still in mine ears the sad cry rings
And tears my heart with poison stings.
Through the long daylight and the gloom
Of night wild thoughts of her consume
My spirit, and my love supplies
The torturing flame which never dies.
Leave me, my brother; I will sleep
Couched on the bosom of the deep,
For the cold wave may bring me peace
And bid the fire of passion cease.
One only thought my stay must be,
That earth, one earth, holds her and me,
To hear, to know my darling lives
Some life-supporting comfort gives,
As streams from distant fountains run
O'er meadows parching in the sun.
Ah when, my foeman at my feet,
Shall I my queen, my glory, meet,
The blossom of her dear face raise
And on her eyes enraptured gaze,
Press her soft lips to mine again,
And drink a balm to banish pain!
Alas, alas! where lies she now,
My darling of the lovely brow?
On the cold earth, no help at hand,
Forlorn amid the Rákshas band,
King Janak's child still calls on me,
Her lord and love, to set her free.
But soon in glory will she rise
A crescent moon in autumn skies,
And those dark rovers of the night,
Like scattered clouds shall turn in flight."

Rávan's Speech

But when the giant king surveyed
    His glorious town in ruin laid,
    And each dire sign of victory won
By Hanumán the Wind-God's son,
He vailed his angry eyes oppressed
By shame, and thus his lords addressed:
"The Vánar spy has passed the gate
Of Lanká long inviolate,
Eluded watch and ward, and seen
With his bold eyes the captive queen.
My royal roof with flames is red,
The bravest of my lords are dead,
And the fierce Vánar in his hate
Has left our city desolate.
Now ponder well the work that lies
Before us, ponder and advise.
With deep-observing judgment scan
The peril, and mature a plan.
From counsel, sages say, the root,
Springs victory, most glorious fruit.
First ranks the king, when woe impends
Who seeks the counsel of his friends,
Of kinsmen ever faithful found,
Or those whose hopes with his are bound,
Then with their aid his strength applies,
And triumphs in his enterprise.
Next ranks the prince who plans alone,
No counsel seeks to aid his own,
Weighs loss and gain and wrong and right,
And seeks success with earnest might.
Unwisest he who spurns delays,

Who counts no cost, no peril weighs,
Speeds to his aim, defying fate,
And risks his all, precipitate.
Thus too in counsel sages find
A best, a worst, a middle kind.
When gathered counsellors explore
The way by light of holy lore,
And all from first to last agree,
Is the best counsel of the three.
Next, if debate first waxes high,
And each his chosen plan would try
Till all agree at last, we deem
This counsel second in esteem.
Worst of the three is this, when each
Assails with taunt his fellow's speech;
When all debate, and no consent
Concludes the angry argument.
Consult then, lords; my task shall be
To crown with act your wise decree.
With thousands of his wild allies
The vengeful Ráma hither hies;
With unresisted might and speed
Across the flood his troops will lead,
Or for the Vánar host will drain
The channels of the conquered main."

CANTO

VII

Rávan Encouraged

He ceased: they scorned, with blinded eyes,
The foeman and his bold allies,
Raised reverent hands with one accord,
And thus made answer to their lord:
"Why yield thee, King, to causeless fear?

335

A mighty host with sword and spear
And mace and axe and pike and lance
Waits but thy signal to advance.
Art thou not he who slew of old
The Serpent-Gods, and stormed their hold;
Scaled Mount Kailása and o'erthrew
Kuvera and his Yaksha crew,

Compelling Śiva's haughty friend
Beneath a mightier arm to bend?
Didst thou not bring from realms afar
The marvel of the magic car,
When they who served Kuvera fell
Crushed in their mountain citadel?
Attracted by thy matchless fame
To thee, a suppliant, Maya came,
The lord of every Dánav band,
And won thee with his daughter's hand.
Thy arm in hell itself was felt,
Where Vásuki and Śankha dwelt,
And they and Takshak, overthrown,
Were forced thy conquering might to own.
The Gods in vain their blessing gave
To heroes bravest of the brave,
Who strove a year and, sorely pressed,
Their victor's peerless might confessed.
In vain their magic arts they tried,
In vain thy matchless arm defied
King Varuṇ's sons with fourfold force,
Cars, elephants, and foot, and horse,
But for a while thy power withstood,
And, conquered, mourned their hardihood.
Thou hast encountered, face to face,
King Yáma with his murdering mace.
Fierce as the wild tempestuous sea,
What terror had his wrath for thee,
Though death in every threatening form,
And woe and torment, urged the storm?
Thine arm a glorious victory won
O'er the dread king who pities none;
And the three worlds, from terror freed,

In joyful wonder praised thy deed.
The tribe of Warriors, strong and dread
As Indra's self, o'er earth had spread;
As giant trees that towering stand
In mountain glens, they filled the land.
Can Raghu's son encounter foes
Fierce, numerous, and strong as those?
Yet, trained in war and practised well,
O'ermatched by thee, they fought and fell,
Stay in thy royal home, nor care
The battle and the toil to share;
But let the easy fight be won
By Indrajít thy matchless son.
All, all shall die, if thou permit,
Slain by the hand of Indrajít."

CANTO
VIII

Prahasta's Speech

D ark as a cloud of autumn, dread
Prahasta joined his palms and said:

"Gandharvas, Gods, the hosts who dwell
In heaven, in air, in earth, in hell,
Have yielded to thy might, and how
Shall two weak men oppose thee now?
Hanúmán came, a foe disguised,
And mocked us heedless and surprised,
Or never had he lived to flee
And boast that he has fought with me.
Command, O King, and this right hand
Shall sweep the Vánars from the land,
And hill and dale, to Ocean's shore,
Shall know the death-doomed race no more.

But let my care the means devise
To guard thy city from surprise."

Then Durmukh cried, of Rákshas race:
"Too long we brook the dire disgrace.
He gave our city to the flames,
He trod the chambers of thy dames.
Ne'er shall so weak and vile a thing
Unpunished brave the giants' king.
Now shall this single arm attack
And drive the daring Vánars back,
Till to the winds of heaven they flee,
Or seek the depths of earth and sea."

Then, brandishing the mace he bore,
Whose horrid spikes were stained with gore,
While fury made his eyeballs red,
Impetuous Vajradanshṭra said:

"Why waste a thought on one so vile
As Hanúmán the Vánar, while
Sugríva, Lakshmaṇ, yet remain,
And Ráma mightier still, unslain?
This mace to-day shall crush the three,
And all the host will turn and flee.
Listen, and I will speak: incline,
O King, to hear these words of mine,
For the deep plan that I propose
Will swiftly rid thee of thy foes.
Let thousands of thy host assume
The forms of men in youthful bloom,
In war's magnificent array
Draw near to Raghu's son, and say:
"Thy younger brother Bharat sends
This army, and thy cause befriends."
Then let our legions hasten near
With bow and mace and sword and spear,
And on the Vánar army rain
Our steel and stone till all be slain.
If Raghu's sons will fain believe,
Entangled in the net we weave,

The penalty they both must pay,
And lose their forfeit lives to-day."

Then with his warrior soul on fire,
Nikumbha spoke in burning ire:

"I, only I, will take the field,
And Raghu's son his life shall yield.
Within these walls, O Chiefs, abide,
Nor part ye from our monarch's side."

CANTO

IX

Vibhishan's Counsel

A score of warriors forward sprang,
　　And loud the clashing iron rang
　　Of mace and axe and spear and sword,
As thus they spake unto their lord:
"Their king Sugríva will we slay,
And Raghu's sons, ere close of day,
And strike the wretch Hanúmán down,
The spoiler of our golden town."

But sage Vibhishaṇ strove to calm
The chieftains' fury; palm to palm
He joined in lowly reverence, pressed
Before them, and the throng addressed:

"Dismiss the hope of conquering one
So stern and strong as Raghu's son.
In due control each sense he keeps
With constant care that never sleeps.
Whose daring heart has e'er conceived
The exploit Hanumán achieved,

339

Across the fearful sea to spring,
The tributary rivers' king?
O Rákshas lords, in time be wise,
Nor Ráma's matchless power despise.
And say, what evil had the son
Of Raghu to our monarch done,
Who stole the dame he loved so well
And keeps her in his citadel;
If Khara in his foolish pride
Encountered Ráma, fought, and died,
May not the meanest love his life
And guard it in the deadly strife?
The Maithil dame, O Rákshas King,
Sore peril to thy realm will bring.
Restore her while there yet is time,
Nor let us perish for thy crime.
O, let the Maithil lady go
Ere the avenger bend his bow
To ruin with his arrowy showers
Our Lanká with her gates and towers.
Let Janak's child again be free
Ere the wild Vánars cross the sea,
In their resistless might assail
Our city and her ramparts scale.
Ah, I conjure thee by the ties
Of brotherhood, be just and wise.
In all my thoughts thy good I seek,
And thus my prudent counsel speak.
Let captive Sítá be restored
Ere, fierce as autumn's sun, her lord
Send his keen arrows from the string
To drink the life-blood of our king.
This fury from thy soul dismiss,
The bane of duty, peace, and bliss.
Seek duty's path and walk therein,
And joy and endless glory win.
Restore the captive, ere we feel
The piercing point of Ráma's steel.
O spare thy city, spare the lives
Of us, our friends, our sons and wives."

Thus spake Vibhishaṇ wise and brave:
The Rákshas king no answer gave,
But bade his lords the council close,
And sought his chamber for repose.

Vibhishan's Counsel

S oon as the light of morning broke,
Vibhishaṇ from his slumber woke,
And, duty guiding every thought,
The palace of his brother sought.
Vast as a towering hill that shows
His peaks afar, that palace rose.
Here stood within the monarch's gate
Sage nobles skilful in debate.
There strayed in glittering raiment through
The courts his royal retinue,
Where in wild measure rose and fell
The music of the drum and shell,
And talk grew loud, and many a dame
Of fairest feature went and came
Through doors a marvel to behold,
With pearl inlaid on burning gold:
Therein Gandharvas or the fleet
Lords of the storm might joy to meet.
He passed within the wondrous pile,
Chief glory of the giants' isle:
Thus, ere his fiery course be done,
An autumn cloud admits the sun.

He heard auspicious voices raise
With loud accord the note of praise,
And sages, deep in Scripture, sing

Each glorious triumph of the king.
He saw the priests in order stand,
Curd, oil, in every sacred hand;
And by them flowers were laid and grain,
Due offerings to the holy train.
Vibhishaṇ to the monarch bowed,
Raised on a throne above the crowd:
Then, skilled in arts of soft address,
He raised his voice the king to bless,
And sate him on a seat where he
Full in his brother's sight should be.
The chieftain there, while none could hear,
Spoke his true speech for Rávaṇ's ear,
And to his words of wisdom lent
The force of weightiest argument:

"O brother, hear! since Ráma's queen
A captive in thy house has been,
Disastrous omens day by day
Have struck our souls with wild dismay.
No longer still and strong and clear
The flames of sacrifice appear,
But, restless with the frequent spark,
Neath clouds of smoke grow faint and dark.
Our ministering priests turn pale
To see their wonted offerings fail,
And ants and serpents creep and crawl
Within the consecrated hall.
Dried are the udders of our cows,
Our elephants have juiceless brows,
Nor can the sweetest pasture stay
The charger's long unquiet neigh.
Big tears from mules and camels flow
Whose staring coats their trouble show,
Nor can the leech's art restore
Their health and vigour as before.
Rapacious birds are fierce and bold:
Not single hunters as of old,
In banded troops they chase the prey,
Or gathering on our temples stay.

Through twilight hours with shriek and howl
Around the city jackals prowl,
And wolves and foul hyænas wait
Athirst for blood at every gate.
One sole atonement still may cure
These evils, and our weal assure.
Restore the Maithil dame, and win
An easy pardon for thy sin."

The Rákshas monarch heard, and moved
To sudden wrath his speech reproved:

"No danger, brother, can I see:
The Maithil dame I will not free.
Though all the Gods for Ráma fight,
He yields to my superior might."
Thus the tremendous king who broke
The ranks of heavenly warriors spoke,
And, sternly purposed to resist,
His brother from the hall dismissed.

CANTO
XI

The Summons

Still Rávan's haughty heart rebelled,
The counsel of the wise repelled,
And, as his breast with passion burned,
His thoughts again to Sítá turned.
Thus, to each sign of danger blind,
To love and war he still inclined.
Then mounted he his car that glowed
With gems and golden net, and rode
Where, gathered at the monarch's call,

The nobles filled the council hall.
A host of warriors bright and gay
With coloured robes and rich array,
With shield and mace and spear and sword,
Followed the chariot of their lord.
Mid the loud voice of shells and beat
Of drums he raced along the street,
And, ere he came, was heard afar
The rolling thunder of his car.
He reached the doors: the nobles bent
Their heads before him reverent:
And, welcomed with their loud acclaim,
Within the glorious hall he came.
He sat upon a royal seat
With golden steps beneath his feet,
And bade the heralds summon all
His captains to the council hall.
The heralds heard the words he spake,
And sped from house to house to wake
The giants where they slept or spent
The careless hours in merriment.
These heard the summons and obeyed:
From chamber, grove, and colonnade,
On elephants or cars they rode,
Or through the streets impatient strode.
As birds on rustling pinions fly
Through regions of the darkened sky,
Thus cars and mettled coursers through
The crowded streets of Lanká flew.
The council hall was reached, and then,
As lions seek their mountain den,
Through massy doors that opened wide,
With martial stalk the captains hied.
Welcomed with honour as was meet
They stooped to press their monarch's feet,

And each a place in order found
On stool, on cushion, or the ground.
Nor did the sage Vibhishaṇ long
Delay to join the noble throng.

High on a car that shone like flame
With gold and flashing gems he came,
Drew near and spoke his name aloud,
And reverent to his brother bowed.

Rávan's Speech

The king in counsel unsurpassed
His eye around the synod cast,
And fierce Prahasta, first and best
Of all his captains, thus addressed:

"Brave master of each warlike art,
Arouse thee and perform thy part.
Array thy fourfold forces well
To guard our isle and citadel."

The captain of the hosts obeyed,
The troops with prudent skill arrayed;
Then to the hall again he hied,
And stood before the king and cried:
"Each inlet to the town is closed
Without, within, are troops disposed.
With fearless heart thine aim pursue
And do the deed thou hast in view."

Thus spoke Prahasta in the zeal
That moved him for the kingdom's weal.
And thus the monarch, who pursued
His own delight, his speech renewed:
"In ease and bliss, in toil and pain,
In doubts of duty, pleasure, gain,

345

Your proper path I need not tell,
For of yourselves ye know it well.
The Storm-Gods, Moon, and planets bring
New glory to their heavenly king,
And, ranged about your monarch, ye
Give joy and endless fame to me.
My secret counsel have I kept,
While senseless Kumbhakarṇa slept.
Six months the warrior's slumbers last
And bind his torpid senses fast;
But now his deep repose he breaks,
The best of all our champions wakes.
I captured, Ráma's heart to wring,
This daughter of Videha's king.
And brought her from that distant land
Where wandered many a Rákshas band.
Disdainful still my love she spurns,
Still from each prayer and offering turns,
Yet in all lands beneath the sun
No dame may rival Sítá, none,
Her dainty waist is round and slight,
Her cheek like autumn's moon is bright,
And she like fruit in graven gold
Mocks her whom Maya framed of old.
Faultless in form, how firmly tread
Her feet whose soles are rosy red!
Ah, as I gaze her beauty takes
My spirit, and my passion wakes.
Looking for Ráma far away
She sought with tears a year's delay
Nor gazing on her love-lit eye
Could I that earnest prayer deny.
But baffled hopes and vain desire
At length my patient spirit tire.
How shall the sons of Raghu sweep
To vengeance o'er the pathless deep?
How shall they lead the Vánar train
Across the monster-teeming main?
One Vánar yet could find a way
To Lanká's town, and burn and slay.
Take counsel then, remembering still

That we from men need fear no ill;
And give your sentence in debate,
For matchless is the power of fate.
Assailed by you the Gods who dwell
In heaven beneath our fury fell.
And shall we fear these creatures bred
In forests, by Sugríva led?
E'en now on ocean's farther strand,
The sons of Daśaratha stand,
And follow, burning to attack
Their giant foes, on Sítá's track.
Consult then, lords for ye are wise:
A seasonable plan devise.
The captive lady to retain,
And triumph when the foes are slain.
No power can bring across the foam
Those Vánars to our island home;
Or if they madly will defy
Our conquering might, they needs must die."

Then Kumbhakarṇa's anger woke,
And wroth at Rávaṇ's words he spoke:
"O Monarch, when thy ravished eyes
First looked upon thy lovely prize,
Then was the time to bid us scan
Each peril and mature a plan.
Blest is the king who acts with heed,
And ne'er repents one hasty deed;
And hapless he whose troubled soul
Mourns over days beyond control.

Thou hast, in beauty's toils ensnared,
A desperate deed of boldness dared;
By fortune saved ere Ráma's steel
One wound, thy mortal bane, could deal.
But, Rávaṇ, as the deed is done,
The toil of war I will not shun.
This arm, O rover of the night,
Thy foemen to the earth shall smite,
Though Indra with the Lord of Flame,
The Sun and Storms, against me came.

E'en Indra, monarch of the skies,
Would dread my club and mountain size,
Shrink from these teeth and quake to hear
The thunders of my voice of fear.
No second dart shall Ráma cast:
The first he aims shall be the last.
He falls, and these dry lips shall drain
The blood of him my hand has slain;
And Sítá, when her champion dies,
Shall be thine undisputed prize."

CANTO

XIII

Rávan's Speech

But Mahápárśva saw the sting
Of keen reproach had galled the king;
And humbly, eager to appease
His anger, spoke in words like these:

"And breathes there one so cold and weak
The forest and the gloom to seek
Where savage beasts abound, and spare
To taste the luscious honey there?
Art thou not lord? and who is he
Shall venture to give laws to thee?
Love thy Videhan still, and tread
Upon thy prostrate foeman's head.
O'er Sítá's will let thine prevail,
And strength achieve if flattery fail.
What though the lady yet be coy
And turn her from the proffered joy?
Soon shall her conquered heart relent
And yield to love and blandishment.
With us let Kumbhakarṇa fight,

And Indrajít of matchless might:
We need not other champions, they
Shall lead us forth to rout and slay.
Not ours to bribe or soothe or part
The foeman's force with gentle art,
Doomed, conquered by our might, to feel
The vengeance of the warrior's steel."

The Rákshas monarch heard, and moved
By flattering hopes the speech approved:

"Hear me," he cried, "great chieftain, tell
What in the olden time befell,—
A secret tale which, long suppressed,
Lies prisoned only in my breast.
One day—a day I never forget—
Fair Punjikasthalá I met,
When, radiant as a flame of fire,
She sought the palace of the Sire.
In passion's eager grasp I tore
From her sweet limbs the robes she wore,
And heedless of her prayers and cries
Strained to my breast the vanquised prize.
Like Naliní with soil distained,
The mansion of the Sire she gained,
And weeping made the outrage known
To Brahmá on his heavenly throne.
He in his wrath pronounced a curse,—
That lord who made the universe:
"If, Rávan, thou a second time
Be guilty of so foul a crime,
Thy head in shivers shall be rent:
Be warned, and dread the punishment."
Awed by the threat of vengeance still
I force not Sítá's stubborn will.
Terrific as the sea in might:
My steps are like the Storm-Gods' flight;
But Ráma knows not this, or he
Had never sought to war with me.
Where is the man would idly brave
The lion in his mountain cave,

And wake him when with slumbering eyes
Grim, terrible as Death, he lies?
No, blinded Ráma knows me not:
Ne'er has he seen mine arrows shot;
Ne'er marked them speeding to their aim
Like snakes with cloven tongues of flame.
On him those arrows will I turn,
Whose fiery points shall rend and burn.
Quenched by my power when I assail
The glory of his might shall fail,
As stars before the sun grow dim
And yield their feeble light to him."

CANTO

XIV

Vibhishan's Speech

He ceased: Vibhishaṇ ill at ease
Addressed the king in words like these:

"O Rávaṇ, O my lord, beware
Of Sítá dangerous as fair,
Nor on thy heedless bosom hang
This serpent with a deadly fang.
O King, the Maithil dame restore
To Raghu's matchless son before
Those warriors of the woodlands, vast
As mountain peaks, approaching fast,
Armed with fierce teeth and claws, enclose
Thy city with unsparing foes.
O, be the Maithil dame restored
Ere loosened from the clanging cord

The vengeful shafts of Ráma fly,
And low in death thy princes lie.

350

In all thy legions hast thou one
A match in war for Raghu's son?
Can Kumbhakarṇa's self withstand,
Or Indrajít, that mighty hand?
In vain with Ráma wilt thou strive:
Thou wilt not save thy soul alive
Though guarded by the Lord of Day
And Storm-Gods' terrible array,
In vain to Indra wilt thou fly,
Or seek protection in the sky,
In Yáma's gloomy mansion dwell,
Or hide thee in the depths of hell."

He ceased; and when his lips were closed
Prahasta thus his rede opposed:

"O timid heart, to counsel thus!
What terrors have the Gods for us?
Can snake, Gandharva, fiend appal
The giants' sons who scorn them all?
And shall we now our birth disgrace,
And dread a king of human race?"
Thus fierce Prahasta counselled ill:
But sage Vibhishaṇ's constant will
The safety of the realm ensued;
Who thus in turn his speech renewed:
"Yes, when a soul defiled with sin
Shall mount to heaven and enter in,
Then, chieftain, will experience teach
The truth of thy disdainful speech.
Can I, or thou, or these or all
Our bravest compass Ráma's fall,
The chief in whom all virtues shine,
The pride of old Ikshváku'a line,
With whom the Gods may scarce compare
In skill to act, in heart to dare?
Yea, idly mayst thou vaunt thee, till
Sharp arrows winged with matchless skill
From Ráma's bowstring, fleet and fierce
As lightning's flame, thy body pierce.
Nikumbha shall not save thee then,

Nor Rávaṇ, from the lord of men,
O Monarch, hear my last appeal,
My counsel for thy kingdom's weal.
This sentence I again declare:
O giant King, beware, beware!
Save from the ruin that impends
Thy town, thy people, and thy friends;
O hear the warning urged once more:
To Raghu's son the dame restore."

CANTO

XV

Indrajít's Speech

H e ceased: and Indrajít the pride
Of Rákshas warriors thus replied:

"Is this a speech our king should hear,
This counsel of ignoble fear?
A scion of our glorious race
Should ne'er conceive a thought so base,
But one mid all our kin we find,
Vibhishaṇ, whose degenerate mind
No spark of gallant pride retains,
Whose coward soul his lineage stains.
Against one giant what can two
Unhappy sons of Raghu do?
Away with idle fears, away!
Matched with our meanest, what are they?
Beneath my conquering prowess fell
The Lord of earth and heaven and hell.
Through every startled region dread
Of my resistless fury spread;
And Gods in each remotest sphere
Confessed the universal fear.

Rending the air with roar and groan,
Airávat to the earth was thrown.
From his huge head the tusks I drew,
And smote the Gods with fear anew.
Shall I who tame celestials' pride,
By whom the fiends are terrified,
Now prove a weakling little worth,
And fail to slay those sons of earth?"

He ceased: Vibhishan trained and tried
In war and counsel thus replied
"Thy speech is marked with scorn of truth,
With rashness and the pride of youth.
Yea, to thy ruin like a child
Thou pratest, and thy words are wild.
Most dear, O Indrajít, to thee
Should Rávan's weal and safety be,
For thou art called his son, but thou
Art proved his direst foeman now,
When warned by me thou hast not tried
To turn the coming woe aside.
Both thee and him 'twere meet to slay,
Who brought thee to this hall to-day,
And dared so rash a youth admit
To council where the wisest sit.
Presumptuous, wild, devoid of sense,
Filled full of pride and insolence,
Thy reckless tongue thou wilt not rule
That speaks the counsel of a fool.
Who in the fight may brook or shun
The arrows shot by Raghu's son
With flame and fiery vengeance sped,
Dire as his staff who rules the dead?
O Rávan, let thy people live,
And to the son of Raghu give
Fair robes and gems and precious ore,
And Sítá to his arms restore."

Rávan's Speech

Then, while his breast with fury swelled,
Thus Rávaṇ spoke, as fate impelled:

"Better with foes thy dwelling make,
Or house thee with the venomed snake,
Than live with false familiar friends
Who further still thy foeman's ends.
I know their treacherous mood, I know
Their secret triumph at thy woe.
They in their inward hearts despise
The brave, the noble, and the wise,
Grieve at their bliss with rancorous hate,
And for their sorrows watch and wait:
Scan every fault with curious eye,
And each slight error magnify.
Ask elephants who roam the wild
How were their captive friends beguiled.
"For fire," they cry, "we little care,
For javelin and shaft and snare:
Our foes are traitors, taught to bind
The trusting creatures of their kind."
Still, still, shall blessings flow from cows,
And Bráhmans love their rigorous vows;
Still woman change her restless will,
And friends perfidious work us ill.
What though with conquering feet I tread
On every prostrate foeman's head;
What though the worlds in abject fear
Their mighty lord in me revere?
This thought my peace of mind destroys
And robs me of expected joys.

The lotus of the lake receives
The glittering rain that gems its leaves,
But each bright drop remains apart:
So is it still with heart and heart.
Deceitful as an autumn cloud
Which, though its thunderous voice be loud,
On the dry earth no torrent sends,
Such is the race of faithless friends.
No riches of the bloomy spray
Will tempt the wandering bee to stay
That loves from flower to flower to range;
And friends like thee are swift to change.
Thou blot upon thy glorious line,
If any giant's tongue but thine
Had dared to give this base advice,
He should not live to shame me twice."
Then just Vibhishan in the heat
Of anger started from his seat,
And with four captains of the band
Sprang forward with his mace in hand;
Then, fury flashing from his eye,
Looked on the king and made reply:

"Thy rights, O Rávan, I allow:
My brother and mine elder thou.
Such, though from duty's path they stray,
We love like fathers and obey,
But still too bitter to be borne
Is thy harsh speech of cruel scorn.
The rash like thee, who spurn control,
Nor check one longing of the soul,
Urged by malignant fate repel
The faithful friend who counsels well.
A thousand courtiers wilt thou meet,
With flattering lips of smooth deceit:
But rare are they whose tongue or ear
Will speak the bitter truth, or hear.
Unclose thy blinded eyes and see
That snares of death encompass thee.
I dread, my brother, to behold
The shafts of Ráma, bright with gold,

355

Flash fury through the air, and red
With fires of vengeance strike thee dead.
Lord, brother, King, again reflect,
Nor this mine earnest prayer reject,
O, save thyself, thy royal town,
Thy people and thine old renown."

Vibhishan's Flight

Soon as his bitter words were said,
To Raghu's sons Vibhishaṇ fled.
Their eyes the Vánar leaders raised
And on the air-borne Rákhshas gazed,
Bright as a thunderbolt, in size
Like Meru's peak that cleaves the skies.
In gorgeous panoply arrayed
Like Indra's self he stood displayed,
And four attendants brave and bold
Shone by their chief in mail and gold.
Sugríva then with dark surmise
Bent on their forms his wondering eyes,
And thus in hasty words confessed
The anxious doubt that moved his breast:

"Look, look ye Vánars, and beware:
That giant chief sublime in air
With other four in bright array
Comes armed to conquer and to slay."

Soon as his warning speech they heard,
The Vánar chieftains undeterred
Seized fragments of the rock and trees,
And made reply in words like these:

356

"We wait thy word: the order give,
And these thy foes shall cease to live.
Command us, mighty King, and all
Lifeless upon the earth shall fall."

Meanwhile Vibhishaṇ with the four
Stood high above the ocean shore.
Sugríva and the chiefs he spied,
And raised his mighty voice and cried:
"From Rávaṇ, lord of giants, I
His brother, named Vibhishaṇ, fly.
From Janasthán he stole the child
Of Janak by his art beguiled,
And in his palace locked and barred
Surrounds her with a Rákshas guard.
I bade him, plied with varied lore,
His hapless prisoner restore.
But he, by Fate to ruin sent,
No credence to my counsel lent,
Mad as the fevered wretch who sees
And scorns the balm to bring him ease.
He scorned the sage advice I gave,
He spurned me like a base-born slave.
I left my children and my wife,
And fly to Raghu's son for life.
I pray thee, Vánar chieftain, speed
To him who saves in hour of need,
And tell him famed in distant lands
That suppliant here Vibhishaṇ stands."

The Rákshas ceased: Sugríva hied
To Raghu's noble son and cried:

"A stranger from the giant host,
Borne o'er the sea, has reached the coast;
A secret foe, he comes to slay,
As owls attack their heedless prey.
'Tis thine, O King, in time of need
To watch, to counsel, and to lead,
Our Vánar legions to dispose,
And guard us from our crafty foes.

Vibhishaṇ from the giants' isle,
King Rávaṇ's brother, comes with guile
And, feigning from his king to flee,
Seeks refuge, Raghu's son, with thee.
Arise, O Ráma, and prevent
By bold attack his dark intent.
Who comes in friendly guise prepared
To slay thee by his arts ensnared."

Thus urged Sugríva famed for lore
Of moving words, and spoke no more.
Then Ráma thus in turn addressed
The bold Hanúmán and the rest:
"Chiefs of the Vánar legions each
Of you heard Sugríva's speech.
What think ye now in time of fear,
When peril and distress are near,
In every doubt the wise depend
For counsel on a faithful friend."
They heard his gracious words, and then
Spake reverent to the lord of men:
"O Raghu's son, thou knowest well
All things of heaven and earth and hell.
'Tis but thy friendship bids us speak
The counsel Ráma need not seek.
So duteous, brave, and true art thou,
Heroic, faithful to thy vow.
Deep in the scriptures, trained and tried,
Still in thy friends wilt thou confide.
Let each of us in turn impart
The secret counsel of his heart,
And strive to win his chief's assent,
By force of wisest argument."

They ceased and Angad thus began:
"With jealous eye the stranger scan:
Not yet with trusting heart receive
Vibhishaṇ, nor his tale believe.
These giants wandering far and wide
Their evil nature falsely hide,
And watching with malignant skill

Assail us when we fear no ill.
Well ponder every hope and fear
Until thy doubtful course be clear;
Then own his merit or detect
His guile, and welcome or reject."

Then Śarabha the bold and brave
In turn his prudent sentence gave:
"Yea, Ráma, send a skilful spy
With keenest tact to test and try.
Then let the stranger, as is just,
Obtain or be refused thy trust."

Then he whose heart was rich in store
Of scripture's life-directing lore,
King Jámbaván, stood forth and cried:
"Suspect, suspect a foe allied
With Rávaṇ lord of Lanká's isle,
And Rákshas sin and Rákshas guile."
Then Mainda, wisest chief, who knew
The wrong, the right, the false, the true,
Pondered a while, then silence broke,
And thus his sober counsel spoke:

"Let one with gracious speech draw near
And gently charm Vibhishaṇ's ear,
Till he the soothing witchery feel
And all his secret heart reveal.
So thou his aims and hopes shalt know,
And hail the friend or shun the foe."

"Not he," Hanúmán cried, "not he
Who taught the Gods may rival thee,
Supreme in power of quickest sense,
First in the art of eloquence.
But hear me soothly speak, O King,
And learn the hope to which I cling.
Vibhishaṇ comes no crafty spy:
Urged by his brother's fault to fly.
With righteous soul that loathes the sin,
He fled from Lanká and his kin.

If strangers question, doubt will rise
And chill the heart of one so wise.
Marred by distrust the parle will end,
And thou wilt lose a faithful friend.
Nor let it seem so light a thing
To sound a stranger's heart, O King.
And he, I ween, whate'er he say,
Will ne'er an evil thought betray.
He comes a friend in happy time,
Loathing his brother for his crime.
His ear has heard thine old renown,
The might that struck King Báli down,
And set Sugríva on the throne.
And looking now to thee alone
He comes thy matchless aid to win
And punish Rávaṇ for his sin.
Thus have I tried thy heart to move,
And thus Vibhishaṇ's truth to prove.
Still in his friendship I confide;
But ponder, wisest, and decide."

CANTO

XVIII

Ráma's Speech

Then Ráma's rising doubt was stilled,
And friendly thoughts his bosom filled.
Thus, deep in Scripture's lore, he spake:
"The suppliant will I ne'er forsake,
Nor my protecting aid refuse
When one in name of friendship sues.
Though faults and folly blot his fame,
Pity and help he still may claim."

He ceased: Sugríva bowed his head
And pondered for a while, and said:
"Past number be his faults or few,
What think ye of the Rákshas who,
When threatening clouds of danger rise,
Deserts his brother's side and flies?
Say, Vánars, who may hope to find
True friendship in his faithless kind?"

The son of Raghu heard his speech:
He cast a hasty look on each
Of those brave Vánar chiefs, and while
Upon his lips there played a smile,
To Lakshmaṇ turned and thus expressed
The thoughts that moved his gallant breast:
"Well versed in Scripture's lore, and sage
And duly reverent to age,
Is he, with long experience stored,
Who counsels like this Vánar lord.
Yet here, methinks, for searching eyes
Some deeper, subtler matter lies.
To you and all the world are known
The perils of a monarch's throne,
While foe and stranger, kith and kin
By his misfortune trust to win.
By hope of such advantage led,
Vibhishaṇ o'er the sea has fled.
He in his brother's stead would reign,
And our alliance seeks to gain;
And we his offer may embrace,
A stranger and of alien race.
But if he comes a spy and foe,
What power has he to strike a blow
In furtherance of his close design?
What is his strength compared with mine?
And can I, Vánar King, forget
The great, the universal debt,
Ever to aid and welcome those
Who pray for shelter, friends or foes?
Hast thou not heard the deathless praise

Won by the dove in olden days,
Who conquering his fear and hate
Welcomed the slayer of his mate,
And gave a banquet, to refresh
The weary fowler, of his flesh?
Now hear me, Vánar King, rehearse
What Kaṇdu spoke in ancient verse,
Saint Kaṇva's son who loved the truth
And clave to virtue from his youth:
"Strike not the suppliant when he stands
And asks thee with beseeching hands
For shelter: strike him not although
He were thy father's mortal foe.
No, yield him, be he proud or meek,
The shelter which he comes to seek,
And save thy foeman, if the deed
Should cost thy life, in desperate need."
And shall I hear the wretched cry,
And my protecting aid deny?
Shall I a suppliant's prayer refuse,
And heaven and glory basely lose?
No, I will do for honour sake
E'en as the holy Kaṇdu spake,
Preserve a hero's name from stain,
And bliss in heaven and glory gain.
Bound by a solemn vow I sware
That all my saving help should share
Who sought me in distress and cried,
"Thou art my hope, and none beside."
Then go, I pray thee, Vánar King,
Vibhishaṇ to my presence bring,
Yea, were he Rávaṇ's self, my vow
Forbids me to reject him now."

He ceased: the Vánar king approved;
And Ráma toward Vibhishaṇ moved.
So moves, a brother God to greet,
Lord Indra from his heavenly seat.

CANTO
XIX

Vibhishan's Counsel

When Raghu's son had owned his claim
Down from the air Vibhishaṇ came,
And with his four attendants bent
At Ráma's feet most reverent.

"O Ráma," thus he cried, "in me
Vibhishaṇ, Rávaṇ's brother see.
By him disgraced thine aid I seek,
Sure refuge of the poor and weak.
From Lanká, friends, and wealth I fly,
And reft of all on thee rely.
On thee, the wretch's firmest friend,
My kingdom, joys, and life depend."

With glance of favour Ráma eyed
The Rákshas chief and thus replied:

"First from thy lips I fain would hear
Each brighter hope, each darker fear.
Speak, stranger, that I well may know
The strength and weakness of the foe."

He ceased: the Rákshas chief obeyed,
And thus in turn his answer made:

"O Prince, the Self-existent gave
This boon to Rávaṇ; he may brave
All foes in fight; no fiend or snake,
Gandharva, God, his life may take.
His brother Kumbhakarṇa vies
In might with him who rules the skies.

363

The captain of his armies—fame
Perhaps has taught the warrior's name—
Is terrible Prahasta, who
King Maṇibhadra's self o'erthrew.
Where is the warrior found to face
Young Indrajít, when armed with brace
And guard and bow he stands in mail
And laughs at spear and arrowy hail?
Within his city Lanká dwell
Ten million giants fierce and fell,
Who wear each varied shape at will
And eat the flesh of those they kill.
These hosts against the Gods he led,
And heavenly might discomfited."

Then Ráma cried: "I little heed
Gigantic strength or doughty deed.
In spite of all their might has done
The king, the captain, and the son
Shall fall beneath my fury dead,
And thou shalt reign in Rávaṇ's stead.
He, though in depths of earth he dwell,
Or seek protection down in hell,
Or kneel before the Sire supreme,
His forfeit life shall ne'er redeem.
Yea, by my brothers' lives I swear,
I will not to my home repair
Till Rávaṇ and his kith and kin
Have paid in death the price of sin."

Vibhishaṇ bowed his head and cried:
"Thy conquering army will I guide
To storm the city of the foe,
And aid the tyrant's overthrow."
Thus spake Vibhishaṇ: Ráma pressed
The Rákshas chieftain to his breast,
And cried to Lakshmaṇ: "Haste and bring
Sea-water for the new-made king."
He spoke, and o'er Vibhishaṇ's head
The consecrating drops were shed

Mid shouts that hailed with one accord
The giants' king and Lanká's lord.

"Is there no way," Hanúmán cried,
"No passage o'er the boisterous tide?
How may we lead the Vánar host
In triumph to the farther coast?"
"Thus," said Vibhishaṇ, "I advise:
Let Raghu's son in suppliant guise
Entreat the mighty Sea to lend
His succour and this cause befriend.
His channels, as the wise have told,
By Sagar's sons were dug of old,
Nor will high-thoughted Ocean scorn
A prince of Sagar's lineage born."

He ceased; the prudent counsel won
The glad assent of Raghu's son.
Then on the ocean shore a bed
Of tender sacred grass was spread,
Where Ráma at the close of day
Like fire upon an altar lay.

CANTO
XX

The Spies

Śárdúla, Rávaṇ's spy, surveyed
The legions on the strand arrayed.
And bore, his bosom racked with fear,
These tidings to the monarch's ear:

"They come, they come. A rushing tide,
Ten leagues they spread from side to side,

And on to storm thy city press,
Fierce rovers of the wilderness.
Rich in each princely power and grace,
The pride of Daśaratha's race,
Ráma and Lakshman lead their bands,
And halt them on the ocean sands.
O Monarch, rise, this peril meet;
Risk not the danger of defeat.

First let each wiser art be tried;
Bribe them, or win them, or divide."
Such was the counsel of the spy:
And Rávan called to Śuka: "Fly,
Sugríva lord of Vánars seek,
And thus my kingly message speak:
"Great power and might and fame are thine,
Brave scion of a royal line,
King Riksharajas' son, in thee
A brother and a friend I see.
How wronged by me canst thou complain?
What profit here pretend to gain?
If from the wood the wife I stole
Of Ráma of the prudent soul,
What cause hast thou to mourn the theft?
Thou art not injured or bereft.
Return, O King, thy steps retrace
And seek thy mountain dwelling-place.
No, never may thy hosts within
My Lanká's walls a footing win.
A mighty town whose strength defies
The gathered armies of the skies."

He ceased: obedient Śuka heard;
With wings and plumage of a bird
He rose in eager speed and through
The air upon his errand flew.
Borne o'er the sea with rapid wing
He stood above the Vánar king,
And spoke aloud, sublime in air,
The message he was charged to bear.
The Vánar heard the words he spoke,

And quick redoubling stroke on stroke
On head and pinions hemmed him round
And bore him struggling to the ground.
The Rákshas wounded and distressed
These words to Raghu's son addressed:

"Quick, quick! This Vánar host restrain,
For heralds never must be slain.
To him alone, a wretch untrue,
The punishment of death is due
Who leaves his master's speech unsaid
And speaks another in its stead."
Moved by the suppliant speech and prayer
Up sprang the prince and cried, forbear.
Saved from his wild assailant's blows
Again the Rákshas herald rose
And borne on light wings to the sky
Addressed Sugríva from on high:
"O Vánar Monarch, chief endued
With power and wonderous fortitude,
What answer is my king, the fear
And scourge of weeping worlds, to hear?"
"Go tell thy lord," Sugríva cried,
"Thou, Ráma's foe, art thus defied.
His arm the guilty Báli slew;
Thus, tyrant, shalt thou perish too.
Thy sons, thy friends, proud King, and all
Thy kith and kin with thee shall fall;
And, emptied of the giant's brood,
Burnt Lanká be a solitude.
Fly to the Sun-God's pathway, go
And hide thee deep in hell below:
In vain from Ráma shalt thou flee
Though heavenly warriors fight for thee.
Thine arm subdued, securely bold,
The Vulture-king infirm and old:
But will thy puny strength avail
When Raghu's wrathful sons assail?
A captive in thy palace lies
The lady of the lotus eyes:
Thou knowest not how fierce and strong

Is he whom thou hast dared to wrong.
The best of Raghu's lineage, he
Whose conquering hand shall punish thee."

He ceased: and Angad raised a cry;
"This is no herald but a spy.
Above thee from his airy post
His rapid eye surveyed our host,
Where with advantage he might scan
Our gathered strength from rear to van.
Bind him, Vánars, bind the spy,
Nor let him back to Lanká fly."
They hurled the Rákshas to the ground,
They grasped his neck, his pinions bound,
And firmly held him while in vain
His voice was lifted to complain.
But Ráma's heart inclined to spare,
He listened to his plaint and prayer,
And cried aloud: "O Vánars, cease;
The captive from his bonds release."

CANTO
XXI

Ocean Threatened

His hands in reverence Ráma raised
And southward o'er the ocean gazed;
Then on the sacred grass that made
His lowly couch his limbs he laid.
His head on that strong arm reclined
Which Sítá, best of womankind,
Had loved in happier days to hold
With soft arms decked with pearls and gold.
Then rising from his bed of grass,

"This day," he cried, "the host shall pass
Triumphant to the southern shore,
Or Ocean's self shall be no more."
Thus vowing in his constant breast
Again he turned him to his rest,
And there, his eyes in slumber closed,
Silent beside the sea reposed.
Thrice rose the Day-God thrice he set,
The lord of Ocean came not yet,
Thrice came the night, but Raghu's son
No answer by his service won.
To Lakshmaṇ thus the hero cried,
His eyes aflame with wrath and pride:

"In vain the softer gifts that grace
The good are offered to the base.
Long-suffering, patience, gentle speech

Their thankless hearts can never reach.
The world to him its honour pays
Whose ready tongue himself can praise,
Who scorns the true, and hates the right,
Whose hand is ever raised to smite.
Each milder art is tried in vain:
It wins no glory, but disdain.
And victory owns no softer charm
Than might which nerves a warrior's arm.
My humble suit is still denied
By Ocean's overweening pride.
This day the monsters of the deep
In throes of death shall wildly leap.
My shafts shall rend the serpents curled
In caverns of the watery world,
Disclose each sunless depth and bare
The tangled pearl and coral there.
Away with mercy! at a time
Like this compassion is a crime.
Welcome, the battle and the foe!
My bow! my arrows and my bow!
This day the Vánars' feet shall tread

369

The conquered Sea's exhausted bed,
And he who never feared before
Shall tremble to his farthest shore."

Red flashed his eyes with angry glow:
He stood and grasped his mighty bow,
Terrific as the fire of doom
Whose quenchless flames the world consume.
His clanging cord the archer drew,
And swift the fiery arrows flew
Fierce as the flashing levin sent
By him who rules the firmament.
Down through the startled waters sped
Each missile with its flaming head.
The foamy billows rose and sank,
And dashed upon the trembling bank.
Sea monsters of tremendous form
With crash and roar of thunder storm.
Still the wild waters rose and fell
Crowned with white foam and pearl and shell.
Each serpent, startled from his rest,
Raised his fierce eyes and glowing crest.
And prisoned Dánavs where they dwelt
In depths below the terror felt.
Again upon his string he laid
A flaming shaft, but Lakshmaṇ stayed
His arm, with gentle reasoning tried
To soothe his angry mood, and cried:
"Brother, reflect: the wise control
The rising passions of the soul.
Let Ocean grant, without thy threat,
The boon on which thy heart is set.
That gracious lord will ne'er refuse
When Ráma son of Raghu sues."
He ceased: and voices from the air
Fell clear and loud, Spare, Ráma, spare.

Ocean Threatened

With angry menace Ráma, best
Of Raghu's sons, the Sea addressed:
"With fiery flood of arrowy rain
Thy channels will I dry and drain.
And I and all the Vánar host
Will reach on foot the farther coast.
Thou shalt not from destruction save
The creatures of the teeming wave,
And lapse of time shall ne'er efface
The memory of the dire disgrace."

Thus spoke the warrior, and prepared
The mortal shaft which never spared,
Known mystic weapon, by the name
Of Brahmá, red with quenchless flame.
Great terror, as he strained the bow,
Struck heaven above and earth below.
Through echoing skies the thunder pealed,
And startled mountains rocked and reeled,
The earth was black with sudden night
And heaven was blotted from the sight.
Then ever and anon the glare
Of meteors shot through murky air,
And with a wild terrific sound
Red lightnings struck the trembling ground.
In furious gusts the fierce wind blew:
Tall trees it shattered and o'erthrew,
And, smiting with a giant's stroke,
Huge masses from the mountain broke.
A cry of terror long and shrill
Came from each valley, plain, and hill.

Each ruined dale, each riven peak
Re-echoed with a wail or shriek.

While Raghu's son undaunted gazed,
The waters of the deep were raised,
And, still uplifted more and more,
Leapt in wild flood upon the shore.
Still Ráma looked upon the tide
And kept his post unterrified.
Then from the seething flood upreared
Majestic Ocean's form appeared,
As rising from his eastern height
Springs through the sky the Lord of Light.
Attendant on their monarch came
Sea serpents with their eyes aflame.
Like lazulite mid burning gold
His form was wondrous to behold.
Bright with each fairest precious stone
A chain about his neck was thrown.
Calm shone his lotus eyes beneath
The blossoms of his heavenly wreath,
And many a pearl and sea-born gem
Flashed in the monarch's diadem.
There Gangá, tributary queen,
And Sindhu by his lord, were seen,

And every stream and brook renowned
In ancient story girt him round.
Then, as the waters rose and swelled,
The king with suppliant hands upheld,
His glorious head to Ráma bent
And thus addressed him reverent:
"Air, ether, fire, earth, water, true
To nature's will, their course pursue;
And I, as ancient laws ordain,
Unfordable must still remain.
Yet, Raghu's son, my counsel hear:
I ne'er for love or hope or fear
Will pile my waters in a heap
And leave a pathway through the deep.
Still shall my care for thee provide

An easy passage o'er the tide,
And like a city's paven street
Shall be the road beneath thy feet."
He ceased: and Ráma spoke again:
"This spell is ne'er invoked in vain.
Where shall the magic shaft, to spend
The fury of its might, descend?"
"Shoot," Ocean cried, "thine arrow forth
With all its fury to the north,
Where sacred Drumakulya lies,
Whose glory with thy glory vies.
There dwells a wild Abhíra race,
As vile in act as foul of face,
Fierce Dasyus who delight in ill,
And drink my tributary rill.
My soul no longer may endure
Their neighbourhood and touch impure.
At these, O son of Raghu, aim
Thine arrow with the quenchless flame."

Swift from the bow, as Ráma drew
His cord, the fiery arrow flew.
Earth groaned to feel the wound, and sent
A rush of water through the rent;
And famed for ever is the well
Of Vrana where the arrow fell.
Then every brook and lake beside
Throughout the region Ráma dried.
But yet he gave a boon to bless
And fertilize the wilderness:
No fell disease should taint the air,
And sheep and kine should prosper there:
Earth should produce each pleasant root,
The stately trees should bend with fruit;
Oil, milk, and honey should abound,
And fragrant herbs should clothe the ground.
Then spake the king of brooks and seas
To Raghu's son in words like these:
"Now let a wondrous task be done
By Nala, Viśvakarmá's son,
Who, born of one of Vánar race,

373

Inherits by his father's grace
A share of his celestial art.
Call Nala to perform his part,
And he, divinely taught and skilled,
A bridge athwart the sea shall build."

He spoke and vanished. Nala, best
Of Vánar chiefs, the king addressed:
"O'er the deep sea where monsters play
A bridge, O Ráma, will I lay;
For, sharer of my father's skill,
Mine is the power and mine the will.
'Tis vain to try each gentler art
To bribe and soothe the thankless heart;
In vain on such is mercy spent;
It yields to naught but punishment.
Through fear alone will Ocean now
A passage o'er his waves allow.
My mother, ere she bore her son,
This boon from Viśvakarmá won:
"O Mandarí, thy child shall be
In skill and glory next to me."
But why unbidden should I fill
Thine ear with praises of my skill?
Command the Vánar hosts to lay
Foundations for the bridge to-day."

He spoke: and swift at Ráma's hest
Up sprang the Vánars from their rest,
The mandate of the king obeyed
And sought the forest's mighty shade.
Unrooted trees to earth they threw,
And to the sea the timber drew.
The stately palm was bowed and bent,
Aśokas from the ground were rent,
And towering Sáls and light bamboos,
And trees with flowers of varied hues,
With loveliest creepers wreathed and crowned,
Shook, reeled, and fell upon the ground.
With mighty engines piles of stone

And seated hills were overthrown:
Unprisoned waters sprang on high,
In rain descending from the sky:
And ocean with a roar and swell
Heaved wildly when the mountains fell.
Then the great bridge of wondrous strength
Was built, a hundred leagues in length.
Rocks huge as autumn clouds bound fast
With cordage from the shore were cast,
And fragments of each riven hill,
And trees whose flowers adorned them still.
Wild was the tumult, loud the din
As ponderous rocks went thundering in.
Ere set of sun, so toiled each crew,
Ten leagues and four the structure grew;
The labours of the second day
Gave twenty more of ready way,
And on the fifth, when sank the sun,
The whole stupendous work was done.
O'er the broad way the Vánars sped,
Nor swayed it with their countless tread.

Exultant on the ocean strand
Vibhishaṇ stood, and, mace in hand,
Longed eager for the onward way,
And chafed impatient at delay.
Then thus to Ráma trained and tried
In battle King Sugríva cried:
"Come, Hanumán's broad back ascend;
Let Angad help to Lakshmaṇ lend.
These high above the sea shall bear
Their burthen through the ways of air."

So, with Sugríva, borne o'erhead
Ikshváku's sons the legions led.
Behind, the Vánar hosts pursued
Their march in endless multitude.
Some skimmed the surface of the wave,
To some the air a passage gave.
Amid their ceaseless roar the sound

Of Ocean's fearful voice was drowned,
As o'er the bridge by Nala planned
They hastened on to Lanká's strand,
Where, by the pleasant brooks, mid trees
Loaded with fruit, they took their ease.

CANTO

XXIII

The Omens

Then Ráma, peerless in the skill
That marks each sign of good and ill,
Strained his dear brother to his breast,
And thus with prudent words addressed:
"Now, Lakshman, by the water's side
In fruitful groves the host divide,
That warriors of each woodland race
May keep their own appointed place.
Dire is the danger: loss of friends,
Of Vánars and of bears, impends.
Distained with dust the breezes blow,
And earth is shaken from below.
The tall hills rock from foot to crown,
And stately trees come toppling down.
In threatening shape, with voice of fear,
The clouds like cannibals appear,
And rain in fitful torrents, red
With sanguinary drops, is shed.
Long streaks of lurid light invest
The evening skies from east to west.
And from the sun at times a ball
Of angry fire is seen to fall.
From every glen and brake is heard
The boding voice of beast and bird:
From den and lair night-prowlers run

And shriek against the falling sun.
Up springs the moon, but hot and red
Kills the sad night with woe and dread;
No gentle lustre, but the gloom
That heralds universal doom.
A cloud of dust and vapour mars
The beauty of the evening stars,
And wild and fearful is the sky
As though the wreck of worlds were nigh.
Around our heads in boding flight
Wheel hawk and vulture, crow and kite;
And every bird of happy note
Shrieks terror from his altered throat.
Sword, spear and shaft shall strew the plain
Dyed red with torrents of the slain.
To-day the Vánar troops shall close
Around the city of our foes."

CANTO
XXIV

The Spy's Return

As shine the heavens with autumn's moon
Refulgent in the height of noon,
So shone with light which Ráma gave
That army of the bold and brave,
As from the sea it marched away
In war's magnificent array,
And earth was shaken by the beat
And trampling of unnumbered feet.
Then to the giants' ears were borne,
The mingled notes of drum and horn,
And clash of tambours smote the sky,
And shouting and the battle cry.
The sound of martial strains inspired

Each chieftain, and his bosom fired:
While giants from their walls replied,
And answering shouts the foe defied,
Then Ráma looked on Lanká where
Bright banners floated in the air,
And, pierced with anguish at the view,
His loving thoughts to Sítá flew.
"There, prisoned by the giant, lies
My lady of the tender eyes,
Like Rohiṇí the queen of stars
O'erpowered by the fiery Mars."
Then turned he to his brother chief
And cried in agony of grief:
"See on the hill, divinely planned
And built by Viśvakarmá's hand,
The towers and domes of Lanká rise
In peerless beauty to the skies.
Bright from afar the city shines
With gleam of palaces and shrines,
Like pale clouds through the region spread
By Vishṇu's self inhabited.
Fair gardens grow, and woods between
The stately domes are fresh and green,
Where trees their bloom and fruit display,
And sweet birds sing on every spray.
Each bird is mad with joy, and bees
Sing labouring in the bloomy trees
On branches by the breezes bowed,
Where the gay Koïl's voice is loud."

This said, he ranged with warlike art
Each body of the host apart.

"There in the centre," Ráma cried,
"Be Angad's place by Níla's side.
Let Rishabh of impetuous might
Be lord and leader on the right,
And Gandhamádan, next in rank,
Be captain of the farther flank.
Lakshmaṇ and I the hosts will lead,
And Jámbaván of ursine breed,

With bold Sushen unused to fear,
And Vegadarśí, guide the rear."
Thus Ráma spoke: the chiefs obeyed;
And all the Vánar hosts arrayed
Showed awful as the autumn sky
When clouds embattled form on high.
Their arms were mighty trees o'erthrown,
And massy blocks of mountain stone.
One hope in every warlike breast,
One firm resolve, they onward pressed,
To die in fight or batter down
The walls and towers of Lanká's town.

Those marshalled legions Ráma eyed,
And thus to King Sugríva cried:
"Now, Monarch, ere the hosts proceed,
Let Śuka, Rávan's spy, be freed."
He spoke: the Vánar gave consent
And loosed him from imprisonment:
And Śuka, trembling and afraid,
His homeward way to Rávan made.
Loud laughed the lord of Lanká's isle:
"Where hast thou stayed this weary while?
Why is thy plumage marred, and why
Do twisted cords thy pinions tie?
Say, comest thou in evil plight
The victim of the Vánars' spite?"

He ceased: the spy his fear controlled,
And to the king his story told:
"I reached the ocean's distant shore,
Thy message to the king I bore.
In sudden wrath the Vánars rose,
They struck me down with furious blows;
They seized me helpless on the ground,
My plumage rent, my pinions bound.
They would not, headlong in their ire,
Consider, listen, or inquire;
So fickle, wrathful, rough and rude
Is the wild forest multitude.
There, marshalling the Vánar bands,

King Ráma with Sugríva stands,
Ráma the matchless warrior, who
Virádha and Kabandha slew,
Khara, and countless giants more,
And tracks his queen to Lanká's shore.
A bridge athwart the sea was cast,
And o'er it have his legions passed.
Hark! heralded by horns and drums
The terrible avenger comes.
E'en now the giants' isle he fills
With warriors huge as clouds and hills,
And burning with vindictive hate
Will thunder soon at Lanká's gate.
Yield or oppose him: choose between
Thy safety and the Maithil queen."

He ceased: the tyrant's eyeballs blazed
With fury as his voice he raised:
"No, if the dwellers of the sky,
Gandharvas, fiends assail me, I
Will keep the Maithil lady still,
Nor yield her back for fear of ill.
When shall my shafts with iron hail
My foeman, Raghu's son, assail,
Thick as the bees with eager wing
Beat on the flowery trees of spring?
O, let me meet my foe at length,
And strip him of his vaunted strength,
Fierce as the sun who shines afar
Stealing the light of every star.
Strong as the sea's impetuous might
My ways are like the tempest's flight;
But Ráma knows not this, or he
In terror from my face would flee."

Rávan's Spies

When Ráma and the host he led
    Across the sea had safely sped,
    Thus Rávaṇ, moved by wrath and pride,
To Śuka and to Sáraṇ cried:
"O counsellors, the Vánar host
Has passed the sea from coast to coast,
And Daśaratha's son has wrought
A wondrous deed surpassing thought.
And now in truth I needs must know
The strength and number of the foe.
Go ye, to Ráma's host repair
And count me all the legions there.
Learn well what power each captain leads
His name and fame for warlike deeds.
Learn by what artist's wondrous aid
That bridge athwart the sea was made;
Learn how the Vánar host came o'er
And halted on the island shore.
Mark Ráma son of Raghu well;
His valour, strength, and weapons tell.
Watch his advisers one by one,
And Lakshmaṇ, Raghu's younger son.
Learn with observant eyes, and bring
"Unerring tidings to your king.

He ceased: then swift in Vánar guise
Forth on their errand sped the spies.
They reached the Vánars, and, dismayed,
Their never-ending lines surveyd:
Nor would they try, in mere despair,
To count the countless legions there,

That crowded valley, plain and hill,
That pressed about each cave and rill.
Though sea-like o'er the land were spread
The endless hosts which Ráma led,
The bridge by thousands yet was lined,
And eager myriads pressed behind.
But sage Vibhishaṇ's watchful eyes
Had marked the giants in disguise.
He gave command the pair to seize,
And told the tale in words like these:

"O Ráma these, well known erewhile,
Are giant sons of Lanká's isle,
Two counsellors of Rávaṇ sent
To watch the invading armament."

Vibhishaṇ ceased: at Ráma's look
The Rákshas envoys quailed and shook;
Then suppliant hand to hand they pressed
And thus Ikshváku's son addressed:
"O Ráma, bear the truth we speak:
Our monarch Rávaṇ bade us seek
The Vánar legions and survey
Their numbers, strength, and vast array."

Then Ráma, friend and hope and guide
Of suffering creatures, thus replied:

"Now giants, if your eyes have scanned
Our armies, numbering every band,
Marked lord and chief, and gazed their fill,
Return to Rávaṇ when ye will.
If aught remain, if aught anew
Ye fain would scan with closer view,
Vibhishaṇ, ready at your call,
Will lead you forth and show you all.
Think not of bonds and capture; fear
No loss of life, no peril here:
For, captive, helpless and unarmed,
An envoy never should be harmed.
Again to Lanká's town repair,

Speed to the giant monarch there,
And be these words to Rávaṇ told,
Fierce brother of the Lord of Gold:
"Now, tyrant, tremble for thy sin:
Call up thy friends, thy kith and kin,
And let the power and might be seen
Which made thee bold to steal my queen.
To-morrow shall thy mournful eye
Behold thy bravest warriors die,
And Lanká's city, tower and wall,
Struck by my fiery shafts, will fall.
Then shall my vengeful blow descend
Its rage on thee and thine to spend,
Fierce as the fiery bolt that flew
From heaven against the Dánav crew,
Mid those rebellious demons sent
By him who rules the firmament."

Thus spake Ikshváku's son, and ceased:
The giants from their bonds released
Lauded the King with glad accord,
And hasted homeward to their lord.
Before the tyrant side by side
Śuka and Sáraṇ stood and cried:
"Vibhishaṇ seized us, King, and fain
His helpless captives would have slain.
But glorious Ráma saw us; he,
Great-hearted hero, made us free.
There in one spot our eyes beheld
Four chiefs on earth unparalleled,
Who with the guardian Gods may vie
Who rule the regions of the sky.
There Ráma stood, the boast and pride
Of Raghu's race, by Lakshmaṇ's side.
There stood the sage Vibhishaṇ, there
Sugríva strong beyond compare.
These four alone can batter down
Gate, rampart, wall, and Lanká's town.
Nay, Ráma matchless in his form,
A single foe, thy town would storm:
So wondrous are his weapons, he

383

Needs not the succour of the three.
Why speak we of the countless train
That fills the valley, hill and plain,
The millions of the Vánar breed
Whom Ráma and Sugríva lead?
O King, be wise, contend no more,
And Sítá to her lord restore."

CANTO
XXVI

The Vánar Chiefs

"Not if the Gods in heaven who dwell,
Gandharvas, and the fiends of hell
In banded opposition rise
Against me, will I yield my prize.
Still trembling from the ungentle touch
Of Vánar hands ye fear too much,
And bid me, heedless of the shame,
Give to her lord the Maithil dame."

Thus spoke the king in stern reproof;
Then mounted to his palace roof
Aloft o'er many a story raised,
And on the lands beneath him gazed.
There by his faithful spies he stood
And looked on sea and hill and wood.
There stretched before him far away
The Vánars' numberless array:
Scarce could the meadows' tender green
Beneath their trampling feet be seen.
He looked a while with furious eye,
Then questioned thus the nearer spy:
"Bend, Sáraṇ, bend thy gaze, and show

The leaders of the Vánar foe.
Tell me their heroes' names, and teach
The valour, power and might of each."

Obedient Sáraṇ eyed the van,
The leaders marked, and thus began:
"That chief conspicuous at the head
Of warriors in the forest bred,
Who hither bends his ruthless eye
And shouts his fearful battle cry:

Whose voice with pealing thunder shakes
All Lanká, with the groves and lakes
And hills that tremble at the sound,
Is Níla, for his might renowned:
First of the Vánar lords controlled
By King Sugríva lofty-souled.
He who his mighty arm extends,
And his fierce eye on Lanká bends,
In stature like a stately tower,
In colour like a lotus flower,
Who with his wild earth-shaking cries
Thee, Rávaṇ, to the field defies,
Is Angad, by Sugríva's care
Anointed his imperial heir:
In wondrous strength, in martial fire
Peer of King Báli's self, his sire;
For Ráma's sake in arms arrayed
Like Varuṇ called to Śakra's aid.
Behind him, girt by warlike bands,
Nala the mighty Vánar stands,
The son of Viśvakarmá, he
Who built the bridge athwart the sea.
Look farther yet, O King, and mark
That chieftain clothed in Sandal bark.
'Tis Śweta, famed among his peers,
A sage whom all his race reveres.
See, in Sugríva's ear he speaks,
Then, hasting back, his post reseeks,
And turns his practised eye to view

The squadrons he has formed anew.
Next Kumud stands who roamed of yore
On Gomatí's delightful shore,
Feared where the waving woods invest
His seat on Mount Sanrochan's crest.
Next him a chieftain strong and dread,
Comes Chaṇḍa at his legions' head;
Exulting in his warrior might
He hastens, burning for the fight,
And boasts that his unaided powers
Shall cast to earth thy walls and towers.
Mark, mark that chief of lion gait,
Who views thee with a glance of hate
As though his very eyes would burn
The city walls to which they turn:
'Tis Rambha, Vánar king; he dwells
In Krishṇagiri's tangled dells,
Where Vindhya's pleasant slopes are spread
And fair Sudarśan lifts his head.
There, listening with erected ears,
Śarabha, mighty chief, appears.
His soul is burning for the strife,
Nor dreads the jeopardy of life.
He trembles as he moves, for ire,
And bends around his glance of fire.
Next, like a cloud that veils the skies,
A chieftain of terrific size,
Conspicuous mid the Vánars, comes
With battle shout like rolling drums,
'Tis Panas, trained in war and tried,
Who dwells on Páriyátra's side.
He, far away, the chief who throws
A glory o'er the marshalled rows
That ranged behind their captain stand
Exulting on the ocean strand,
Is Vinata the fierce in fight,
Preëminent like Dardur's height.
That chieftain bending down to drink
On lovely Veṇá's verdant brink,
Is Krathan; now he lifts his eyes
And thee to mortal fray defies.

Next Gavaya comes, whose haughty mind
Scorns all the warriors of his kind.
He comes to trample—such his boast—
On Lanká with his single host."

XXVII

The Vánar Chiefs

"Yet more remain, brave chiefs who stake
Their noble lives for Ráma's sake.
See, glorious, golden-coated, one
Who glisters like the morning sun,
Whom thousands of his race surround,
'Tis Hara for his strength renowned.
Next comes a mighty chieftain, he
Whose legions, armed with rock and tree,
Press on, in numbers passing tale,
The ramparts of our town to scale.
O Rávaṇ, see the king advance
Terrific with his fiery glance,
Girt by the bravest of his train,
Majestic as the God of Rain,
Parjanya, when his host of clouds
About the king, embattled, crowds:
On Rikshaván's high mountain nursed,
In Narmadá he slakes his thirst,
Dhúmra, proud ursine chief, who leads
Wild warriors whom the forest breeds.
His brother, next in strength and age,
In Jámbaván the famous sage.
Of yore his might and skill he lent
To him who rules the firmament,
And Indra's liberal boons repaid
The chieftain for the timely aid.

There like a gloomy cloud that flies
Borne by the tempest through the skies,
Pramáthí stands: he roamed of yore
The forest wilds on Gangá's shore,
Where elephants were struck with dread
And trembling at his coming fled.
There on his foes he loved to sate
The old hereditary hate.

Look, Gaja and Gaváksha show
Their lust of battle with the foe.
See Nala burning for the fray,
And Níla chafing at delay.
Behind the eager captains press
Wild hosts in numbers numberless,
And each for Ráma's sake would fall
Or force his way through Lanká's wall."

CANTO

XXVIII

The Chieftains

There Sáraṇ ceased: then Śuka broke
The silence and to Rávaṇ spoke:
"O Monarch, yonder chiefs survey:
Like elephants in size are they,
And tower like stately trees that grow
Where Gangá's nursing waters flow;
Yea, tall as mountain pines that fling
Long shadows o'er the snow-crowned king.
They all in wild Kishkindhá dwell
And serve their lord Sugríva well.
The Gods' and bright Gandharvas' seed,
They take each form that suits their need.
Now farther look, O Monarch, where

Those chieftains stand, a glorious pair,
Conspicuous for their godlike frames;
Dwivid and Mainda are their names.
Their lips the drink of heaven have known,
And Brahmá claims them for his own.
That chieftain whom thine eyes behold
Refulgent like a hill of gold,
Before whose wrathful might the sea
Roused from his rest would turn and flee,
The peerless Vánar, he who came
To Lanká for the Maithil dame,
The Wind-God's son Hanumán; thou
Hast seen him once, behold him now.
Still nearer let thy glance be bent,
And mark that prince preëminent
Mid chieftains for his strength and size
And splendour of his lotus eyes.
Far through the worlds his virtues shine,
The glory of Ikshváku's line.
The path of truth he never leaves,
And still through all to duty cleaves.
Deep in the Vedas, skilled to wield
The mystic shafts to him revealed:
Whose flaming darts to heaven ascend,
And through the earth a passage rend:
In might like him who rules the sky;
Like Yáma, when his wrath grows high:
Whose queen, the darling of his soul,
Thy magic art deceived and stole:
There royal Ráma stands and longs
For battle to avenge his wrongs.
Near on his right a prince, in hue
Like pure gold freshly burnished, view:
Broad is his chest, his eye is red,
His black hair curls about his head:
'Tis Lakshmaṇ, faithful friend, who shares
His brother's joys, his brother's cares.
By Ráma's side he loves to stand
And serve him as his better hand,
For whose dear sake without a sigh
The warrior youth would gladly die.

389

On Ráma's left Vibhishaṇ view,
With giants for his retinue:
King-making drops have dewed his head,
Appointed monarch in thy stead.
Behold that chieftain sternly still,
High towering like a rooted hill,
Supreme in power and pride of place,
The monarch of the Vánar race.
Raised high above his woodland kind,
In might and glory, frame and mind,
His head above his host he shows
Conspicuous as the Lord of Snows.
His home is far from hostile eyes
Where deep in woods Kishkindhá lies.
A glistering chain which flowers bedeck
With burnished gold adorns his neck.
Queen Fortune, loved by Gods and kings,
To him her chosen favourite clings.
That chain he owes to Ráma's grace,
And Tárá and his kingly place.
In him the great Sugríva know,
Whom Ráma rescued from his foe."

CANTO

XXIX

Sárdúla Captured

The giant viewed with earnest ken
The Vánars and the lords of men;
Then thus, with grief and anger moved,
In bitter tone the spies reproved:
"Can faithful servants hope to please
Their master with such fates as these?
Or hope ye with wild words to wring
The bosom of your lord and king?

390

Such words were better said by those
Who come arrayed our mortal foes.
In vain your ears have heard the sage,
And listened to the lore of age,
Untaught, though lectured many a day,
The first great lesson, to obey,
'Tis marvel Rávaṇ reigns and rules
Whose counsellors are blind and fools.
Has death no terrors that ye dare
To tempt your monarch to despair,

From whose imperial mandate flow
Disgrace and honour, weal and woe?
Yea, forest trees, when flames are fanned
About their scorching trunks, may stand;
But naught can set the sinner free
When kings the punishment decree.
I would not in mine anger spare
The traitorous foe-praising pair,
But years of faithful service plead
For pardon, and they shall not bleed.
Henceforth to me be dead: depart,
Far from my presence and my heart."

Thus spoke the angry king: the two
Cried, Long live Rávaṇ, and withdrew,
The giant monarch turned and cried
To strong Mahodar at his side:
"Go thou, and spies more faithful bring.
More duteous to their lord the king."

Swift at his word Mahodar shed,
And came returning at the head
Of long tried messengers, who bent
Before their monarch reverent.
"Go quickly hence," said Rávaṇ "scan
With keenest eyes the foeman's plan.
Learn who, as nearest friends, advise
And mould each secret enterprise.
Learn when he wakes and goes to rest,
Sound every purpose of his breast.

Learn what the prince intends to-day:
Watch keenly all, and come away."

With joy they heard the words he said:
Then with Śárdúla at their head
About the giant king they went
With circling paces reverent.
By fair Suvela's grassy side
The chiefs of Raghu's race they spied,
Where, shaded by the waving wood,
Vibhishaṇ and Sugríva stood.
A while they rested there and viewed
The Vánars' countless multitude.
Vibhishaṇ with observant eyes
Knew at a glance the giant spies,
And bade the warriors of his train
Bind the rash foes with cord and chain:
"Śárdúla's is the sin," he cried.
He neath the Vánars' hands had died,
But Ráma from their fury freed
The captive in his utmost need,
And, merciful at sight of woe,
Loosed all the spies and bade them go.
Then home to Lanká's monarch fled
The giant chiefs discomfited.

CANTO
XXX

Sárdúla's Speech

They told their lord that Ráma still
Lay waiting by Suvela's hill.
The tyrant, flushed with angry glow,
Heard of the coming of the foe,
And thus with close inquiry pressed

Śárdúla spokesman for the rest:
"Why art thou sad, night-rover? speak:
Has grief or terror changed thy cheek?
Have the wild Vánars' hostile bands
Assailed thee with their mighty hands?"

Śárdúla heard, but scarce might speak;
His trembling tones were faint and weak:
"O Giant King, in vain we try
The purpose of the foe to spy.
Their strength and number none may tell,
And Ráma guards his legions well.
He leaves no hope to prying eyes,
And parley with the chiefs denies:
Each road and path a Vánar guard,
Of mountain size, has closed and barred.
Soon as my feet an entrance found
By giants was I seized and bound,
And wounded sore I fell beneath
Their fists and knees and hands and teeth.
Then trembling, bleeding, wellnigh dead
To Ráma's presence was I led.
He in his mercy stooped to save,
And freedom to the captive gave.
With rocks and shattered mountains he
Has bridged his way athwart the sea,
And he and all his legions wait
Embattled close to Lanká's gate.
Soon will the host thy wall assail,
And, swarming on, the rampart scale.
Now, O my King, his consort yield,
Or arm thee with the sword and shield.
This choice is left thee: choose between
Thy safety and the Maithil queen."

XXXI

The Magic Head

The tyrant's troubled eye confessed
The secret fear that filled his breast.
With dread of coming woe dismayed
He called his counsellors to aid;
Then sternly silent, deep in thought,
His chamber in the palace sought.
Then, as the surest hope of all,
The monarch bade his servants call

Vidyujjihva, whom magic skill
Made master of the means of ill.
Then spake the lord of Lanká's isle:
"Come, Sítá with thine arts beguile.
With magic skill and deftest care
A head like Ráma's own prepare.
This head, long shafts and mighty bow,
To Janak's daughter will we show."

He ceased: Vidyujjihva obeyed,
And wondrous magic skill displayed;
And Rávaṇ for the art he showed
An ornament of price bestowed.
Then to the grove where Sítá lay
The lord of Lanká took his way.
Pale, wasted, weeping, on the ground
The melancholy queen he found,
Whose thoughts in utmost stress of ill
Were fixed upon her husband still.
The giant king approached the dame,
Declared in tones of joy his name;

Then heeding naught her wild distress
Bespake her, stern and pitiless:
"The prince to whom thy fancies cling
Though loved and wooed by Lanká's king,
Who slew the noble Khara,—he
Is slain by warriors sent by me.
Thy living root is hewn away,
Thy scornful pride is tamed to-day.
Thy lord in battle's front has died,
And Sítá shall be Rávaṇ's bride.
Hence, idle thoughts: thy hope is fled;
What wilt thou, Sítá, with the dead?
Rise, child of Janak, rise and be
The queen of all my queens and me.
Incline thine ear, and I will tell,
Dear lady, how thy husband fell.
He bridged his way across the sea
With countless troops to fight with me.
The setting sun had flushed the west
When on the shore they took their rest.
Weary with toil no watch they kept,
Securely on the sands they slept.
Prahasta's troops assailed our foes,
And smote them in their deep repose.
Scarce could their bravest prove their might:
They perished in the dark of night.
Axe, spear, and sword, directed well,
Upon the sleeping myriads fell.
First in the fight Prahasta's sword
Reft of his head thy slumbering lord.
Roused at the din Vibhishaṇ rose,
The captive of surrounding foes,
And Lakshmaṇ through the woods that spread
Around him with his Vánars fled.
Hanúmán fell: one deadly stroke
The neck of King Sugríva broke,
And Mainda sank, and Dwivid lay
Gasping in blood his life away.
The Vánars died, or fled dispersed
Like cloudlets when the storm has burst.

Some rose aloft in air, and more
Ran to the sea and filled the shore.
On shore, in woods, on hill and plain
Our conquering giants left the slain.
Thus my victorious host o'erthrew
The Vánars, and thy husband slew:
See, rudely stained with dust, and red
With dropping blood, the severed head."

Then, turning to a Rákshas slave,
The ruthless king his mandate gave,
And straight Vidyujjihva who bore
The head still wet with dripping gore,
The arrows and the mighty bow,
Bent down before his master low.
"Vidyujjihva," cried Rávaṇ, "place
The head before the lady's face,
And let her see with weeping eyes
That low in death her husband lies."

Before the queen the giant laid
The beauteous head his art had made.
And Rávaṇ cried: "Thine eyes will know
These arrows and the mighty bow.
With fame of this by Ráma strung
The earth and heaven and hell have rung.
Prahasta brought it hither when
His hand had slain thy prince of men.
Now, widowed Queen, thy hopes resign:
Forget thy husband and be mine."

Sítá's Lament

Again her eyes with tears o'erflowed:
She gazed upon the head he showed,
Gazed on the bow so famed of yore,
The glorious bow which Ráma bore.
She gazed upon his cheek and brows,
The eyes of her beloved spouse;
His lips, the lustre of his hair,
The priceless gem that glittered there.
The features of her lord she knew,
And, pierced with anguish at the view,
She lifted up her voice and cried:
"Kaikeyí, art thou satisfied?
Now all thy longings are fulfilled;
The joy of Raghu's race is killed,
And ruined is the ancient line,
Destroyer, by that fraud of thine.
Ah, what offence, O cruel dame,
What fault in Ráma couldst thou blame,
To drive him clad in hermit dress
With Sítá to the wilderness?"

Great trembling seized her frame, and she
Fell like a stricken plantain tree.
As lie the dead she lay; at length
Slowly regaining sense and strength,
On the dear head she fixed her eye

And cried with very bitter cry:
"Ah, when thy cold dead cheek I view,
My hero, I am murdered too.
Then first a faithful woman's eyes

See sorrow, when her husband dies.
When thou, my lord, wast nigh to save,
Some stealthy hand thy death wound gave.
Thou art not dead: rise, hero, rise;
Long life was thine, as spake the wise
Whose words, I ween, are ever true,
For faith lies open to their view.
Ah lord, and shall thy head recline
On earth's cold breast, forsaking mine,
Counting her chill lap dearer far
Than I and my caresses are?
Ah, is it thus these eyes behold
Thy famous bow adorned with gold,
Whereon of yore I loved to bind
Sweet garlands that my hands had twined?
And hast thou sought in heaven a place
Amid the founders of thy race,
Where in the home deserved so well
Thy sires and Daśaratha dwell?
Or dost thou shine a brighter star
In skies where blest immortals are,
Forsaking in thy lofty scorn
The race wherein thy sires were born?
Turn to my gaze, O turn thine eye:
Why are thy cold lips silent, why?
When first we met as youth and maid,
When in thy hand my hand was laid,
Thy promise was thy steps should be
Through life in duty's path with me.
Remember, faithful still, thy vow,
And take me with thee even now.
Is that broad bosom where I hung,
That neck to which I fondly clung,
Where flowery garlands breathed their scent
By hungry dogs and vultures rent?
Shall no funereal honours grace
The parted lord of Raghu's race,
Whose bounty liberal fees bestowed,
For whom the fires of worship glowed?
Kauśalyá wild with grief will see

One sole survivor of the three
Who in their hermit garments went
To the dark woods in banishment.
Then at her cry shall Lakshmaṇ tell
How, slain by night, the Vánars fell;
How to thy side the giants crept,
And slew the hero as he slept.
Thy fate and mine the queen will know,
And broken-hearted die of woe.
For my unworthy sake, for mine,
Ráma, the glory of his line,
Who bridged his way across the main,
Is basely in a puddle slain;
And I, the graceless wife he wed,
Have brought this ruin on his head.
Me, too, on him, O Rávaṇ, slay:
The wife beside her husband lay.
By his dear body let me rest,
Cheek close to cheek and breast to breast,
My happy eyes I then will close,
And follow whither Ráma goes."

Thus cried the miserable dame;
When to the king a warder came,
Before the giant monarch bowed
And said that, followed by a crowd
Of counsellors and lords of state,
Prahasta stood before the gate,
And, sent by some engrossing care,
Craved audience of his master there.
The anxious tyrant left his seat
And hastened forth the chief to meet:
Then summoning his nobles all,
Took counsel in his regal hall.

When Lanká's lord had left the queen,
The head and bow no more were seen.
The giant king his nobles eyed,
And, terrible as Yáma, cried:
"O faithful lords, the time is come:

Gather our hosts with beat of drum.
Nigh to the town our foeman draws:
Be prudent, nor reveal the cause."

The nobles listened and obeyed:
Swift were the gathered troops arrayed,
And countless rovers of the night
Stood burning for the hour of fight.

CANTO

XXXIII

Saramá

But Saramá, of gentler mood,
With pitying eyes the mourner viewed,
Stole to her side and softly told
Glad tidings that her heart consoled,
Revealing with sweet voice and smile
The secret of the giant's guile.
She, one of those who night and day
Watching in turns by Sítá lay,
Though Rákshas born felt pity's touch,
And loved the hapless lady much.

"I heard," she said, "thy bitter cry,
Heard Rávaṇ's speech and thy reply,
For, hiding in the thicket near,
No word or tone escaped mine ear.
When Rávaṇ hastened forth I bent
My steps to follow as he went,
And learnt the secret cause that drove
The monarch from the Aśoka grove.
Believe me, Queen, thou needst not weep
For Ráma slaughtered in his sleep.
Thy lion lord of men defies

400

By day attack, by night surprise.
Can even giants slay with ease
Vast hosts who fight with brandished trees,
For whom, with eye that never sleeps,
His constant watch thy Ráma keeps?

Lord of the mighty arm and chest,
Of earthly warriors first and best,
Whose fame through all the regions rings,
Proud scion of a hundred kings;
Who guards his life and loves to lend
His saving succour to a friend:
Whose bow no hand but his can strain,—
Thy lord, thy Ráma is not slain.
Obedient to his master's will,
A great magician, trained in ill,
With deftest art surpassing thought
That marvellous illusion wrought.
Let rising hope thy grief dispel:
Look up and smile, for all is well,
And gentle Lakshmí, Fortune's Queen,
Regards thee with a favouring mien.
Thy Ráma with his Vánar train
Has thrown a bridge athwart the main,
Has led his countless legions o'er,
And ranged them on this southern shore.
These eyes have seen the hero stand
Girt by his hosts on Lanká's strand,
And breathless spies each moment bring
Fresh tidings to the giant king;
And every peer and lord of state
Is called to counsel and debate."

She ceased: the sound, long loud and clear,
Of gathering armies smote her ear,
Where call of drum and shell rang out,
The tambour and the battle shout;
And, while the din the echoes woke,
Again to Janak's child she spoke:
"Hear, lady, hear the loud alarms
That call the Rákshas troops to arms,

From stable and from stall they lead
The elephant and neighing steed,
Brace harness on with deftest care,
And chariots for the fight prepare.
Swift o'er the trembling ground career
Mailed horsemen armed with axe and spear,
And here and there in road and street
The terrible battalions meet.
I hear the gathering near and far,
The snorting steed, the rattling car.
Bold chieftains, leaders of the brave,
Press densely on, like wave on wave,
And bright the evening sunbeams glance
On helm and shield, on sword and lance.
Hark, lady, to the ringing steel,
Hark to the rolling chariot wheel:
Hark to the mettled courser's neigh
And drums' loud thunder far away.
The Queen of Fortune holds thee dear,
For Lanká's troops are struck with fear,
And Ráma with the lotus eyes,
Like Indra monarch of the skies,
With conquering arm will slay his foe
And free his lady from her woe.
Soon will his breast support thy head,
And tears of joy thine eyes will shed.
Soon by his mighty arm embraced
The long-lost rapture wilt thou taste,
And Ráma, meet for highest bliss,
Will gain his guerdon in thy kiss."

Saramá's Tidings

Thus Saramá her story told:
And Sítá's spirit was consoled,
As when the first fresh rain is shed
The parching earth is comforted.
Then, filled with zeal for Sítá's sake,
Again in gentle tones she spake,
And, skilled in arts that soothe and please,
Addressed the queen in words like these:
"Thy husband, lady, will I seek,
Say the fond words thy lips would speak,
And then, unseen of any eye,
Back to thy side will swiftly fly.
My airy flights are speedier far
Than Garuḍa's and the tempest are."

Then Sítá spake: her former woe
Still left her accents faint and low:
"I know thy steps, which naught can stay,
Can urge through heaven and hell their way.
Then if thy love and changeless will
Would serve the helpless captive still,
Go forth and learn each plot and guile
Planned by the lord of Lanká's isle.
With magic art like maddening wine
He cheats these weeping eyes of mine,
Torments me with his suit, nor spares
Reproof or flattery, threats or prayers.
These guards surround me night and day;
My heart is sad, my senses stray;
And helpless in my woe I fear
The tyrant Rávaṇ even here."

Then Saramá replied: "I go
To learn the purpose of thy foe,
Soon by thy side again to stand
And tell thee what the king has planned."
She sped, she heard with eager ears
The tyrant speak his hopes and fears,
Where, gathered at their master's call,
The nobles filled the council hall;
Then swiftly, to her promise true,
Back to the Aśoka grove she flew.
The lady on the grassy ground,
Longing for her return, she found;
Who with a gentle smile, to greet
The envoy, led her to a seat.
Through her worn frame a shiver ran
As Saramá her tale began:
"There stood the royal mother: she
Besought her son to set thee free,

And to her counsel, tears and prayers,
The elder nobles added theirs:
"O be the Maithil queen restored
With honour to her angry lord,
Let Janasthán's unhappy fight
Be witness of the hero's might.
Hanúmán o'er the waters came
And looked upon the guarded dame.
Let Lanká's chiefs who fought and fell
The prowess of the leader tell."
In vain they sued, in vain she wept,
His purpose still unchanged he kept,
As clings the miser to his gold,
He would not loose thee from his hold.
No, never till in death he lies,
Will Lanká's lord release his prize.
Soon slain by Ráma's arrows all
The giants with their king will fall,
And Ráma to his home will lead
His black-eyed queen from bondage freed."

An awful sound that moment rose
From Lanká's fast-approaching foes,
Where drum and shell in mingled peal
Made earth in terror rock and reel.
The hosts within the walls arrayed
Stood trembling, in their hearts dismayed;
Thought of the tempest soon to burst,
And Lanká's lord, their ruin, cursed.

CANTO
XXXV

Malyaván's Speech

The fearful notes of drum and shell
Upon the ear of Rávaṇ fell.
One moment quailed his haughty look,
One moment in his fear he shook,
But soon recalling wonted pride,
His counsellors he sternly eyed,
And with a voice that thundered through
The council hall began anew:
"Lords, I have heard—your tongues have told—
How Raghu's son is fierce and bold.
To Lanká's shore has bridged his way
And hither leads his wild array.
I know your might, in battle tried,
Fighting and conquering by my side.
Why now, when such a foe is near,
Looks eye to eye in silent fear?"

He ceased, his mother's sire well known
For wisdom in the council shown,
Malyaván, sage and faithful guide.
Thus to the monarch's speech replied:

"Long reigns the king in safe repose,
Unmoved by fear of vanquished foes,
Whose feet by saving knowledge led
In justice path delight to tread:
Who knows to sheath the sword or wield,
To order peace, to strike or yield:
Prefers, when foes are stronger, peace,
And bids a doubtful conflict cease.
Now, King, the choice before thee lies,
Make peace with Ráma, and be wise.
This day the captive queen restore
Who brings the foe to Lanká's shore.
The Sire by whom the worlds are swayed
Of yore the Gods and demons made.
With these Injustice sided; those
Fair Justice for her champions chose.
Still Justice dwells with Gods above;
Injustice, fiends and giants love.
Thou, through the worlds that fear thee, long
Hast scorned the right and loved the wrong,
And Justice, with thy foes allied,
Gives might resistless to their side.
Thou, guided by thy wicked will,
Hast found delight in deeds of ill,
And sages in their holy rest
Have trembled, by thy power oppressed.
But they, who check each vain desire,
Are clothed with might which burns like fire.
In them the power and glory live
Which zeal and saintly fervour give.
Their constant task, their sole delight
Is worship and each holy rite,
To chant aloud the Veda hymn,
Nor let the sacred fires grow dim.
Now through the air like thunder ring
The echoes of the chants they sing.
The vapours of their incense rise
And veil with cloudy pall the skies,
And Rákshas might grows weak and faint
Killed by the power of sage and saint.
By Brahmá's boon thy life was screened

From God, Gandharva, Yaksha, fiend;
But Vánars, men, and bears, arrayed
Against thee now, thy shores invade.
Red meteors, heralds of despair
Flash frequent through the lurid air,
Foretelling to my troubled mind
The ruin of the Rákshas kind.
With awful thundering overhead
Clouds black as night are densely spread,
And oozing from the gloomy pall
Great drops of blood on Lanká fall.
Dogs roam through house and shrine to steal
The sacred oil and curd and meal,
Cats pair with tigers, hounds with swine,
And asses' foals are born of kine.
In these and countless signs I trace
The ruin of the giant race.
'Tis Vishṇu's self who comes to storm
Thy city, clothed in Ráma's form;
For, well I ween, no mortal hand
The ocean with a bridge has spanned.
O giant King, the dame release,
And sue to Raghu's son for peace"

CANTO
XXXVI

Rávan's Reply

But Rávaṇ's breast with fury swelled,
And thus he spake by Death impelled,
While, under brows in anger bent,
Fierce glances from his eyes were sent:
"The bitter words which thou, misled
By friendly thought, hast fondly said,
Which praise the foe and counsel fear,

Unheeded fall upon mine ear.
How canst thou deem a mighty foe
This Ráma who, in stress of woe,
Seeks, banished as his sire decreed,
Assistance from the Vánar breed?
Am I so feeble in thine eyes,
Though feared by dwellers of the skies,—
Whose might in many a battle shown
The glorious race of giants own?
Shall I for fear of him restore
The lady whom I hither bore,
Exceeding fair like Beauty's Queen
Without her well-loved lotus seen?
Around the chief let Lakshmaṇ stand,
Sugríva, and each Vánar band,
Soon, Malyaván, thine eyes will see
This boasted Ráma slain by me.
I in the brunt of war defy
The mightiest warriors of the sky;
And if I stoop to combat men,
Shall I be weak and tremble then?
This mangled trunk the foe may rend,
But Rávaṇ ne'er can yield or bend,
And be it vice or virtue, I
This nature never will belie.
What marvel if he bridged the sea?
Why should this deed disquiet thee?
This, only this, I surely know,
Back with his life he shall not go."

Thus in loud tones the king exclaimed,
And mute stood Malyaván ashamed,
His reverend head he humbly bent,
And slowly to his mansion went.
But Rávaṇ stayed, and deep in care
Held counsel with his nobles there,
All entrance to secure and close,
And guard the city from their foes.
He bade the chief Prahasta wait,
Commander at the eastern gate,
To fierce Mahodar, strong and brave,

To keep the southern gate, he gave,
Where Mahápárśva's might should aid
The chieftain with his hosts arrayed.
To guard the west—no chief more fit—
He placed the warrior Indrajít,
His son, the giant's joy and boast,
Surrounded by a Rákshas host:
And mighty Sáraṇ hastened forth
With Śuka to protect the north.
"I will myself," the monarch cried,
"Be present on the northern side."
These orders for the walls' defence
The tyrant gave, then parted thence,
And, by the hope of victory fired,
To chambers far within, retired.

CANTO

XXXVII

Preparations

Lords of the legions of the wood,
    The chieftains with Vibhishaṇ stood,
    And, strangers in the foeman's land,
Their hopes and fears in council scanned:
"See, see where Lanká's towers ascend,
Which Rávaṇ's power and might defend,
Which Gods, Gandharvas, fiends would fail
To conquer, if they durst assail.
How shall our legions pass within,
The city of the foe to win,
With massive walls and portals barred
Which Rávaṇ keeps with surest guard?"
With anxious looks the walls they eyed:
And sage Vibhishaṇ thus replied:
"These lords of mine can answer: they

Within the walls have found their way,
The foeman's plan and order learned,
And hither to my side returned.
Now, Ráma, let my tongue declare
How Rávaṇ's hosts are stationed there.
Prahasta heads, in warlike state,
His legions at the eastern gate.
To guard the southern portal stands
Mahodar, girt by Rákshas bands,
Where mighty Mahápárśva, sent
By Rávaṇ's hest, his aid has lent.
Guard of the gate that fronts the west
Is valiant Indrajít, the best
Of warriors, Rávaṇ's joy and pride;
And by the youthful chieftain's side
Are giants, armed for fierce attacks
With sword and mace and battle-axe.
North, where approach is dreaded most,
The king, encompassed with a host
Of giants trained in war, whose hands
Wield maces, swords and lances, stands.

All these are chiefs whom Rávaṇ chose
As mightiest to resist his foes;
And each a countless army leads
With elephants and cars and steeds."

Then Ráma, while his spirit burned
For battle, words like these returned:
"The eastern gate be Níla's care,
Opponent of Prahasta there.
The southern gate, with troops arrayed
Let Angad, Báli's son, invade.
The gate that fronts the falling sun
Shall be by brave Hanúmán won;
Soon through its portals shall he lead
His myriads of Vánar breed.
The gate that fronts the north shall be
Assailed by Lakshmaṇ and by me,
For I myself have sworn to kill
The tyrant who delights in ill.

Armed with the boon which Brahmá gave,
The Gods of heaven he loves to brave,
And through the trembling worlds he flies,
Oppressor of the just and wise.
Thou, Jámbaván, and thou, O King
Of Vánars, all your bravest bring,
And with your hosts in dense array
Straight to the centre force your way.
But let no Vánar in the storm
Disguise him in a human form,
Ye chiefs who change your shapes at will,
Retain your Vánar semblance still.
Thus, when we battle with the foe,
Both men and Vánars will ye know,
In human form will seven appear;
Myself, my brother Lakshmaṇ here;
Vibhishaṇ, and the four he led
From Lanká's city when he fled."

Thus Raghu's son the chiefs addressed:
Then, gazing on Suvela's crest,
Transported by the lovely sight,
He longed to climb the mountain height.

CANTO
XXXVIII

The Ascent of Suvela

"Come let us scale," the hero cried,
  "This hill with various metals dyed.
  This night upon the breezy crest
Sugríva, Lakshmaṇ, I, will rest,
With sage Vibhishaṇ, faithful friend,
His counsel and his lore to lend.
From those tall peaks each eager eye

The foeman's city shall espy,
Who from the wood my darling stole
And brought long anguish on my soul."

Thus spake the lord of men, and bent
His footsteps to the steep ascent,
And Lakshmaṇ, true in weal and woe,
Next followed with his shafts and bow.
Vibhishaṇ followed, next in place,
The sovereign of the Vánar race,
And hundreds of the forest kind
Thronged with impetuous feet, behind.
The chiefs in woods and mountains bred
Fast followed to Suvela's head,
And gazed on Lanká bright and fair
As some gay city in the air.
On glittering gates, on ramparts raised
By giant hands, the chieftains gazed.
They saw the mighty hosts that, skilled
In arts of war, the city filled,
And ramparts with new ramparts lined,
The swarthy hosts that stood behind.
With spirits burning for the fight
They saw the giants from the height,
And from a hundred throats rang out
Defiance and the battle shout.
Then sank the sun with dying flame,
And soft the shades of twilight came,
And the full moon's delicious light
Was shed upon the tranquil night.

Lanká

They slept secure: the sun arose
    And called the chieftains from repose.
    Before the wondering Vánars, gay
With grove and garden, Lanká lay,
Where golden buds the Champak showed,
And bright with bloom Aśoka glowed,
And palm and Sál and many a tree
With leaf and flower were fair to see.
They looked on wood and lawn and glade,
On emerald grass and dusky shade,
Where creepers filled the air with scent,
And luscious fruit the branches bent,
Where bees inebriate loved to throng,
And each sweet bird was loud in song.
The wondering Vánars passed the bound
That circled that enchanting ground,
And as they came a sweet breeze through
The odorous alleys softly blew.
Some Vánars, at their king's behest,
Onward to bannered Lanká pressed,
While, startled by the strangers' tread,
The birds and deer before them fled.
Earth trembled at each step they took,
And Lanká at their shouting shook.
Bright rose before their wondering eyes
Trikúṭa's peak that kissed the skies,
And, clothed with flowers of every hue,
Afar its golden radiance threw.
Most fair to see the mountain's head

413

A hundred leagues in length was spread.
There Rávan's town, securely placed,
The summit of Trikúṭa graced.
O'er leagues of land she stretched in pride,
A hundred long and twenty wide.
They saw a lofty wall enfold
The city, built of blocks of gold,
They saw the beams of morning fall
On dome and fane within the wall,
Bright with the shine that mansion gives
Where Vishṇu in his glory lives.
White-crested like the Lord of Snows
Before them Rávan's palace rose.
High on a thousand pillars raised
With gold and precious stone it blazed,
Guarded by giant warders, crown
And ornament of Lanká's town.

CANTO
XL

Rávan Attacked

S
till stood the son of Raghu where
Suvela's peak rose high in air,
And with Sugríva turned his eye
To scan each quarter of the sky.
There on Trikúṭa, nobly planned
And built by Viśvakarmá's hand,
He saw the lovely Lanká, dressed
In all her varied beauty, rest.
High on a tower above the gate
The tyrant stood in kingly state.
The royal canopy displayed
Above him lent its grateful shade,
And servants, from the giant band,

His cheek with jewelled chowries fanned.
Red sandal o'er his breast was spread,
His ornaments and robe were red:
Thus shows a cloud of darksome hue
With golden sunbeams flashing through.
While Ráma and the chiefs intent
Upon the king their glances bent,
Up sprang Sugríva from the ground
And reached the turret at a bound.
Unterrified the Vánar stood,
And wroth, with wondrous hardihood,
The king in bitter words addressed,
And thus his scorn and hate expressed:
"King of the giant race, in me
The friend and slave of Ráma see.
Lord of the world, he gives me power
To smite thee in thy fenced tower."
While through the air his challenge rang,
At Rávaṇ's face the Vánar sprang.
Snatched from his head the kingly crown
And dashed it in his fury down.
Straight at his foe the giant flew,
His mighty arms about him threw.
With strength resistless swung him round
And dashed him panting to the ground.
Unharmed amid the storm of blows
Swift to his feet Sugríva rose.
Again in furious fight they met:
With streams of blood their limbs were wet,
Each grasping his opponent's waist.
Thus with their branches interlaced,
Which, crimson with the flowers of spring,
From side to side the breezes swing,
In furious wrestle you may see
The Kinśuk and the Seemal tree.
They fought with fists and hands, alike
Prepared to parry and to strike.
Long time the doubtful combat, waged
With matchless strength and fury, raged.
Each fiercely struck, each guarded well,
Till, closing, from the tower they fell,

And, grasping each the other's throat,
Lay for an instant in the moat.
They rose, and each in fiercer mood
The sanguinary strife renewed.
Well matched in size and strength and skill
They fought the dubious battle still.
While sweat and blood their limbs bedewed
They met, retreated, and pursued:
Each stratagem and art they tried,
Stood front to front and swerved aside.
His hand a while the giant stayed
And called his magic to his aid.
But brave Sugríva, swift to know
The guileful purpose of the foe,
Gained with light leap the upper air,
And breath and strength and spirit there;
Then, joyous as for victory won,
Returned to Raghu's royal son.

CANTO
XLI

Ráma's Envoy

When Ráma saw each bloody trace
On King Sugríva's limbs and face,
He cried, while, sorrowing at the view,
His arms about his friend he threw:
"Too venturous chieftain, kings like us
Bring not their lives in peril thus;
Nor, save when counsel shows the need,
Attempt so bold, so rash a deed.
Remember, I, Vibhishaṇ all
Have sorrowed fearing for thy fall.
O do not—for us all I speak—
These desperate adventures seek."

"I could not," cried Sugríva, "brook
Upon the giant king to look,

Nor challenge to the deadly strife
The fiend who robbed thee of thy wife."
"Now Lakshmaṇ, marshal," Ráma cried,
"Our legions where the woods are wide,
And stand we ready to oppose
The fury of our giant foes.
This day our armies shall ascend
The walls which Rávaṇ's powers defend,
And floods of Rákshas blood shall stain
The streets encumbered with the slain."
Down from the peak he came, and viewed
The Vánars' ordered multitude.
Each captain there for battle burned,
Each fiery eye to Lanká turned.
On, where the royal brothers led
To Lanká's walls the legions sped.
The northern gate, where giant foes
Swarmed round their monarch, Ráma chose
Where he in person might direct
The battle, and his troops protect.
What arm but his the post might keep
Where, strong as he who sways the deep,
Mid thousands armed with bow and mace,
Stood Rávaṇ mightiest of his race?
The eastern gate was Níla's post,
Where marshalled stood his Vánar host,
And Mainda with his troops arrayed,
And Dwivid stood to lend him aid.
The southern gate was Angad's care,
Who ranged his bold battalions there.
Hanúmán by the port that faced
The setting sun his legions placed,
And King Sugríva held the wood
East of the gate where Rávaṇ stood.
On every side the myriads met,
And Lanká's walls of close beset
That scarce the roving gale could win
A passage to the hosts within.

417

Loud as the angry ocean's roar
When wild waves lash the rocky shore,
Ten thousand thousand throats upsent
A shout that tore the firmament,
And Lanká with each grove and brook
And tower and wall and rampart shook.
The giants heard, and were appalled:
Then Raghu's son to Angad called,
And, led by kingly duty, gave
This order merciful as brave:
"Go, Angad, Rávaṇ's presence seek,
And thus my words of warning speak:
"How art thou changed and fallen now,
O Monarch of the giants, thou
Whose impious fury would not spare
Saint, nymph, or spirit of the air;
Whose foot in haughty triumph trod
On Yaksha, king, and Serpent God:
How art thou fallen from thy pride
Which Brahmá's favour fortified!
With myriads at thy Lanká's gate
I stand my righteous ire to sate,
And punish thee with sword and flame,
The tyrant fiend who stole my dame.
Now show the might, employ the guile,
O Monarch of the giants' isle,
Which stole a helpless dame away:
Call up thy power and strength to-day.
Once more I warn thee, Rákshas King,
This hour the Maithil lady bring,
And, yielding while there yet is time,
Seek, suppliant, pardon for the crime,
Or I will leave beneath the sun
No living Rákshas, no, not one.
In vain from battle wilt thou fly,
Or borne on pinions seek the sky;
The hand of Ráma shall not spare;
His fiery shaft shall smite thee there.'"

He ceased: and Angad bowed his head;
Thence like embodied flame he sped,

And lighted from his airy road
Within the Rákshas king's abode.
There sate, the centre of a ring
Of counsellors, the giant king.
Swift through the circle Angad pressed,
And spoke with fury in his breast:
"Sent by the lord of Kośal's land,
His envoy here, O King, I stand,
Angad the son of Báli: fame
Has haply taught thine ears my name.
Thus in the words of Ráma I
Am come to warn thee or defy:
Come forth, and fighting in the van
Display the spirit of a man.
This arm shall slay thee, tyrant: all
Thy nobles, kith and kin shall fall:
And earth and heaven, from terror freed,
Shall joy to see the oppressor bleed.
Vibhishan, when his foe is slain,
Anointed king in peace shall reign.
Once more I counsel thee: repent,
Avoid the mortal punishment,
With honour due the dame restore,
And pardon for thy sin implore."

Loud rose the king's infuriate cry:
"Seize, seize the Vánar, let him die."
Four of his band their lord obeyed,
And eager hands on Angad laid.
He purposing his strength to show
Gave no resistance to the foe,
But swiftly round his captors cast
His mighty arms and held them fast.
Fierce shout and cry around him rang:
Light to the palace roof he sprang,
There his detaining arms unwound,
And hurled the giants to the ground.
Then, smiting with a fearful stroke,
A turret from the roof he broke,—
As when the fiery levin sent

419

By Indra from the clouds has rent
The proud peak of the Lord of Snow,—
And flung the stony mass below.
Again with loud terrific cry
He sprang exulting to the sky,
And, joyous for his errand done,
Stood by the side of Raghu's son.

The Sally

Still was the cry, "The Vánar foes
Around the leaguered city close."
King Rávaṇ from the terrace gazed
And saw, with eyes where fury blazed,
The Vánar host in serried ranks
Press to the moat and line the banks,
And, first in splendour and in place,
The lion lord of Raghu's race.
And Ráma looked on Lanká where
Gay flags were streaming to the air,
And, while keen sorrow pierced him through,
His loving thoughts to Sítá flew:
"There, there in deep affliction lies
My darling with the fawn-like eyes.
There on the cold bare ground she keeps
Sad vigil and for Ráma weeps."
Mad with the thought, "Charge, charge," he cried.
"Let earth with Rákshas blood be dyed."

Responsive to his call rang out
A loud, a universal shout,
As myriads filled the moat with stone,

420

Trees, rocks, and mountains overthrown,
And charging at their leader's call
Pressed forward furious to the wall.
Some in their headlong ardour scaled
The rampart's height, the guard assailed,
And many a ponderous fragment rent
From portal, tower, and battlement.
Huge gates adorned with burnished gold
Were loosed and lifted from their hold;
And post and pillar, with a sound
Like thunder, fell upon the ground.
At every portal, east and west
And north and south, the chieftains pressed
Each in his post appointed led
His myriads in the forest bred.

"Charge, let the gates be opened wide:
Charge, charge, my giants," Rávaṇ cried.
They heard his voice, and loud and long
Rang the wild clamour of the throng,
And shell and drum their notes upsent,
And every martial instrument.
Forth, at the bidding of their lord
From every gate the giants poured,
As, when the waters rise and swell,
Huge waves preceding waves impel.
Again from every Vánar throat
A scream of fierce defiance smote
The welkin: earth and sea and sky
Reëchoed with the awful cry.
The roar of elephants, the neigh
Of horses eager for the fray.
The frequent clash of warriors' steel,
The rattling of the chariot wheel.
Fierce was the deadly fight: opposed
In terrible array they closed,
As when the Gods of heaven enraged
With rebel fiends wild battle waged.
Axe, spear, and mace were wielded well:
At every blow a Vánar fell.

But shivered rock and brandished tree
Brought many a giant on his knee,
To perish in his turn beneath
The deadly wounds of nails and teeth.

CANTO
XLIII

The Single Combats

Brave chiefs of each opposing side
Their strength in single combat tried.
Fierce Indrajít the fight began
With Angad in the battle's van.
Sampáti, strongest of his race,
Stood with Prajangha face to face.
Hanúmán, Jambumáli met
In mortal opposition set.
Vibhishaṇ, brother of the lord
Of Lanká, raised his threatening sword
And singled out, with eyes aglow
With wrath, Śatrughna for his foe.
The mighty Gaja Tapan sought,
And Níla with Nikumbha fought.
Sugríva, Vánar king, defied
Fierce Praghas long in battle tried,
And Lakshmaṇ fearless in the fight
Encountered Vírúpáksha's might.
To meet the royal Ráma came
Wild Agniketu fierce as flame;
Mitraghana, he who loved to strike
His foeman and his friend alike:
With Raśmiketu, known and feared
Where'er his ponderous flag was reared;
And Yajnakopa whose delight
Was ruin of the sacred rite.

422

These met and fought, with thousands more,
And trampled earth was red with gore.
Swift as the bolt which Indra sends
When fire from heaven the mountain rends
Smote Indrajít with furious blows
On Angad queller of his foes.
But Angad from his foeman tore
The murderous mace the warrior bore,

And low in dust his coursers rolled,
His driver, and his car of gold.
Struck by the shafts Prajangha sped,
The Vánar chief Sampáti bled,
But, heedless of his gashes he
Crushed down the giant with a tree.
Then car-borne Jambumáli smote
Hanumán on the chest and throat;
But at the car the Vánar rushed,
And chariot, steeds, and rider crushed.
Sugríva whirled a huge tree round,
And struck fierce Praghas to the ground.
One arrow shot from Lakshman's bow
Laid mighty Vírúpáksha low.
His giant foes round Ráma pressed
And shot their shafts at head and breast;
But, when the iron shower was spent,
Four arrows from his bow he sent,
And every missile, deftly sped;
Cleft from the trunk a giant head.

The Night

The lord of Light had sunk and set:
Night came; the foeman struggled yet;
And fiercer for the gloom of night
Grew the wild fury of the fight.
Scarce could each warrior's eager eye
The foeman from the friend descry.
"Rákshas or Vánar? say;" cried each,
And foe knew foeman by his speech.
"Why wilt thou fly? O warrior, stay:
Turn on the foe, and rend and slay:"
Such were the cries, such words of fear
Smote through the gloom each listening ear.
Each swarthy rover of the night
Whose golden armour flashed with light,
Showed like a towering hill embraced
By burning woods about his waist.
The giants at the Vánars flew,
And ravening ate the foes they slew:
With mortal bite like serpent's fang,
The Vánars at the giants sprang,
And car and steeds and they who bore
The pennons fell bedewed with gore.
No serried band, no firm array
The fury of their charge could stay.
Down went the horse and rider, down
Went giant lords of high renown.
Though midnight's shade was dense and dark,
With skill that swerved not from the mark
Their bows the sons of Raghu drew,
And each keen shaft a chieftain slew.

Uprose the blinding dust from meads
Ploughed by the cars and trampling steeds,
And where the warriors fell the flood
Was dark and terrible with blood.
Six giants singled Ráma out,
And charged him with a furious shout
Loud as the roaring of the sea
When every wind is raging free.
Six times he shot: six heads were cleft;
Six giants dead on earth were left.
Nor ceased he yet: his bow he strained,
And from the sounding weapon rained
A storm of shafts whose fiery glare
Filled all the region of the air;
And chieftains dropped before his aim
Like moths that perish in the flame.
Earth glistened where the arrows fell,
As shines in autumn nights a dell
Which fireflies, flashing through the gloom,
With momentary light illume.

But Indrajít, when Báli's son
The victory o'er the foe had won,
Saw with a fury-kindled eye
His mangled steeds and driver die;
Then, lost in air, he fled the fight,
And vanished from the victor's sight.
The Gods and saints glad voices raised,
And Angad for his virtue praised;
And Raghu's sons bestowed the meed
Of honour due to valorous deed.

Compelled his shattered car to quit,
Rage filled the soul of Indrajít,
Who brooked not, strong by Brahmá's grace
Defeat from one of Vánar race.
In magic mist concealed from view
His bow the treacherous warrior drew,
And Raghu's sons were first to feel
The tempest of his winged steel.

Then when his arrows failed to kill
The princes who defied him still,
He bound them with the serpent noose,
The magic bond which none might loose.

CANTO
XLV

Indrajít's Victory

B rave Ráma, burning still to know
    The station of his artful foe,
Gave to ten chieftains, mid the best
Of all the host, his high behest.
Swift rose in air the Vánar band:
Each region of the sky they scanned:
But Rávaṇ's son by magic skill
Checked them with arrows swifter still,
When streams of blood from chest and side
The dauntless Vánars' limbs had dyed,
The giant in his misty shroud
Showed like the sun obscured by cloud.
Like serpents hissing through the air,
His arrows smote the princely pair;
And from their limbs at every rent
A stream of rushing blood was sent.
Like Kinśuk trees they stood, that show
In spring their blossoms' crimson glow.
Then Indrajít with fury eyed
Ikshváku's royal sons, and cried:

"Not mighty Indra can assail
Or see me when I choose to veil
My form in battle: and can ye,
Children of earth, contend with me?

The arrowy noose this hand has shot
Has bound you with a hopeless knot;
And, slaughtered by my shafts and bow,
To Yáma's hall this hour ye go."

He spoke, and shouted. Then anew
The arrows from his bowstring flew,
And pierced, well aimed with perfect art,
Each limb and joint and vital part.
Transfixed with shafts in every limb,
Their strength relaxed, their eyes grew dim.
As two tall standards side by side,
With each sustaining rope untied,
Fall levelled by the howling blast,
So earth's majestic lords at last
Beneath the arrowy tempest reeled,
And prostrate pressed the battle field.

CANTO

XLVI

Indrajít's Triumph

The Vánar chiefs whose piercing eyes
    Scanned eagerly the earth and skies,
    Saw the brave brothers wounded sore
Transfixed with darts and stained with gore.
The monarch of the Vánar race,
With wise Vibhishaṇ, reached the place;
Angad and Níla came behind,
And others of the forest kind,
And standing with Hanúmán there
Lamented for the fallen pair.
Their melancholy eyes they raised;
In fruitless search a while they gazed.
But magic arts Vibhishaṇ knew;

Not hidden from his keener view,
Though veiled by magic from the rest,
The son of Rávaṇ stood confessed.
Fierce Indrajít with savage pride
The fallen sons of Raghu eyed,
And every giant heart was proud
As thus the warrior cried aloud:

"Slain by mine arrows Ráma lies,
And closed in death are Lakshmaṇ's eyes.
Dead are the mighty princes who
Dúshaṇ and Khara smote and slew.
The Gods and fiends may toil in vain
To free them from the binding chain.
The haughty chief, my father's dread,
Who drove him sleepless from his bed,
While Lanká, troubled like a brook
In rain time, heard his name and shook:
He whose fierce hate our lives pursued
Lies helpless by my shafts subdued.
Now fruitless is each wondrous deed
Wrought by the race the forests breed,
And fruitless every toil at last
Like cloudlets when the rains are past."
Then rose the shout of giants loud
As thunder from a bursting cloud,
When, deeming Ráma, dead, they raised
Their voices and the conqueror praised.
Still motionless, as lie the slain,
The brothers pressed the bloody plain,
No sigh they drew, no breath they heaved,
And lay as though of life bereaved.
Proud of the deed his art had done,
To Lanká's town went Rávaṇ's son,
Where, as he passed, all fear was stilled,
And every heart with triumph filled.
Sugríva trembled as he viewed
Each fallen prince with blood bedewed,
And in his eyes which overflowed
With tears the flame of anger glowed.

428

"Calm," cried Vibhishaṇ, "calm thy fears,
And stay the torrent of thy tears.
Still must the chance of battle change,
And victory still delight to range.
Our cause again will she befriend
And bring us triumph in the end.
This is not death: each prince will break
The spell that holds him, and awake;
Nor long shall numbing magic bind
The mighty arm, the lofty mind."

He ceased: his finger bathed in dew
Across Sugríva's eyes he drew;
From dulling mist his vision freed,
And spoke these words to suit the need:
"No time is this for fear: away
With fainting heart and weak delay.
Now, e'en the tear which sorrow wrings
From loving eyes destruction brings.
Up, on to battle at the head
Of those brave troops which Ráma led.
Or guardian by his side remain
Till sense and strength the prince regain.
Soon shall the trance-bound pair revive,
And from our hearts all sorrow drive.
Though prostrate on the earth he lie,

Deem not that Ráma's death is nigh;
Deem not that Lakshmí will forget
Or leave her darling champion yet.
Rest here and be thy heart consoled;
Ponder my words, be firm and bold.
I, foremost in the battlefield,
Will rally all who faint or yield.
Their staring eyes betray their fear;
They whisper each in other's ear.
They, when they hear my cheering cry
And see the friend of Ráma nigh,
Will cast their gloom and fears away
Like faded wreaths of yesterday."

Thus calmed he King Sugríva's dread;
Then gave new heart to those who fled.
Fierce Indrajít, his soul on fire
With pride of conquest, sought his sire,
Raised reverent hands, and told him all,
The battle and the princes' fall.
Rejoicing at his foes' defeat
Upsprang the monarch from his seat,
Girt by his giant courtiers: round
His warrior son his arms he wound,
Close kisses on his head applied,
And heard again how Ráma died.

CANTO
XLVII

Sítá

Still on the ground where Ráma slept
Their faithful watch the Vánars kept.
There Angad stood o'erwhelmed with grief
And many a lord and warrior chief;
And, ranged in densest mass around,
Their tree-armed legions held the ground.
Far ranged each Vánar's eager eye,
Now swept the land, now sought the sky,
All fearing, if a leaf was stirred,
A Rákshas in the sound they heard.
The lord of Lanká in his hall,
Rejoicing at his foeman's fall,
Commanded and the warders came
Who ever watched the Maithil dame.
"Go," cried the Rákshas king, "relate
To Janak's child her husband's fate.
Low on the earth her Ráma lies,
And dark in death are Lakshman's eyes.

Bring forth my car and let her ride
To view the chieftains side by side.
The lord to whom her fancy turned
For whose dear sake my love she spurned,
Lies smitten, as he fiercely led
The battle, with his brother dead.
Lead forth the royal lady: go
Her husband's lifeless body show.
Then from all doubt and terror free
Her softening heart will turn to me."

They heard his speech: the car was brought;
That shady grove the warders sought
Where, mourning Ráma night and day,
The melancholy lady lay.
They placed her in the car and through
The yielding air they swiftly flew.
The lady looked upon the plain,
Looked on the heaps of Vánar slain,
Saw where, triumphant in the fight,
Thronged the fierce rovers of the night,
And Vánar chieftains, mournful-eyed,
Watched by the fallen brothers' side.
There stretched upon his gory bed
Each brother lay as lie the dead,
With shattered mail and splintered bow
Pierced by the arrows of the foe.
When on the pair her eyes she bent,
Burst from her lips a wild lament
Her eyes o'erflowed, she groaned and sighed
And thus in trembling accents cried:

Sítá's Lament

"False are they all, proved false to-day,
The prophets of my fortune, they
Who in the tranquil time of old
A blessed life for me foretold,
Predicting I should never know
A childless dame's, a widow's woe,
False are they all, their words are vain,
For thou, my lord and life, art slain.
False was the priest and vain his lore
Who blessed me in those days of yore
By Ráma's side in bliss to reign:
For thou, my lord and life, art slain.
They hailed me happy from my birth,
Proud empress of the lord of earth.
They blessed me—but the thought is pain—
For thou, my lord and life, art slain.
Ah, fruitless hope! each glorious sign
That stamps the future queen is mine,
With no ill-omened mark to show
A widow's crushing hour of woe.
They say my hair is black and fine,
They praise my brows' continuous line;
My even teeth divided well,
My bosom for its graceful swell.
They praise my feet and fingers oft;
They say my skin is smooth and soft,
And call me happy to possess
The twelve fair marks that bring success.
But ah, what profit shall I gain?
Thou, O my lord and life, art slain.

The flattering seer in former days
My gentle girlish smile would praise,

And swear that holy water shed
By Bráhman hands upon my head
Should make me queen, a monarch's bride:
How is the promise verified?
Matchless in might the brothers slew
In Janasthán the giant crew.
And forced the indomitable sea
To let them pass to rescue me.
Theirs was the fiery weapon hurled
By him who rules the watery world;
Theirs the dire shaft by Indra sped;
Theirs was the mystic Brahmá's Head.
In vain they fought, the bold and brave:
A coward's hand their death-wounds gave.
By secret shafts and magic spell
The brothers, peers of Indra, fell.
That foe, if seen by Ráma's eye
One moment, had not lived to fly.
Though swift as thought, his utmost speed
Had failed him in the hour of need.
No might, no tear, no prayer may stay
Fate's dark inevitable day.
Nor could their matchless valour shield
These heroes on the battle field.
I sorrow for the noble dead,
I mourn my hopes for ever fled;
But chief my weeping eyes o'erflow
For Queen Kauśalyá's hopeless woe.
The widowed queen is counting now
Each hour prescribed by Ráma's vow,
And lives because she longs to see
Once more her princely sons and me."

Then Trijaṭá, of gentler mould
Though Rákshas born, her grief consoled:
"Dear Queen, thy causeless woe dispel:
Thy husband lives, and all is well.

433

Look round: in every Vánar face
The light of joyful hope I trace.
Not thus, believe me, shine the eyes
Of warriors when their leader dies.
An Army, when the chief is dead,
Flies from the field dispirited.
Here, undisturbed in firm array,
The Vánars by the brothers stay.
Love prompts my speech; no longer grieve;
Ponder my counsel, and believe.
These lips of mine from earliest youth
Have spoken, and shall speak, the truth.
Deep in my heart thy gentle grace
And patient virtues hold their place.
Turn, lady, turn once more thine eye:
Though pierced with shafts the heroes lie,
On brows and cheeks with blood-drops wet
The light of beauty lingers yet.
Such beauty ne'er is found in death,
But vanishes with parting breath.
O, trust the hope these tokens give:
The heroes are not dead, but live."

Then Sítá joined her hands, and sighed,
"O, may thy words be verified!"
The car was turned, which fleet as thought
The mourning queen to Lanká brought.
They led her to the garden, where
Again she yielded to despair,
Lamenting for the chiefs who bled
On earth's cold bosom with the dead.

Ráma's Lament

Ranged round the spot where Ráma fell
Each Vánar chief stood sentinel.
At length the mighty hero broke
The trance that held him, and awoke.
He saw his senseless brother, dyed
With blood from head to foot, and cried:
"What have I now to do with life
Or rescue of my prisoned wife,
When thus before my weeping eyes,
Slain in the fight, my brother lies?
A queen like Sítá I may find
Among the best of womankind,
But never such a brother, tried
In war, my guardian, friend, and guide.
If he be dead, the brave and true,
I will not live but perish too.
How, reft of Lakshmaṇ, shall I meet
My mother, and Kaikeyí greet?
My brother's eager question brook,
And fond Sumitrá's longing look?
What shall I say, o'erwhelmed with shame
To cheer the miserable dame?
How, when she hears her son is dead,
Will her sad heart be comforted?
Ah me, for longer life unfit
This mortal body will I quit;
For Lakshmaṇ slaughtered for my sake,
From sleep of death will never wake.
Ah when I sank oppressed with care,
Thy gentle voice could soothe despair.
And art thou, O my brother, killed?

Is that dear voice for ever stilled?
Cold are those lips, my brother, whence
Came never word to breed offence?
Ah stretched upon the gory plain
My brother lies untimely slain:
Numbed is the mighty arm that slew
The leaders of the giant crew.
Transfixed with shafts, with blood-streams red,
Thou liest on thy lowly bed:

So sinks to rest, his journey done,
Mid arrowy rays the crimson sun.
Thou, when from home and sire I fled,
The wood's wild ways with me wouldst tread:
Now close to thine my steps shall be,
For I in death will follow thee.
Vibhishaṇ now will curse my name,
And Ráma as a braggart blame,
Who promised—but his word is vain—
That he in Lanká's isle should reign.
Return, Sugríva: reft of me
Lead back thy Vánars o'er the sea,
Nor hope to battle face to face
With him who rules the giant race.
Well have ye done and nobly fought,
And death in desperate combat sought.
All that heroic might can do,
Brave Vánars, has been done by you.
My faithful friends I now dismiss:
Return: my last farewell is this."

Bedewed with tears was every cheek
As thus the Vánars heard him speak.
Vibhishaṇ on the field had stayed
The Vánar hosts who fled dismayed.
Now lifting up his mace on high
With martial step the chief drew nigh.
The hosts who watched by Ráma's side
Beheld his shape and giant stride.
'Tis he, 'tis Rávaṇ's son, they thought:
And all in flight their safety sought.

The Broken Spell

Sugríva viewed the flying crowd,
And thus to Angad cried aloud:
"Why run the trembling hosts, as flee
Storm-scattered barks across the sea?"
"Dost thou not mark," the chief replied,
"Transfixed with shafts, with bloodstreams dyed,
With arrowy toils about them wound,
The sons of Raghu on the ground?"

That moment brought Vibhishaṇ near.
Sugríva knew the cause of fear,
And ordered Jámbaván, who led
The bears, to check the hosts that fled.
The king of bears his hest obeyed:
The Vánars' headlong flight was stayed.
A little while Vibhishaṇ eyed
The brothers fallen side by side.
His giant fingers wet with dew
Across the heroes' eyes he drew,
Still on the pair his sad look bent,
And spoke these word in wild lament:
"Ah for the mighty chiefs brought low
By coward hand and stealthy blow!
Brave pair who loved the open fight,
Slain by that rover of the night.
Dishonest is the victory won
By Indrajít my brother's son.
I on their might for aid relied,
And in my cause they fought and died.
Lost is the hope that soothed each pain:
I live, but live no more to reign,

While Lanká's lord, untouched by ill,
Exults in safe defiance still."

"Not thus," Sugríva said, "repine,
For Lanká's isle shall still be thine.
Nor let the tyrant and his son
Exult before the fight be done.
These royal chiefs, though now dismayed,
Freed from the spell by Garuḍ's aid,
Triumphant yet the foe shall meet
And lay the robber at their feet."

His hope the Vánar monarch told,
And thus Vibhishaṇ's grief consoled.
Then to Sushen who at his side
Expectant stood, Sugríva cried:
"When these regain their strength and sense,
Fly, bear them to Kishkindhá hence.
Here with my legions will I stay,
The tyrant and his kinsmen slay,
And, rescued from the giant king,
The Maithil lady will I bring,
Like Glory lost of old, restored
By Śakra, heaven's almighty lord."

Sushen made answer: "Hear me yet:
When Gods and fiends in battle met,
So fiercely fought the demon crew,
So wild a storm of arrows flew,
That heavenly warriors faint with pain,
Sank smitten by the ceaseless rain.
Vṛihaspati, with herb and spell,
Cured the sore wounds of those who fell.
And, skilled in arts that heal and save,
New life and sense and vigour gave.
Far, on the Milky Ocean's shore,
Still grow those herbs in boundless store;
Let swiftest Vánars thither speed
And bring them for our utmost need.
Those herbs that on the mountain spring
Let Panas and Sampáti bring,

438

For well the wondrous leaves they know,
That heal each wound and life bestow.
Beside that sea which, churned of yore,
The amrit on its surface bore,
Where the white billows lash the land,
Chandra's fair height and Droṇa stand.
Planted by Gods each glittering steep
Looks down upon the milky deep.
Let fleet Hanúmán bring us thence
Those herbs of wondrous influence."

Meanwhile the rushing wind grew loud,
Red lightnings flashed from banks of cloud.
The mountains shook, the wild waves rose,
And smitten with resistless blows

Unrooted fell each stately tree
That fringed the margin of the sea.
All life within the waters feared
Then, as the Vánars gazed, appeared
King Garuḍ's self, a wondrous sight,
Disclosed in flames of fiery light.
From his fierce eye in sudden dread
All serpents in a moment fled.
And those transformed to shaft that bound
The princes vanished in the ground.
On Raghu's sons his eyes he bent,
And hailed the lords armipotent.
Then o'er them stooped the feathered king,
And touched their faces with his wing.
His healing touch their pangs allayed,
And closed each rent the shafts had made.
Again their eyes were bright and bold,
Again the smooth skin shone like gold.
Again within their shell enshrined
Came memory and each power of mind:
And, from those numbing bonds released,
Their spirit, zeal, and strength increased.
Firm on their feet they stood, and then
Thus Ráma spake, the lord of men:

"By thy dear grace in sorest need
From deadly bonds we both are freed.
To these glad eyes as welcome now
As Aja or my sire art thou.
Who art thou, mighty being? say,
Thus glorious in thy bright array."
He ceased: the king of birds replied,
While flashed his eye with joy and pride:
"In me, O Raghu's son, behold
One who has loved thee from of old:
Garuḍ, the lord of all that fly,
Thy guardian and thy friend am I.
Not all the Gods in heaven could loose
These numbing bonds, this serpent noose,
Wherewith fierce Rávaṇ's son, renowned
For magic arts, your limbs had bound.
Those arrows fixed in every limb
Were mighty snakes, transformed by him.
Blood thirsty race, they live beneath
The earth, and slay with venomed teeth.
On, smite the lord of Lanká's isle,
But guard you from the giants' guile
Who each dishonest art employ
And by deceit brave foes destroy.
So shall the tyrant Rávaṇ bleed,
And Sítá from his power be freed."
Thus Garuḍ spake: then, swift as thought,
The region of the sky he sought,
Where in the distance like a blaze
Of fire he vanished from the gaze.

Then the glad Vánars' joy rang out
In many a wild tumultuous shout,
And the loud roar of drum and shell
Startled each distant sentinel.

440

CANTO
LI

Dhúmráksha's Sally

King Rávaṇ, where he sat within,
    Heard from his hall the deafening din,
    And with a spirit ill at ease
Addressed his lords in words like these:

"That warlike shout, those joyous cries,
Loud as the thunder of the skies,
Upsent from every Vánar throat,
Some new-born confidence denote.
Hark, how the sea and trembling shore
Re-echo with the Vánars' roar.
Though arrowy chains, securely twined
Both Ráma and his brother bind,
Still must the fierce triumphant shout
Disturb my soul with rising doubt.
Swift envoys to the army send,
And learn what change these cries portend."

Obedient, at their master's call,
Fleet giants clomb the circling wall.
They saw the Vánars formed and led:
They saw Sugríva at their head,
The brothers from their bonds released:
And hope grew faint and fear increased.
Their faces pale with doubt and dread,
Back to the giant king they sped,
And to his startled ear revealed
The tidings of the battle field.

The flush of rage a while gave place
To chilling fear that changed his face:

441

"What?" cried the tyrant, "are my foes
Freed from the binding snakes that close
With venomed clasp round head and limb,
Bright as the sun and fierce like him:
The spell a God bestowed of yore,
The spell that never failed before?
If arts like these be useless, how
Shall giant strength avail us now?
Go forth, Dhúmráksha, good at need,
The bravest of my warriors lead:
Force through the foe thy conquering way,
And Ráma and the Vánars slay."

Before his king with reverence due
Dhúmráksha bowed him, and withdrew.
Around him at his summons came
Fierce legions led by chiefs of fame.
Well armed with sword and spear and mace,
They hurried to the gathering place,
And rushed to battle, borne at speed
By elephant and car and steed.

CANTO
LII

Dhúmráksha's Death

The Vánars saw the giant foe
  Pour from the gate in gallant show,
Rejoiced with warriors' fierce delight
And shouted, longing for the fight.
Near came the hosts and nearer yet:
Dire was the tumult as they met,
As, serried line to line opposed,
The Vánars and the giants closed.

Fierce on the foe the Vánars rushed,
And, wielding trees, the foremost crushed;
But, feathered from the heron's wing,
With eager flight from sounding string,
Against them shot with surest aim
A ceaseless storm of arrows came:
And, pierced in head and chest and side,
Full many a Vánar fell and died.
They perished slain in fierce attacks
With sword and pike and battle-axe;
But myriads following undismayed
Their valour in the fight displayed.
Unnumbered Vánars rent and torn
With shaft and spear to earth were borne.
But crushed by branchy trees and blocks
Of jagged stone and shivered rocks
Which the wild Vánars wielded well
The bravest of the giants fell.
Their trampled banners strewed the fields,
And broken swords and spears and shields;
And, crushed by blows which none might stay,
Cars, elephants, and riders lay.
Dhúmráksha turned his furious eye
And saw his routed legions fly.
Still dauntless, with terrific blows,
He struck and slew his foremost foes.
At every blow, at every thrust,
He laid a Vánar in the dust.
So fell they neath the sword and lance
In battle's wild Gandharva dance,
Where clang of bow and clash of sword
Did duty for the silvery chord,
And hoofs that rang and steeds that neighed
Loud concert for the dancers made.
So fiercely from Dhúmráksha's bow
His arrows rained in ceaseless flow,
The Vánar legions turned and fled
To all the winds discomfited.
Hanúmán saw the Vánars fly;
He heaved a mighty rock on high.
His keen eyes flashed with wrathful fire,

And, rapid as the Wind his sire,
Strong as the rushing tempests are,
He hurled it at the advancing car.
Swift through the air the missile sang:
The giant from the chariot sprang,
Ere crushed by that terrific blow
Lay pole and wheel and flag and bow.
Hanúmán's eyes with fury blazed:
A mountain's rocky peak he raised,
Poised it on high in act to throw,
And rushed upon his giant foe.
Dhúmráksha saw: he raised his mace
And smote Hanúmán on the face,
Who maddened by the wound's keen pang
Again upon his foeman sprang;
And on the giant's head the rock
Descended with resistless shock.
Crushed was each limb: a shapeless mass
He lay upon the blood-stained grass.

CANTO
LIII

Vajradanshtra's Sally

When Rávaṇ in his palace heard
The mournful news, his wrath was stirred;
And, gasping like a furious snake,
To Vajradanshṭra thus he spake:

"Go forth, my fiercest captain, lead
The bravest of the giants' breed.
Go forth, the sons of Raghu slay
And by their side Sugríva lay."
He ceased: the chieftain bowed his head
And forth with gathered troops he sped.

Cars, camels, steeds were well arrayed,
And coloured banners o'er them played.
Rings decked his arms: about his waist
The life-protecting mail was braced,
And on the chieftain's forehead set
Glittered his cap and coronet.
Borne on a bannered car that glowed
With golden sheen the warrior rode,
And footmen marched with spear and sword
And bow and mace behind their lord.
In pomp and pride of warlike state
They sallied from the southern gate,
But saw, as on their way they sped,
Dread signs around and overhead.
For there were meteors falling fast,
Though not a cloud its shadow cast;
And each ill-omened bird and beast,
Forboding death, the fear increased,
While many a giant slipped and reeled,
Falling before he reached the field.
They met in mortal strife engaged,
And long and fierce the battle raged.
Spears, swords uplifted, gleamed and flashed,
And many a chief to earth was dashed.
A ceaseless storm of arrows rained,
And limbs were pierced and blood-distained.
Terrific was the sound that filled
The air, and every heart was chilled,
As hurtling o'er the giants flew
The rocks and trees which Vánars threw.
Fierce as a hungry lion when
Unwary deer approach his den,

Angad, his eyes with fury red,
Waving a tree above his head,
Rushed with wild charge which none could stay
Where stood the giants' dense array.
Like tall trees levelled by the blast
Before him fell the giants fast,
And earth that streamed with blood was strown
With warriors, steeds, and cars o'erthrown.

445

Vajradanshtra's Death

The giant leader fiercely rained
　　His arrows and the fight maintained.
　　Each time the clanging cord he drew
His certain shaft a Vánar slew.
Then, as the creatures he has made
Fly to the Lord of Life for aid,
To Angad for protection fled
The Vánar hosts dispirited.
Then raged the battle fiercer yet
When Angad and the giant met.
A hundred thousand arrows, hot
With flames of fire, the giant shot;
And every shaft he deftly sent
His foeman's body pierced and rent.
From Angad's limbs ran floods of gore:
A stately tree from earth he tore,
Which, maddened as his gashes bled,
He hurled at his opponent's head.
His bow the dauntless giant drew;
To meet the tree swift arrows flew,
Checked the huge missile's onward way,
And harmless on the earth it lay.
A while the Vánar chieftain gazed,
Then from the earth a rock he raised
Rent from a thunder-splitten height,
And cast it with resistless might.
The giant marked, and, mace in hand,
Leapt from his chariot to the sand,
Ere the rough mass descending broke
The seat, the wheel, the pole and yoke.
Then Angad seized a shattered hill,

Whereon the trees were flowering still,
And with full force the jagged peak
Fell crashing on the giant's cheek.
He staggered, reeled, and fell: the blood
Gushed from the giant in a flood.
Reft of his might, each sense astray,
A while upon the sand he lay.
But strength and wandering sense returned
Again his eyes with fury burned,
And with his mace upraised on high
He wounded Angad on the thigh.
Then from his hand his mace he threw,
And closer to his foeman drew.
Then with their fists they fought, and smote
On brow and cheek and chest and throat.
Worn out with toil, their limbs bedewed,
With blood, the strife they still renewed,
Like Mercury and fiery Mars
Met in fierce battle mid the stars.

A while the deadly fight was stayed:
Each armed him with his trusty blade
Whose sheath with tinkling bells supplied,
And golden net, adorned his side;
And grasped his ponderous leather shield
To fight till one should fall or yield.
Unnumbered wounds they gave and took:
Their wearied bodies reeled and shook.
At length upon the sand that drank
Streams of their blood the warriors sank,
But as a serpent rears his head
Sore wounded by a peasant's tread,
So Angad, fallen on his knees,
Yet gathered strength his sword to seize;
And, severed by the glittering blade,
The giant's head on earth was laid.

[I omit Cantos LV, LVI, LVII, and LVIII, which relate how Akampan
and Prahasta sally out and fall. There is little novelty of incident in
these Cantos and the results are exactly the same as before. In Canto
LV, Akampan, at the command of Rávaṇ, leads forth his troops. Evil

447

omens are seen and heard. The enemies meet, and many fall on each side, the Vánars transfixed with arrows, the Rákshases crushed with rocks and trees.

In Canto LVI Akampan sees that the Rákshases are worsted, and fights with redoubled rage and vigour. The Vánars fall fast under his "nets of arrows." Hanumán comes to the rescue. He throws mountain peaks at the giant which are dexterously stopped with flights of arrows; and at last beats him down and kills him with a tree.

In Canto LVII, Rávaṇ is seriously alarmed. He declares that he himself, Kumbhakarṇa or Prahasta, must go forth. Prahasta sallies out vaunting that the fowls of the air shall eat their fill of Vánar flesh.

In Canto LVIII, the two armies meet. Dire is the conflict; ceaseless is the rain of stones and arrows. At last Níla meets Prahasta and breaks his bow. Prahasta leaps from his car, and the giant and the Vánar fight on foot. Níla with a huge tree crushes his opponent who falls like a tree when its roots are cut.]

CANTO

LIX

Rávan's Sally

They told him that the chief was killed,
And Rávaṇ's breast with rage was filled.
Then, fiercely moved by wrath and pride,
Thus to his lords the tyrant cried:

"No longer, nobles, may we show
This lofty scorn for such a foe
By whom our bravest, with his train
Of steeds and elephants, is slain.
Myself this day will take the field,
And Raghu's sons their lives shall yield."

High on the royal car, that glowed
With glory from his face, he rode;

And tambour shell and drum pealed out,
And joyful was each giant's shout.
A mighty host, with eyeballs red
Like flames of kindled fire, he led.
He passed the city gate, and viewed,
Arrayed, the Vánar multitude,
Those wielding massy rocks, and these
Armed with the stems of uptorn trees,
And Ráma with his eyes aglow
With warlike ardour viewed the foe,
And thus the brave Vibhishan, best
Of weapon-wielding chiefs, addressed:
"What captain leads this bright array
Where lances gleam and banners play,
And thousands armed with spear and sword
Await the bidding of their lord?"

"Seest, thou," Vibhishan answered, "one
Whose face is as the morning sun,
Preëminent for hugest frame?
Akampan is the giant's name.
Behold that chieftain, chariot-borne,
Whom Brahmá's chosen gifts adorn.
He wields a bow like Indra's own;
A lion on his flag is shown,
His eyes with baleful fire are lit:
'Tis Rávan's son, 'tis Indrajít.
There, brandishing in mighty hands
His huge bow, Atikáya stands.
And that proud warrior o'er whose head
A moon-bright canopy is spread:
Whose might, in many a battle tried,
Has tamed imperial Indra's pride;
Who wears a crown of burnished gold,
Is Lanká's lord the lofty-souled."

He ceased: and Ráma knew his foe,
And laid an arrow on his bow:
"Woe to the wretch," he cried, "whom fate
Abandons to my deadly hate."
He spoke, and, firm by Lakshman's side,

449

The giant to the fray defied.
The lord of Lanká bade his train
Of warriors by the gates remain,
To guard the city from surprise
By Ráma's forest born allies.
Then as some monster of the sea
Cleaves swift-advancing billows, he
Charged with impetuous onset through
The foe, and cleft the host in two.
Sugríva ran, the king to meet:
A hill uprooted from its seat
He hurled, with trees that graced the height
Against the rover of the night:
But cleft with shafts that checked its way
Harmless upon the earth it lay.
Then fiercer Rávan's fury grew,
An arrow from his side he drew,
Swift as a thunderbolt, aglow
With fire, and launched it at the foe.
Through flesh and bone a way it found,
And stretched Sugríva on the ground.
Sushen and Nala saw him fall,
Gaváksha, Gavaya heard their call,
And, poising hills, in act to fling
They charged amain the giant king.
They charged, they hurled the hills in vain,
He checked them with his arrowy rain,
And every brave assailant felt
The piercing wounds his missiles dealt,
Then smitten by the shafts that came
Keen, fleet, and thick, with certain aim,
They fled to Ráma, sure defence
Against the oppressor's violence,
Then, reverent palm to palm applied,
Thus Lakshman to his brother cried:
"To me, my lord, the task entrust
To lay this giant in the dust."
"Go, then," said Ráma, "bravely fight;
Beat down this rover of the night.
But he, unmatched in bold emprise,
Fears not the Lord of earth and skies,

Keep on thy guard: with keenest eye
Thy moments of attack espy.
Let hand and eye in due accord
Protect thee with the bow and sword."

Then Lakshmaṇ round his brother threw
His mighty arms in honour due,
Bent lowly down his reverent head,
And onward to the battle sped.
Hanúmán from afar beheld
How Rávaṇ's shafts the Vánars quelled:
To meet the giant's car he ran,
Raised his right arm and thus began:
"If Brahmá's boon thy life has screened
From Yaksha, God, Gandharva, fiend,
With these contending fear no ill,
But tremble at a Vánar still."
With fury flashing from his eye
The lord of Lanká made reply:
"Strike, Vánar, strike: the fray begin,
And hope eternal fame to win.
This arm shall prove thee in the strife

And end thy glory and thy life."
"Remember," cried the Wind-God's son,
"Remember all that I have done,
My prowess, King, thou knowest well,
Shown in the fight when Aksha fell."

With heavy hand the giant smote
Hanúmán on the chest and throat,
Who reeled and staggered to and fro,
Stunned for a moment by the blow.
Till, mustering strength, his hand he reared
And struck the foe whom Indra feared.
His huge limbs bent beneath the shock,
As mountains, in an earthquake, rock,
And from the Gods and sages pealed
Shouts of loud triumph as he reeled.
But strength returning nerved his frame:
His eyeballs flashed with fiercer flame.

451

No living creature might resist
That blow of his tremendous fist
Which fell upon Hanúmán's flank:
And to the ground the Vánar sank,
No sign of life his body showed:
And Rávaṇ in his chariot rode
At Níla; and his arrowy rain
Fell on the captain and his train.
Fierce Níla stayed his Vánar band,
And, heaving with his single hand
A mountain peak, with vigorous swing
Hurled the huge missile at the king.

Hanúmán life and strength regained,
Burned for the fight and thus complained:
"Why, coward giant, didst thou flee
And leave the doubtful fight with me?"
Seven mighty arrows keen and fleet
The giant launched, the hill to meet;
And, all its force and fury stayed,
The harmless mass on earth was laid.
Enraged the Vánar chief beheld
The mountain peak by force repelled,
And rained upon the foe a shower
Of trees uptorn with branch and flower.
Still his keen shafts which pierced and rent
Each flying tree the giant sent:
Still was the Vánar doomed to feel
The tempest of the winged steel.
Then, smarting from that arrowy storm,
The Vánar chief condensed his form,
And lightly leaping from the ground
On Rávan's standard footing found;
Then springing unimpeded down
Stood on his bow and golden crown.
The Vánar's nimble leaps amazed
Ikshváku's son who stood and gazed.
The giant, raging in his heart,
Laid on his bow a fiery dart;
The Vánar on his flagstaff eyed,
And thus in tones of fury cried:

452

"Well skilled in magic lore art thou:
But will thine art avail thee now?
See if thy magic will defend
Thy life against the dart I send."

Thus Rávaṇ spake, the giant king,
And loosed the arrow from the string.
It pierced, with direst fury sped,
The Vánar with its flaming head.
His father's might, his power innate
Preserved him from the threatened fate.
Upon his knees he fell, distained
With streams of blood, but life remained.

Still Rávaṇ for the battle burned:
At Lakshmaṇ next his car he turned,
And charged amain with furious show,
Straining in mighty hands his bow.
"Come," Lakshmaṇ cried, "assay the fight:
Leave foes unworthy of thy might."
Thus Lakshmaṇ spoke: and Lanká's lord
Heard the dread thunder of the cord.
And mad with burning rage and pride
In hasty words like these replied:
"Joy, joy is mine, O Raghu's son:
Thy fate to-day thou canst not shun.
Slain by mine arrows thou shalt tread
The gloomy pathway of the dead."

Thus as he spoke his bow he drew,
And seven keen shafts at Lakshmaṇ flew,
But Raghu's son with surest aim
Cleft every arrow as it came.
Thus with fleet shafts each warrior shot
Against his foe, and rested not.
Then one choice weapon from his store,
By Brahmá's self bestowed of yore,
Fierce as the flames that end the world,
The giant king at Lakshmaṇ hurled.
The hero fell, and racked with pain,
Scarce could his hand his bow retain.

453

But sense and strength resumed their seat
And, lightly springing to his feet,
He struck with one tremendous stroke
And Rávan's bow in splinters broke.
From Lakshman's cord three arrows flew
And pierced the giant monarch through.
Sore wounded Rávan closed, and round
Ikshváku's son his strong arms wound.
With strength unrivalled, Brahmá's gift,
He strove from earth his foe to lift.
"Shall I," he cried, "who overthrow
Mount Meru and the Lord of Snow,
And heaven and all who dwell therein,
Be foiled by one of Ráma's kin?"
But though he heaved, and toiled, and strained,
Unmoved Ikshváku's son remained.
His frame by those huge arms compressed
The giant's God-given force confessed,
But conscious that himself was part

Of Vishnu, he was firm in heart.

The Wind-God's son the fight beheld,
And rushed at Rávan, rage-impelled.
Down crashed his mighty hand; the foe
Full in the chest received the blow.
His eyes grew dim, his knees gave way,
And senseless on the earth he lay.

The Wind-God's son to Ráma bore
Deep-wounded Lakshman stained with gore.
He whom no foe might lift or bend
Was light as air to such a friend.
The dart that Lakshman's side had cleft,
Untouched, the hero's body left,
And flashing through the air afar
Resumed its place in Rávan's car;
And, waxing well though wounded sore,
He felt the deadly pain no more.
And Rávan, though with deep wounds pained,
Slowly his sense and strength regained,

And furious still and undismayed
On bow and shaft his hand he laid.

Then Hanumán to Ráma cried:
"Ascend my back, great chief, and ride
Like Vishṇu borne on Garuḍ's wing,
To battle with the giant king."
So, burning for the dire attack,
Rode Ráma on the Vánar's back,
And with fierce accents loud and slow
Thus gave defiance to the foe,
While his strained bowstring made a sound
Like thunder when it shakes the ground:
"Stay, Monarch of the giants, stay,
The penalty of sin to pay.
Stay! whither wilt thou fly, and how
Escape the death that waits thee now?"

No word the giant king returned:
His eyes with flames of fury burned.
His arm was stretched, his bow was bent,
And swift his fiery shafts were sent.
Red torrents from the Vánar flowed:
Then Ráma near to Rávaṇ strode,
And with keen darts that never failed,
The chariot of the king assailed.
With surest aim his arrows flew:
The driver and the steeds he slew.
And shattered with the pointed steel
Car, flag, and pole and yoke and wheel.
As Indra hurls his bolt to smite
Mount Meru's heaven-ascending height,
So Ráma with a flaming dart
Struck Lanká's monarch near the heart,
Who reeled and fell beneath the blow
And from loose fingers dropped his bow.
Bright as the sun, with crescent head,
From Ráma's bow an arrow sped,
And from his forehead, proud no more,
Cleft the bright coronet he wore.
Then Ráma stood by Rávaṇ's side

And to the conquered giant cried:
"Well hast thou fought: thine arm has slain
Strong heroes of the Vánar train.
I will not strike or slay thee now,
For weary, faint with fight art thou.
To Lanká's town thy footsteps bend,
And there the night securely spend.
To-morrow come with car and bow,
And then my prowess shalt thou know."

He ceased: the king in humbled pride
Rose from the earth and naught replied.
With wounded limbs and shattered crown
He sought again his royal town.

CANTO
LX

Kumbhakarna Roused

With humbled heart and broken pride
Through Lanká's gate the giant hied,
Crushed, like an elephant beneath
A lion's spring and murderous teeth,
Or like a serpent 'neath the wing
And talons of the Feathered King.
Such was the giant's wild alarm
At arrows shot by Ráma's arm;
Shafts with red lightning round them curled,
Like Brahmá's bolts that end the world.

Supported on his golden throne,
With failing eye and humbled tone,
"Giants," he cried, "the toil is vain,
Fruitless the penance and the pain,
If I whom Indra owned his peer,

Secure from Gods, a mortal fear.
My soul remembers, now too late,
Lord Brahmá's words who spoke my fate:
"Tremble, proud Giant," thus they ran,
"And dread thy death from slighted man.
Secure from Gods and demons live,
And serpents, by the boon I give.
Against their power thy life is charmed,
But against man is still unarmed."
This Ráma is the man foretold
By Anaraṇya's lips of old:

"Fear, Rávaṇ, basest of the base:
For of mine own imperial race
A prince in after time shall spring
And thee and thine to ruin bring.
And Vedavatí, ere she died
Slain by my ruthless insult, cried:

"A scion of my royal line
Shall slay, vile wretch, both thee and thine."
She in a later birth became
King Janak's child, now Ráma's dame.
Nandíśvara foretold this fate,
And Umá when I moved her hate,
And Rambhá, and the lovely child
Of Varuṇ by my touch defiled.
I know the fated hour is nigh:
Hence, captains, to your stations fly.
Let warders on the rampart stand:
Place at each gate a watchful band;
And, terror of immortal eyes,
Let mightiest Kumbhakarṇa rise.
He, slumbering, free from care and pain,
By Brahmá's curse, for months has lain.
But when Prahasta's death he hears,
Mine own defeat and doubts and fears,
The chief will rise to smite the foe
And his unrivalled valour show.
Then Raghu's royal sons and all
The Vánars neath his might will fall."

The giant lords his hest obeyed,
They left him, trembling and afraid,
And from the royal palace strode
To Kumbhakarṇa's vast abode.
They carried garlands sweet and fresh,
And reeking loads of blood and flesh.
They reached the dwelling where he lay,
A cave that reached a league each way,
Sweet with fair blooms of lovely scent
And bright with golden ornament.
His breathings came so fierce and fast,
Scarce could the giants brook the blast.
They found him on a golden bed
With his huge limbs at length outspread.
They piled their heaps of venison near,
Fat buffaloes and boars and deer.
With wreaths of flowers they fanned his face,
And incense sweetened all the place.
Each raised his mighty voice as loud
As thunders of an angry cloud,
And conchs their stirring summons gave
That echoed through the giant's cave.
Then on his breast they rained their blows,
And high the wild commotion rose
When cymbal vied with drum and horn.
And war cries on the gale upborne.
Through all the air loud discord spread,
And, struck with fear, the birds fell dead.
But still he slept and took his rest.
Then dashed they on his shaggy chest
Clubs, maces, fragments of the rock:
He moved not once, nor felt the shock.
The giants made one effort more
With shell and drum and shout and roar.
Club, mallet, mace, in fury plied,
Rained blows upon his breast and side.
And elephants were urged to aid,
And camels groaned and horses neighed.
They drenched him with a hundred pails,
They tore his ears with teeth and nails.
They bound together many a mace

And beat him on the head and face;
And elephants with ponderous tread
Stamped on his limbs and chest and head.
The unusual weight his slumber broke:
He started, shook his sides, and woke;
And, heedless of the wounds and blows,
Yawning with thirst and hunger rose,
His jaws like hell gaped fierce and wide,
Dire as the flame neath ocean's tide.
Red as the sun on Meru's crest
The giant's face his wrath expressed,
And every burning breath he drew
Was like the blast that rushes through
The mountain cedars. Up he raised
His awful head with eyes that blazed
Like comets, dire as Death in form
Who threats the worlds with fire and storm.
The giants pointed to their stores
Of buffaloes and deer and boars,
And straight he gorged him with a flood
Of wine, with marrow, flesh, and blood.
He ceased: the giants ventured near
And bent their lowly heads in fear.
Then Kumbhakar[n.]a glared with eyes
Still heavy in their first surprise,
Still drowsy from his troubled rest,
And thus the giant band addressed.
"How have ye dared my sleep to break?
No trifling cause should bid me wake.
Say, is all well? or tell the need
That drives you with unruly speed
To wake me. Mark the words I say,
The king shall tremble in dismay,

The fire be quenched and Indra slain
Ere ye shall break my rest in vain."

Yúpáksha answered: "Chieftain, hear;
No God or fiend excites our fear.
But men in arms our walls assail:
We tremble lest their might prevail.

For vengeful Ráma vows to slay
The foe who stole his queen away,
And, matchless for his warlike deeds,
A host of mighty Vánars leads.
Ere now a monstrous Vánar came,
Laid Lanká waste with ruthless flame,
And Aksha, Rávaṇ's offspring, slew
With all his warrior retinue.
Our king who never trembled yet
For heavenly hosts in battle met,
At length the general dread has shared,
O'erthrown by Ráma's arm and spared."

He ceased: and Kumbhakarṇa spake:
"I will go forth and vengeance take;
Will tread their hosts beneath my feet,
Then triumph-flushed our king will meet.
Our giant bands shall eat their fill
Of Vánars whom this arm shall kill.
The princes' blood shall be my draught,
The chieftains' shall by you be quaffed."
He spake, and, with an eager stride
That shook the earth, to Rávaṇ hied.

CANTO
LXI

The Vánars' Alarm

The son of Raghu near the wall
Saw, proudly towering over all,
The mighty giant stride along
Attended by the warrior throng;
Heard Kumbhakarṇa's heavy feet
Awake the echoes of the street;
And, with the lust of battle fired,

Turned to Vibhishaṇ and inquired:
"Vibhishaṇ, tell that chieftain's name
Who rears so high his mountain frame;
With glittering helm and lion eyes,
Preëminent in might and size
Above the rest of giant birth,
He towers the standard of the earth;
And all the Vánars when they see
The mighty warrior turn and flee."
"In him," Vibhishaṇ answered, "know
Viśravas' son, the Immortals' foe,
Fierce Kumbhakarṇa, mightier far
Than Gods and fiends and giants are.
He conquered Yáma in the fight,
And Indra trembling owned his might.
His arm the Gods and fiends subdued,
Gandharvas and the serpent brood.
The rest of his gigantic race
Are wondrous strong by God-giving grace;
But nature at his birth to him
Gave matchless power and strength of limb.
Scarce was he born, fierce monster, when
He killed and ate a thousand men.
The trembling race of men, appalled,
On Indra for protection called;
And he, to save the suffering world,
His bolt at Kumbhakarṇa hurled.
So awful was the monster's yell
That fear on all the nations fell,
He, rushing on with furious roar,
A tusk from huge Airávat tore,
And dealt the God so dire a blow
That Indra reeling left his foe,
And with the Gods and mortals fled
To Brahmá's throne dispirited.
"O Brahmá," thus the suppliants cried,
"Some refuge for this woe provide.
If thus his maw the giant sate
Soon will the world be desolate."
The Self-existent calmed their woe,
And spake in anger to their foe:

"As thou wast born, Pulastya's son,
That worlds might weep by thee undone,
Thou like the dead henceforth shalt be:
Such is the curse I lay on thee."
Senseless he lay, nor spoke nor stirred;
Such was the power of Brahmá's word.
But Rávaṇ, troubled for his sake,
Thus to the Self-existent spake:
"Who lops the tree his care has reared
When golden fruit has first appeared?
Not thus, O Brahmá, deal with one
Descended from thine own dear son.
Still thou, O Lord, thy word must keep,
He may not die, but let him sleep.
Yet fix a time for him to break
The chains of slumber and awake."
He ceased: and Brahmá made reply;
"Six months in slumber shall he lie
And then arising for a day
Shall cast the numbing bonds away."
Now Rávaṇ in his doubt and dread
Has roused the monster from his bed,
Who comes in this the hour of need
On slaughtered Vánars flesh to feed.
Each Vánar, when his awe-struck eyes
Behold the monstrous chieftain, flies.
With hopeful words their minds deceive,
And let our trembling hosts believe
They see no giant, but, displayed,
A lifeless engine deftly made."

Then Ráma called to Níla: "Haste,
Let troops near every gate be placed,
And, armed with fragments of the rock
And trees, each lane and alley block."

Thus Ráma spoke: the chief obeyed,
And swift the Vánars stood arrayed,
As when the black clouds their battle form,
The summit of a hill to storm.

Rávan's Request

Along bright Lanká's royal road
The giant, roused from slumber, strode,
While from the houses on his head
A rain of fragrant flowers was shed.
He reached the monarch's gate whereon
Rich gems and golden fretwork shone.
Through court and corridor that shook
Beneath his tread his way he took,
And stood within the chamber where
His brother sat in dark despair.
But sudden, at the grateful sight
The monarch's eye again grew bright.
He started up, forgot his fear,
And drew his giant brother near.
The younger pressed the elder's feet
And paid the King observance meet,
Then cried: "O Monarch, speak thy will,
And let my care thy word fulfil.
What sudden terror and dismay
Have burst the bonds in which I lay?"

Fierce flashed the flame from Rávan's eye,
As thus in wrath he made reply:
"Fair time, I ween, for sleep is this,
To lull thy soul in tranquil bliss,
Unheeding, in oblivion drowned,
The dangers that our lives surround.
Brave Ráma, Daśaratha's son,
A passage o'er the sea has won,
And, with the Vánar monarch's aid,
Round Lanká's walls his hosts arrayed.

Though never in the deadly field
My Rákshas troops were known to yield,
The bravest of the giant train
Have fallen by the Vánars slain.
Hence comes my fear. O fierce and brave,
Go forth, our threatened Lanká save.
Go forth, a dreadful vengeance take:
For this, O chief, I bade thee wake.
The Gods and trembling fiends have felt
The furious blows thine arm has dealt.
Earth has no warrior, heaven has none
To match thy might, Paulastya's son."

CANTO
LXIII

Kumbhakarna's Boast

Then Kumbhakarṇa laughed aloud
And cried; "O Monarch, once so proud,
We warned thee, but thou wouldst not hear;
And now the fruits of sin appear.
We warned thee, I, thy nobles, all
Who loved thee, in thy council hall.
Those sovereigns who with blinded eyes
Neglect the foe their hearts despise,
Soon, falling from their high estate
Bring on themselves the stroke of fate.
Accept at length, thy life to save,
The counsel sage Vibhishaṇ gave,
The prudent counsel spurned before,
And Sítá to her lord restore."
The monarch frowned, by passion moved
And thus in angry words reproved:
"Wilt thou thine elder brother school,
Forgetful of the ancient rule

That bids thee treat him as the sage
Who guides thee with the lore of age?
Think on the dangers of the day,
Nor idly throw thy words away:
If, led astray, by passion stirred,
I in the pride of power have erred;
If deeds of old were done amiss,
No time for vain reproach is this.
Up, brother; let thy loving care
The errors of thy king repair."

To calm his wrath, his soul to ease,
The younger spake in words like these:
"Yea, from our bosoms let us cast
All idle sorrow for the past.
Let grief and anger be repressed:
Again be firm and self-possessed.
This day, O Monarch, shalt thou see
The Vánar legions turn and flee,
And Ráma and his brother slain
With their hearts' blood shall dye the plain.
Yea, if the God who rules the dead,
And Varuṇ their battalions led;
If Indra with the Storm-Gods came
Against me, and the Lord of Flame,
Still would I fight with all and slay
Thy banded foes, my King, to-day.
If Raghu's son this day withstand
The blow of mine uplifted hand,
Deep in his breast my darts shall sink,
And torrents of his life-blood drink.
O fear not, in my promise trust:
This arm shall lay him in the dust,
Shall leave the fierce Sugríva dyed
With gore, and Lakshmaṇ by his side,
And strike the great Hanúmán down,
The spoiler of our glorious town."

Mahodar's Speech

He ceased: and when his lips were closed
Mahodar thus his rede opposed:
"Why wilt thou shame thy noble birth
And speak like one of little worth?
Why boast thee thus in youthful pride
Rejecting wisdom for thy guide?
How will thy single arm oppose
The victor of a thousand foes,
Who proved in Janasthán his might
And slew the rovers of the night?
The remnant of those legions, they
Who saw his power that fatal day,
Now in this leaguered city dread
The mighty chief from whom they fled.
And wouldst thou meet the lord of men,
Beard the great lion in his den,
And, when thine eyes are open, break
The slumber of a deadly snake?
Who may an equal battle wage
With him, so awful in his rage,
Fierce as the God of Death whom none
May vanquish, Daśaratha's son?
But, Rávaṇ, shall the lady still
Refuse compliance with thy will?
No, listen, King, to this design
Which soon shall make the captive thine.
This day through Lanká's streets proclaim
That four of us of highest fame
With Kumbhakarṇa at our head
Will strike the son of Raghu dead.

Forth to the battle will we go
And prove our prowess on the foe.
Then, if our bold attempt succeed,
No further plans thy hopes will need.
But if in vain our warriors strive,
And Raghu's son be left alive,
We will return, and, wounded sore,
Our armour stained with gouts of gore,
Will show the shafts that rent each frame,
Keen arrows marked with Ráma's name,
And say we giants have devoured
The princes whom our might o'erpowered.
Then let the joyful tidings spread
That Raghu's royal sons are dead.
To all around thy pleasure show,
Gold, pearls, and precious robes, bestow.
Gay garlands round the portals twine,
Enjoy the banquet and the wine.
Then go, the scornful lady seek,
And woo her when her heart is weak.
Rich robes and gold and gems display,
And gently wile her grief away.
Then will she feel her hopeless state,
Widowed, forlorn, and desolate;
Know that on thee her bliss depends,
Far from her country and her friends;
Then, her proud spirit overthrown,
The lady will be all thine own."

CANTO
LXV

Kumbhakarna's Speech

B ut haughty Kumbhakarṇa spurned
His counsel, and to Rávaṇ turned:
"Thy life from peril will I free
And slay the foe who threatens thee.
A hero never vaunts in vain,
Like bellowing clouds devoid of rain,
Nor, Monarch, be thine ear inclined
To counsellors of slavish kind,
Who with mean arts their king mislead
And mar each gallant plan and deed.
O, let not words like his beguile
The glorious king of Lanká's isle."

Thus scornful Kumbhakarṇa cried,
And Rávaṇ with a laugh replied:
"Mahodar fears and fain would shun
The battle with Ikshváku's son.
Of all my giant warriors, who
Is strong as thou, and brave and true?
Ride, conqueror, to the battle ride,
And tame the foeman's senseless pride.
Go forth like Yáma to the field,
And let thine arm thy trident wield.
Scared by the lightning of thine eye
The Vánar hosts will turn and fly;
And Ráma, when he sees thee near,
With trembling heart will own his fear."

The champion heard, and, well content,
Forth from the hall his footsteps bent.
He grasped his spear, the foeman's dread,

Black iron all, both shaft and head,
Which, dyed in many a battle, bore
Great spots of slaughtered victims' gore.
The king upon his neck had thrown
The jewelled chain which graced his own.
And garlands of delicious scent
About his limbs for ornament.
Around his arms gay bracelets clung,
And pendants in his ears were hung.
Adorned with gold, about his waist
His coat of mail was firmly braced,
And like Náráyaṇ or the God
Who rules the sky he proudly trod.
Behind him went a mighty throng
Of giant warriors tall and strong,

On elephants of noblest breeds.
With cars, with camels, and with steeds:
And, armed with spear and axe and sword
Were fain to battle for their lord.

CANTO
LXVI

Kumbhakarna's Sally

In pomp and pride of warlike state
The giant passed the city gate.
He raised his voice: the hills, the shore
Of Lanká's sea returned the roar.
The Vánars saw the chief draw nigh
Whom not the ruler of the sky,
Nor Yáma, monarch of the dead,
Might vanquish, and affrighted fled.
When royal Angad, Báli's son,
Saw the scared Vánars turn and run,

Undaunted still he kept his ground,
And shouted as he gazed around:
"O Nala, Níla, stay nor let
Your souls your generous worth forget,
O Kumud and Gaváksha, why
Like base-born Vánars will ye fly?
Turn, turn, nor shame your order thus:
This giant is no match for us."

They heard his voice: the flight was stayed;
Again for war they stood arrayed,
And hurled upon the foe a shower
Of mountain peaks and trees in flower.
Still on his limbs their missiles rained:
Unmoved, their blows he still sustained,
And seemed unconscious of the stroke
When rocks against his body broke.
Fierce as the flame when woods are dry
He charged with fury in his eye.
Like trees consumed with fervent heat
They fell beneath the giant's feet.
Some o'er the ground, dyed red with gore,
Fled wild with terror to the shore,
And, deeming that all hope was lost,
Ran to the bridge they erst had crossed.
Some clomb the trees their lives to save,
Some sought the mountain and the cave;
Some hid them in the bosky dell,
And there in deathlike slumber fell.

When Angad saw the chieftains fly
He called them with a mighty cry:
"Once more, O Vánars, charge once more,
On to the battle as before.
In all her compass earth has not,
To hide you safe, one secret spot.
What! leave your arms? each nobler dame
Will scorn her consort for the shame.
This blot upon your names efface,
And keep your valour from disgrace.
Stay, chieftains; wherefore will ye run,

A band of warriors scared by one?"
Scarce would they hear: they would not stay,
And basely spoke in wild dismay:
"Have we not fought, and fought in vain
Have we not seen our mightiest slain?
The giant's matchless force we fear,
And fly because our lives are dear."
But Báli's son with gentle art
Dispelled their dread and cheered each heart.
They turned and formed and waited still
Obedient to the prince's will.

CANTO

LXVII

Kumbhakarna's Death

Thus from their flight the Vánars turned,
    And every heart for battle burned,
    Determined on the spot to die
Or gain a warrior's meed on high.
Again the Vánars stooped to seize
Their weapons, rocks and fallen trees;
Again the deadly fight began,
And fiercely at the giant ran.
Unmoved the monster kept his place:
He raised on high his awful mace,
Whirled the huge weapon round his head
And laid the foremost Vánars dead.
Eight thousand fell bedewed with gore,
Then sank and died seven hundred more.
Then thirty, twenty, ten, or eight
At each fierce onset met their fate,
And fast the fallen were devoured
Like snakes by Garuḍ's beak o'erpowered.
Then Dwivid from the Vánar van,

Armed with an uptorn mountain, ran,
Like a huge cloud when fierce winds blow,
And charged amain the mountain foe.
With wondrous force the hill he threw:
O'er Kumbhakarṇa's head it flew,
And falling on his host afar
Crushed many a giant, steed, and car.
Rocks, trees, by fierce Hanúmán sped,
Rained fast on Kumbhakarṇa's head.
Whose spear each deadlier missile stopped,
And harmless on the plain it dropped.

Then with his furious eyes aglow
The giant rushed upon the foe,
Where, with a woody hill upheaved,
Hanúmán's might his charge received.
Through his vast frame the giant felt
The angry blow Hanúmán dealt.
He reeled a moment, sore distressed,
Then smote the Vánar on the breast,
As when the War-God's furious stroke
Through Krauncha's hill a passage broke.
Fierce was the blow, and deep and wide
The rent: with crimson torrents dyed,
Hanúmán, maddened by the pain,
Roared like a cloud that brings the rain,
And from each Rákshas throat rang out
Loud clamour and exultant shout.
Then Níla hurled with mustered might
The fragment of a mountain height;
Nor would the rock the foe have missed,
But Kumbhakarṇa raised his fist
And smote so fiercely that the mass
Fell crushed to powder on the grass.
Five chieftains of the Vánar race
Charged Kumbhakarṇa face to face,
And his huge frame they wildly beat
With rocks and trees and hands and feet.
Round Rishabh first the giant wound
His arms and hurled him to the ground,
Where speechless, senseless, wounded sore,

472

He lay his face besmeared with gore.
Then Níla with his fist he slew,
And Śarabh with his knee o'erthrew,
Nor could Gaváksha's strength withstand
The force of his terrific hand.
At Gandhamádan's eager call
Rushed thousands to avenge their fall,
Nor ceased those Vánars to assail
With knee and fist and tooth and nail.
Around his foes the giant threw
His mighty arms, and nearer drew
The captives subject to his will:
Then snatched them up and ate his fill.
There was no respite then, no pause:
Fast gaped and closed his hell-like jaws:
Yet, prisoned in that gloomy cave,
Some Vánars still their lives could save:
Some through his nostrils found a way,
Some through his ears resought the day.
Like Indra with his thunder, like
The God of Death in act to strike,
The giant seized his ponderous spear,
And charged the foe in swift career.
Before his might the Vánars fell,
Nor could their hosts his charge repel.
Then trembling, nor ashamed to run,
They turned and fled to Raghu's son.

When Báli's warrior son beheld
Their flight, his heart with fury swelled.
He rushed, with his terrific shout,
To meet the foe and stay the rout.
He came, he hurled a mountain peak,
And smote the giant on the cheek.
His ponderous spear the giant threw:
Fierce was the cast, the aim was true;
But Angad, trained in war and tried,
Saw ere it came, and leapt aside.
Then with his open hand he smote
The giant on the chest and throat.
That blow the giant scarce sustained;

But sense and strength were soon regained.
With force which nothing might resist
He caught the Vánar by the wrist,
Whirled him, as if in pastime, round,
And dashed him senseless on the ground.
There low on earth his foe lay crushed:
At King Sugríva next he rushed,
Who, waiting for the charge, stood still,
And heaved on high a shattered hill,
He looked on Kumbhakarṇa dyed
With streams of blood, and fiercely cried:
"Great glory has thine arm achieved,
And thousands of their lives bereaved.
Now leave a while thy meaner foes,
And brook the hill Sugríva throws."

He spoke, and hurled the mass he held:
The giant's chest the stroke repelled,
Then on the Vánars fell despair,
And Rákshas clamour filled the air.
The giant raised his arm, and fast
Came the tremendous spear he cast.
Hanúmán caught it as it flew,
And knapped it on his knee in two.
The giant saw the broken spear:
His clouded eye confessed his fear;
Yet at Sugríva's head he sent
A peak from Lanká's mountain rent.

The rushing mass no might could stay:
Sugríva fell and senseless lay.
The giant stooped his foe to seize,
And bore him thence, as bears the breeze
A cloud in autumn through the sky.
He heard the sad Immortals sigh,
And shouts of triumph long and loud
Went up from all the Rákshas crowd.
Through Lanká's gate the giant passed
Holding his struggling captive fast,
While from each terrace, house, and tower
Fell on his haughty head a shower

Of fragrant scent and flowery rain,
Blossoms and leaves and scattered grain.

By slow degrees the Vánars' lord
Felt life and sense and strength restored.
He heard the giants' joyful boast:
He thought upon his Vánar host.
His teeth and feet he fiercely plied,
And bit and rent the giant's side,
Who, mad with pain and smeared with gore,
Hurled to the ground the load he bore.
Regardless of a storm of blows
Swift to the sky the Vánar rose,
Then lightly like a flying ball
High overleapt the city wall,
And joyous for deliverance won
Regained the side of Raghu's son.
And Kumbhakarṇa, mad with hate
And fury, sallied from the gate,
The carnage of the foe renewed
And filled his maw with gory food.
Slaying, with headlong frenzy blind,
Both Vánar foes and giant kind.

Nor would Sumitrá's valiant son
The might of Kumbhakarṇa shun,
Who through his harness felt the sting
Of keen shafts loosened from the string.
His heart confessed the warrior's power,
And, bleeding from the ceaseless shower
That smote him on the chest and side,
With words like these the giant cried:
"Well fought, well fought, Sumitrá's son;
Eternal glory hast thou won,
For thou in desperate fight hast met
The victor never conquered yet,
Whom, borne on huge Airávat's back,
E'en Indra trembles to attack.
Go, son of Queen Sumitrá, go:
Thy valour and thy strength I know.
Now all my hope and earnest will

475

Is Ráma in the fight to kill.
Let him beneath my weapons fall,
And I will meet and conquer all."

The chieftain, of Sumitrá born,
Made answer as he laughed in scorn:
"Yea, thou hast won a victor's fame
From trembling Gods and Indra's shame.
There waits thee now a mightier foe
Whose prowess thou hast yet to know.
There, famous in a hundred lands,
Ráma the son of Raghu stands."

Straight at the king the giant sped,
And earth was shaken at his tread.
His bow the hero grasped and strained,
And deadly shafts in torrents rained.
As Kumbhakarṇa felt each stroke
From his huge mouth burst fire and smoke;
His hands were loosed in mortal pain
And dropped his weapons on the plain.
Though reft of spear and sword and mace
No terror changed his haughty face.
With heavy hands he rained his blows
And smote to death a thousand foes.
Where'er the furious monster strode
While down his limbs the red blood flowed
Like torrents down a mountain's side,
Vánars and bears and giants died.
High o'er his head a rock he swung,
And the huge mass at Ráma flung.
But Ráma's arrows bright as flame
Shattered the mountain as it came.
Then Raghu's son, his eyes aglow
With burning anger, charged the foe,
And as his bow he strained and tried
With fearful clang the cord replied.
Wroth at the bowstring's threatening clang
To meet his foe the giant sprang.
High towering with enormous frame
Huge as a wood-crowned hill he came.

But Ráma firm and self-possessed
In words like these the foe addressed:
"Draw near, O Rákshas lord, draw near,
Nor turn thee from the fight in fear.
Thou meetest Ráma face to face,
Destroyer of the giant race.
Come, fight, and thou shalt feel this hour,
Laid low in death, thy conqueror's power."

He ceased: and mad with wrath and pride
The giant champion thus replied:
"Come thou to me and thou shalt find
A foeman of a different kind.
No Khara, no Virádha,—thou
Hast met a mightier warrior now.
The strength of Kumbhakarṇa fear,
And dread the iron mace I rear
This mace in days of yore subdued
The Gods and Dánav multitude.
Prove, lion of Ikshváku's line,
Thy power upon these limbs of mine.
Then, after trial, shalt thou bleed,
And with thy flesh my hunger feed."

He ceased: and Ráma, undismayed,
Upon his cord those arrows laid

Which pierced the stately Sál trees through,
And Báli king of Vánars slew.
They flew, they smote, but smote in vain
Those mighty limbs that felt no pain.
Then Ráma sent with surest aim
The dart that bore the Wind-God's name.
The missile from the giant tore
His huge arm and the mace it bore,
Which crushed the Vánars where it fell:
And dire was Kumbhakarṇa's yell.
The giant seized a tree, and then
Rushed madly at the lord of men.
Another dart, Lord Indra's own,
To meet his furious onset thrown,

His left arm from the shoulder lopped,
And like a mountain peak it dropped.
Then from the bow of Ráma sped
Two arrows, each with crescent head;
And, winged with might which naught could stay,
They cut the giant's legs away.
They fell, and awful was the sound
As those vast columns shook the ground;
And sky and sea and hill and cave
In echoing roars their answer gave.
Then from his side the hero drew
A dart that like the tempest flew—
No deadlier shaft has ever flown
Than that which Indra called his own—
Nor could the giant's mail-armed neck
The fury of the missile check.
Through skin and flesh and bone it smote
And rent asunder head and throat.
Down with the sound of thunder rolled
The head adorned with rings of gold,
And crushed to pieces in its fall
A gate, a tower, a massive wall.
Hurled to the sea the body fell:
Terrific was the ocean's swell,
Nor could swift fin and nimble leap
Save the crushed creatures of the deep.

Thus he who plagued in impious pride
The Gods and Bráhmans fought and died.
Glad were the hosts of heaven, and long
The air re-echoed with their song.

LXVIII

Rávan's Lament

They ran to Rávaṇ in his hall
    And told him of his brother's fall:
    "Fierce as the God who rules the dead,
Upon the routed foe he fed;
And, victor for a while, at length
Fell slain by Ráma's matchless strength.
Now like a mighty hill in size
His mangled trunk extended lies,
And where he fell, a bleeding mass,
Blocks Lanká's gate that none may pass."
The monarch heard: his strength gave way;
And fainting on the ground he lay.
Grieved at the giants' mournful tale,
Long, shrill was Atikáya's wail;
And Triśirás in sorrow bowed
His triple head, and wept aloud.
Mahodar, Mahápárśva shed
Hot tears and mourned their brother dead.
At length, his wandering sense restored,
In loud lament cried Lanká's lord:
"Ah chief, for might and valour famed,
Whose arm the haughty foeman tamed,
Forsaking me, thy friends and all,
Why hast thou fled to Yáma's hall?
Why hast thou fled to taste no more
The slaughtered foeman's flesh and gore?
Ah me, my life is done to-day:
My better arm is lopped away.
Whereon in danger I relied,
And, fearless, Gods and fiends defied.
How could a shaft from Ráma's bow

The matchless giant overthrow,
Whose iron frame so strong of yore
The crushing bolt of Indra bore?
This day the Gods and sages meet
And triumph at their foe's defeat.
This day the Vánar chiefs will boast
And, with new ardour fired, their host
In fiercer onset will assail
Our city, and the ramparts scale.
What care I for a monarch's name,
For empire, or the Maithil dame?
What joy can power and riches give,
Or life that I should care to live,
Unless this arm in mortal fray
The slayer of my brother slay?
For me, of Kumbhakarṇa reft,
Death is the only solace left;
And I will seek, o'erwhelmed with woes,
The realm to which my brother goes.
Ah me ill-minded, not to take
His counsel when Vibhishaṇ spake
When he this evil day foretold
My foolish heart was overbold:
I drove my sage adviser hence,
And reap the fruits of mine offence."

CANTO
LXIX

Narántak's Death

Pierced to the soul by sorrow's sting
Thus wailed the evil-hearted king.
    Then Triśirás stood forth and cried:
"Yea, father, he has fought and died,
Our bravest: and the loss is sore:

But rouse thee, and lament no more.
Hast thou not still thy coat of mail,
Thy bow and shafts which never fail?
A thousand asses draw thy car
Which roars like thunder heard afar.
Thy valour and thy warrior skill,
Thy God-given strength, are left thee still.
Unarmed, thy matchless might subdued
The Gods and Dánav multitude.
Armed with thy glorious weapons, how
Shall Raghu's son oppose thee now?
Or, sire, within thy palace stay;
And I myself will sweep away
Thy foes, like Garuḍ when he makes
A banquet of the writhing snakes.
Soon Raghu's son shall press the plain,
As Narak fell by Vishṇu slain,
Or Śambar in rebellious pride
Who met the King of Gods and died."

The monarch heard: his courage grew,
And life and spirit came anew.
Devántak and Narántak heard,
And their fierce souls with joy were stirred;
And Atikáya burned to fight,
And heard the summons with delight;
While from the rest loud rang the cry,
"I too will fight," "and I," "and I."

The joyous king his sons embraced,
With gold and chains and jewels graced,
And sent them forth with stirring speech
Of benison and praise to each.
Forth from the gate the princes sped
And ranged for war the troops they led.
The Vánar legions charged anew,
And trees and rocks for missiles flew.
They saw Narántak's mighty form
Borne on a steed that mocked the storm.
To check his charge in vain they strove:
Straight through their host his way he clove,

481

As springs a dolphin through the tide:
And countless Vánars fell and died,
And mangled limbs and corpses lay
To mark the chief's ensanguined way,
Sugríva saw them fall or fly
When fierce Narántak's steed was nigh,
And marked the giant where he sped
O'er heaps of dying or of dead.
He bade the royal Angad face
That bravest chief of giant race.
As springs the sun from clouds dispersed,
So Angad from the Vánars burst.
No weapon for the fight he bore
Save nails and teeth, and sought no more.
"Leave, giant chieftain," thus he spoke,
"Leave foes unworthy of thy stroke,
And bend against a nobler heart
The terrors of thy deadly dart."

Narántak heard the words he spake:
Fast breathing, like an angry snake,
With bloody teeth his lips he pressed
And hurled his dart at Angad's breast.
True was the aim and fierce the stroke,
Yet on his breast the missile broke.
Then Angad at the giant flew,
And with a blow his courser slew:
The fierce hand crushed through flesh and bone,
And steed and rider fell o'erthrown.
Narántak's eyes with fury blazed:
His heavy hand on high he raised
And struck in savage wrath the head
Of Báli's son, who reeled and bled,
Fainted a moment and no more:
Then stronger, fiercer than before
Smote with that fist which naught could stay,
And crushed to death the giant lay.

The Death of Trisirás

Then raged the Rákshas chiefs, and all
   Burned to avenge Narántak's fall.
   Devántak raised his club on high
And rushed at Angad with a cry.
Behind came Triśirás, and near
Mahodar charged with levelled spear.
There Angad stood to fight with three:
High o'er his head he waved a tree,
And at Devántak, swift and true
As Indra's flaming bolt, it flew.
But, cut by giant shafts in twain,
With minished force it flew in vain.
A shower of trees and blocks of stone
From Angad's hand was fiercely thrown;
But well his club Devántak plied
And turned each rock and tree aside.
Nor yet, by three such foes assailed,

The heart of Angad sank or quailed.
He slew the mighty beast that bore
Mahodar: from his head he tore
A bleeding tusk, and blow on blow
Fell fiercely on his Rákshas foe.
The giant reeled, but strength regained,
And furious strokes on Angad rained,
Who, wounded by the storm of blows,
Sank on his knees, but swiftly rose.
Then Triśirás, as up he sprang,
Drew his great bow with awful clang,
And fixed three arrows from his sheaf
Full in the forehead of the chief.

Hanúmán saw, nor long delayed
To speed with Níla to his aid,
Who at the three-faced giant sent
A peak from Lanká's mountain rent.
But Triśirás with certain aim
Shot rapid arrows as it came:
And shivered by their force it broke
And fell to earth with flash and smoke.
Then as the Wind-God's son came nigh,
Devántak reared his mace on high.
Hanúmán smote him on the head
And stretched the monstrous giant dead.
Fierce Triśirás with fury strained
His bow, and showers of arrows rained
That smote on Níla's side and chest:
He sank a moment, sore distressed;
But quickly gathered strength to seize
A mountain with its crown of trees.
Crushed by the hill, distained with gore,
Mahodar fell to rise no more.

Then Triśirás raised high his spear
Which chilled the trembling foe with fear
And, like a flashing meteor through
The air at Hanúmán it flew.
The Vánar shunned the threatened stroke,
And with strong hands the weapon broke.
The giant drew his glittering blade:
Dire was the wound the weapon made
Deep in the Vánar's ample chest,
Who, for a moment sore oppressed,
Raised his broad hand, regaining might,
And struck the rover of the night.
Fierce was the blow: with one wild yell
Low on the earth the monster fell.
Hanúmán seized his fallen sword
Which served no more its senseless lord,
And from the monster triple-necked
Smote his huge heads with crowns bedecked.
Then Mahápárśva burned with ire;
Fierce flashed his eyes with vengeful fire.

A moment on the dead he gazed,
Then his black mace aloft was raised,
And down the mass of iron came
That struck and shook the Vánar's frame.
Hanúmán's chest was wellnigh crushed,
And from his mouth red torrents gushed:
Yet served one instant to restore
His spirit: from the foe he tore
His awful mace, and smote, and laid
The giant in the dust dismayed.
Crushed were his jaws and teeth and eyes:
Breathless and still he lay as lies
A summit from a mountain rent
By him who rules the firmament.

CANTO

LXXI

Atikáya's Death

But Atikáya's wrath grew high
To see his noblest kinsmen die.
He, fiercest of the giant race,
Presuming still on Brahmá's grace;
Proud tamer of the Immortals' pride,
Whose power and might with Indra's vied,
For blood and vengeful carnage burned,
And on the foe his fury turned.
High on a car that flashed and glowed
Bright as a thousand suns he rode.
Around his princely brows was set
A rich bejewelled coronet.
Gold pendants in his ears he wore;
He strained and tried the bow he bore,
And ever, as a shaft he aimed,
His name and royal race proclaimed.

Scarce might the Vánars brook to hear
His clanging bow and voice of fear:
To Raghu's elder son they fled,
Their sure defence in woe and dread.
Then Ráma bent his eyes afar
And saw the giant in his car
Fast following the flying crowd
And roaring like a rainy cloud.
He, with the lust of battle fired,
Turned to Vibhishaṇ and inquired:
"Say, who is this, of mountain size,
This archer with the lion eyes?
His car, which strikes our host with awe,
A thousand eager coursers draw.
Surrounded by the flashing spears
Which line his car, the chief appears
Like some huge cloud when lightnings play
About it on a stormy day;
And the great bow he joys to hold
Whose bended back is bright with gold,
As Indra's bow makes glad the skies,
That best of chariots glorifies.
O see the sunlike splendour flung
From the great flag above him hung,
Where, blazoned with refulgent lines,
Ráhu the dreadful Dragon shines.
Full thirty quivers near his side,
His car with shafts is well supplied:

And flashing like the light of stars
Gleam his two mighty scimitars.
Say, best of giants, who is he
Before whose face the Vánars flee?"

Thus Ráma spake. Vibhishaṇ eyed
The giants' chief, and thus replied:
"This Ráma, this is Rávaṇ's son:
High fame his youthful might has won.
He, best of warriors, bows his ear
The wisdom of the wise to hear.
Supreme is he mid those who know

486

The mastery of sword and bow.
Unrivalled in the bold attack
On elephant's or courser's back,
He knows, beside, each subtler art,
To win the foe, to bribe, or part.
On him the giant hosts rely,
And fear no ill when he is nigh.
This peerless chieftain bears the name
Of Atikáya huge of frame,
Whom Dhanyamáliní of yore
To Rávaṇ lord of Lanká bore."

Roused by his bow-string's awful clang,
To meet their foes the Vánars sprang.
Armed with tall trees from Lanká's wood,
And rocks and mountain peaks, they stood.
The giant's arrows, gold-bedecked,
The storm of hurtling missiles checked;
And ever on his foemen poured
Fierce tempest from his clanging cord;
Nor could the Vánar chiefs sustain
His shafts' intolerable rain.
They fled: the victor gained the place
Where stood the lord of Raghu's race,
And cried with voice of thunder: "Lo,
Borne on my car, with shaft and bow,
I, champion of the giants, scorn
To fight with weaklings humbly born.
Come forth your bravest, if he dare,
And fight with one who will not spare."

Forth sprang Sumitrá's noble child,
And strained his ready bow, and smiled;
And giants trembled as the clang
Through heaven and earth reëchoing rang.
The giant to his string applied
A pointed shaft, and proudly cried;
"Turn, turn, Sumitrá's son and fly,
For terrible as Death am I.
Fly, nor that youthful form oppose,
Untrained in war, to warriors' blows.

What! wilt thou waste thy childish breath
And wake the dormant fire of death?
Cast down, rash boy, that useless bow:
Preserve thy life, uninjured go."

He ceased: and stirred by wrath & pride
Sumitrá's noble son replied:
"By warlike deed, not words alone,
The valour of the brave is shown.
Cease with vain boasts my scorn to move,
And with thine arm thy prowess prove.
Borne on thy car, with sword and bow,
With all thine arms, thy valour show.
Fight, and my deadly shafts this day
Low in the dust thy head shall lay,
And, rushing fast in ceaseless flood,
Shall rend thy flesh and drink thy blood."
His giant foe no answer made,
But on his string an arrow laid.
He raised his arm, the cord he drew,
At Lakshman's breast the arrow flew.
Sumitrá's son, his foemen's dread,
Shot a fleet shaft with crescent head,
Which cleft that arrow pointed well,
And harmless to the earth it fell.
A shower of shafts from Lakshman's bow
Fell fast and furious on the foe
Who quailed not as the missiles smote
With idle force his iron coat.
Then came the friendly Wind-God near,
And whispered thus in Lakshman's ear:
"Such shafts as these in vain assail
Thy foe's impenetrable mail.
A more tremendous missile try,
Or never may the giant die.
Employ the mighty spell, and aim
The weapon known by Brahmá's name."
He ceased; Sumitrá's son obeyed:
On his great bow the shaft was laid,
And with a roar like thunder, true

488

As Indra's flashing bolt, it flew.
The giant poured his shafts like rain
To check its course, but all in vain.
With spear and mace and sword he tried
To turn the fiery dart aside.
Winged with a force which naught could check,
It smote the monster in the neck,
And, sundered from his shoulders, rolled
To earth his head and helm of gold.

CANTO
LXXII

Rávan's Speech

The giants bent, in rage and grief,
    Their eyes upon the fallen chief:
    Then flying wild with fear and pale
To Rávan bore the mournful tale.
He heard how Atikáya died,
Then turned him to his lords, and cried:
"Where are they now—my bravest—where,
Wise to consult and prompt to dare?
Where is Dhúmráksha, skilled to wield
All weapons in the battle field?
Akampan, and Prahasta's might,
And Kumbhakarṇa bold in fight?
These, these and many a Rákshas more,
Each master of the arms he bore,

Who every foe in fight o'erthrew,
The victors none could e'er subdue,
Have perished by the might of one,
The vengeful arm of Raghu's son.

In vain I cast mine eyes around,
No match for Ráma here is found,
No chief to stand before that bow
Whose deadly shafts have caused our woe.
Now, warriors, to your stations hence;
Provide ye for the wall's defence,
And be the Aśoka garden, where
The lady lies, your special care.
Be every lane and passage barred,
Set at each gate a chosen guard.
And with your troops, where danger calls,
Be ready to defend the walls.
Each movement of the Vánars mark;
Observe them when the skies grow dark;
Be ready in the dead of night,
And ere the morning bring the light.
Taught by our loss we may not scorn
These legions of the forest-born."

He ceased: the Rákshas lords obeyed;
Each at his post his troops arrayed:
And, torn with pangs that pierced him through
The monarch from the hall withdrew.

CANTO
LXXIII

Indrajít's Victory

B ut Indrajít the fierce and bold
With words like these his sire consoled:
"Dismiss, O King, thy grief and dread,
And be not thus disquieted.
Against this numbing sorrow strive,
For Indrajít is yet alive;
And none in battle may withstand

The fury of his strong right hand.
This day, O sire, thine eyes shall see
The sons of Raghu slain by me."
He ceased: he bade the king farewell:
Clear, mid the roar of drum and shell,
The clash of sword and harness rang
As to his car the warrior sprang.
Close followed by his Rákshas train
Through Lanká's gate he reached the plain.
Then down he leapt, and bade a band
Of giants by the chariot stand:
Then with due rites, as rules require,
Did worship to the Lord of Fire.
The sacred oil, as texts ordain,
With wreaths of scented flowers and grain,
Within the flame in order due,
That mightiest of the giants threw.
There on the ground were spear and blade,
And arrowy leaves and fuel laid;
An iron ladle deep and wide,
And robes with sanguine colours dyed.
Beside him stood a sable goat:
The giant seized it by the throat,
And straight from the consuming flame
Auspicious signs of victory came.
For swiftly, curling to the right,
The fire leapt up with willing light
Undimmed by smoky cloud, and, red
Like gold, upon the offering fed.
They brought him, while the flame yet glowed,
The dart by Brahmá's grace bestowed,
And all the arms he wielded well
Were charmed with text and holy spell.

Then fiercer for the fight he burned,
And at the foe his chariot turned,
While all his followers lifting high
Their maces charged with furious cry.
Dire, yet more dire the battle grew,
As rocks and trees and arrows flew.
The giant shot his shafts like rain,

And Vánars fell in myriads slain,
Sugríva, Angad, Níla felt
The wounds his hurtling arrows dealt.
His shafts the blood of Gaya drank;
Hanúmán reeled and Mainda sank.
Bright as the glances of the sun
Came the swift darts they could not shun.
Caught in the arrowy nets he wove,
In vain the sons of Raghu strove;
And Ráma, by the darts oppressed,
His brother chieftain thus addressed:
"See, first this giant warrior sends
Destruction, mid our Vánar friends,
And now his arrows thick and fast
Their binding net around us cast.
To Brahmá's grace the chieftain owes
The matchless power and might he shows;
And mortal strength in vain contends
With him whom Brahmá's self befriends.
Then let us still with dauntless hearts
Endure this storm of pelting darts.
Soon must we sink bereaved of sense;
And then the victor, hurrying hence,
Will seek his father in his hall
And tell him of his foemen's fall."
He ceased: o'erpowered by shaft and spell
The sons of Raghu reeled and fell.
The Rákshas on their bodies gazed;
And, mid the shouts his followers raised,
Sped back to Lanká to relate
In Rávaṇ's hall the princes' fate.

The Medicinal Herbs

The shades of falling night concealed
The carnage of the battle field,
Which, bearing each a blazing brand,
Hanúmán and Vibhishaṇ scanned,
Moving with slow and anxious tread
Among the dying and the dead.
Sad was the scene of slaughter shown
Where'er the torches' light was thrown.
Here mountain forms of Vánars lay
Whose heads and limbs were lopped away,
Arms, legs and fingers strewed the ground,
And severed heads lay thick around.
The earth was moist with sanguine streams,
And sighs were heard and groans and screams.
There lay Sugríva still and cold,
There Angad, once so brave and bold.
There Jámbaván his might reposed,
There Vegadarśí's eyes were closed;
There in the dust was Nala's pride,
And Dwivid lay by Mainda's side.
Where'er they looked the ensanguined plain
Was strewn with myriads of the slain;
They sought with keenly searching eyes
King Jámbaván supremely wise.
His strength had failed by slow decay,
And pierced with countless shafts he lay.
They saw, and hastened to his side,
And thus the sage Vibhishaṇ cried:
"Thee, monarch of the bears, we seek:
Speak if thou yet art living, speak."

Slow came the aged chief's reply;
Scarce could he say with many a sigh:
"Torn with keen shafts which pierce each limb,
My strength is gone, my sight is dim;
Yet though I scarce can raise mine eyes,
Thy voice, O chief, I recognize.
O, while these ears can hear thee, say,
Has Hanúmán survived this day?"

"Why ask," Vibhishaṇ cried, "for one
Of lower rank, the Wind-God's son?
Hast thou forgotten, first in place,
The princely chief of Raghu's race?
Can King Sugríva claim no care,
And Angad, his imperial heir?"

"Yea, dearer than my noblest friends
Is he on whom our hope depends.
For if the Wind-God's son survive,
All we though dead are yet alive.
But if his precious life be fled
Though living still we are but dead:
He is our hope and sure relief."
Thus slowly spoke the aged chief:
Then to his side Hanúmán came,
And with low reverence named his name.
Cheered by the face he longed to view
The wounded chieftain lived anew.
"Go forth," he cried, "O strong and brave,
And in their woe the Vánars save.
No might but thine, supremely great,
May help us in our lost estate.
The trembling bears and Vánars cheer,
Calm their sad hearts, dispel their fear.
Save Raghu's noble sons, and heal
The deep wounds of the winged steel.
High o'er the waters of the sea
To far Himálaya's summits flee.
Kailása there wilt thou behold,
And Rishabh, with his peaks of gold.
Between them see a mountain rise

Whose splendour will enchant thine eyes;
His sides are clothed above, below,
With all the rarest herbs that grow.
Upon that mountain's lofty crest
Four plants, of sovereign powers possessed,
Spring from the soil, and flashing there
Shed radiance through the neighbouring air.
One draws the shaft: one brings again
The breath of life to warm the slain;
One heals each wound; one gives anew
To faded cheeks their wonted hue.
Fly, chieftain, to that mountain's brow
And bring those herbs to save us now."

Hanúmán heard, and springing through
The air like Vishṇu's discus flew.
The sea was passed: beneath him, gay
With bright-winged birds, the mountains lay,
And brook and lake and lonely glen,
And fertile lands with toiling men.
On, on he sped: before him rose
The mansion of perennial snows.
There soared the glorious peaks as fair
As white clouds in the summer air.
Here, bursting from the leafy shade,
In thunder leapt the wild cascade.
He looked on many a pure retreat
Dear to the Gods' and sages' feet:
The spot where Brahmá dwells apart,
The place whence Rudra launched his dart;
Vishṇu's high seat and Indra's home,
And slopes where Yáma's servants roam.
There was Kuvera's bright abode;
There Brahmá's mystic weapon glowed.
There was the noble hill whereon

Those herbs with wondrous lustre shone,
And, ravished by the glorious sight,
Hanúmán rested on the height.
He, moving down the glittering peak,
The healing herbs began to seek:

But, when he thought to seize the prize,
They hid them from his eager eyes.
Then to the hill in wrath he spake:
"Mine arm this day shall vengeance take,
If thou wilt feel no pity, none,
In this great need of Raghu's son."
He ceased: his mighty arms he bent
And from the trembling mountain rent
His huge head with the life it bore,
Snakes, elephants, and golden ore.
O'er hill and plain and watery waste
His rapid way again he traced.
And mid the wondering Vánars laid
His burthen through the air conveyed,
The wondrous herbs' delightful scent
To all the host new vigour lent.
Free from all darts and wounds and pain
The sons of Raghu lived again,
And dead and dying Vánars healed
Rose vigorous from the battle field.

CANTO

LXXV

The Night Attack

Sugríva spake in words like these:
    "Now, Vánar lords, the occasion seize.
    For now, of sons and brothers reft,
To Rávaṇ little hope is left:
And if our host his gates assail
His weak defence will surely fail."

At dead of night the Vánar bands
Rushed on with torches in their hands.
Scared by the coming of the host

Each giant warder left his post.
Where'er the Vánar legions came
Their way was marked with hostile flame
That spread in fury to devour
Palace and temple, gate and tower.
Down came the walls and porches, down
Came stately piles that graced the town.
In many a house the fire was red,
On sandal wood and aloe fed.
And scorching flames in billows rolled
O'er diamonds and pearls and gold.
On cloth of wool, on silk brocade,
On linen robes their fury preyed.
Wheels, poles and yokes were burned, and all
The coursers' harness in the stall;
And elephants' and chariots' gear,
The sword, the buckler, and the spear.
Scared by the crash of falling beams,
Mid lamentations, groans and screams,
Forth rushed the giants through the flames
And with them dragged bewildered dames,
Each, with o'erwhelming terror wild,
Still clasping to her breast a child.
The swift fire from a cloud of smoke
Through many a gilded lattice broke,
And, melting pearl and coral, rose
O'er balconies and porticoes.
The startled crane and peacock screamed
As with strange light the courtyard gleamed,
And fierce unusual glare was thrown
On shrinking wood and heated stone.
From burning stall and stable freed
Rushed frantic elephant and steed,
And goaded by the driving blaze
Fled wildly through the crowded ways.
As earth with fervent heat will glow
When comes her final overthrow;
From gate to gate, from court to spire
Proud Lanká was one blaze of fire,
And every headland, rock and bay
Shone bright a hundred leagues away.

Forth, blinded by the heat and flame
Ran countless giants huge of frame;
And, mustering for fierce attack,
The Vánars charged to drive them back,
While shout and scream and roar and cry
Reëchoed through the earth and sky.
There Ráma stood with strength renewed,
And ever, as the foe he viewed,
Shaking the distant regions rang
His mighty bow's tremendous clang.
Then through the gates Nikumbha hied,
And Kumbha by his brother's side,
Sent forth—the bravest and the best—
To battle by the king's behest.
There fought the chiefs in open field,
And Angad fell and Dwivid reeled.
Sugríva saw: by rage impelled
He crushed the bow which Kumbha held.
About his foe Sugríva wound
His arms, and, heaving from the ground
The giant hurled him o'er the bank;
And deep beneath the sea he sank.
Like mandar hill with furious swell
Up leapt the waters where he fell.
Again he rose: he sprang to land
And raised on high his threatening hand:
Full on Sugríva's chest it came
And shook the Vánar's massy frame,
But on the wounded bone he broke
His wrist—so furious was the stroke.
With force that naught could stay or check,
Sugríva smote him neath the neck.
The fierce blow crashed through flesh and bone
And Kumbha lay in death o'erthrown.
Nikumbha saw his brother die,
And red with fury flashed his eye.
He dashed with mighty sway and swing

His axe against the Vánar king;
But shattered on that living rock
It split in fragments at the shock.

Sugríva, rising to the blow,
Raised his huge hand and smote his foe.
And in the dust the giant lay
Gasping in blood his soul away.

[I have briefly despatched Kumbha and Nikumbha, each of whom has
in the text a long Canto to himself. When they fall Rávan sends forth
Makaráksha or Crocodile-Eye, the son of Khara who was slain by Ráma
in the forest before the abduction of Sítá. The account of his sallying
forth, of his battle with Ráma and of his death by the fiery dart of that
hero occupies two Cantos which I entirely pass over. Indrajít again comes
forth and, rendered invisible by his magic art slays countless Vánars with
his unerring arrows. He retires to the city and returns bearing in his
chariot an effigy of Sítá, the work of magic, weeping and wailing by his
side. He grasps the lovely image by the hair and cuts it down with his
scimitar in the sight of the enraged Hanúmán and all the Vánar host. At
last after much fighting of the usual kind Indrajít's chariot is broken in
pieces, his charioteer is slain, and he himself falls by Lakshman's hand,
to the inexpressible delight of the high-souled saints, the nymphs of
heaven and other celestial beings.]

CANTO
XCIII

Rávan's Lament

They sought the king, a mournful train,
And cried, "My lord, thy son is slain.
By Lakshman's hand, before these eyes,
The warrior fell no more to rise.
No time is this for vain regret:
Thy hero son a hero met;
And he whose might in battle pressed
Lord Indra and the Gods confessed,
Whose power was stranger to defeat,
Has gained in heaven a blissful seat."

The monarch heard the mournful tale:
His heart was faint, his cheek was pale;
His fleeting sense at length regained,
In trembling tones he thus complained:
"Ah me, my son, my pride: the boast
And glory of the giant host.
Could Lakshman's puny might defeat
The foe whom Indra feared to meet?
Could not thy deadly arrows split
Proud Mandar's peaks, O Indrajít,
And the Destroyer's self destroy?
And wast thou conquered by a boy?
I will not weep: thy noble deed
Has blessed thee with immortal meed
Gained by each hero in the skies
Who fighting for his sovereign dies.
Now, fearless of all meaner foes,
The guardian Gods will taste repose:
But earth to me, with hill and plain,
Is desolate, for thou art slain.
Ah, whither hast thou fled, and left
Thy mother, Lanká, me bereft;
Left pride and state and wives behind,
And lordship over all thy kind?
I fondly hoped thy hand should pay
Due honours on my dying day:
And couldst thou, O beloved, flee
And leave thy funeral rites to me?
Life has no comfort left me, none,
O Indrajít my son, my son."

Thus wailed he broken by his woes:
But swift the thought of vengeance rose.
In awful wrath his teeth he gnashed,
And from his eyes red lightning flashed.
Hot from his mouth came fire and smoke,
As thus the king in fury spoke:

"Through many a thousand years of yore
The penance and the pain I bore,
And by fierce torment well sustained

The highest grace of Brahmá gained,
His plighted word my life assured,
From Gods of heaven and fiends secured.
He armed my limbs with burnished mail
Whose lustre turns the sunbeams pale,
In battle proof gainst heavenly bands
With thunder in their threatening hands.
Armed in this mail myself will go
With Brahmá's gift my deadly bow,
And, cleaving through the foes my way,
The slayers of my son will slay."

Then, by his grief to frenzy wrought,
The captive in the grove he sought.
Swift through the shady path he sped:
Earth trembled at his furious tread.
Fierce were his eyes: his monstrous hand
Held drawn for death his glittering brand.

There weeping stood the Maithil dame:
She shuddered as the giant came.
Near drew the rover of the night
And raised his sword in act to smite;
But, by his nobler heart impelled,
One Rákshas lord his arm withheld:
"Wilt thou, great Monarch," thus he cried,
"Wilt thou, to heavenly Gods allied,
Blot for all time thy glorious fame,
The slayer of a gentle dame?
What! shall a woman's blood be spilt
To stain thee with eternal guilt,
Thee deep in all the Veda's lore?
Far be the thought for evermore.
Ah look, and let her lovely face
This fury from thy bosom chase."

He ceased: the prudent counsel pleased
The monarch, and his wrath appeased;
Then to his council hall in haste
The giant lord his steps retraced.

[I omit two Cantos in the first of which Ráma with an enchanted Gandharva weapon deals destruction among the Rákshases sent out by Rávaṇ, and in the second the Rákshas dames lament the slain and mourn over the madness of Rávaṇ.]

CANTO

XCVI

Rávan's Sally

The groans and cries of dames who wailed
The ears of Lanká's lord assailed,
For from each house and home was sent
The voice of weeping and lament.
In troubled thought his head he bowed,
Then fiercely loosing on the crowd
Of nobles near his throne he broke
The silence, and in fury spoke:
"This day my deadly shafts shall fly,
And Raghu's sons shall surely die.
This day shall countless Vánars bleed
And dogs and kites and vultures feed.
Go, bid them swift my car prepare,
Bring the great bow I long to bear:
And let my host with sword and shield
And spear be ready for the field."

From street to street the captains passed
And Rákshas warriors gathered fast.
With spear and sword to pierce and strike,
And axe and club and mace and pike.

[I omit several weapons for which I cannot find distinctive names, and among them the *Sataghní* or *Centicide*, supposed by some to be a kind of fire-arms or rocket, but described by a commentator on the Mahábhárata as a stone or cylindrical piece of wood studded with iron spikes.]

Then Rávaṇ's warrior chariot wrought
With gold and rich inlay was brought.
Mid tinkling bells and weapons' clang
The monarch on the chariot sprang,
Which, decked with gems of every hue,
Eight steeds of noble lineage drew.
Mid roars of drum and shell rang out
From countless throats a joyful shout.
As, girt with hosts in warlike pride,
Through Lanká's streets the tyrant hied.
Still, louder than the roar of drums,
Went up the cry "He comes, he comes,
Our ever conquering lord who trod
Beneath his feet both fiend and God."
On to the gate the warriors swept
Where Raghu's sons their station kept.
When Rávaṇ's car the portal passed
The sun in heaven was overcast.
Earth rocked and reeled from side to side
And birds with boding voices cried.
Against the standard of the king
A vulture flapped his horrid wing.
Big gouts of blood before him dropped,
His trembling steeds in terror stopped.
The hue of death was on his cheek,
And scarce his flattering tongue could speak,
When, terrible with flash and flame,
Through murky air a meteor came.
Still by the hand of Death impelled
His onward way the giant held.
The Vánars in the field afar
Heard the loud thunder of his car.
And turned with warriors' fierce delight
To meet the giant in the fight.
He came: his clanging bow he drew
And myriads of the Vánars slew.
Some through the side and heart he cleft,
Some headless on the plain were left.
Some struggling groaned with mangled thighs,
Or broken arms or blinded eyes.

[I omit Cantos XCVII, XCVIII, and XCIX, which describe in the usual way three single combats between Sugríva and Angad on the Vánar side and Virúpáksha, Mahodar, and Mahápárśva on the side of the giants. The weapons of the Vánars are trees and rocks; the giants fight with swords, axes, and bows and arrows. The details are generally the same as those of preceding duels. The giants fall, one in each Canto.]

CANTO

C

Rávan in the Field

The plain with bleeding limbs was spread,
And heaps of dying and of dead.
His mighty bow still Ráma strained,
And shafts upon the giants rained.
Still Angad and Sugríva, wrought
To fury, for the Vánars fought.
Crushed with huge rocks through chest and side
Mahodar, Mahápárśva died,
And Virúpáksha stained with gore
Dropped on the plain to rise no more.
When Rávaṇ saw the three o'erthrown
He cried aloud in furious tone:
"Urge, urge the car, my charioteer,
The haughty Vánars' death is near.
This very day shall end our griefs
For leaguered town and slaughtered chiefs.
Ráma the tree whose lovely fruit
Is Sítá, shall this arm uproot,—
Whose branches with protecting shade
Are Vánar lords who lend him aid."
Thus cried the king: the welkin rang
As forth the eager coursers sprang,
And earth beneath the chariot shook
With flowery grove and hill and brook.

Fast rained his shafts: where'er he sped
The conquered Vánars fell or fled,
On rolled the car in swift career
Till Raghu's noble sons were near.
Then Ráma looked upon the foe
And strained and tried his sounding bow,
Till earth and all the region rang
Re-echoing to the awful clang.
His bow the younger chieftain bent,
And shaft on shaft at Rávaṇ sent.
He shot: but Rávaṇ little recked;
Each arrow with his own he checked,
And headless, baffled of its aim,
To earth the harmless missile came;
And Lakshmaṇ stayed his arm o'erpowered
By the thick darts the giant showered.
Fierce waxed the fight and fiercer yet,
For Rávaṇ now and Ráma met,
And each on other poured amain
The tempest of his arrowy rain.
While all the sky above was dark
With missiles speeding to their mark
Like clouds, with flashing lightning twined
About them, hurried by the wind.
Not fiercer was the wondrous fight
When Vritra fell by Indra's might.
All arts of war each foeman knew,
And trained alike, his bowstring drew.
Red-eyed with fury Lanká's king
Pressed his huge fingers on the string,
And fixed in Ráma's brows a flight
Of arrows winged with matchless flight.
Still Raghu's son endured, and bore
That crown of shafts though wounded sore.
O'er a dire dart a spell he spoke
With mystic power to aid the stroke.
In vain upon the foe it smote
Rebounding from the steelproof coat.
The giant armed his bow anew,
And wondrous weapons hissed and flew,
Terrific, deadly, swift of flight,

Beaked like the vulture and the kite,
Or bearing heads of fearful make,
Of lion, tiger, wolf and snake.
Then Ráma, troubled by the storm
Of flying darts in every form
Shot by an arm that naught could tire,
Launched at the foe his dart of fire,
Which, sacred to the Lord of Flame,
Burnt and consumed where'er it came.
And many a blazing shaft beside
The hero to his string applied.
With fiery course of dazzling hue
Swift to the mark each missile flew,
Some flashing like a shooting star,
Some as the tongues of lightning are;
One like a brilliant plant, one
In splendour like the morning sun.
Where'er the shafts of Ráma burned
The giant's darts were foiled and turned.
Far into space his weapons fled,
But as they flew struck thousands dead.

CANTO
CI

Lakshman's Fall

W hen Rávaṇ saw his darts repelled,
With double rage his bosom swelled.
He summoned, wroth but undismayed,
A mightier charm to lend its aid.
And, fierce as fire before the blast,
A storm of missiles thick and fast,
Spear, pike and javelin, mace and brand,
Came hurtling from the giant's hand.
But, mightier still, the arms employed

By Raghu's son their force destroyed,
And every dart fell dulled and spent
By powers the bards of heaven had lent.
With his huge mace Vibhishan slew
The steeds that Rávan's chariot drew.

Then Rávan hurled in deadly ire
A ponderous spear that flashed like fire:
But Ráma's arrows checked its way,
And harmless on the earth it lay,
The giant seized a mightier spear,
Which Death himself would shun with fear.
Vibhishan with the stroke had died,
But Lakshman's hand his bowstring plied,
And flying arrows thick as hail
Smote fiercely on the giant's mail.
Then Rávan turned his aim aside,
On Lakshman looked and fiercely cried:
"Thou, thou again my wrath hast braved,
And from his death Vibhishan saved.
Now in his stead this spear receive
Whose deadly point thy heart shall cleave."

He ceased: he hurled the mortal dart
By Maya forged with magic art.
The spear, with all his fury flung,
Swift, flickering like a serpent's tongue,
Adorned with many a tinkling bell,
Smote Lakshman, and the hero fell.
When Ráma saw, he heaved a sigh,
A tear one moment dimmed his eye.
But tender grief was soon repressed
And thoughts of vengeance filled his breast.
The air around him flashed and gleamed
As from his bow the arrows streamed;
And Lanká's lord, the foeman's dread,
O'erwhelmed with terror turned and fled.

Lakshman Healed

But Ráma, pride of Raghu's race,
Gazed tenderly on Lakshman's face,
And, as the sight his spirit broke,
Turned to Sushen and sadly spoke:
"Where is my power and valour? how
Shall I have heart for battle now,
When dead before my weeping eyes
My brother, noblest Lakshman, lies?
My tears in blinding torrents flow,
My hand unnerved has dropped my bow.
The pangs of woe have blanched my cheek,
My heart is sick, my strength is weak.
Ah me, my brother! Ah, that I
By Lakshman's side might sink and die:
Life, war and conquest, all are vain
If Lakshman lies in battle slain.
Why will those eyes my glances shun?
Hast thou no word of answer, none?
Ah, is thy noble spirit flown
And gone to other worlds alone?
Couldst thou not let thy brother seek
Those worlds with thee? O speak, O speak!
Rise up once more, my brother, rise,
Look on me with thy loving eyes.
Were not thy steps beside me still
In gloomy wood, on breezy hill?
Did not thy gentle care assuage
Thy brother's grief and fitful rage?
Didst thou not all his troubles share,
His guide and comfort in despair?"

As Ráma, vanquished, wept and sighed
The Vánar chieftain thus replied:
"Great Prince, unmanly thoughts dismiss,
Nor yield thy soul to grief like this.
In vain those burning tears are shed:
Our glory Lakshmaṇ is not dead.
Death on his brow no mark has set,
Where beauty's lustre lingers yet.
Clear is the skin, and tender hues
Of lotus flowers his palms suffuse.
O Ráma, cheer thy trembling heart;
Not thus do life and body part.
Now, Hanumán, to thee I speak:
Hie hence to tall Mahodaya's peak
Where herbs of sovereign virtue grow
Which life and health and strength bestow
Bring thou the leaves to balm his pain,
And Lakshmaṇ shall be well again."

He ceased: the Wind-God's son obeyed
Swift through the clouds his way he made.
He reached the hill, nor stayed to find
The wondrous herbs of healing kind,
From its broad base the mount he tore
With all the shrubs and trees it bore,
Sped through the clouds again and showed
To wise Susheṇ his woody load.
Susheṇ in wonder viewed the hill,
And culled the sovereign salve of ill.
Soon as the healing herb he found,
The fragrant leaves he crushed and ground.
Then over Lakshmaṇ's face he bent,
Who, healed and strengthened by the scent
Of that blest herb divinely sweet,
Rose fresh and lusty on his feet.

Indra's Car

Then Raghu's son forgot his woe:
Again he grasped his fallen bow
And hurled at Lanká's lord amain
The tempest of his arrowy rain.

Drawn by the steeds his lords had brought,
Again the giant turned and fought.
And drove his glittering chariot nigh
As springs the Day-God through the sky.
Then, as his sounding bow he bent,
Like thunderbolts his shafts were sent,
As when dark clouds in rain time shed
Fierce torrents on a mountain's head.
High on his car the giant rode,
On foot the son of Raghu strode.
The Gods from their celestial height
Indignant saw the unequal fight.
Then he whom heavenly hosts revere,
Lord Indra, called his charioteer:

"Haste, Mátali," he cried, "descend;
To Raghu's son my chariot lend.
With cheering words the chief address;
And all the Gods thy deed will bless."

He bowed; he brought the glorious car
Whose tinkling bells were heard afar;
Fair as the sun of morning, bright
With gold and pearl and lazulite.
He yoked the steeds of tawny hue
That swifter than the tempest flew.

Then down the slope of heaven he hied
And stayed the car by Ráma's side.
"Ascend, O Chief," he humbly cried,
"The chariot which the Gods provide.
The mighty bow of Indra see,
Sent by the Gods who favour thee;
Behold this coat of glittering mail,
And spear and shafts which never fail."

Cheered by the grace the Immortals showed
The chieftain on the chariot rode.
Then as the car-borne warriors met
The awful fight raged fiercer yet.
Each shaft that Rávaṇ shot became
A serpent red with kindled flame,
And round the limbs of Ráma hung
With fiery jaws and quivering tongue.
But every serpent fled dismayed
When Raghu's valiant son displayed
The weapon of the Feathered King,
And loosed his arrows from the string.
But Rávaṇ armed his bow anew,
And showers of shafts at Ráma flew,
While the fierce king in swift career
Smote with a dart the charioteer.
An arrow shot by Rávaṇ's hand
Laid the proud banner on the sand,
And Indra's steeds of heavenly strain
Fell by the iron tempest slain.
On Gods and spirits of the air
Fell terror, trembling, and despair.
The sea's white billows mounted high
With froth and foam to drench the sky.
The sun by lurid clouds was veiled,
The friendly lights of heaven were paled;
And, fiercely gleaming, fiery Mars
Opposed the beams of gentler stars.

Then Ráma's eyes with fury blazed
As Indra's heavenly spear he raised.
Loud rang the bells: the glistering head

Bright flashes through the region shed.
Down came the spear in swift descent:
The giant's lance was crushed and bent.
Then Rávaṇ's horses brave and fleet
Fell dead beneath his arrowy sleet.
Fierce on his foeman Ráma pressed,
And gored with shafts his mighty breast.
And spouting streams of crimson dyed
The weary giant's limbs and side.

[I omit Cantos CIV and CV in which the fight is renewed and Rávaṇ
severely reprimands his charioteer for timidity and want of confidence
in his master's prowess, and orders him to charge straight at Ráma on the
next occasion.]

CANTO
CVI

Glory to the Sun

There faint and bleeding fast, apart
Stood Rávaṇ raging in his heart.
Then, moved with ruth for Ráma's sake,
Agastya came and gently spake:
"Bend, Ráma, bend thy heart and ear
The everlasting truth to hear
Which all thy hopes through life will bless
And crown thine arms with full success.
The rising sun with golden rays,
Light of the worlds, adore and praise:
The universal king, the lord
By hosts of heaven and fiends adored.
He tempers all with soft control,
He is the Gods' diviner soul;
And Gods above and fiends below

512

And men to him their safety owe.
He Brahmá, Vishṇu, Śiva, he
Each person of the glorious Three,
Is every God whose praise we tell,
The King of Heaven, the Lord of Hell:
Each God revered from times of old,
The Lord of War, the King of Gold:

Mahendra, Time and Death is he,
The Moon, the Ruler of the Sea.
He hears our praise in every form,—
The manes, Gods who ride the storm,
The Aśvins, Manu, they who stand
Round Indra, and the Sádhyas' band
He is the air, and life and fire,
The universal source and sire:
He brings the seasons at his call,
Creator, light, and nurse of all.
His heavenly course he joys to run,
Maker of Day, the golden sun.
The steeds that whirl his car are seven,
The flaming steeds that flash through heaven.
Lord of the sky, the conqueror parts
The clouds of night with glistering darts.
He, master of the Vedas' lore,
Commands the clouds' collected store:
He is the rivers' surest friend;
He bids the rains, and they descend.
Stars, planets, constellations own
Their monarch of the golden throne.
Lord of twelve forms, to thee I bow,
Most glorious King of heaven art thou.
O Ráma, he who pays aright
Due worship to the Lord of Light
Shall never fall oppressed by ill,
But find a stay and comfort still.
Adore with all thy heart and mind
This God of Gods, to him resigned;
And thou his saving power shalt know
Victorious o'er thy giant foe."

[This Canto does not appear in the Bengal recension. It comes in awkwardly and may I think be considered as an interpolation, but I paraphrase a portion of it as a relief after so much fighting and carnage, and as an interesting glimpse of the monotheistic ideas which underlie the Hindu religion. The hymn does not readily lend itself to metrical translation, and I have not attempted here to give a faithful rendering of the whole. A literal version of the text and the commentary given in the Calcutta edition will be found in the Additional Notes.

A canto is here omitted. It contains fighting of the ordinary kind between Ráma and Rávaṇ, and a description of sights and sounds of evil omen foreboding the destruction of the giant.]

CANTO
CVIII

The Battle

He spoke, and vanished: Ráma raised
His eyes with reverence meet, and praised
The glorious Day-God full in view:
Then armed him for the fight anew.
Urged onward by his charioteer
The giant's foaming steeds came near,
And furious was the battle's din
Where each resolved to die or win.
The Rákshas host and Vánar bands
Stood with their weapons in their hands,
And watched in terror and dismay
The fortune of the awful fray.
The giant chief with rage inflamed
His darts at Ráma's pennon aimed;
But when they touched the chariot made
By heavenly hands their force was stayed.
Then Ráma's breast with fury swelled;
He strained the mighty bow he held,

And straight at Rávaṇ's banner flew
An arrow as the string he drew—
A deadly arrow swift of flight,
Like some huge snake ablaze with light,
Whose fury none might e'er repel,—
And, split in twain, the standard fell.
At Ráma's steeds sharp arrows, hot
With flames of fire, the giant shot.
Unmoved the heavenly steeds sustained
The furious shower the warrior rained,
As though soft lotus tendrils smote
Each haughty crest and glossy coat.
Then volleyed swift by magic art,
Tree, mountain peak and spear and dart,
Trident and pike and club and mace
Flew hurtling straight at Ráma's face.
But Ráma with his steeds and car
Escaped the storm which fell afar
Where the strange missiles, as they rushed
To earth, a thousand Vánars crushed.

CANTO
CIX

The Battle

With wondrous power and might and skill
 The giant fought with Ráma still.
  Each at his foe his chariot drove,
And still for death or victory strove.
The warriors' steeds together dashed,
And pole with pole reëchoing clashed.
Then Ráma launching dart on dart
Made Rávaṇ's coursers swerve and start.
Nor was the lord of Lanká slow

515

To rain his arrows on the foe,
Who showed, by fiery points assailed,
No trace of pain, nor shook nor quailed.
Dense clouds of arrows Ráma shot
With that strong arm which rested not,
And spear and mace and club and brand
Fell in dire rain from Rávaṇ's hand.
The storm of missiles fiercely cast
Stirred up the oceans with its blast,
And Serpent-Gods and fiends who dwell
Below were troubled by the swell.
The earth with hill and plain and brook
And grove and garden reeled and shook:
The very sun grew cold and pale,
And horror stilled the rising gale.
God and Gandharva, sage and saint
Cried out, with grief and terror faint:
"O may the prince of Raghu's line
Give peace to Bráhmans and to kine,
And, rescuing the worlds, o'erthrow
The giant king our awful foe."

Then to his deadly string the pride
Of Raghu's race a shaft applied.
Sharp as a serpent's venomed fang
Straight to its mark the arrow sprang,
And from the giant's body shred
With trenchant steel the monstrous head.
There might the triple world behold
That severed head adorned with gold.
But when all eyes were bent to view,
Swift in its stead another grew.
Again the shaft was pointed well:
Again the head divided fell;
But still as each to earth was cast
Another head succeeded fast.
A hundred, bright with fiery flame,
Fell low before the victor's aim,
Yet Rávaṇ by no sign betrayed
That death was near or strength decayed.
The doubtful fight he still maintained,

And on the foe his missiles rained.
In air, on earth, on plain, on hill,
With awful might he battled still;
And through the hours of night and day
The conflict knew no pause or stay.

Rávan's Death

T hen Mátali to Ráma cried:
      "Let other arms the day decide.
      Why wilt thou strive with useless toil
And see his might thy efforts foil?
Launch at the foe thy dart whose fire
Was kindled by the Almighty Sire."
He ceased: and Raghu's son obeyed:
Upon his string the hero laid
An arrow, like a snake that hissed.
Whose fiery flight had never missed:
The arrow Saint Agastya gave
And blessed the chieftain's life to save
That dart the Eternal Father made
The Monarch of the Gods to aid;
By Brahmá's self on him bestowed
When forth to fight Lord Indra rode.
'Twas feathered with the rushing wind;
The glowing sun and fire combined
To the keen point their splendour lent;
The shaft, ethereal element,
By Meru's hill and Mandar, pride
Of mountains, had its weight supplied.
He laid it on the twisted cord,
He turned the point at Lanká's lord,
And swift the limb-dividing dart

Pierced the huge chest and cleft the heart,
And dead he fell upon the plain
Like Vritra by the Thunderer slain.
The Rákahas host when Rávaṇ fell
Sent forth a wild terrific yell,
Then turned and fled, all hope resigned,
Through Lanká's gates, nor looked behind.
His voice each joyous Vánar raised,
And Ráma, conquering Ráma, praised.
Soft from celestial minstrels came
The sound of music and acclaim.
Soft, fresh, and cool, a rising breeze
Brought odours from the heavenly trees,
And ravishing the sight and smell
A wondrous rain of blossoms fell:
And voices breathed round Raghu's son:
"Champion of Gods, well done, well done."

CANTO
CXI

Vibhishan's Lament

Vibhishaṇ saw his brother slain,
Nor could his heart its woe contain.
O'er the dead king he sadly bent
And mourned him with a loud lament:
"O hero, bold and brave," he cried,
"Skilled in all arms, in battle tried.
Spoiled of thy crown, with limbs outspread,

Why wilt thou press thy gory bed?
Why slumber on the earth's cold breast,
When sumptuous couches woo to rest?
Ah me, my brother over bold,
Thine is the fate my heart foretold:

But love and pride forbade to hear
The friend who blamed thy wild career.
Fallen is the sun who gave us light,
Our lordly moon is veiled in night.
Our beacon fire is dead and cold
A hundred waves have o'er it rolled.
What could his light and fire avail
Against Lord Ráma's arrowy hail?
Woe for the giants' royal tree,
Whose stately height was fair to see.
His buds were deeds of kingly grace,
His bloom the sons who decked his race.
With rifled bloom and mangled bough
The royal tree lies prostrate now."
"Nay, idly mourn not," Ráma cried,
"The warrior king has nobly died,
Intrepid hero, firm through all,
So fell he as the brave should fall;
And ill beseems it chiefs like us
To weep for those who perish thus.
Be firm: thy causeless grief restrain,
And pay the dues that yet remain."

Again Vibhishan sadly spoke:
"His was the hero arm that broke
Embattled Gods' and Indra's might,
Unconquered ere to-day in fight.
He rushed against thee, fought and fell,
As Ocean, when his waters swell,
Hurling his might against a rock,
Falls spent and shattered by the shock.
Woe for our king's untimely end,
The generous lord the trusty friend:
Our sure defence when fear arose,
A dreaded scourge to stubborn foes.
O, let the king thy hand has slain
The honours of the dead obtain."

Then Ráma answered. "Hatred dies
When low in dust the foeman lies.
Now triumph bids the conflict cease,

And knits us in the bonds of peace.
Let funeral rites be duly paid.
And be it mine thy toil to aid."

CANTO
CXII

The Rákshas Dames

High rose the universal wail
That mourned the monarch's death, and, pale
With crushing woe, her hair unbound,
Her eyes in floods of sorrow drowned,
Forth from the inner chambers came
With trembling feet each royal dame,
Heedless of those who bade them stay
They reached the field where Rávaṇ lay;
There falling by their husband's side,
"Ah, King! ah dearest lord!" they cried.
Like creepers shattered by the storm
They threw them on his mangled form.
One to his bleeding bosom crept
And lifted up her voice and wept.
About his feet one mourner clung,
Around his neck another hung,
One on the giant's severed head,
Her pearly tears in torrents shed
Fast as the drops the summer shower
Pours down upon the lotus flower.
"Ah, he whose arm in anger reared
The King of Gods and Yáma feared,
While panic struck their heavenly train,
Lies prostrate in the battle slain.
Thy haughty heart thou wouldst not bend,
Nor listen to each wiser friend.
Ah, had the dame, as they implored,

Been yielded to her injured lord,
We had not mourned this day thy fall,
And happy had it been for all.
Then Ráma and thy friends content
In blissful peace their days had spent.
Thine injured brother had not fled,
Nor giant chiefs and Vánars bled.
Yet for these woes we will not blame.
Thy fancy for the Maithil dame,
Fate, ruthless Fate, whom none may bend
Has urged thee to thy hapless end."

CANTO
CXIII

Mandodarí's Lament

W hile thus they wept, supreme in place,
The loveliest for form and face,
Mandodarí drew near alone,
Looked on her lord and made her moan:
"Ah Monarch, Indra feared to stand
In fight before thy conquering hand.
From thy dread spear the Immortals ran;
And art thou murdered by a man?
Ah, 'twas no child of earth, I know,
That smote thee with that mortal blow.
'Twas Death himself in Ráma's shape,
That slew thee: Death whom none escape.
Or was it he who rules the skies
Who met thee, clothed in man's disguise?
Ah no, my lord, not Indra: he
In battle ne'er could look on thee.
One only God thy match I deem:
'Twas Vishṇu's self, the Lord Supreme,
Whose days through ceaseless time extend

And ne'er began and ne'er shall end:
He with the discus, shell, and mace,
Brought ruin on the giant race.
Girt by the Gods of heaven arrayed
Like Vánar hosts his strength to aid,
He Ráma's shape and arms assumed

And slew the king whom Fate had doomed.
In Janasthán when Khara died
With giant legions by his side,
No mortal was the unconquered foe
In Ráma's form who struck the blow.
When Hanumán the Vanár came
And burnt thy town with hostile flame,
I counselled peace in anxious fear:
I counselled, but thou wouldst not hear.
Thy fancy for the foreign dame
Has brought thee death and endless shame.
Why should thy foolish fancy roam?
Hadst thou not wives as fair at home?
In beauty, form and grace could she,
Dear lord, surpass or rival me?
Now will the days of Sítá glide
In tranquil joy by Ráma's side:
And I—ah me, around me raves
A sea of woe with whelming waves.
With thee in days of old I trod
Each spot beloved by nymph and God;
I stood with thee in proud delight
On Mandar's side and Meru's height;
With thee, my lord, enchanted strayed
In Chaitraratha's lovely shade,
And viewed each fairest scene afar
Transported in thy radiant car.
But source of every joy wast thou,
And all my bliss is ended now."

Then Ráma to Vibhishaṇ cried:
"Whate'er the ritual bids, provide.
Obsequial honours duly pay,
And these sad mourners' grief allay."

Vibhishaṇ answered, wise and true,
For duty's changeless law he knew:
"Nay one who scorned all sacred vows
And dared to touch another's spouse,
Fell tyrant of the human race,
With funeral rites I may not grace."

Him Raghu's royal son, the best
Of those who love the law, addressed:
"False was the rover of the night,
He loved the wrong and scorned the right.
Yet for the fallen warrior plead
The dauntless heart, the valorous deed.
Let him who ne'er had brooked defeat,
The chief whom Indra feared to meet,
The ever-conquering lord, obtain
The honours that should grace the slain."
Vibhishaṇ bade his friends prepare
The funeral rites with thoughtful care.
Himself the royal palace sought
Whence sacred fire was quickly brought,
With sandal wood and precious scents
And pearl and coral ornaments.
Wise Bráhmans, while the tears that flowed
Down their wan cheeks their sorrow sowed,
Upon a golden litter laid
The corpse in finest ropes arrayed.
Thereon were flowers and pennons hung,
And loud the monarch's praise was sung.
Then was the golden litter raised,
While holy fire in order blazed.
And first in place Vibhishaṇ led
The slow procession of the dead,
Behind, their cheeks with tears bedewed,
Came sad the widowed multitude.
Where, raised as Bráhmans ordered, stood
Piled sandal logs, and scented wood,
The body of the king was set
High on a deerskin coverlet.
Then duly to the monarch's shade
The offerings for the dead they paid,

And southward on the eastern side
An altar formed and fire supplied.
Then on the shoulder of the dead
The oil and clotted milk were shed.
All rites were done as rules ordain:
The sacrificial goat was slain.
Next on the corpse were perfumes thrown
And many a flowery wreath was strown;
And with Vibhishaṇ's ready aid
Rich vesture o'er the king was laid.
Then while the tears their cheeks bedewed
Parched grain upon the dead they strewed;
Last, to the wood, as rules require,
Vibhishaṇ set the kindling fire.

Then having bathed, as texts ordain,
To Lanká went the mourning train.
Vibhishaṇ, when his task was done,
Stood by the side of Raghu's son.
And Ráma, freed from every foe,
Unstrung at last his deadly bow,
And laid the glittering shafts aside,
And mail by Indra's love supplied.

CANTO

CXIV

Vibhishan Consecrated

Joy reigned in heaven where every eye
Had seen the Lord of Lanká die.
In cars whose sheen surpassed the sun's
Triumphant rode the radiant ones:
And Rávaṇ's death, by every tongue,
And Ráma's glorious deeds were sung.
They praised the Vánars true and brave,

The counsel wise Sugríva gave.
The deeds of Hanúmán they told,
The valiant chief supremely bold,
The strong ally, the faithful friend,
And Sítá's truth which naught could bend.

To Mátali, whom Indra sent,
His head the son of Raghu bent:
And he with fiery steeds who clove
The clouds again to Swarga drove.

Round King Sugríva brave and true
His arms in rapture Ráma threw,
Looked on the host with joy and pride,
And thus to noble Lakshman cried:

"Now let king-making drops be shed,
Dear brother, on Vibhishan's head
For truth and friendship nobly shown,
And make him lord of Rávan's throne."
This longing of his heart he told:
And Lakshman took an urn of gold
And bade the wind-fleet Vánars bring
Sea water for the giants' king.
The brimming urn was swiftly brought:
Then on a throne superbly wrought
Vibhishan sat, the giants' lord,
And o'er his brows the drops were poured.
As Raghu's son the rite beheld
His loving heart with rapture swelled:
But tenderer thoughts within him woke,
And thus to Hanúmán he spoke:

"Go to my queen: this message give:
Say Lakshman and Sugríva live.
The death of Lanká's monarch tell,
And bid her joy, for all is well."

CANTO
CXV

Sítá's Joy

The Vánar chieftain bowed his head,
　　Within the walls of Lanká sped,
　　Leave from the new-made king obtained,
And Sítá's lovely garden gained.
Beneath a tree the queen he found,
Where Rákshas warders watched around.
Her pallid cheek, her tangled hair,
Her raiment showed her deep despair,
Near and more near the envoy came
And gently hailed the weeping dame.
She started up in sweet surprise,
And sudden joy illumed her eyes.
For well the Vánar's voice she knew,
And hope reviving sprang and grew.

"Fair Queen," he said, "our task is done:
The foe is slain and Lanká won.
Triumphant mid triumphant friends
Kind words of greeting Ráma sends.
"Blest for thy sake, O spouse most true,
My deadly foe I met and slew.
Mine eyes are strangers yet to sleep:
I built a bridge athwart the deep
And crossed the sea to Lanká's shore
To keep the mighty oath I swore.
Now, gentle love, thy cares dispel,
And weep no more, for all is well.
Fear not in Rávaṇ's house to stay
For good Vibhishaṇ now bears sway,
For constant truth and friendship known
Regard his palace as thine own."

He greets thee thus thy heart to cheer,
And urged by love will soon be here."

Then flushed with joy the lady's cheek.
Her eyes o'erflowed, her voice was weak;
But struggling with her sobs she broke
Her silence thus, and faintly spoke:
"So fast the flood of rapture came,
My trembling tongue no words could frame.
Ne'er have I heard in days of bliss
A tale that gave such joy as this.
More precious far than gems and gold
The message which thy lips have told."
His reverent hands the Vánar raised
And thus the lady's answer praised:
"Sweet are the words, O Queen, which thou
True to thy lord, hast spoken now,
Better than gems and pearls of price,
Yea, or the throne of Paradise.
But, lady, ere I leave this place,
Grant me, I pray, a single grace.
Permit me, and this vengeful hand
Shall slay thy guards, this Rákshas band,
Whose cruel insult threat and scorn
Thy gentle soul too long has borne."

Thus, stern of mood, Hanúmán cried:
The Maithil lady thus replied:
"Nay, be not wroth with servants: they,
When monarchs bid must needs obey.
And, vassals of their lords, fulfil
Each fancy of their sovereign will.
To mine own sins the blame impute,
For as we sow we reap the fruit.
The tyrant's will these dames obeyed
When their fierce threats my soul dismayed."

She ceased: with admiration moved
The Vánar chief her words approved:
"Thy speech," he cried, "is worthy one
Whom love has linked to Raghu's son.

Now speak, O Queen, that I may know
Thy pleasure, for to him I go."
The Vánar ceased: then Janak's child
Made answer as she sweetly smiled:
"'My first, my only wish can be,
O chief, my loving lord to see."
Again the Vánar envoy spoke,
And with his words new rapture woke:
"Queen, ere this sun shall cease to shine
Thy Ráma's eyes shall look in thine.
Again the lord of Raghu's race
Shall turn to thee his moon-bright face.
His faithful brother shalt thou see
And every friend who fought for thee,
And greet once more thy king restored
Like Śachí to her heavenly lord."
To Raghu's son his steps he bent
And told the message that she sent.

CANTO

CXVI

The Meeting

He looked upon that archer chief
Whose full eye mocked the lotus leaf,
And thus the noble Vánar spake:
"Now meet the queen for whose dear sake
Thy mighty task was first begun,
And now the glorious fruit is won.
O'erwhelmed with woe thy lady lies,
The hot tears streaming from her eyes.
And still the queen must long and pine
Until those eyes be turned to thine."

But Ráma stood in pensive mood,
And gathering tears his eyes bedewed.
His sad looks sought the ground: he sighed
And thus to King Vibhishaṇ cried:
"Let Sítá bathe and tire her head
And hither to my sight be led
In raiment sweet with precious scent,
And gay with golden ornament."

The Rákshas king his palace sought,
And Sítá from her bower was brought.
Then Rákshas bearers tall and strong,
Selected from the menial throng,
Through Lanká's gate the queen, arrayed
In glorious robes and gems, conveyed.
Concealed behind the silken screen,
Swift to the plain they bore the queen,
While Vánars, close on every side,
With eager looks the litter eyed.
The warders at Vibhishaṇ's hest
The onward rushing throng repressed,
While like the roar of ocean loud
Rose the wild murmur of the crowd.
The son of Raghu saw and moved
With anger thus the king reproved:
"Why vex with hasty blow and threat
The Vánars, and my rights forget?
Repress this zeal, untimely shown:
I count this people as mine own.
A woman's guard is not her bower,
The lofty wall, the fenced tower:
Her conduct is her best defence,
And not a king's magnificence.
At holy rites, in war and woe,
Her face unveiled a dame may show;
When at the Maiden's Choice they meet,
When marriage troops parade the street.
And she, my queen, who long has lain
In prison racked with care and pain,
May cease a while her face to hide,

529

For is not Ráma by her side?
Lay down the litter: on her feet
Let Sítá come her lord to meet.
And let the hosts of woodland race
Look near upon the lady's face."

Then Lakshmaṇ and each Vánar chief
Who heard his words were filled with grief.
The lady's gentle spirit sank,
And from each eye in fear she shrank,
As, her sweet eyelids veiled for shame,
Slowly before her lord she came.
While rapture battled with surprise
She raised to his her wistful eyes.
Then with her doubt and fear she strove,
And from her breast all sorrow drove.
Regardless of the gathering crowd,
Bright as the moon without a cloud,
She bent her eyes, no longer dim,
In joy and trusting love on him.

CANTO
CXVII

Sítá's Disgrace

H e saw her trembling by her side,
And looked upon her face and cried:
"Lady, at length my task is done,
And thou, the prize of war, art won,
This arm my glory has retrieved,
And all that man might do achieved;
The insulting foe in battle slain
And cleared mine honour from its stain.
This day has made my name renowned
And with success my labour crowned.

Lord of myself, the oath I swore
Is binding on my soul no more.
If from my home my queen was reft,
This arm has well avenged the theft,
And in the field has wiped away
The blot that on mine honour lay.
The bridge that spans the foaming flood,
The city red with giants' blood;
The hosts by King Sugríva led
Who wisely counselled, fought and bled;
Vibhishan's love, our guide and stay—
All these are crowned with fruit to-day.
But, lady, 'twas not love for thee
That led mine army o'er the sea.
'Twas not for thee our blood was shed,
Or Lanká filled with giant dead.
No fond affection for my wife
Inspired me in the hour of strife.
I battled to avenge the cause
Of honour and insulted laws.
My love is fled, for on thy fame
Lies the dark blot of sin and shame;
And thou art hateful as the light

That flashes on the injured sight.
The world is all before thee: flee:
Go where thou wilt, but not with me.
How should my home receive again
A mistress soiled with deathless stain?
How should I brook the foul disgrace,
Scorned by my friends and all my race?
For Rávan bore thee through the sky,
And fixed on thine his evil eye.
About thy waist his arms he threw,
Close to his breast his captive drew,
And kept thee, vassal of his power,
An inmate of his ladies' bower."

CXVIII

Sítá's Reply

Struck down with overwhelming shame
She shrank within her trembling frame.
Each word of Ráma's like a dart
Had pierced the lady to the heart;
And from her sweet eyes unrestrained
The torrent of her sorrows, rained.
Her weeping eyes at length she dried,
And thus mid choking sobs replied:
"Canst thou, a high-born prince, dismiss
A high-born dame with speech like this?
Such words befit the meanest hind,
Not princely birth and generous mind,
By all my virtuous life I swear
I am not what thy words declare.
If some are faithless, wilt thou find
No love and truth in womankind?
Doubt others if thou wilt, but own
The truth which all my life has shown.
If, when the giant seized his prey,
Within his hated arms I lay,
And felt the grasp I dreaded, blame
Fate and the robber, not thy dame.
What could a helpless woman do?
My heart was mine and still was true,
Why when Hanúmán sent by thee
Sought Lanká's town across the sea,
Couldst thou not give, O lord of men,
Thy sentence of rejection then?
Then in the presence of the chief
Death, ready death, had brought relief,

Nor had I nursed in woe and pain
This lingering life, alas in vain.
Then hadst thou shunned the fruitless strife
Nor jeopardied thy noble life,
But spared thy friends and bold allies
Their vain and weary enterprise.
Is all forgotten, all? my birth,
Named Janak's child, from fostering earth?
That day of triumph when a maid
My trembling hand in thine I laid?
My meek obedience to thy will,
My faithful love through joy and ill,
That never failed at duty's call—
O King, is all forgotten, all?"

To Lakshmaṇ then she turned and spoke
While sobs and sighs her utterance broke:
"Sumitrá's son, a pile prepare,
My refuge in my dark despair.
I will not live to bear this weight
Of shame, forlorn and desolate.
The kindled fire my woes shall end
And be my best and surest friend."

His mournful eyes the hero raised
And wistfully on Ráma gazed,
In whose stern look no ruth was seen,
No mercy for the weeping queen.
No chieftain dared to meet those eyes,
To pray, to question or advise.

The word was passed, the wood was piled
And fain to die stood Janak's child.
She slowly paced around her lord,
The Gods with reverent act adored,
Then raising suppliant hands the dame
Prayed humbly to the Lord of Flame:
"As this fond heart by virtue swayed
From Raghu's son has never strayed,
So, universal witness, Fire

Protect my body on the pyre,
As Raghu's son has idly laid
This charge on Sítá, hear and aid."

She ceased: and fearless to the last
Within the flame's wild fury passed.
Then rose a piercing cry from all
Dames, children, men, who saw her fall
Adorned with gems and gay attire
Beneath the fury of the fire.

CANTO
CXIX

Glory to Vishnu

The shrill cry pierced through Ráma's ears
And his sad eyes o'erflowed with tears,
When lo, transported through the sky
A glorious band of Gods was nigh.
Ancestral shades, by men revered,
In venerable state appeared,
And he from whom all riches flow,
And Yáma Lord who reigns below:
King Indra, thousand-eyed, and he
Who wields the sceptre of the sea.
The God who shows the blazoned bull,
And Brahmá Lord most bountiful
By whose command the worlds were made
All these on radiant cars conveyed,

Brighter than sun-beams, sought the place
Where stood the prince of Raghu's race,
And from their glittering seats the best
Of blessed Gods the chief addressed:

"Couldst thou, the Lord of all, couldst thou,
Creator of the worlds, allow
Thy queen, thy spouse to brave the fire
And give her body to the pyre?
Dost thou not yet, supremely wise,
Thy heavenly nature recognize?"
They ceased: and Ráma thus began:
"I deem myself a mortal man.
Of old Ikshváku's line, I spring
From Daśaratha Kośal's king."
He ceased: and Brahmá's self replied:
"O cast the idle thought aside.
Thou art the Lord Náráyaṇ, thou
The God to whom all creatures bow.
Thou art the saviour God who wore
Of old the semblance of a boar;
Thou he whose discus overthrows
All present, past and future foes;
Thou Brahmá, That whose days extend
Without beginning, growth or end;
The God, who, bears the bow of horn,
Whom four majestic arms adorn;
Thou art the God who rules the sense
And sways with gentle influence;
Thou all-pervading Vishṇu Lord
Who wears the ever-conquering sword;
Thou art the Guide who leads aright,
Thou Krishṇa of unequalled might.
Thy hand, O Lord, the hills and plains,
And earth with all her life sustains;
Thou wilt appear in serpent form
When sinks the earth in fire and storm.
Queen Sítá of the lovely brows
Is Lakshmí thy celestial spouse.
To free the worlds from Rávaṇ thou
Wouldst take the form thou wearest now.
Rejoice: the mighty task is done:
Rejoice, thou great and glorious one.
The tyrant, slain, thy labours end:
Triumphant now to heaven ascend.
High bliss awaits the devotee

Who clings in loving faith to thee,
Who celebrates with solemn praise
The Lord of ne'er beginning days.
On earth below, in heaven above
Great joy shall crown his faith and love.
And he who loves the tale divine
Which tells each glorious deed of thine
Through life's fair course shall never know
The fierce assault of pain and woe."

CANTO

CXX

Sítá Restored

Thus spoke the Self-existent Sire:
Then swiftly from the blazing pyre
The circling flames were backward rolled,
And, raising in his gentle hold
Alive unharmed the Maithil dame,
The Lord of Fire embodied came.
Fair as the morning was her sheen,
And gold and gems adorned the queen.
Her form in crimson robes arrayed,
Her hair was bound in glossy braid.
Her wreath was fresh and sweet of scent,
Undimmed was every ornament.
Then, standing close to Ráma'a side,
The universal witness cried:
"From every blot and blemish free
Thy faithful queen returns to thee.
In word or deed, in look or mind
Her heart from thee has ne'er declined.
By force the giant bore away
From thy lone cot his helpless prey;
And in his bowers securely kept

536

She still has longed for thee and wept.
With soft temptation, bribe and threat,
He bade the dame her love forget:
But, nobly faithful to her lord,
Her soul the giant's suit abhorred.
Receive, O King, thy queen again,
Pure, ever pure from spot and stain."

Still stood the king in thoughtful mood
And tears of joy his eyes bedewed.
Then to the best of Gods the best
Of warrior chiefs his mind expressed:

"'Twas meet that mid the thousands here
The searching fire my queen should clear;
For long within the giant's bower
She dwelt the vassal of his power.
For else had many a slanderous tongue
Reproaches on mine honour flung,
And scorned the king who, love-impelled,
His consort from the proof withheld.
No doubt had I, but surely knew
That Janak's child was pure and true,
That, come what might, in good and ill
Her faithful heart was with me still.
I knew that Rávan could not wrong
My queen whom virtue made so strong.
I knew his heart would sink and fail,
Nor dare her honour to assail,
As Ocean, when he raves and roars,
Fears to o'erleap his bounding shores.
Now to the worlds her truth is shown,
And Sítá is again mine own.
Thus proved before unnumbered eyes,
On her pure fame no shadow lies.
As heroes to their glory cleave,
Mine own dear spouse I ne'er will leave."

He ceased: and clasped in fond embrace
On his dear breast she hid her face.

CANTO
CXXI

Dasaratha

To him Maheśvar thus replied:
"O strong-armed hero, lotus-eyed,
Thou, best of those who love the right,
Hast nobly fought the wondrous fight.
Dispelled by thee the doom that spread
Through trembling earth and heaven is fled.
The worlds exult in light and bliss,
And praise thy name, O chief, for this.
Now peace to Bharat's heart restore,
And bid Kausalyá weep no more.
Thy face let Queen Kaikeyí see,
Let fond Sumitrá gaze on thee.
The longing of thy friends relieve,
The kingdom of thy sires receive.
Let sons of gentle Sítá born
Ikshváku's ancient line adorn.
Then from all care and foemen freed
Perform the offering of the steed.
In pious gifts thy wealth expend,
Then to the home of Gods ascend,
Thy sire, this glorious king, behold,
Among the blest in heaven enrolled.
He comes from where the Immortals dwell:
Salute him, for he loves thee well."

His mandate Raghu's sons obeyed,
And to their sire obeisance made,
Where high he stood above the car
In wondrous light that shone afar,
His limbs in radiant garments dressed

538

Whereon no spot of dust might rest.
When on the son he loved so well
The eyes of Daśaratha fell,
He strained the hero to his breast
And thus with gentle words addressed:
"No joy to me is heavenly bliss,
For there these eyes my Ráma miss.
Enrolled on high with saint and sage,
Thy woes, dear son, my thoughts engage.
Kaikeyí's guile I ne'er forget:
Her cruel words will haunt me yet,
Which sent thee forth, my son, to roam
The forest far from me and home.
Now when I look on each dear face,
And hold you both in fond embrace,
My heart is full of joy to see
The sons I love from danger free.
Now know I what the Gods designed,
And how in Ráma's form enshrined
The might of Purushottam lay,
The tyrant of the worlds to slay.
Ah, how Kausalyá will rejoice
To hear again her darling's voice,
And, all thy weary wanderings o'er,
To gaze upon thy face once more.
Ah blest, for ever blest are they
Whose eyes shall see the glorious day
Of thy return in joy at last,
Thy term of toil and exile past.
Ayodhyá's lord, begin thy reign,
And day by day new glory gain."

He ceased: and Ráma thus replied:
"Be not this grace, O sire, denied.
Those hasty words, that curse revoke
Which from thy lips in anger broke:
"Kaikeyí, be no longer mine:
I cast thee off, both thee and thine."
O father, let no sorrow fall
On her or hers: thy curse recall."

"Yea, she shall live, if so thou wilt,"
The sire replied, "absolved from guilt."
Round Lakshmaṇ then his arms he threw,
And moved by love began anew:
"Great store of merit shall be thine,
And brightly shall thy glory shine;
Secure on earth thy brother's grace,
And high in heaven shall be thy place.
Thy glorious king obey and fear:
To him the triple world is dear.
God, saint, and sage, by Indra led,
To Ráma bow the reverent head,
Nor from the Lord, the lofty-souled,
Their worship or their praise withhold.
Heart of the Gods, supreme is he,
The One who ne'er shall cease to be."

On Sítá then he looked and smiled;
"List to my words" he said, "dear child,
Let not thy gentle breast retain
One lingering trace of wrath or pain.
When by the fire thy truth be proved,
By love for thee his will was moved.
The furious flame thy faith confessed
Which shrank not from the awful test:
And thou, in every heart enshrined,
Shalt live the best of womankind."

He ceased: he bade the three adieu,
And home to heaven exulting flew.

Indra's Boon

T hen Indra, he whose fiery stroke
    Slew furious Páka, turned and spoke:
    "A glorious day, O chief, is this,
Rich with the fruit of lasting bliss.
Well pleased are we: we love thee well
Now speak, thy secret wishes tell."

Thus spake the sovereign of the sky,
And this was Ráma's glad reply:
"If I have won your grace, incline
To grant this one request of mine.
Restore, O King: the Vánar dead
Whose blood for me was nobly shed.

To life and strength my friends recall,
And bring them back from Yáma's hall.
When, fresh in might the warriors rise,
Prepare a feast to glad their eyes.
Let fruits of every season glow,
And streams of purest water flow."

Thus Raghu's son, great-hearted, prayed,
And Indra thus his answer made:
"High is the boon thou seekest: none
Should win this grace but Raghu's son.
Yet, faithful to the word I spake,
I grant the prayer for thy dear sake.
The Vánars whom the giants slew
Their life and vigour shall renew.
Their strength repaired, their gashes healed
Whose torrents dyed the battle field,

541

The warrior hosts from death shall rise
Like sleepers when their slumber flies." .

Restored from Yáma's dark domain
The Vánar legions filled the plain,
And, round the royal chief arrayed,
With wondering hearts obeisance paid.
Each God the son of Raghu praised,
And cried as loud his voice he raised:
"Turn, King, to fair Ayodhyá speed,
And leave thy friends of Vánar breed.
Thy true devoted consort cheer
After long days of woe and fear.
Bharat, thy loyal brother, see,
A hermit now for love of thee.
The tears of Queen Kauśalyá dry,
And light with joy each stepdame's eye;
Then consecrated king of men
Make glad each faithful citizen."

They ceased: and borne on radiant cars
Sought their bright home amid the stars.

CANTO
CXXIII

The Magic Car

Then slept the tamer of his foes
And spent the night in calm repose.
Vibhishaṇ came when morning broke,
And hailed the royal chief, and spoke:
"Here wait thee precious oil and scents,
And rich attire and ornaments.
The brimming urns are newly filled,

And women in their duty skilled,
With lotus-eyes, thy call attend,
Assistance at thy bath to lend."
"Let others," Ráma cried, "desire
These precious scents, this rich attire,
I heed not such delights as these,
For faithful Bharat, ill at ease,
Watching for me is keeping now
Far far away his rigorous vow.
By Bharat's side I long to stand,
I long to see my fatherland.
Far is Ayodhyá: long, alas,
The dreary road and hard to pass."

"One day," Vibhishaṇ cried, "one day
Shall bear thee o'er that length of way.
Is not the wondrous chariot mine,
Named Pushpak, wrought by hands divine.
The prize which Rávaṇ seized of old
Victorious o'er the God of Gold?
This chariot, kept with utmost care,
Will waft thee through the fields of air,
And thou shalt light unwearied down
In fair Ayodhyá's royal town.
But yet if aught that I have done
Has pleased thee well, O Raghu's son;
If still thou carest for thy friend,
Some little time in Lanká spend;
There after toil of battle rest
Within my halls an honoured guest."
Again the son of Raghu spake:
"Thy life was perilled for my sake.
Thy counsel gave me priceless aid:
All honours have been richly paid.
Scarce can my love refuse, O best
Of giant kind, thy last request.
But still I yearn once more to see
My home and all most dear to me;
Nor can I brook one hour's delay:
Forgive me, speed me on my way."

He ceased: the magic car was brought.
Of yore by Viśvakarmá wrought.
In sunlike sheen it flashed and blazed;
And Raghu's sons in wonder gazed.

CANTO
CXXIV

The Departure

The giant lord the chariot viewed,
And humbly thus his speech renewed:
"Behold, O King, the car prepared:
Now be thy further will declared."
He ceased: and Ráma spake once more:
"These hosts who thronged to Lanká's shore
Their faith and might have nobly shown,
And set thee on the giants' throne.
Let pearls and gems and gold repay
The feats of many a desperate day,
That all may go triumphant hence
Proud of their noble recompense."
Vibhishaṇ, ready at his call,
With gold and gems enriched them all.
Then Ráma clomb the glorious car
That shone like day's resplendent star.
There in his lap he held his dame
Vailing her eyes in modest shame.
Beside him Lakshmaṇ took his stand,
Whose mighty bow still armed his hand,
"O King Vibhishaṇ," Ráma cried,
"O Vánar chiefs, so long allied,

My comrades till the foemen fell,
List, for I speak a long farewell.
The task, in doubt and fear begun,

544

With your good aid is nobly done.
Leave Lanká's shore, your steps retrace,
Brave warriors of the Vánar race.
Thou, King Sugríva, true, through all,
To friendship's bond and duty's call,
Seek far Kishkindhá with thy train
And o'er thy realm in glory reign.
Farewell, Vibhishaṇ, Lanká's throne
Won by our arms is now thine own,
Thou, mighty lord, hast nought to dread
From heavenly Gods by Indra led.
My last farewell, King, receive,
For Lanká's isle this hour I leave."

Loud rose their cry in answer: "We,
O Raghu's son, would go with thee.
With thee delighted would we stray
Where sweet Ayodhyá's groves are gay,
Then in the joyous synod view
King-making balm thy brows bedew;
Our homage to Kauśalyá pay,
And hasten on our homeward way."

Their prayer the son of Raghu heard,
And spoke, his heart with rapture stirred:
"Sugríva, O my faithful friend,
Vibhishaṇ and ye chiefs, ascend.
A joy beyond all joys the best
Will fill my overflowing breast,
If girt by you, O noble band,
I seek again my native land."
With Vánar lords in danger tried
Sugríva sprang to Ráma's side,
And girt by chiefs of giant kind
Vibhíshan's step was close behind.
Swift through the air, as Ráma chose,
The wondrous car from earth arose.
And decked with swans and silver wings
Bore through the clouds its freight of kings.

The Return

T hen Ráma, speeding through the skies,
 Bent on the earth his eager eyes:
 "Look, Sítá, see, divinely planned
And built by Viśvakarmá's hand,
Lanká the lovely city rest
Enthroned on Mount Trikúṭa's crest
Behold those fields, ensanguined yet,
Where Vánar hosts and giants met.
There, vainly screened by charm and spell,
The robber Rávan fought and fell.
There knelt Mandodarí and shed
Her tears in floods for Rávan dead.
And every dame who loved him sent
From her sad heart her wild lament.
There gleams the margin of the deep,
Where, worn with toil, we sank to sleep.
Look, love, the unconquered sea behold,
King Varuṇ's home ordained of old,
Whose boundless waters roar and swell
Rich with their store of pearl and shell.
O see, the morning sun is bright
On fair Hiraṇyanábha's height,
Who rose from Ocean's sheltering breast
That Hanumán might stay and rest.
There stretches, famed for evermore,
The wondrous bridge from shore to shore.
The worlds, to life's remotest day,
Due reverence to the work shall pay,
Which holier for the lapse of time
Shall give release from sin and crime.
Now thither bend, dear love, thine eyes

Where green with groves Kishkindhá lies,
The seat of King Sugríva's reign,
Where Báli by this hand was slain.
There Ríshyamúka's hill behold
Bright gleaming with embedded gold.
There too my wandering foot I set,
There King Sugríva first I met.
And, where yon trees their branches wave,
My promise of assistance gave.
There, flushed with lilies, Pampá shines
With banks which greenest foliage lines,
Where melancholy steps I bent
And mourned thee with a mad lament.
There fierce Kabandha, spreading wide
His giant arms, in battle died.
Turn, Sítá, turn thine eyes and see
In Janasthán that glorious tree:
There Rávaṇ, lord of giants slew
Our friend Jaṭáyus brave and true,
Thy champion in the hopeless strife,
Who gave for thee his noble life.
Now mark that glade amid the trees
Where once we lived as devotees.
See, see our leafy cot between
Those waving boughs of densest green,
Where Rávaṇ seized his prize and stole
My love the darling of my soul.
O, look again: beneath thee gleams
Godávarí the best of streams,
Whose lucid waters sweetly glide
By lilies that adorn her side.
There dwelt Agastya, holy sage,
In plantain-sheltered hermitage.
See Śarabhanga's humble shed

Which sovereign Indra visited.
See where the gentle hermits dwell
Neath Atri's rule who loved us well;
Where once thine eyes were blest to see
His sainted dame who talked with thee.
Now rest thine eyes with new delight

On Chitrakúṭa's woody height,
See Jumna flashing in the sun
Through groves of brilliant foliage run.
Screened by the shade of spreading boughs.
There Bharadvája keeps his vows,
There Gangá, river of the skies,
Rolls the sweet wave that purifies,
There Śringavera's towers ascend
Where Guha reigns, mine ancient friend.
I see, I see thy glittering spires,
Ayodhyá, city of my sires.
Bow down, bow down thy head, my sweet,
Our home, our long-lost home to greet."

C A N T O

CXXVI

Bharat Consoled

But Ráma bade the chariot stay,
And halting in his airy way,
In Bharadvája's holy shade
His homage to the hermit paid.
"O saint," he cried, "I yearn to know
My dear Ayodhyá's weal and woe.
O tell me that the people thrive,
And that the queens are yet alive."

Joy gleamed in Bhardvája's eye,
Who gently smiled and made reply:
"Thy brother, studious of thy will,
Is faithful and obedient still.
In tangled twine he coils his hair:
Thy safe return is all his care.
Before thy shoes he humbly bends,
And to thy house and realm attends.

When first these dreary years began,
When first I saw the banished man,
With Sítá, in his hermit coat,
At this sad heart compassion smote.
My breast with tender pity swelled:
I saw thee from thy home expelled,
Reft of all princely state, forlorn,
A hapless wanderer travel-worn,
Firm in thy purpose to fulfil
Thy duty and thy father's will.
But boundless is my rapture now:
Triumphant, girt with friends, art thou.
Where'er thy wandering steps have been,
Thy joy and woe mine eyes have seen.
Thy glorious deeds to me art known,
The Bráhmans saved, the foes o'erthrown.
Such power have countless seasons spent
In penance and devotion lent.
Thy virtues, best of chiefs, I know,
And now a boon would fain bestow.
This hospitable gift receive:
Then with the dawn my dwelling leave."
The bended head of Ráma showed
His reverence for the grace bestowed;
Then for each brave companion's sake
He sought a further boon and spake:

"O let that mighty power of thine
The road to fair Ayodhyá line
With trees where fruit of every hue
The Vánars' eye and taste may woo,
And flowers of every season, sweet
With stores of honeyed juice, may meet."
The hero ceased: the hermit bent
His reverend head in glad assent;
And swift, as Bharadvája willed,
The prayer of Ráma was fulfilled.
For many a league the lengthening road
Trees thick with fruit and blossom showed
With luscious beauty to entice
The taste like trees of Paradise.

549

The Vánars passed beneath the shade
Of that delightful colonnade,
Still tasting with unbounded glee
The treasures of each wondrous tree.

CANTO
CXXVII

Ráma's Message

But Ráma, when he first looked down
And saw afar Ayodhyá's town,
Had called Hanumán to his side,
The chief on whom his heart relied,
And said: "Brave Vánar, good at need,
Haste onward, to Ayodhyá speed,
And learn, I pray, if all be well
With those who in the palace dwell.
But as thou speedest on thy way
Awhile at Śringavera stay.
Tell Guha the Nishádas' lord,
That victor, with my queen restored,
In health and strength with many a friend
Homeward again my steps I bend.
Thence by the road that he will show
On to Ayodhyá swiftly go.
There with my love my brother greet,
And all our wondrous tale repeat.
Say that victorious in the strife
I come with Lakshmaṇ and my wife,
Then mark with keenest eye each trace
Of joy or grief on Bharat's face.
Be all his gestures closely viewed,

Each change of look and attitude.
Where breathes the man who will not cling

To all that glorifies a king?
Where beats the heart that can resign
An ancient kingdom, nor repine
To lose a land renowned for breeds
Of elephants and warrior steeds?
If, won by custom day by day,
My brother Bharat thirsts for sway,
Still let him rule the nations, still
The throne of old Ikshváku fill.
Go, mark him well: his feelings learn,
And, ere we yet be near return."

He ceased: and, garbed in human form,
Forth sped Hanúmán swift as storm.
Sublime in air he rose, and through
The region of his father flew.
He saw far far beneath his feet
Where Gangá's flood and Jumna meet.
Descending from the upper air
He entered Śringavera, where
King Guha's heart was well content
To hear the message Ráma sent.
Then, with his mighty strength renewed,
The Vánar chief his way pursued,
Válúkiní was far behind,
And Gomatí with forests lined,
And golden fields and pastures gay
With flocks and herds beneath him lay.
Then Nandigráma charmed his eye
Where flowers were bright with every dye,
And trees of lovely foliage made
With meeting boughs delightful shade,
Where women watched in trim array
Their little sons' and grandsons' play.
His eager eye on Bharat fell
Who sat before his lonely cell.
In hermit weed, with tangled hair,
Pale, weak, and worn with ceaseless care.
His royal pomp and state resigned
For Ráma still he watched and pined,
Still to his dreary vows adhered,

And royal Ráma's shoes revered.
Yet still the terror of his arm
Preserved the land from fear and harm.

The Wind-God's son, in form a man,
Raised reverent hands and thus began:
"Fond greeting, Prince, I bring to thee,
And Ráma's self has sent it: he
For whom thy spirit sorrows yet
As for a hapless anchoret
In Daṇḍak wood, in dire distress,
With matted hair and hermit dress.
This sorrow from thy bosom fling,
And hear the tale of joy I bring.
This day thy brother shalt thou meet
Exulting in his foe's defeat,
Freed from his toil and lengthened vow,
The light of victory on his brow,
With Sítá, Lakshmaṇ and his friends
Homeward at last his steps he bends."

Then joy, too mighty for control,
Rushed in full flood o'er Bharat's soul;
His reeling sense and strength gave way,
And fainting on the earth he lay,
At length upspringing from the ground,
His arms about Hanúmán wound,
With tender tears of rapture sprung,
He dewed the neck to which he clung:
"Art thou a God or man," he cried,
"Whom love and pity hither guide?
For this a hundred thousand kine,
A hundred villages be thine.
A score of maids of spotless lives
To thee I give to be thy wives,
Of golden hue and bright of face,
Each lovely for her tender grace."

He ceased a while by joy subdued,
And then his eager speech renewed.

CXXVIII

Hanumán's Story

"In doubt and fear long years have passed
And glorious tidings come at last.
True, true is now the ancient verse
Which men in time of bliss rehearse:
"Once only in a hundred years
Great joy to mortal men appears."
But now his woes and triumph tell,
And loss and gain as each befell."
He ceased: Hanúmán mighty-souled
The tale of Ráma's wanderings told
From that first day on which he stood
In the drear shade of Daṇḍak wood.
He told how fierce Virádha fell;
He told of Śarabhanga's cell
Where Ráma saw with wondering eyes
Indra descended from the skies.
He told how Śúrpaṇakhí came,
Her soul aglow with amorous flame,
And fled repulsed, with rage and tears,
Reft of her nose and severed ears.
He told how Ráma's might subdued
The giants' furious multitude;
How Khara with the troops he led
And Triśirás and Dúshaṇ bled:
How Ráma, tempted from his cot,
The golden deer pursued and shot,
And Rávaṇ came and stole away
The Maithil queen his hapless prey,
When, as he fought, the dame to save,
His noble life Jatáyus gave:

553

How Ráma still the the search renewed,
The robber to his hold pursued,
Bridging the sea from shore to shore,
And found his queen to part no more.

CANTO
CXXIX

The Meeting With Bharat

O'erwhelmed with rapture Bharat heard
The tale that all his being stirred,
And, heralding the glad event,
This order to Śatrughna sent:
"Let every shrine with flowers be gay
Let incense burn and music play.
Go forth, go forth to meet your king,
Let tabours sound and minstrels sing,
Let bards swell high the note of praise
Skilled in the lore of ancient days,
Call forth the royal matrons: call
Each noble from the council hall.
Send all we love and honour most,
Send Bráhmans and the warrior host,
A glorious company to bring
In triumph home our lord the king."
Great rapture filled Śatrughna's breast,
Obedient to his brother's hest.
"Send forth ten thousand men" he cried,
"Let brawny arms be stoutly plied,
And, smoothing all with skilful care,
The road for Kośal's king prepare.
Then o'er the earth let thousands throw
Fresh showers of water cool as snow,
And others strew with garlands gay
With loveliest blooms our monarch's way.

On tower and temple porch and gate
Let banners wave in royal state,
And be each roof and terrace lined
With blossoms loose and chaplets twined."

The nobles hasting forth fulfilled
His order as Śatrughna willed.
Sublime on elephants they rode
Whose gilded girths with jewels glowed.
Attended close by thousands more
Gay with the gear and flags they bore.
A thousand chiefs their steeds bestrode,
Their glittering cars a thousand showed.
And countless hosts in rich array
Pursued on foot their eager way.
Veiled from the air with silken screens
In litters rode the widowed queens.
Kausalyá first, acknowledged head
And sovereign of the household, led:
Sumitrá next, and after, dames
Of lower rank and humbler names.
Then compassed by a white-robed throng
Of Bráhmans, heralded with song,
With shouts of joy from countless throats,
And shells' and tambours' mingled notes,
And drums resounding long and loud,
Exulting Bharat joined the crowd.
Still on his head, well-trained in lore
Of duty, Ráma's shoes he bore.
The moon-white canopy was spread
With flowery twine engarlanded,
And jewelled cheuries, meet to hold
O'er Ráma's brow, shone bright with gold,
Though Nandigráma's town they neared,
Of Ráma yet no sign appeared.
Then Bharat called the Vánar chief
And questioned thus in doubt and grief:
"Hast thou uncertain, like thy kind,
A sweet delusive guile designed?
Where, where is royal Ráma? show
The hero, victor of the foe.

555

I gaze, but see no Vánars still
Who wear each varied shape at will."

In eager love thus Bharat cried,
And thus the Wind-God's son replied:
"Look, Bharat, on those laden trees
That murmur with the song of bees;
For Ráma's sake the saint has made
Untimely fruits, unwonted shade.
Such power in ages long ago
Could Indra's gracious boon bestow.
O, hear the Vánars' voices, hear
The shouting which proclaims them near.
E'en now about to cross they seem
Sweet Gomatí's delightful stream.
I see, I see the car designed
By Brahmá's own creative mind,
The car which, radiant as the moon,
Moves at the will by Brahmá's boon;
The car which once was Rávan's pride,
The victor's spoil when Rávan died.
Look, there are Raghu's sons: between
The brothers stands the rescued queen.
There is Vibhishaṇ full in view,
Sugríva and his retinue."

He ceased: then rapture loosed each tongue:
From men and dames, from old and young,
One long, one universal cry,
'Tis he, 'tis Ráma, smote the sky.
All lighted down with eager speed
From elephant and car and steed,
And every joyful eye intent
On Ráma's moonbright face was bent.
Entranced a moment Bharat gazed:
Then reverential hands he raised,
And on his brother humbly pressed
The honours due to welcome guest.
Then Bharat clomb the car to greet
His king and bowed him at his feet,

556

Till Ráma raised him face to face
And held him in a close embrace.
Then Lakshmaṇ and the Maithil dame
He greeted as he spoke his name
He greeted next, supreme in place,
The sovereign of the Vánar race,
And Jámbaván and Báli's son,

And lords and chiefs, omitting none.
Sugríva to his heart he pressed
And thus with grateful words addressed:
"Four brothers, Vánar king, were we,
And now we boast a fifth in thee.
By kindly acts a friend we know:
Offence and wrong proclaim the foe."
To King Vibhishaṇ then he spake:
"Well hast thou fought for Ráma's sake."
Nor was the brave Śatrughna slow
His reverential love to show
To both his brothers, as was meet,
And venerate the lady's feet.
Then Ráma to his mother came,
Saw her pale cheek and wasted frame,
With gentle words her heart consoled,
And clasped her feet with loving hold.
Then at Sumitrá's feet he bent,
And fair Kaikeyí's, reverent,
Greeted each dame from chief to least,
And bowed him to the household priest.
Up rose a shout from all the throng:
"O welcome, Ráma, mourned so long.
Welcome, Kausalyá's joy and pride,"
Ten hundred thousand voices cried.
Then Bharat placed, in duty taught,
On Ráma's feet the shoes he brought:
"My King," he cried, "receive again
The pledge preserved through years of pain,
The rule and lordship of the land
Entrusted to my weaker hand.
No more I sigh o'er sorrows past,

My birth and life are blest at last
In the glad sight this day has shown,
When Ráma comes to rule his own."

He ceased: the faithful love that moved
The prince's soul each heart approved;
Nor could the Vánar chiefs refrain
From tender tears that fell like rain.
Then Ráma, stirred with joy anew,
His arms about his brother threw,
And to the grove his course he bent
Where Bharat's hermit days were spent.
Alighting in that pure retreat
He pressed the earth with eager feet.
Then, at his hest, the car rose high
And sailing through the northern sky
Sped homeward to the Lord of Gold
Who owned the wondrous prize of old.

CANTO

CXXX

The Consecration

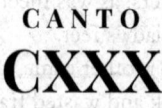

hen, reverent hand to hand applied,
Thus Bharat to his brother cried:
"Thy realm, O King, is now restored,
Uninjured to the rightful lord.
This feeble arm with toil and pain,
The weighty charge could scarce sustain.
And the great burthen wellnigh broke
The neck untrained to bear the yoke.
The royal swan outspeeds the crow:
The steed is swift, the mule is slow,
Nor can my feeble feet be led
O'er the rough ways where thine should tread.

Now grant what all thy subjects ask:
Begin, O King, thy royal task.
Now let our longing eyes behold
The glorious rite ordained of old,
And on the new-found monarch's head
Let consecrating drops be shed."

He ceased; victorious Ráma bent
His head in token of assent.
He sat, and tonsors trimmed with care
His tangles of neglected hair
Then, duly bathed, the hero shone
With all his splendid raiment on.
And Sítá with the matrons' aid
Her limbs in shining robes arrayed,
Sumantra then, the charioteer,
Drew, ordered by Śatrughna near,
And stayed within the hermit grove
The chariot and the steeds he drove.
Therein Sugríva's consorts, graced
With gems, and Ráma's queen were placed,
All fain Ayodhyá to behold:
And swift away the chariot rolled.
Like Indra Lord of Thousand Eyes,
Drawn by fleet lions through the skies.
Thus radiant in his glory showed
King Ráma as he homeward rode,
In power and might unparalleled.
The reins the hand of Bharat held.
Above the peerless victor's head
The snow-white shade Śatrughna spread,
And Lakshman's ever-ready hand
His forehead with a chourie fanned.
Vibhishaṇ close to Lakshman's side
Sharing his task a chourie plied.
Sugríva on Śatrunjay came,
An elephant of hugest frame:
Nine thousand others bore, behind,
The chieftains of the Vánar kind
All gay, in forms of human mould,
With rich attire and gems and gold.

Thus borne along in royal state
King Ráma reached Ayodbyá's gate
With merry noise of shells and drums
And joyful shouts, He comes, he comes,
A Bráhman host with solemn tread,
And kine the long procession led,
And happy maids in ordered bands
Threw grain and gold with liberal hands.
Neath gorgeous flags that waved in rows
On towers and roofs and porticoes.
Mid merry crowds who sang and cheered
The palace of the king they neared.
Then Raghu's son to Bharat, best
Of duty's slaves, these words addressed:
"Pass onward to the monarch's hall.
The high-souled Vánars with thee call,
And let the chieftains, as is meet,
The widows of our father greet.
And to the Vánar king assign
Those chambers, best of all, which shine
With lazulite and pearl inlaid,
And pleasant grounds with flowers and shade."

He ceased: and Bharat bent his head;
Sugríva by the hand he led
And passed within the palace where
Stood couches which Śatrughna's care,
With robes and hangings richly dyed,
And burning lamps, had seen supplied.
Then Bharat spake: "I pray thee, friend,
Thy speedy messengers to send,
Each sacred requisite to bring
That we may consecrate our king."
Sugríva raised four urns of gold,
The water for the rite to hold,
And bade four swiftest Vánars flee
And fill them from each distant sea.
Then east and west and south and north
The Vánar envoys hastened forth.
Each in swift flight an ocean sought

And back through air his treasure brought,
And full five hundred floods beside
Pure water for the king supplied.
Then girt by many a Bráhman sage,
Vaśishṭha, chief for reverend age,
High on a throne with jewels graced
King Ráma and his Sítá placed.
There by Jábáli, far revered,
Vijay and Kaśyap's son appeared;
By Gautam's side Kátváyan stood,
And Vámadeva wise and good,
Whose holy hands in order shed
The pure sweet drops on Ráma's head.
Then priests and maids and warriors, all
Approaching at Vaśishṭha's call,
With sacred drops bedewed their king,
The centre of a joyous ring,
The guardians of the worlds, on high,
And all the children of the sky
From herbs wherewith their hands were filled
Rare juices on his brow distilled.
His brows were bound with glistering gold
Which Manu's self had worn of old,
Bright with the flash of many a gem
His sire's ancestral diadem.
Śatrughna lent his willing aid
And o'er him held the regal shade:
The monarchs whom his arm had saved
The chouries round his forehead waved.
A golden chain, that flashed and glowed
With gems the God of Wind bestowed:
Mahendra gave a glorious string
Of fairest pearls to deck the king,
The skies with acclamation rang,
The gay nymphs danced, the minstrels sang.
On that blest day the joyful plain
Was clothed anew with golden grain.
The trees the witching influence knew,
And bent with fruits of loveliest hue,
And Ráma's consecration lent

New sweetness to each flowret's scent.
The monarch, joy of Raghu's line,
Gave largess to the Bráhmans, kine
And steeds unnumbered, wealth untold
Of robes and pearls and gems and gold.
A jewelled chain, whose lustre passed
The glory of the sun, he cast
About his friend Sugríva's neck;
And, Angad Báli's son to deck,
He gave a pair of armlets bright
With diamond and lazulite.
A string of pearls of matchless hue
Which gleams like tender moonlight threw
Adorned with gems of brightest sheen,
He gave to grace his darling queen.
The offering from his hand received
A moment on her bosom heaved;
Then from her neck the chain she drew,
A glance on all the Vánars threw,
And wistful eyes on Ráma bent
As still she held the ornament.
Her wish he knew, and made reply
To that mute question of her eye:
"Yea, love; the chain on him bestow
Whose wisdom truth and might we know,
The firm ally, the faithful friend
Through toil and peril to the end."

Then on Hanúmán's bosom hung
The chain which Sítá's hand had flung:
So may a cloud, when winds are still
With moon-lit silver gird a hill.

To every Vánar Ráma gave
Rich treasures from the mine and wave.
And with their honours well content
Homeward their steps the chieftains bent.
Ten thousand years Ayodhyá, blest
With Ráma's rule, had peace and rest,
No widow mourned her murdered mate,

No house was ever desolate.
The happy land no murrain knew,
The flocks and herds increased and grew.

The earth her kindly fruits supplied,
No harvest failed, no children died.
Unknown were want, disease, and crime:
So calm, so happy was the time.